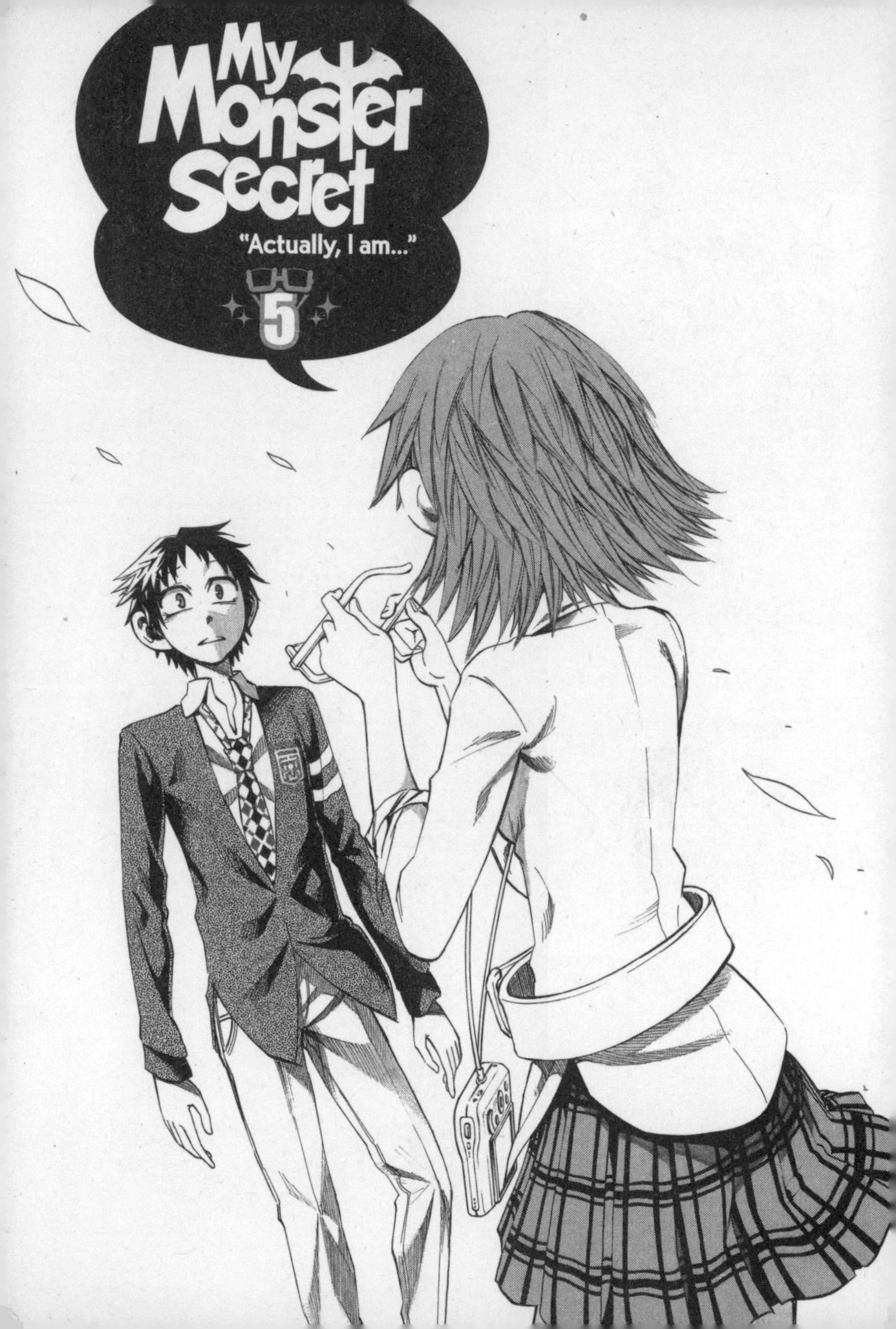
My Monster Secret
"Actually, I am..."
5

My Monster Secret

"Actually, I am..."

Story & Character

After school one day, **Kuromine Asahi** opened the door to his classroom to confess his love to his crush **Shiragami Youko**...and discovered that she's actually a vampire! His goal was to tell Shiragami that he loved her, but he instead resolved to keep her secret--as a friend. It means they can continue to go to school together, but their problems are only beginning...

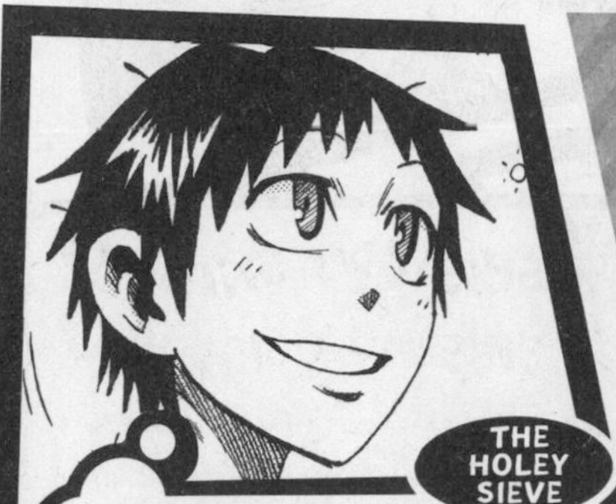

THE HOLEY SIEVE

KUROMINE ASAHI

The man with the worst poker face in the world, he's known as ***The Sieve With A Hole In It***...because secrets slide right out of him. Now he has to hide the fact that Shiragami-san--the girl he's in love with--is a vampire.

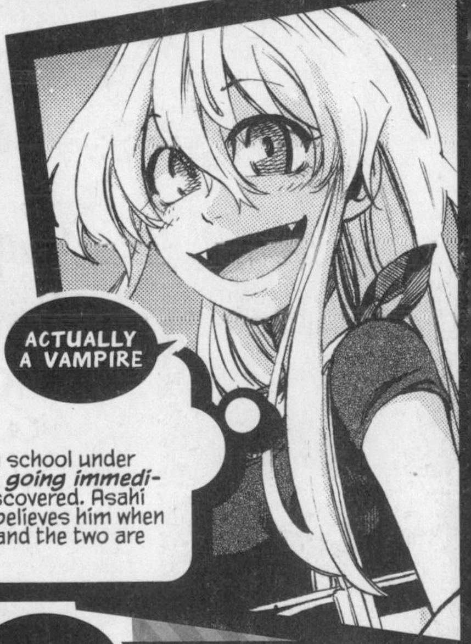

ACTUALLY A VAMPIRE

SHIRAGAMI YOUKO

She's attending a human high school under the condition that she'll ***stop going immediately*** if her true identity is discovered. Asahi found out (whoops), but she believes him when he says he'll keep her secret, and the two are now friends.

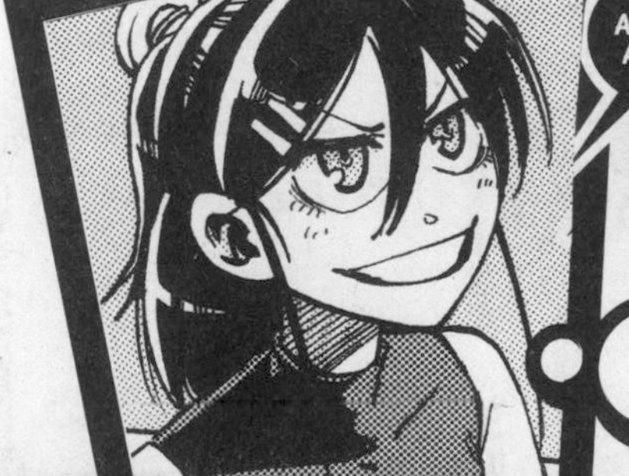

ACTUALLY AN ALIEN

AIZAWA NAGISA

Currently investigating Earth as a class representative, she once mercilessly tore Asahi to shreds before he could confess his love, but she now harbors an unrequited crush on him. Her true (tiny) form emerges from the screw-shaped cockpit on her head. Her brother **Aizawa Ryo** is also staying on Earth.

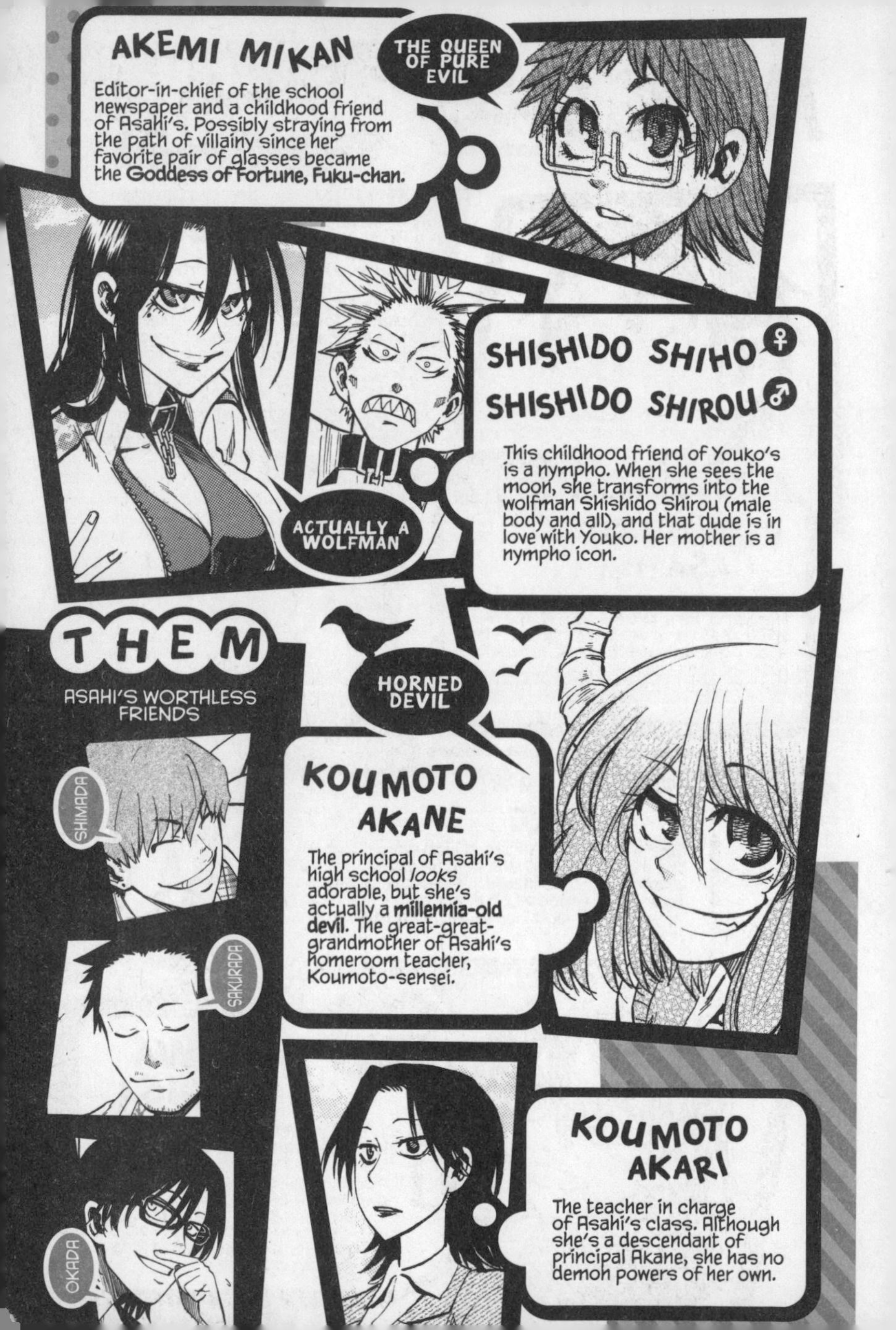
THE QUEEN OF PURE EVIL
AKEMI MIKAN
Editor-in-chief of the school newspaper and a childhood friend of Asahi's. Possibly straying from the path of villainy since her favorite pair of glasses became the **Goddess of Fortune, Fuku-chan.**
SHISHIDO SHIHO ♀
SHISHIDO SHIROU ♂
This childhood friend of Youko's is a nympho. When she sees the moon, she transforms into the wolfman Shishido Shirou (male body and all), and that dude is in love with Youko. Her mother is a nympho icon.
ACTUALLY A WOLFMAN
HORNED DEVIL
KOUMOTO AKANE
The principal of Asahi's high school *looks* adorable, but she's actually a **millennia-old devil.** The great-great-grandmother of Asahi's homeroom teacher, Koumoto-sensei.
THEM
ASAHI'S WORTHLESS FRIENDS
SHIMADA
SAKURADA
OKADA
KOUMOTO AKARI
The teacher in charge of Asahi's class. Although she's a descendant of principal Akane, she has no demon powers of her own.

SEVEN SEAS ENTERTAINMENT PRESENTS

My Monster Secret
"Actually, I am..."

story and art by Eiji Masuda

VOLUME 5

TRANSLATION
Alethea and Athena Nibley

ADAPTATION
Lianne Sentar

LETTERING AND LAYOUT
Annaliese Christman

LOGO DESIGN
Karis Page

COVER DESIGN
Nicky Lim

PROOFREADER
Shanti Whitesides

PRODUCTION MANAGER
Lissa Pattillo

EDITOR IN CHIEF
Adam Arnold

PUBLISHER
Jason DeAngelis

JITSUHA WATASHIHA Volume 5
© EIJI MASUDA 2014
Originally published in Japan in 2014 by Akita Publishing Co., Ltd.
English translation rights arranged with Akita Publishing Co., Ltd.
through TOHAN CORPORATION, Tokyo.

Seven Seas books may be purchased in bulk for promotional, educational, or
business use. Please contact your local bookseller or the Macmillan Corporate
and Premium Sales Department at 1-800-221-7945, extension 5442, or by
e-mail at MacmillanSpecialMarkets@macmillan.com.

Seven Seas and the Seven Seas logo are trademarks of
Seven Seas Entertainment, LLC. All rights reserved.

ISBN: 978-1-626923-85-0

Printed in Canada

First Printing: January 2017

10 9 8 7 6 5 4 3 2 1

FOLLOW US ONLINE: www.gomanga.com

READING DIRECTIONS

This book reads from *right to left*, Japanese style.
If this is your first time reading manga, you start
reading from the top right panel on each page and
take it from there. If you get lost, just follow the
numbered diagram here. It may seem backwards at
first, but you'll get the hang of it! Have fun!!

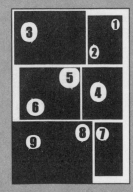

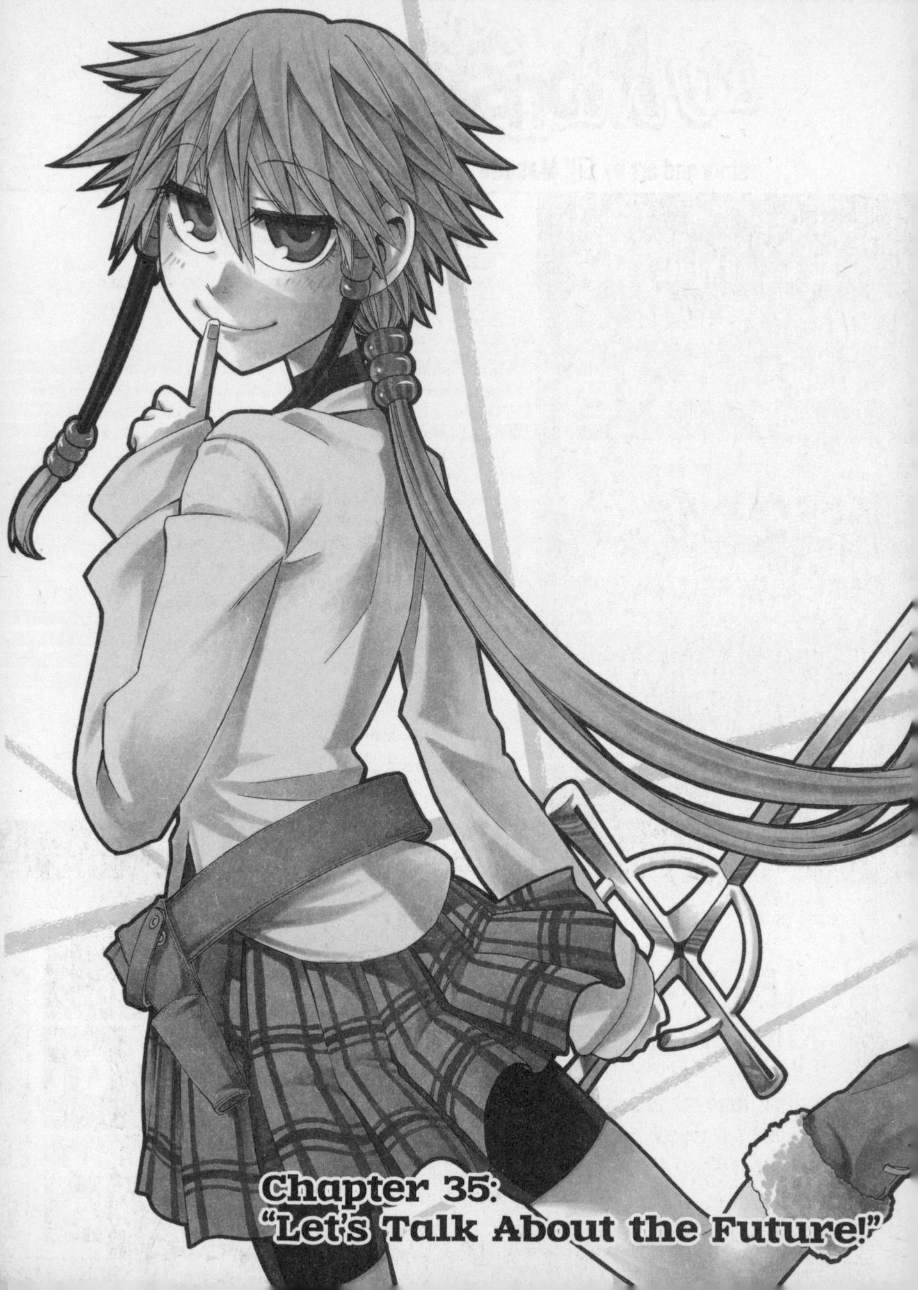

Chapter 35: "Let's Talk About the Future!"

TOP SECRET

My Monster Secret 5

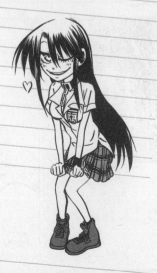

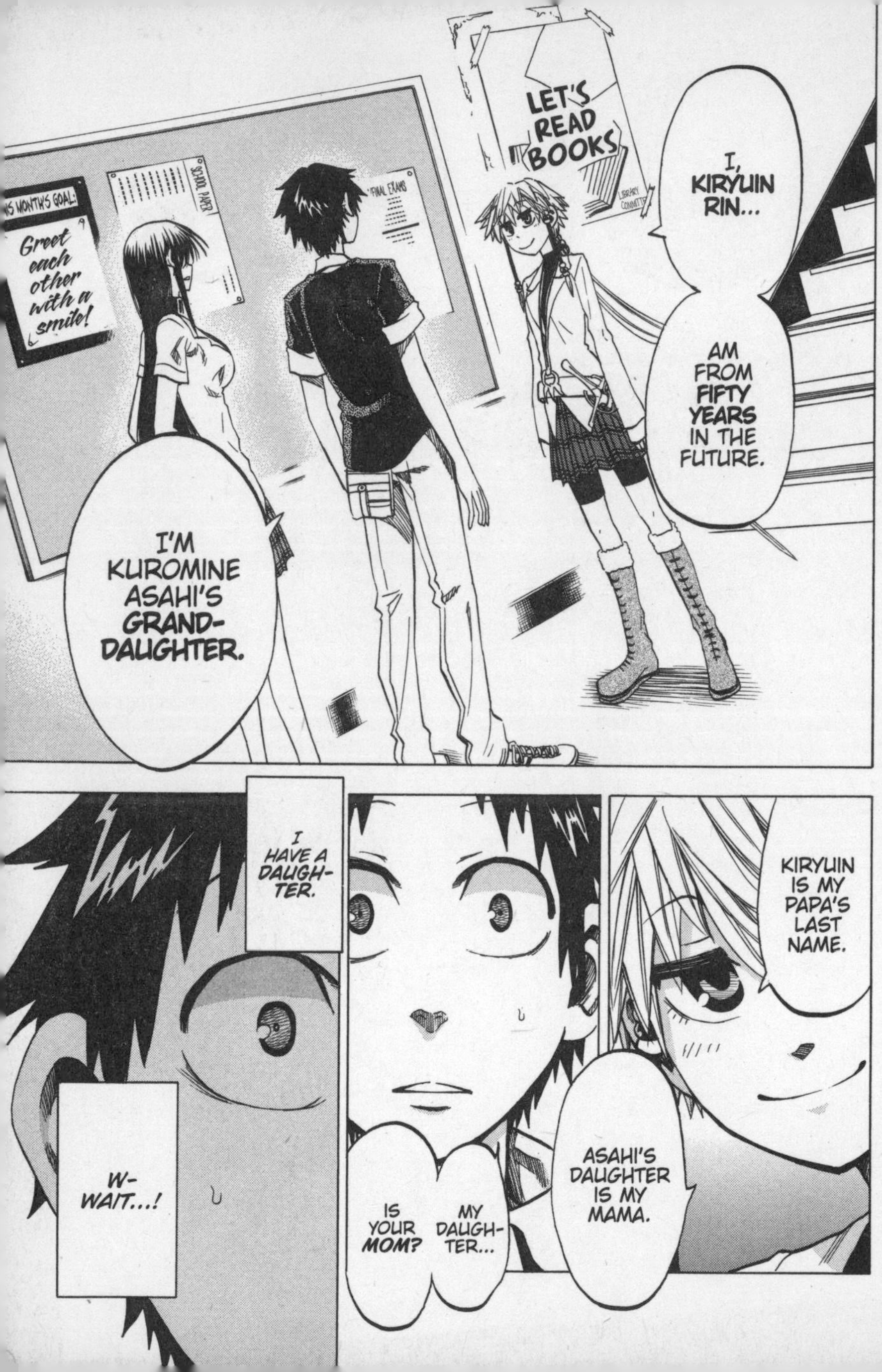
LET'S READ BOOKS
LIBRARY COMMITTEE
I, KIRYUIN RIN...
AM FROM FIFTY YEARS IN THE FUTURE.
FINAL EXAMS
SCHOOL PAPER
MONTH'S GOAL:
Greet each other with a smile!
I'M KUROMINE ASAHI'S GRAND-DAUGHTER.
KIRYUIN IS MY PAPA'S LAST NAME.
ASAHI'S DAUGHTER IS MY MAMA.
MY DAUGH-TER...
IS YOUR MOM?
I HAVE A DAUGH-TER.
W-WAIT...!

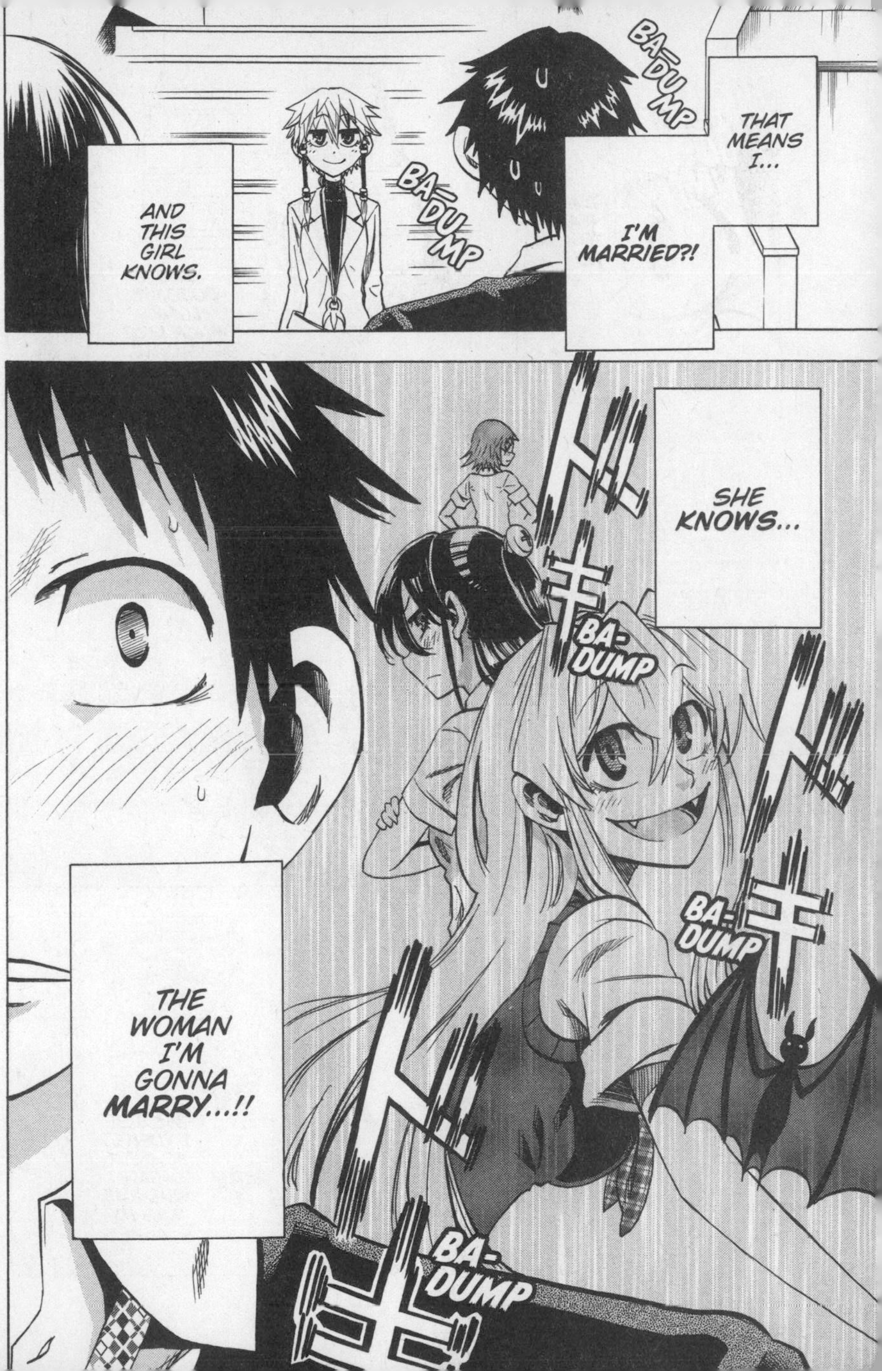
BA-DUMP
THAT MEANS I...
I'M MARRIED?!
BA-DUMP
AND THIS GIRL KNOWS.
SHE KNOWS...
BA-DUMP
BA-DUMP
THE WOMAN I'M GONNA MARRY...!!
BA-DUMP

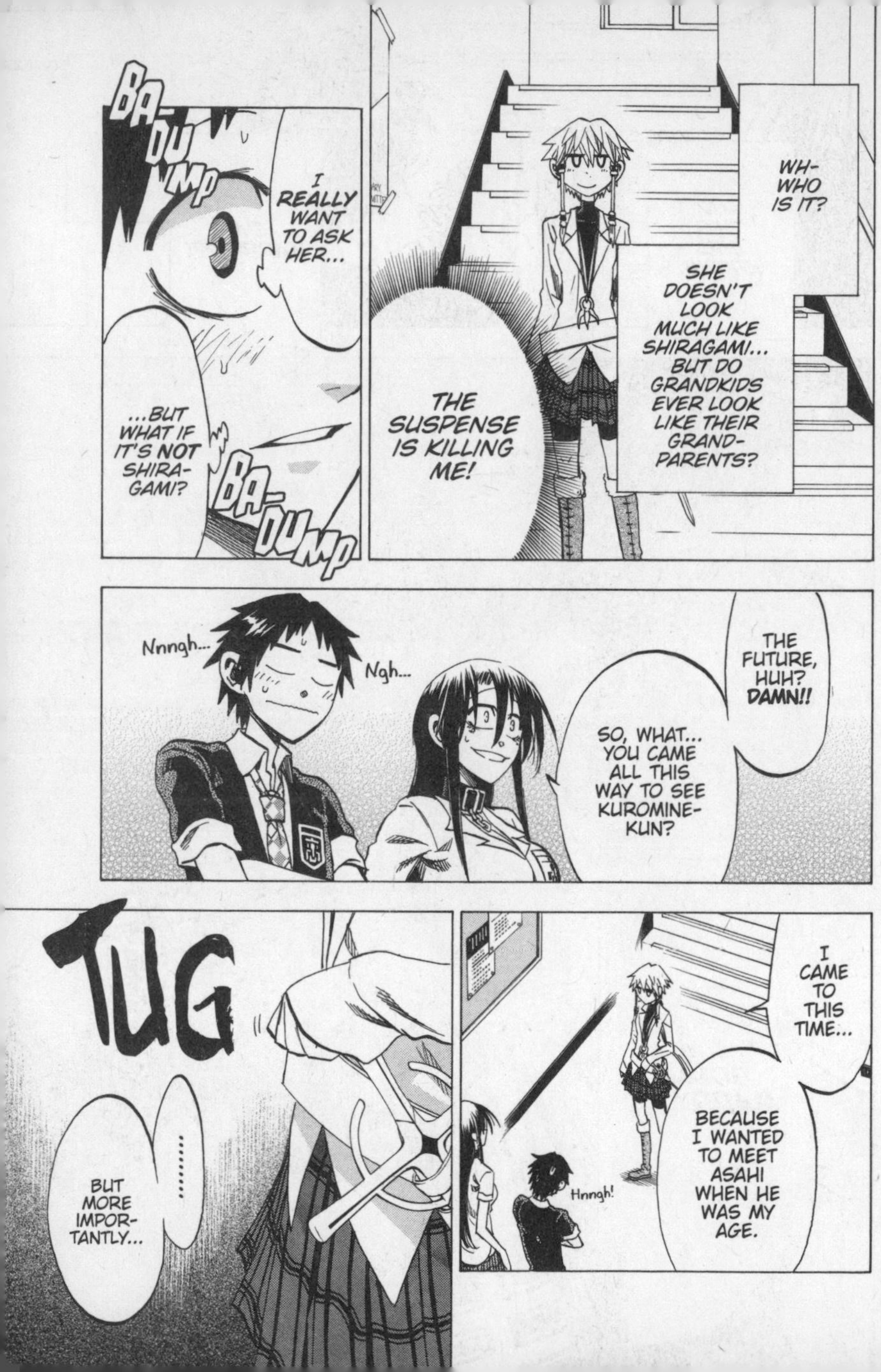
WH-WHO IS IT?
SHE DOESN'T LOOK MUCH LIKE SHIRAGAMI... BUT DO GRANDKIDS EVER LOOK LIKE THEIR GRAND-PARENTS?
THE SUSPENSE IS KILLING ME!
BA-DUMP
I REALLY WANT TO ASK HER...
...BUT WHAT IF IT'S NOT SHIRA-GAMI?
BA-DUMP
THE FUTURE, HUH? DAMN!!
SO, WHAT... YOU CAME ALL THIS WAY TO SEE KUROMINE-KUN?
Ngh...
Nnngh...
I CAME TO THIS TIME...
BECAUSE I WANTED TO MEET ASAHI WHEN HE WAS MY AGE.
Hnngh!
TUG
......
BUT MORE IMPOR-TANTLY...

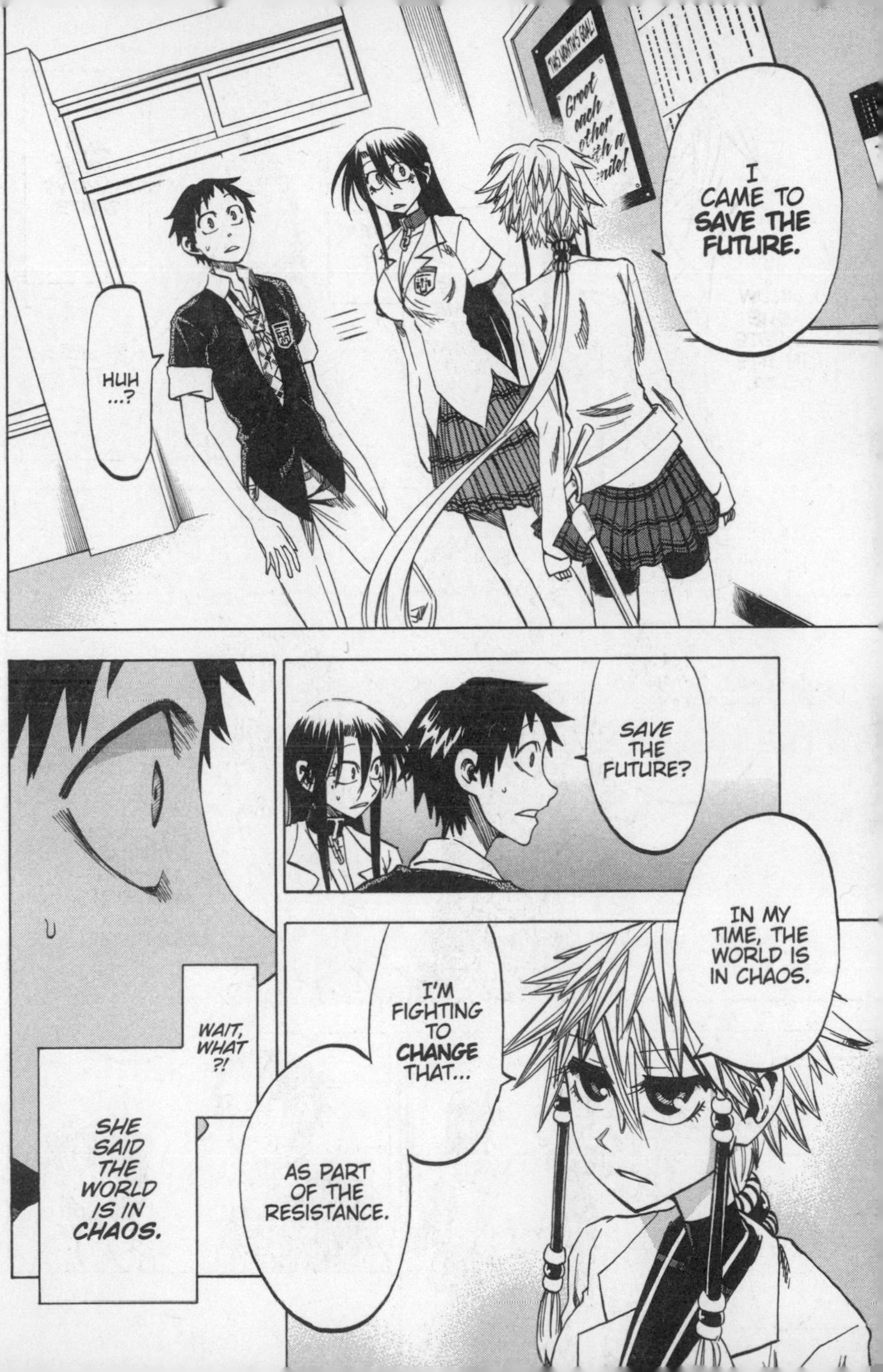
I CAME TO SAVE THE FUTURE.
HUH ...?
SAVE THE FUTURE?
IN MY TIME, THE WORLD IS IN CHAOS.
I'M FIGHTING TO CHANGE THAT...
AS PART OF THE RESISTANCE.
WAIT, WHAT ?!
SHE SAID THE WORLD IS IN CHAOS.

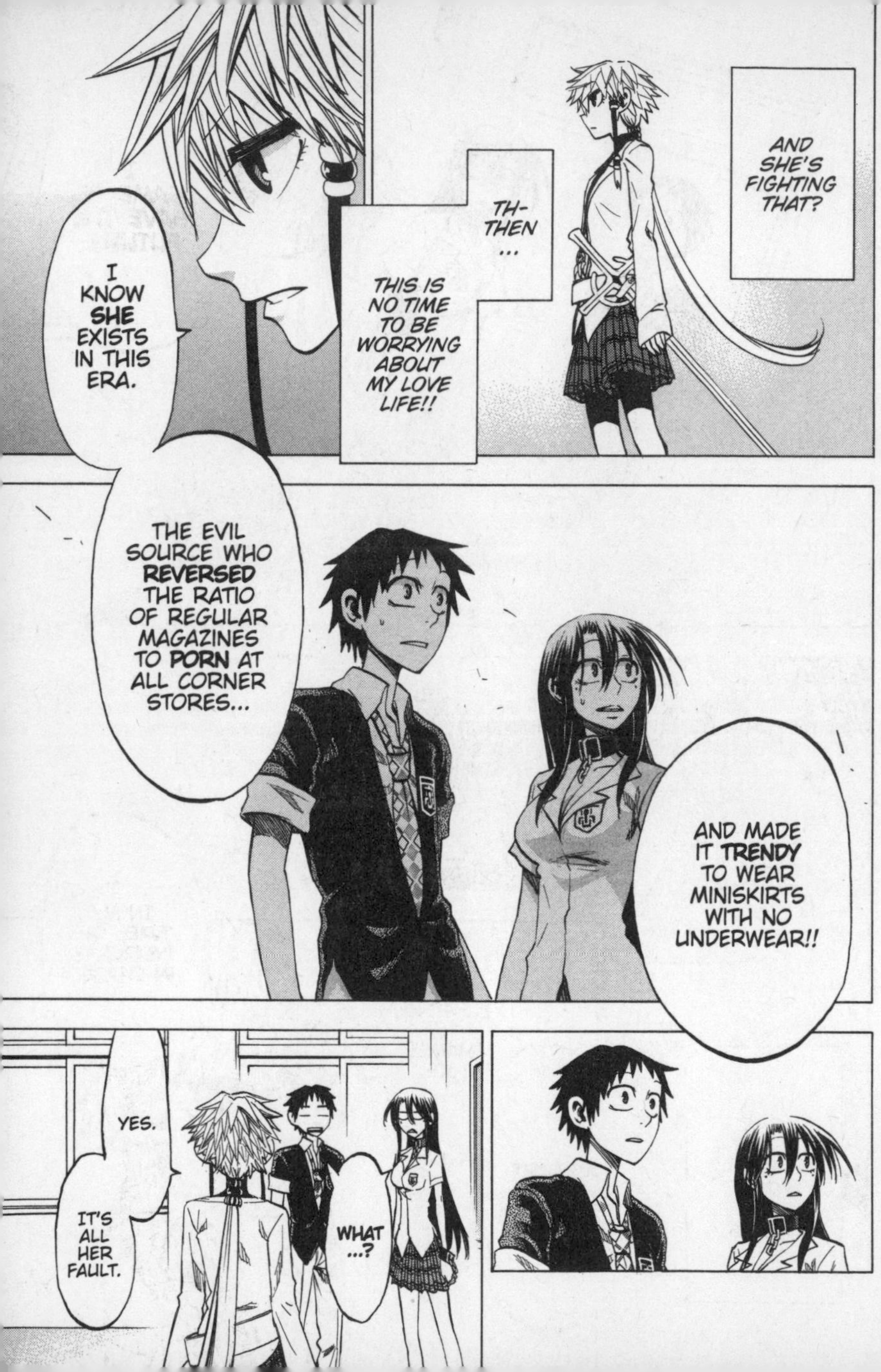
AND SHE'S FIGHTING THAT?
TH-THEN...
THIS IS NO TIME TO BE WORRYING ABOUT MY LOVE LIFE!!
I KNOW SHE EXISTS IN THIS ERA.
THE EVIL SOURCE WHO REVERSED THE RATIO OF REGULAR MAGAZINES TO PORN AT ALL CORNER STORES...
AND MADE IT TRENDY TO WEAR MINISKIRTS WITH NO UNDERWEAR!!
WHAT ...?
YES.
IT'S ALL HER FAULT.

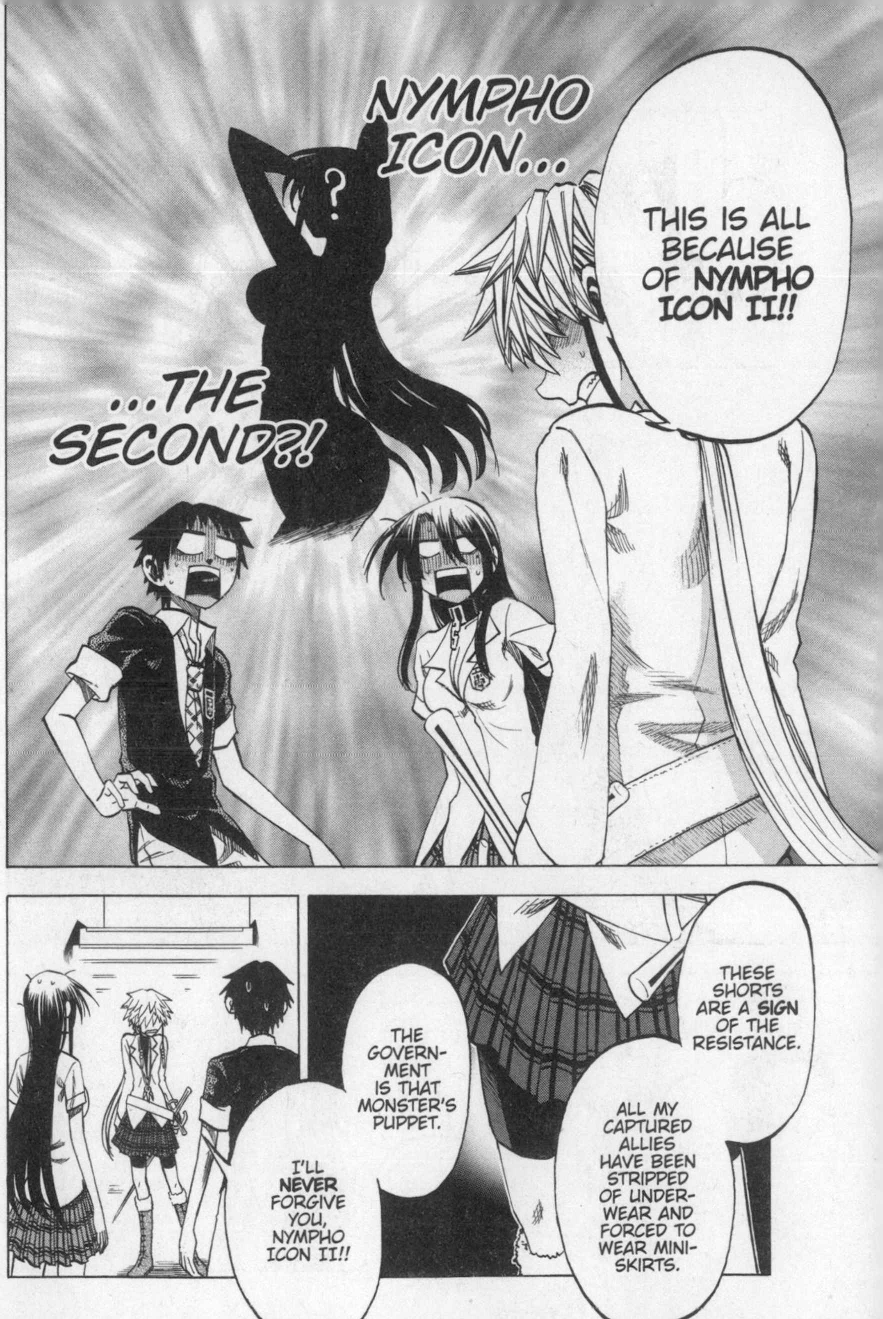
THIS IS ALL BECAUSE OF NYMPHO ICON II!!
NYMPHO ICON...
...THE SECOND?!
THESE SHORTS ARE A SIGN OF THE RESISTANCE.
ALL MY CAPTURED ALLIES HAVE BEEN STRIPPED OF UNDER-WEAR AND FORCED TO WEAR MINI-SKIRTS.
THE GOVERN-MENT IS THAT MONSTER'S PUPPET.
I'LL NEVER FORGIVE YOU, NYMPHO ICON II!!

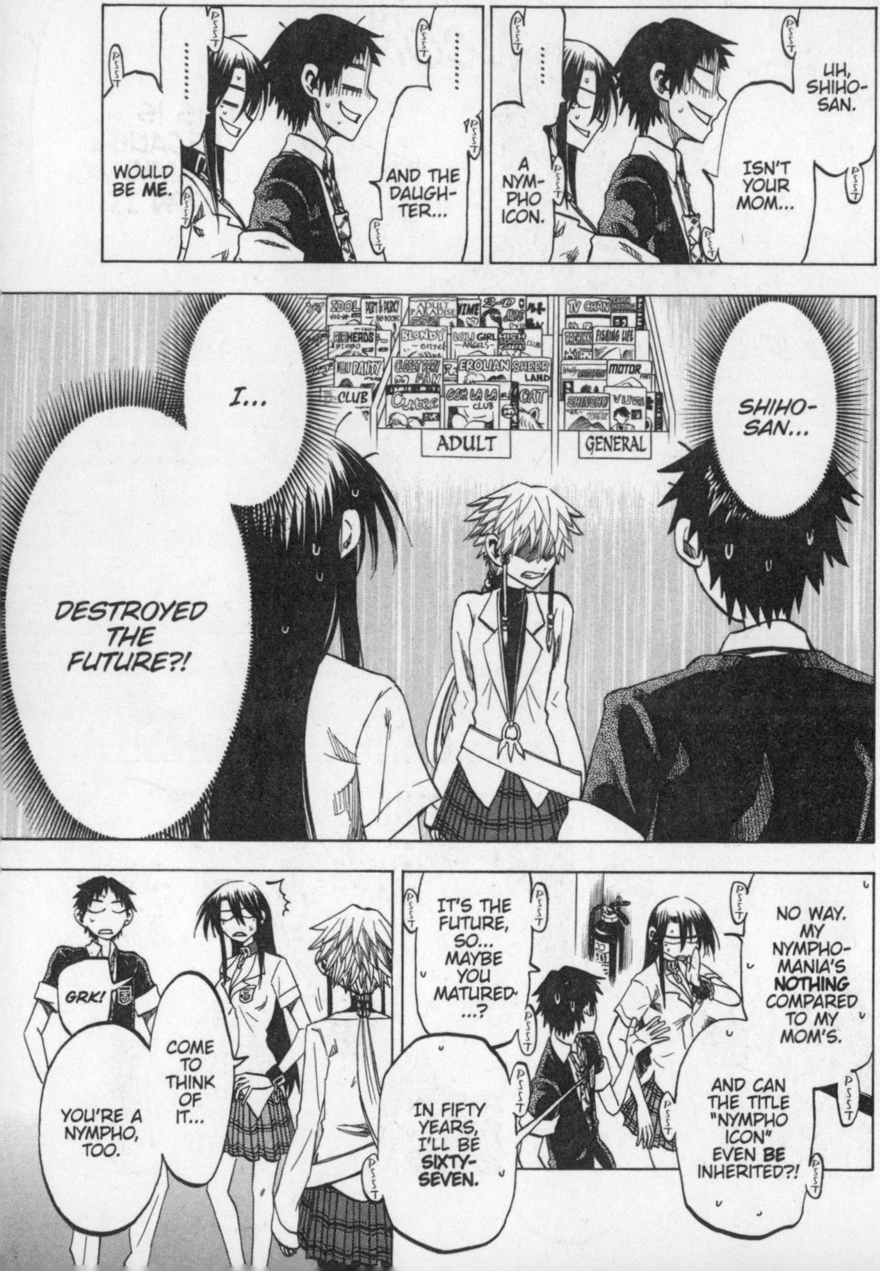
PSSST
UH, SHIHO-SAN.
ISN'T YOUR MOM...
A NYMPHO ICON.
PSSST
AND THE DAUGHTER...
WOULD BE ME.
SHIHO-SAN...
ADULT
GENERAL
I...
DESTROYED THE FUTURE?!
PSSST
NO WAY. MY NYMPHOMANIA'S NOTHING COMPARED TO MY MOM'S.
AND CAN THE TITLE "NYMPHO ICON" EVEN BE INHERITED?!
IT'S THE FUTURE, SO... MAYBE YOU MATURED...?
IN FIFTY YEARS, I'LL BE SIXTY-SEVEN.
COME TO THINK OF IT...
YOU'RE A NYMPHO, TOO.
GRK!

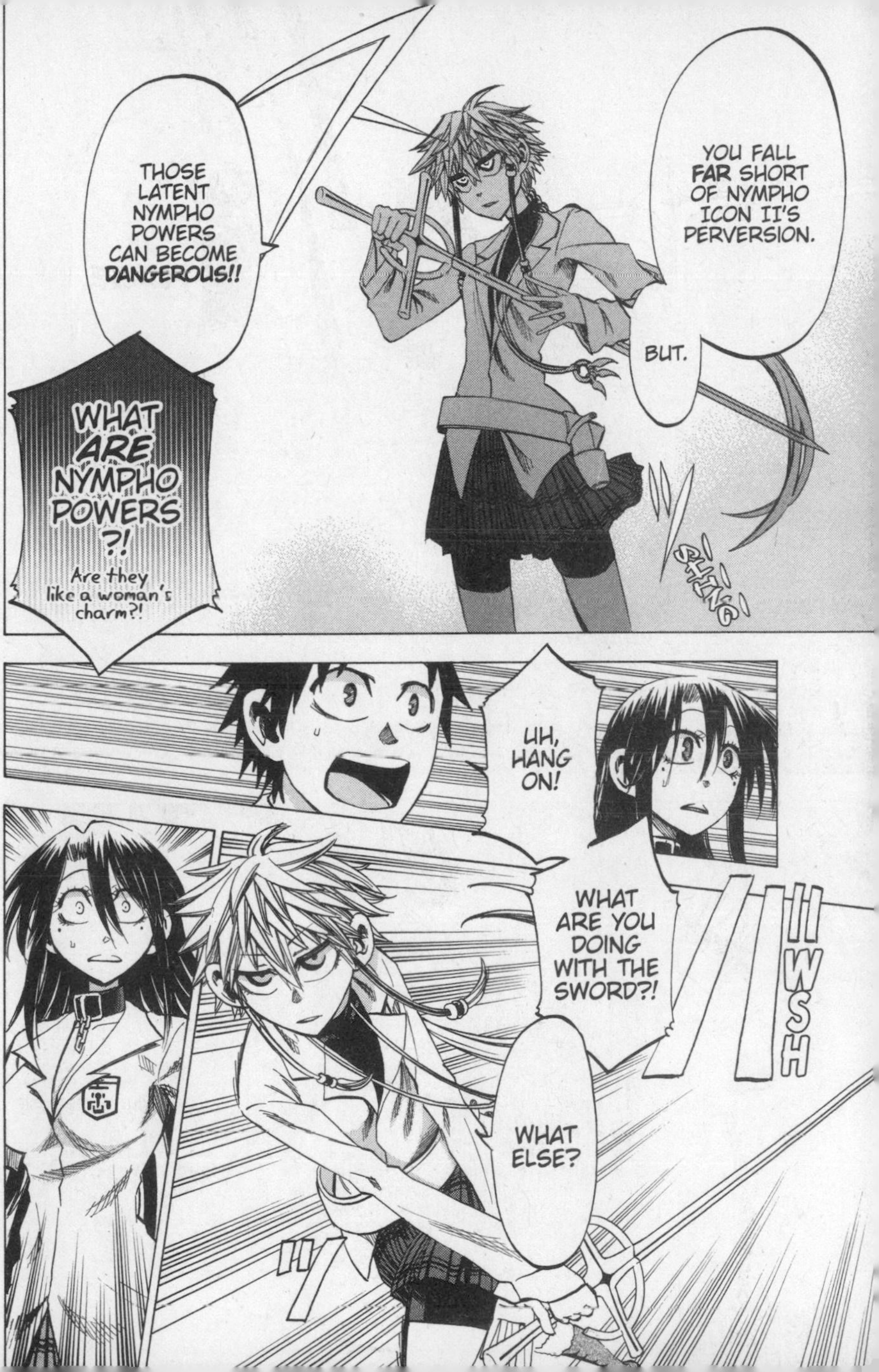
YOU FALL FAR SHORT OF NYMPHO ICON II'S PERVERSION.
BUT.
THOSE LATENT NYMPHO POWERS CAN BECOME DANGEROUS!!
SHING
WHAT ARE NYMPHO POWERS?!
Are they like a woman's charm?!
UH, HANG ON!
WHAT ARE YOU DOING WITH THE SWORD?!
HWSH
WHAT ELSE?

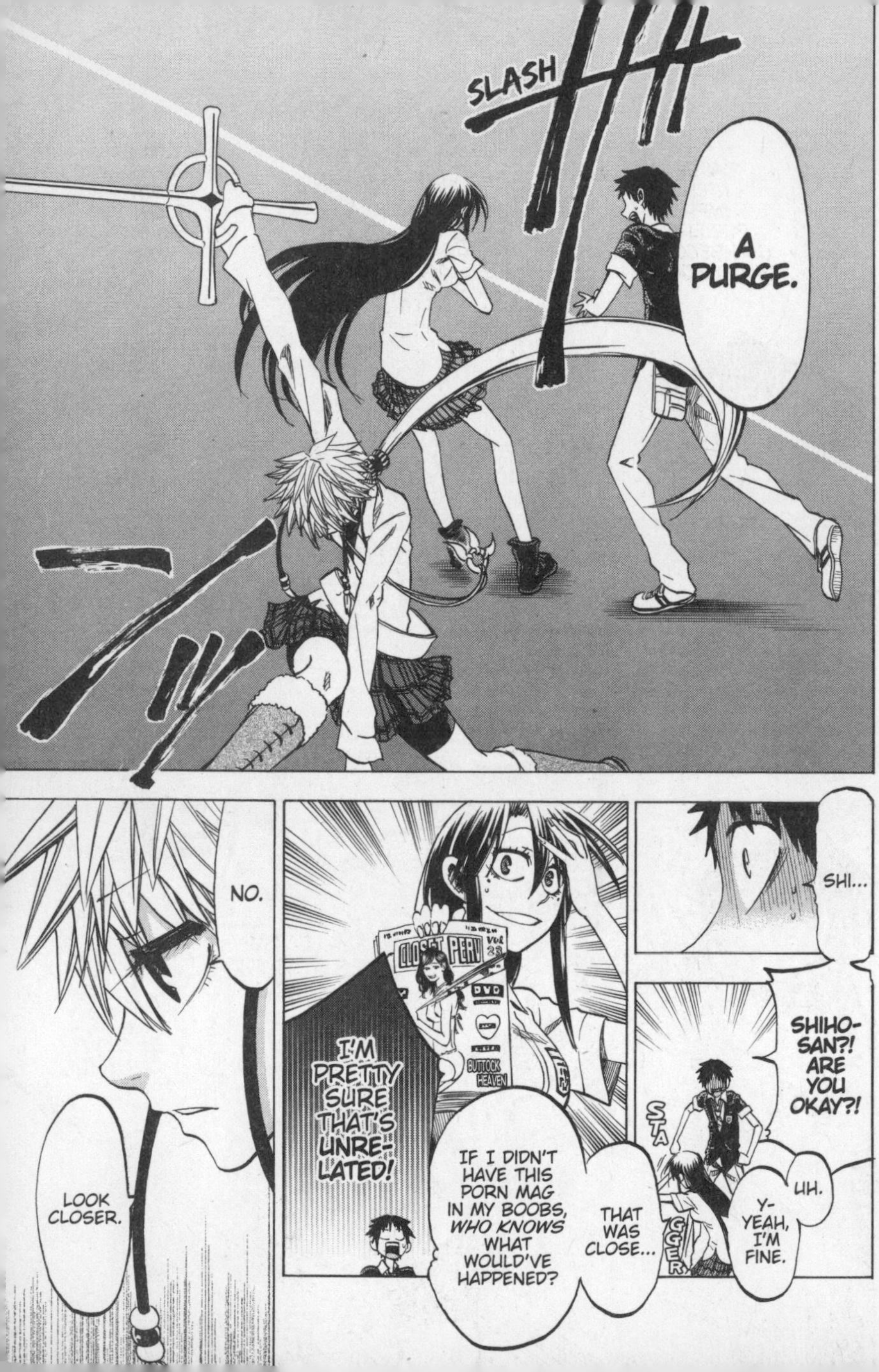
SLASH
A PURGE.
SHI...
SHIHO-SAN?! ARE YOU OKAY?!
STAGGER
UH.
Y-YEAH, I'M FINE.
THAT WAS CLOSE...
CLOSET PERV
DVD
BUTTOCK HEAVEN
IF I DIDN'T HAVE THIS PORN MAG IN MY BOOBS, *WHO KNOWS* WHAT WOULD'VE HAPPENED?
I'M PRETTY SURE THAT'S UNRELATED!
NO.
LOOK CLOSER.

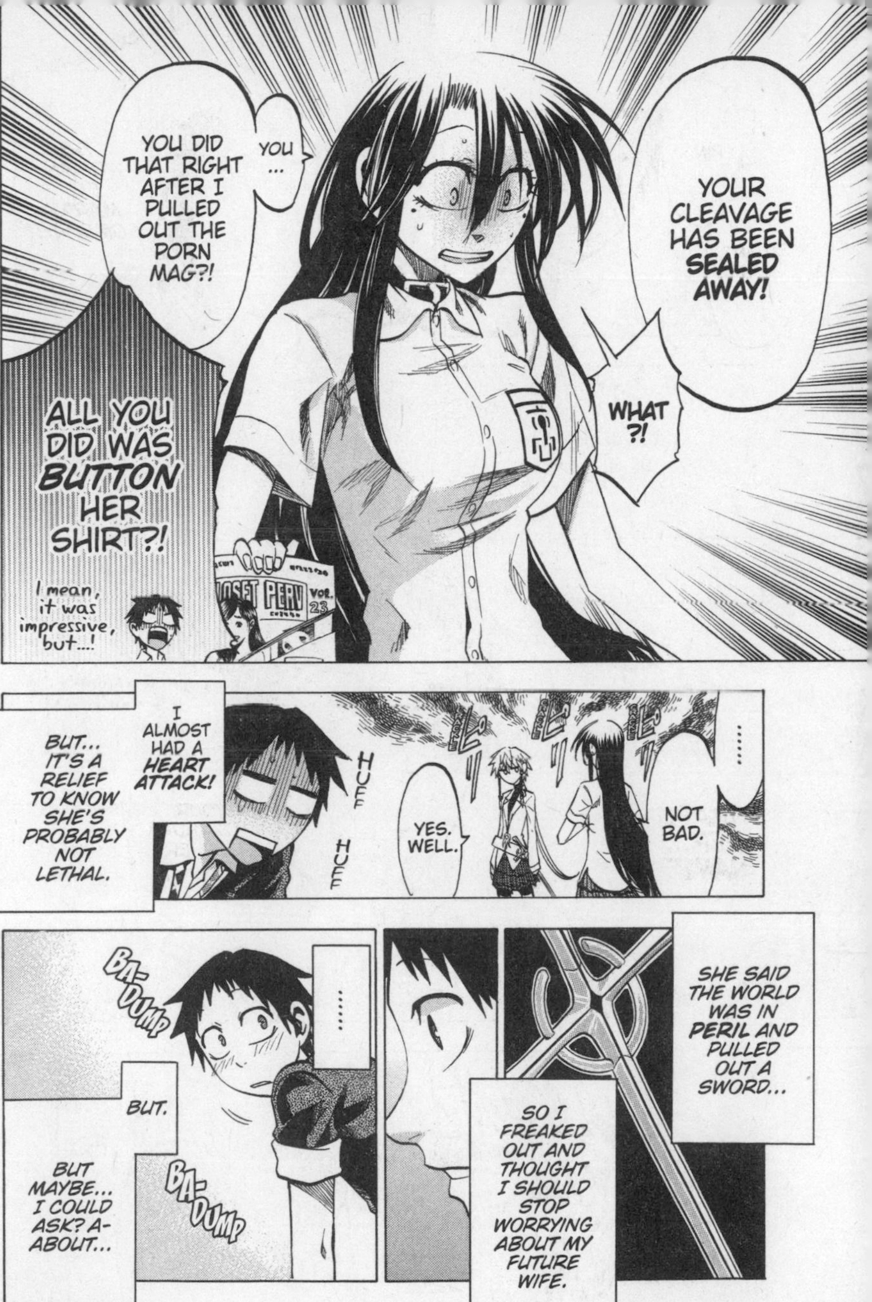
YOUR CLEAVAGE HAS BEEN SEALED AWAY!
WHAT?!
YOU ...
YOU DID THAT RIGHT AFTER I PULLED OUT THE PORN MAG?!
ALL YOU DID WAS BUTTON HER SHIRT?!
I mean, it was impressive, but...!
......
NOT BAD.
YES. WELL.
HUFF HUFF
I ALMOST HAD A HEART ATTACK!
BUT... IT'S A RELIEF TO KNOW SHE'S PROBABLY NOT LETHAL.
SHE SAID THE WORLD WAS IN PERIL AND PULLED OUT A SWORD...
SO I FREAKED OUT AND THOUGHT I SHOULD STOP WORRYING ABOUT MY FUTURE WIFE.
......
BA-DUMP
BUT.
BUT MAYBE... I COULD ASK? A-ABOUT...
BA-DUMP

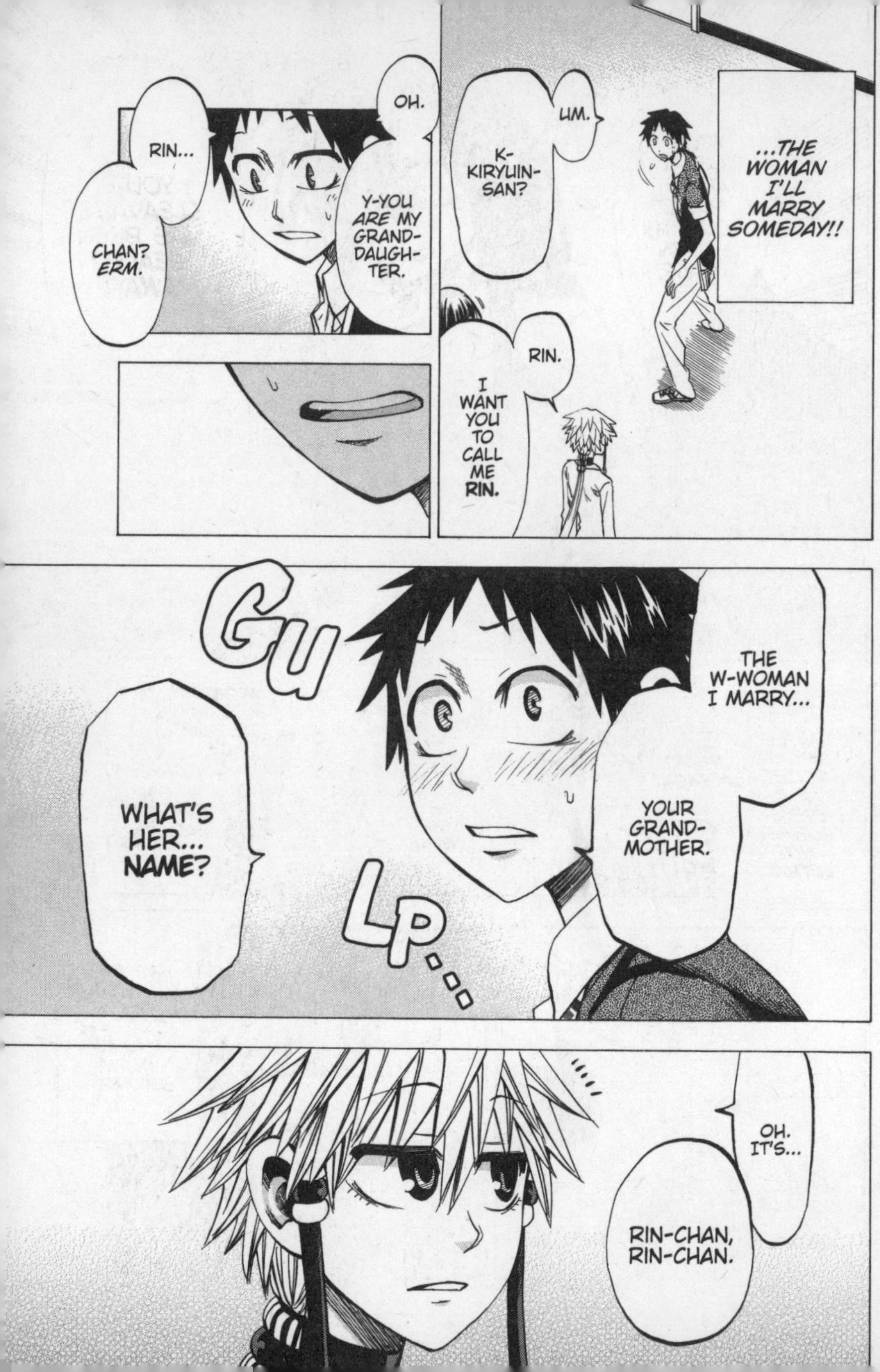
...THE WOMAN I'LL MARRY SOMEDAY!!
UM.
K-KIRYUIN-SAN?
RIN.
I WANT YOU TO CALL ME RIN.
OH.
Y-YOU ARE MY GRAND-DAUGH-TER.
RIN...
CHAN? ERM.
THE W-WOMAN I MARRY...
YOUR GRAND-MOTHER.
GULP...
WHAT'S HER... NAME?
OH. IT'S...
RIN-CHAN, RIN-CHAN.

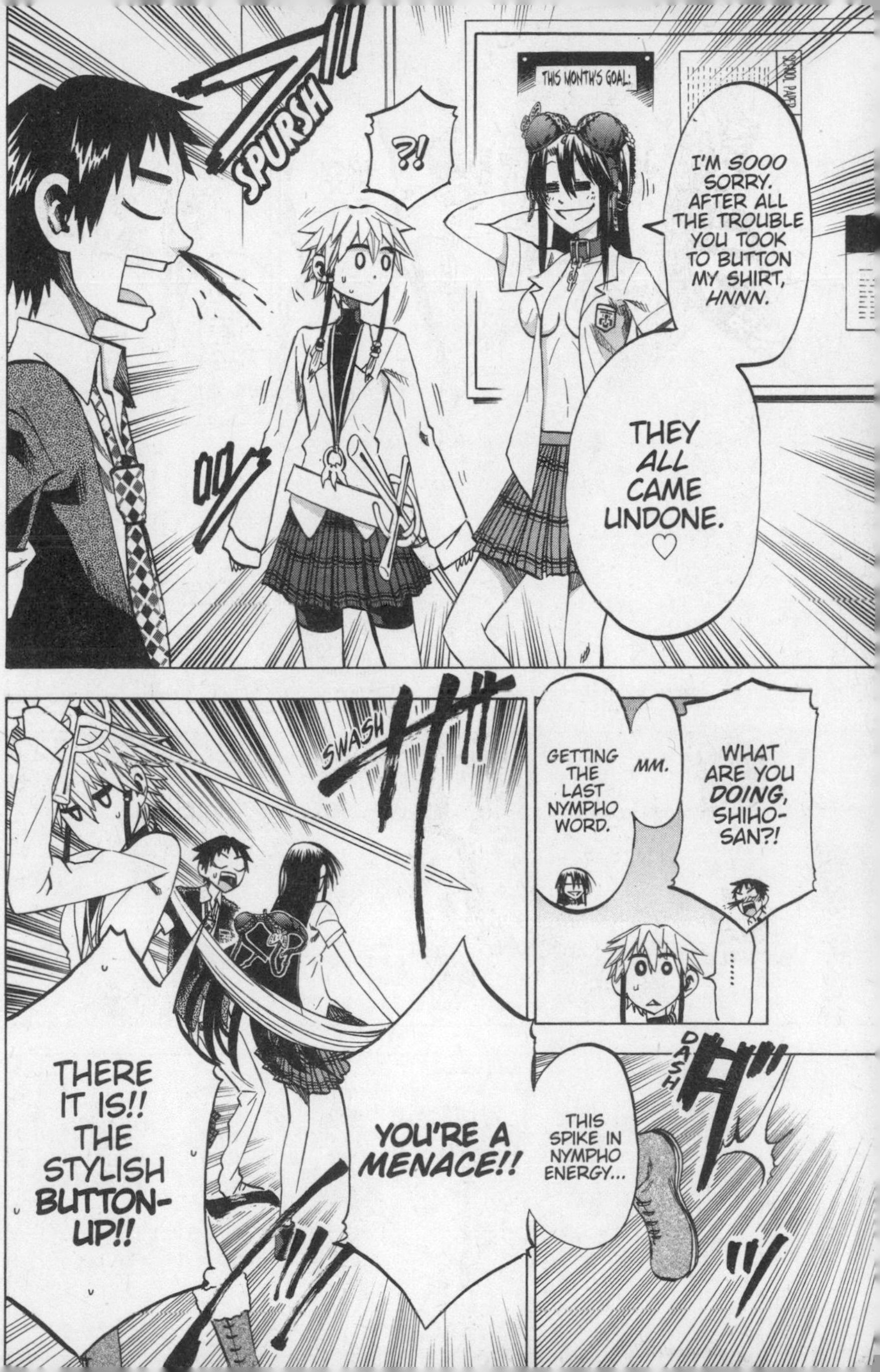
THIS MONTH'S GOAL:
SCHOOL PAPER
I'M SOOO SORRY. AFTER ALL THE TROUBLE YOU TOOK TO BUTTON MY SHIRT, HNNN.
THEY ALL CAME UNDONE. ♡
?!
SPURSH
WHAT ARE YOU DOING, SHIHO-SAN?!
MM.
GETTING THE LAST NYMPHO WORD.
......
DASH
THIS SPIKE IN NYMPHO ENERGY...
SWASH
YOU'RE A MENACE!!
THERE IT IS!! THE STYLISH BUTTON-UP!!

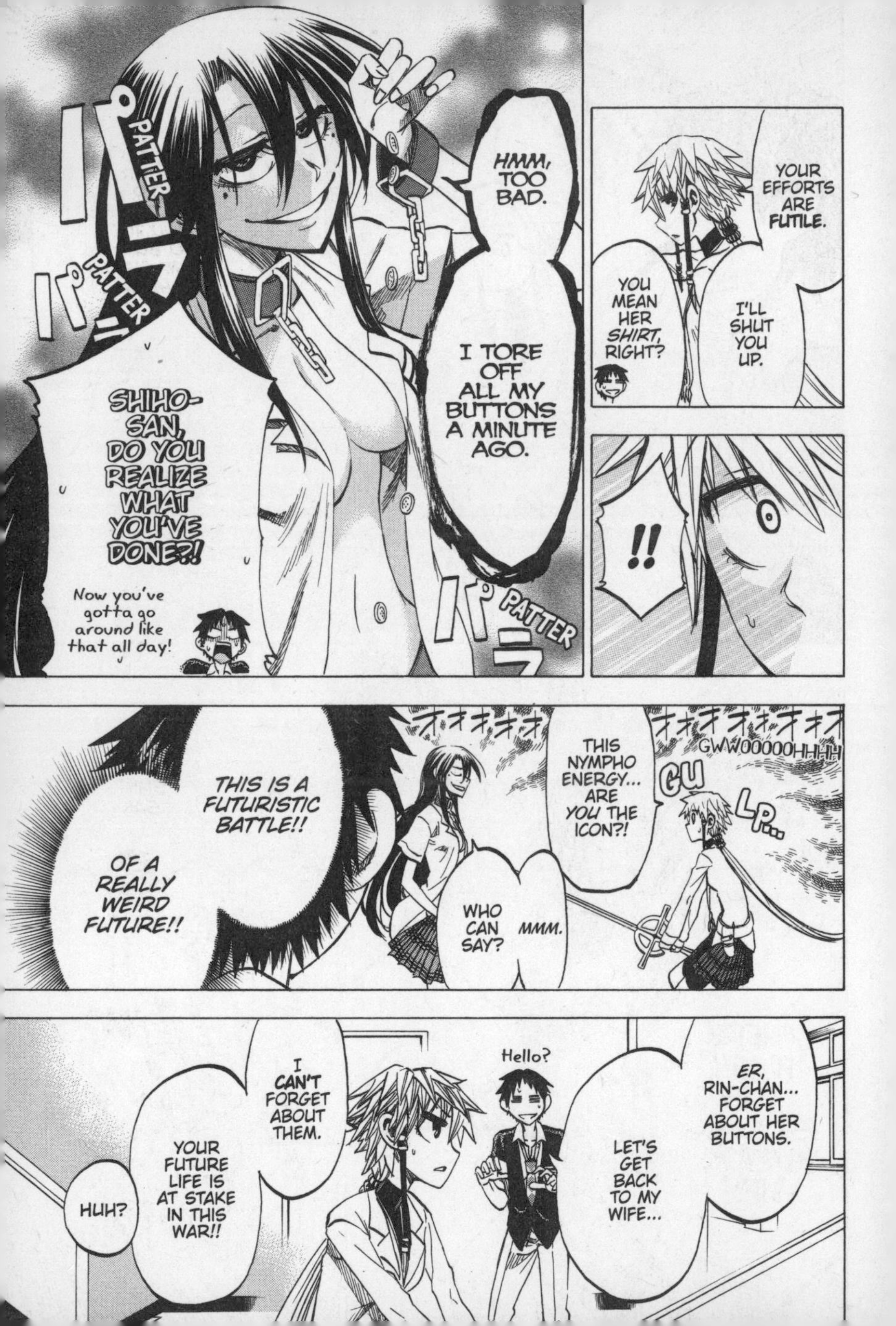
YOUR EFFORTS ARE FUTILE.
I'LL SHUT YOU UP.
YOU MEAN HER SHIRT, RIGHT?
!!
HMM, TOO BAD.
I TORE OFF ALL MY BUTTONS A MINUTE AGO.
PATTER
PATTER
PATTER
SHIHO-SAN, DO YOU REALIZE WHAT YOU'VE DONE?!
Now you've gotta go around like that all day!
GWWOOOOOHHHH
THIS NYMPHO ENERGY... ARE YOU THE ICON?!
GULP...
MMM.
WHO CAN SAY?
THIS IS A FUTURISTIC BATTLE!!
OF A REALLY WEIRD FUTURE!!
ER, RIN-CHAN... FORGET ABOUT HER BUTTONS.
LET'S GET BACK TO MY WIFE...
Hello?
I CAN'T FORGET ABOUT THEM.
YOUR FUTURE LIFE IS AT STAKE IN THIS WAR!!
HUH?

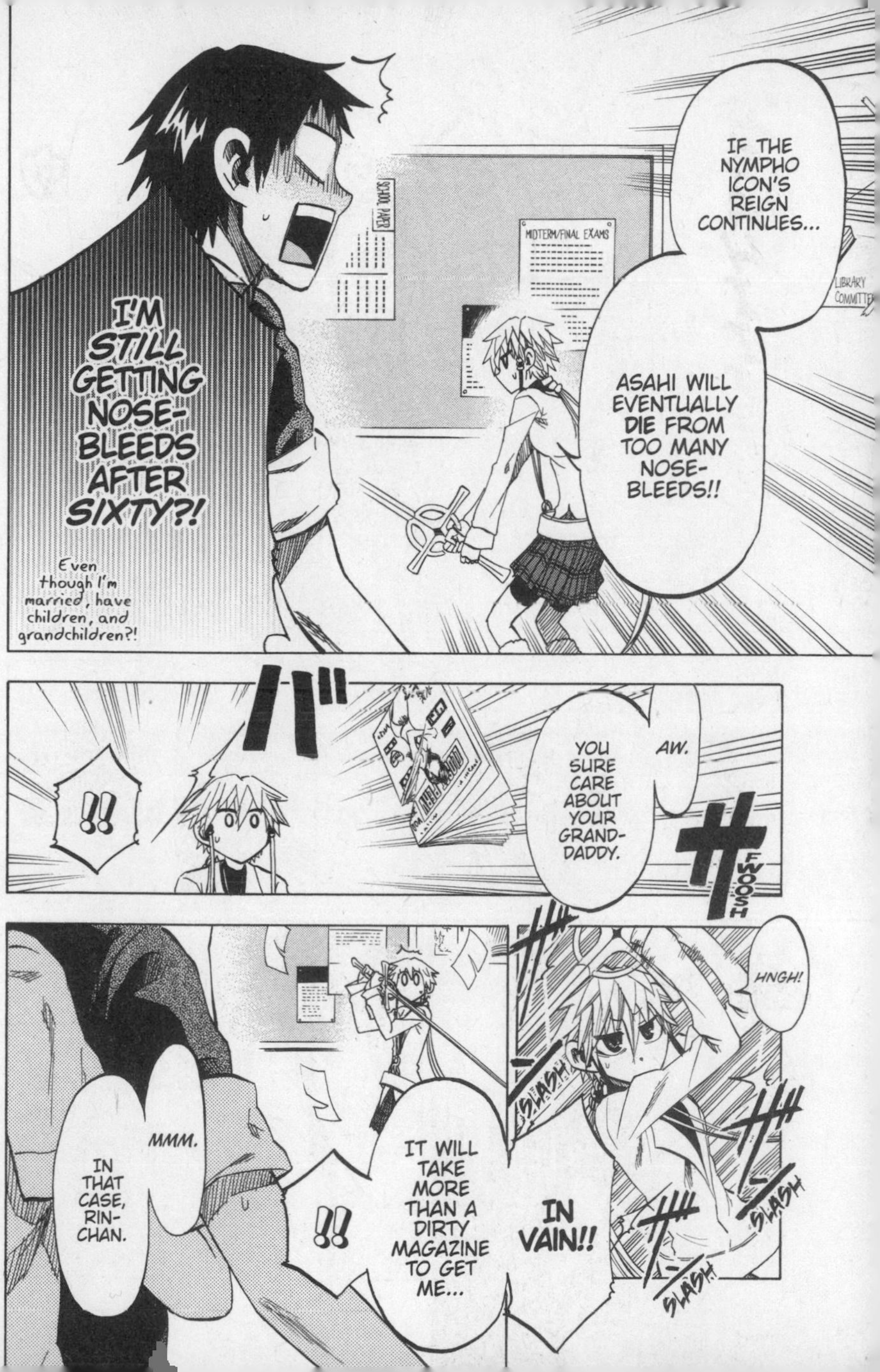
LIBRARY COMMITTE
IF THE NYMPHO ICON'S REIGN CONTINUES...
ASAHI WILL EVENTUALLY DIE FROM TOO MANY NOSE-BLEEDS!!
MIDTERM/FINAL EXAMS
SCHOOL PAPER
I'M STILL GETTING NOSE-BLEEDS AFTER SIXTY?!
Even though I'm married, have children, and grandchildren?!
AW.
YOU SURE CARE ABOUT YOUR GRAND-DADDY.
FWOOSH
!!
HNGH!
SLASH
SLASH
SLASH
IN VAIN!!
IT WILL TAKE MORE THAN A DIRTY MAGAZINE TO GET ME...
!!
MMM.
IN THAT CASE, RIN-CHAN.

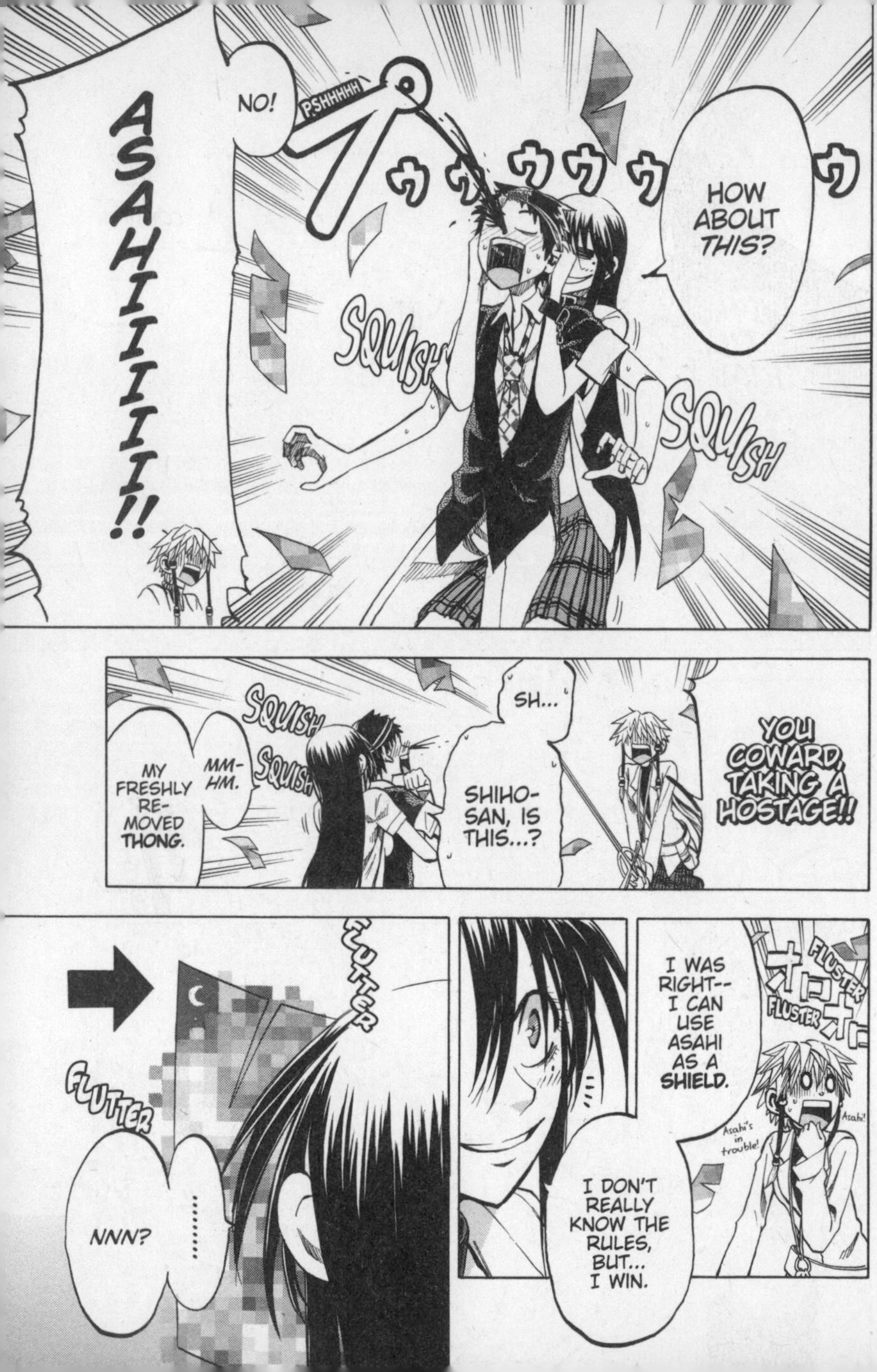
HOW ABOUT THIS?
ウウウウウウ
SQUISH
PSHHHHH
NO!
SQUISH
ASAHIIIII!!
YOU COWARD, TAKING A HOSTAGE!!
SH...
SHIHO-SAN, IS THIS...?
MM-HM.
SQUISH
SQUISH
MY FRESHLY RE-MOVED THONG.
FLUSTER
FLUSTER
I WAS RIGHT-- I CAN USE ASAHI AS A SHIELD.
Asahi!
Asahi's in trouble!
...
I DON'T REALLY KNOW THE RULES, BUT... I WIN.
FLUTTER
FLUTTER
......
NNN?

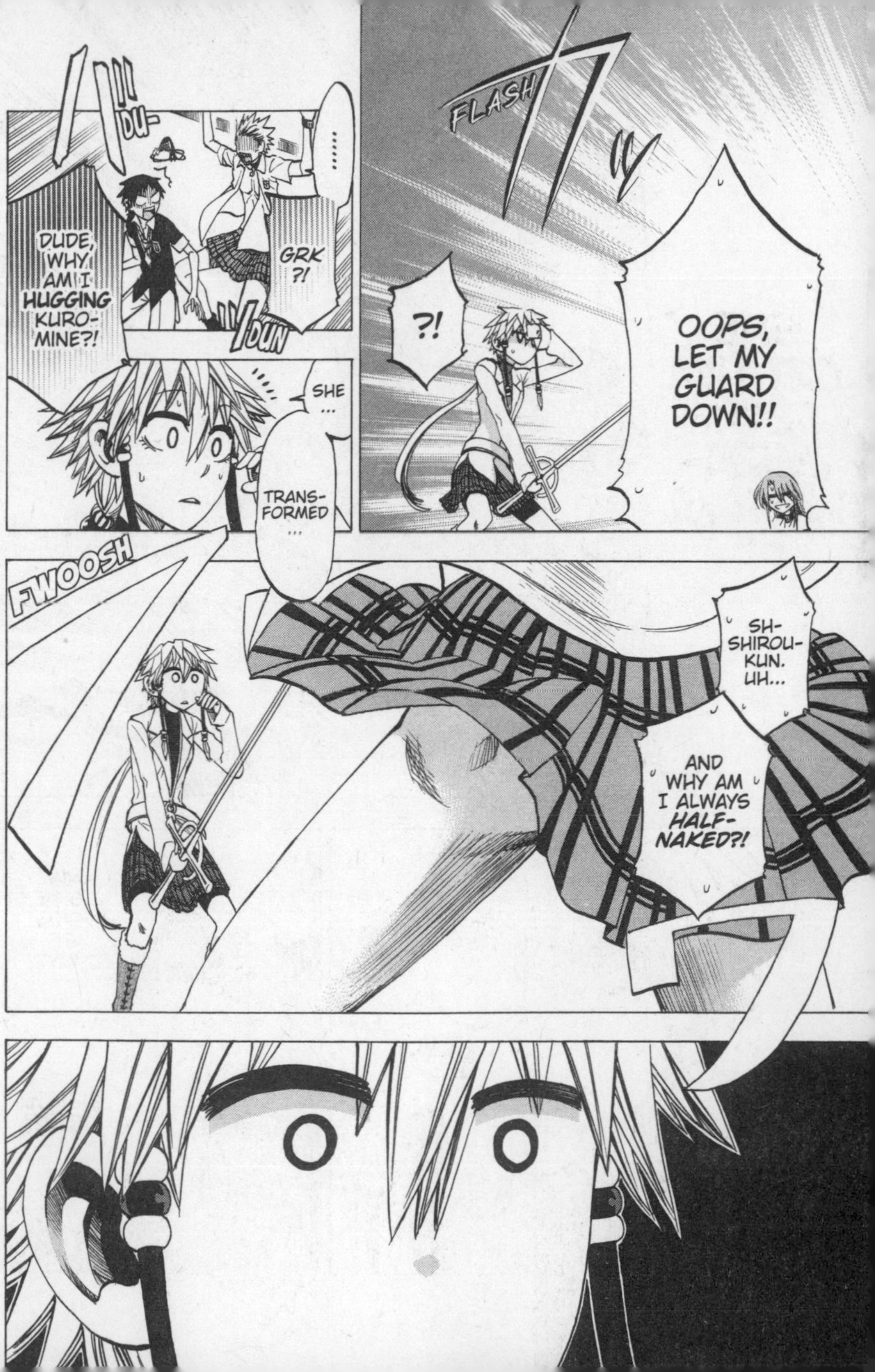
FLASH
OOPS, LET MY GUARD DOWN!!
?!
......
DU-
GRK ?!
DUDE, WHY AM I HUGGING KURO-MINE?!
DUN
SHE ...
TRANS-FORMED ...
SH-SHIROU-KUN. UH...
AND WHY AM I ALWAYS HALF-NAKED?!
FWOOSH

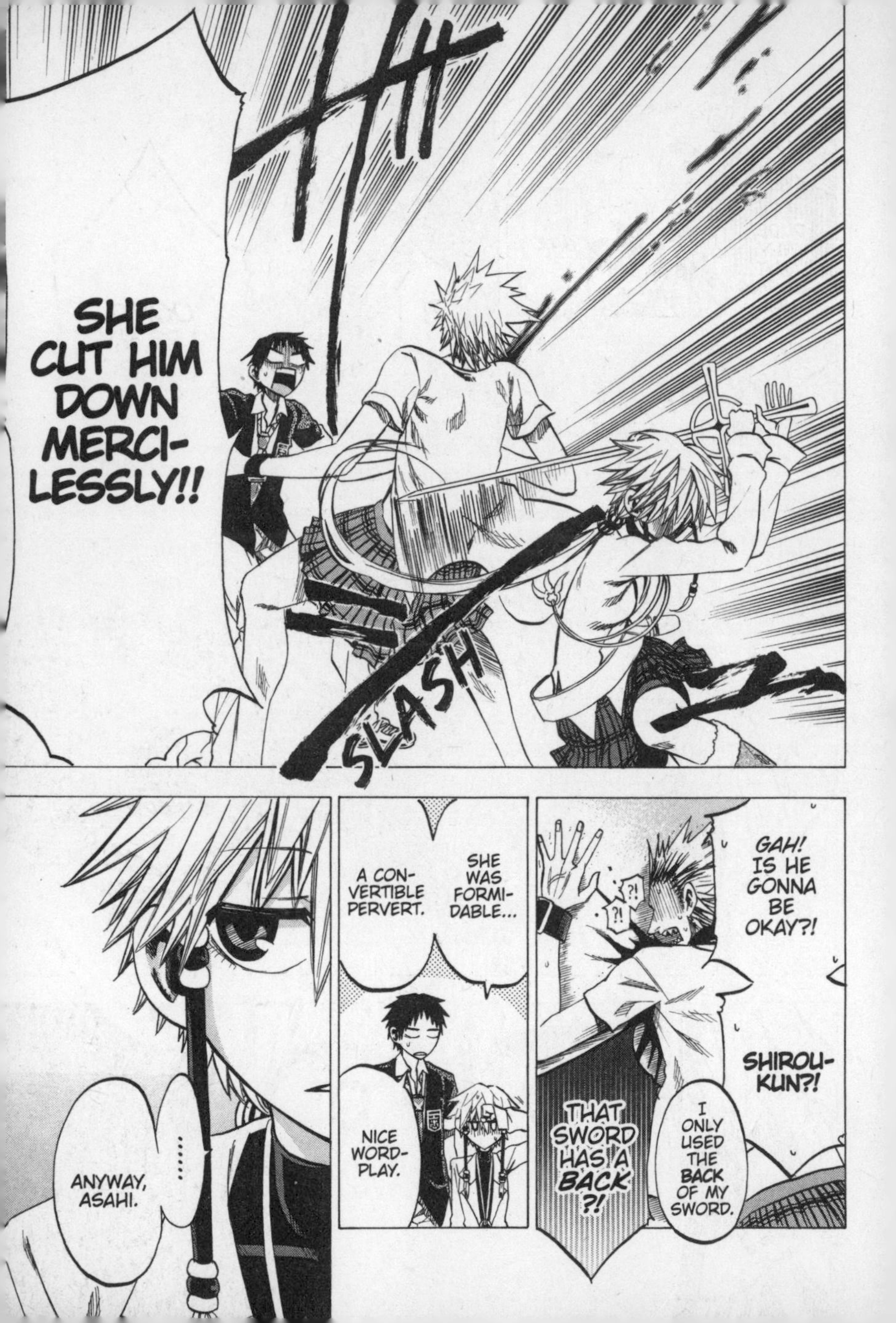
SHE CUT HIM DOWN MERCILESSLY!!
SLASH
GAH! IS HE GONNA BE OKAY?!
?!
?!
SHIROU-KUN?!
I ONLY USED THE BACK OF MY SWORD.
THAT SWORD HAS A BACK?!
SHE WAS FORMIDABLE...
A CONVERTIBLE PERVERT.
NICE WORDPLAY.
......
ANYWAY, ASAHI.

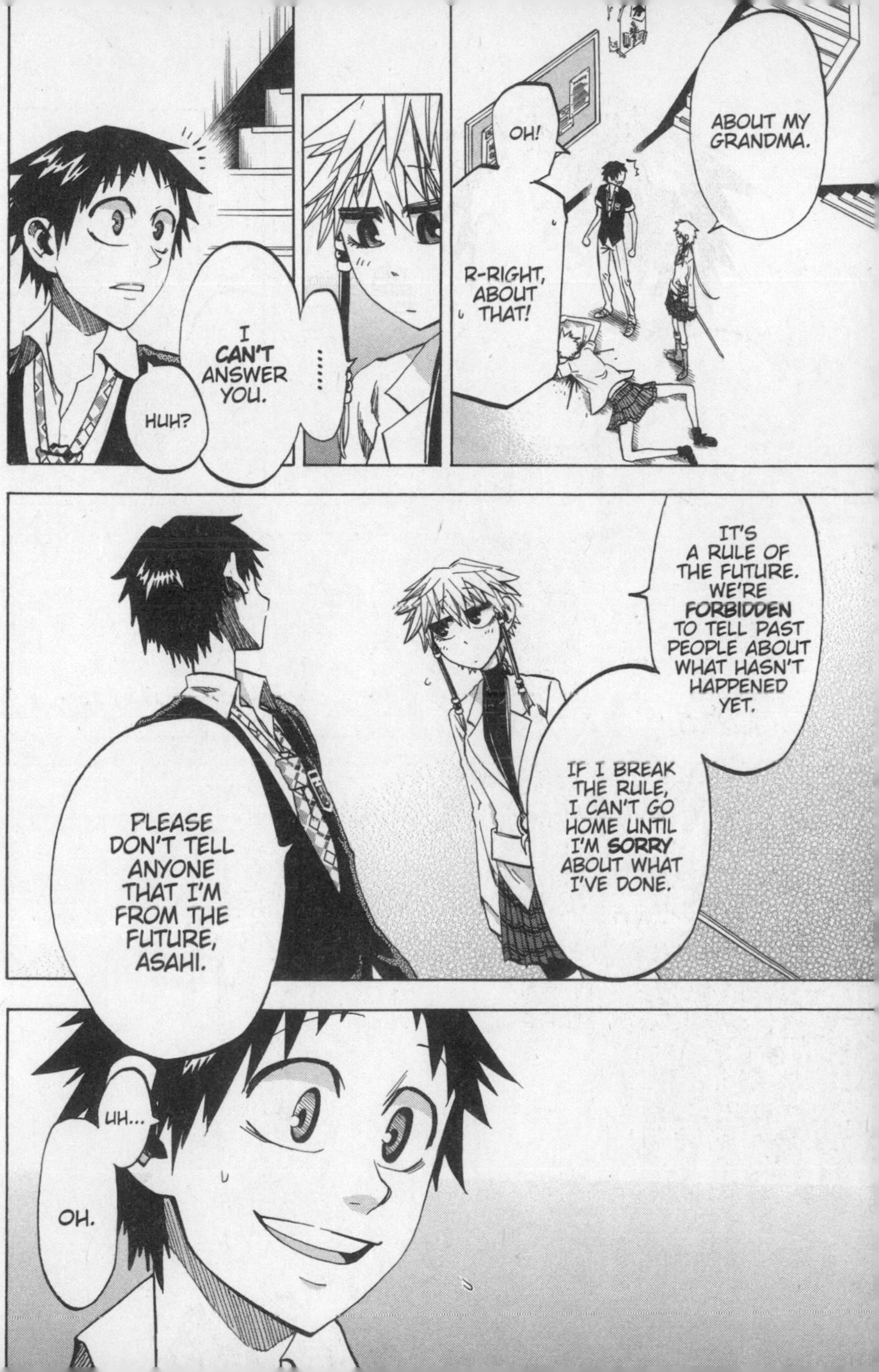
ABOUT MY GRANDMA.
OH!
R-RIGHT, ABOUT THAT!
......
I CAN'T ANSWER YOU.
HUH?
IT'S A RULE OF THE FUTURE. WE'RE FORBIDDEN TO TELL PAST PEOPLE ABOUT WHAT HASN'T HAPPENED YET.
IF I BREAK THE RULE, I CAN'T GO HOME UNTIL I'M SORRY ABOUT WHAT I'VE DONE.
PLEASE DON'T TELL ANYONE THAT I'M FROM THE FUTURE, ASAHI.
UH...
OH.

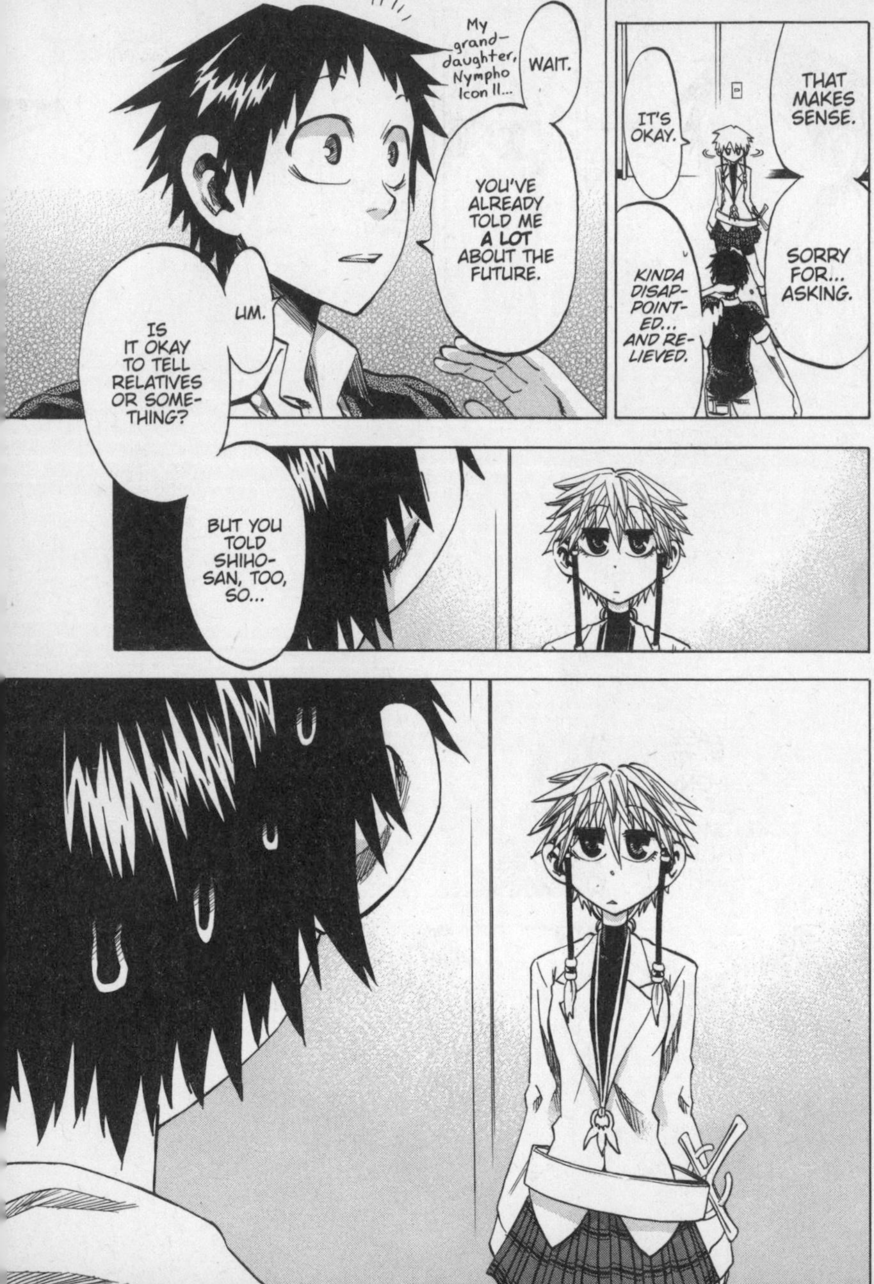
THAT MAKES SENSE.
IT'S OKAY.
SORRY FOR... ASKING.
KINDA DISAPPOINTED... AND RELIEVED.
WAIT.
My grand-daughter, Nympho Icon II...
YOU'VE ALREADY TOLD ME **A LOT** ABOUT THE FUTURE.
UM.
IS IT OKAY TO TELL RELATIVES OR SOMETHING?
BUT YOU TOLD SHIHO-SAN, TOO, SO...

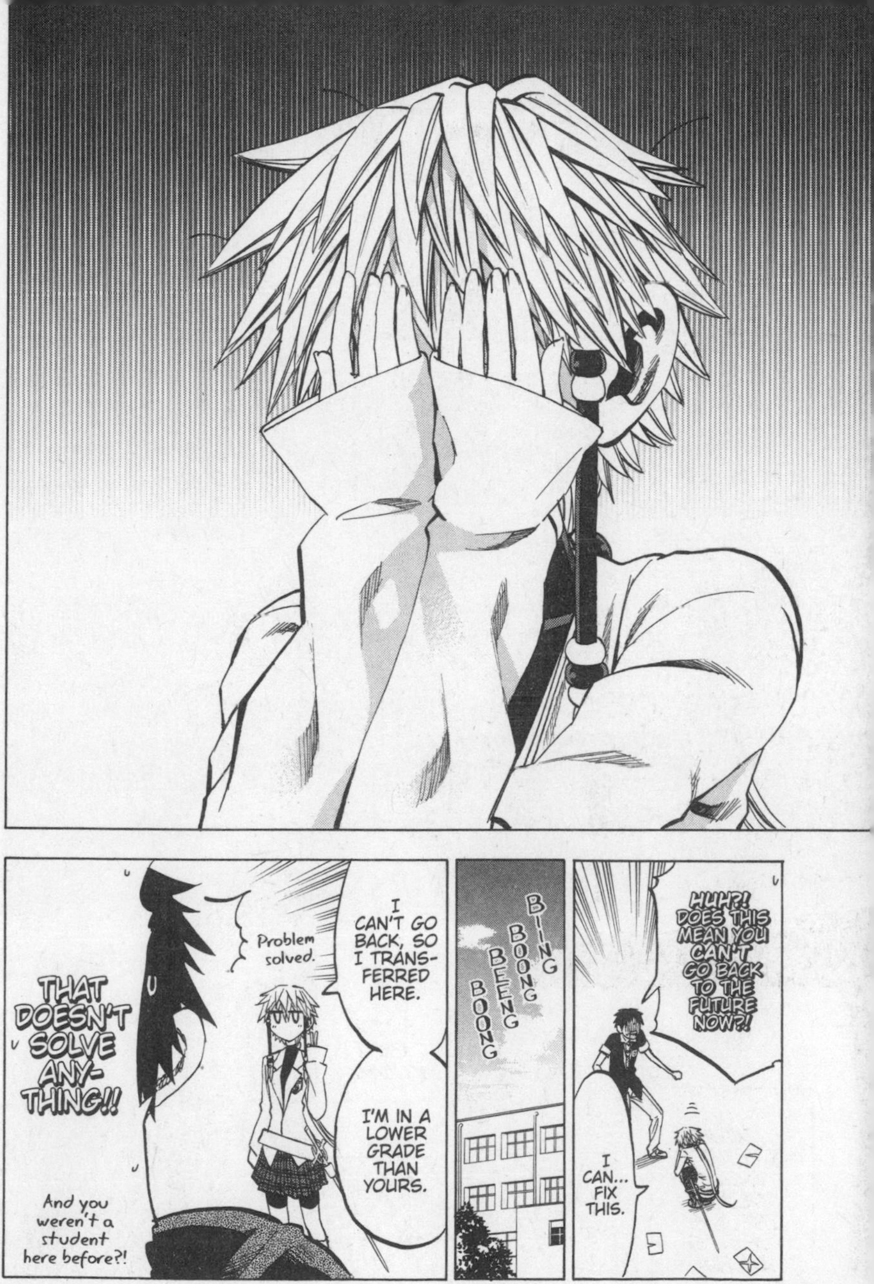
HUH?! DOES THIS MEAN YOU CAN'T GO BACK TO THE FUTURE NOW?!
I CAN... FIX THIS.
BIING
BOONG
BEEENG
BOONG
I CAN'T GO BACK, SO I TRANS-FERRED HERE.
I'M IN A LOWER GRADE THAN YOURS.
Problem solved.
THAT DOESN'T SOLVE ANY-THING!!
And you weren't a student here before?!

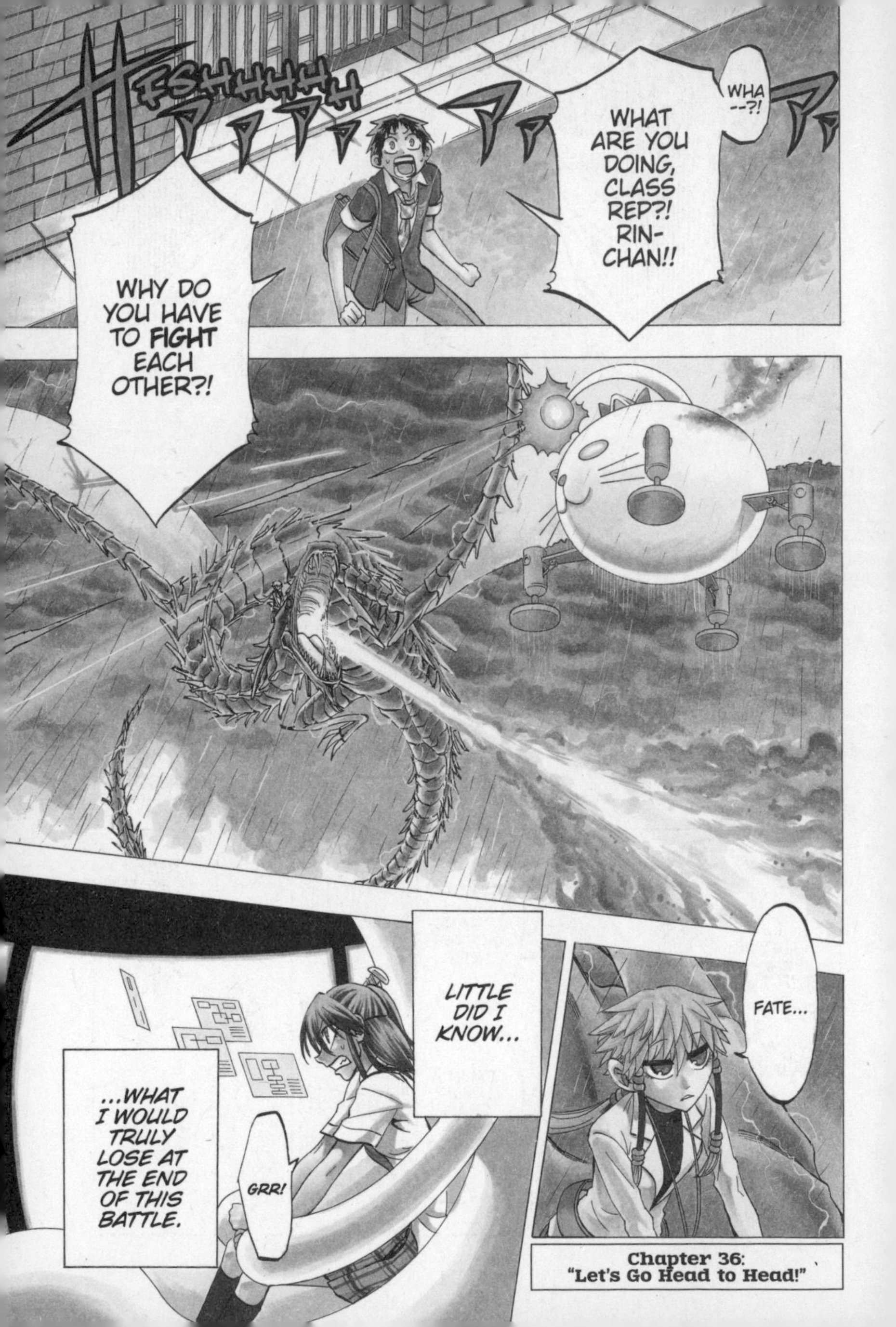

WHA--?!
WHAT ARE YOU DOING, CLASS REP?! RIN-CHAN!!
FSHHHHH
WHY DO YOU HAVE TO FIGHT EACH OTHER?!
FATE...
Chapter 36: "Let's Go Head to Head!"
LITTLE DID I KNOW...
...WHAT I WOULD TRULY LOSE AT THE END OF THIS BATTLE.
GRR!

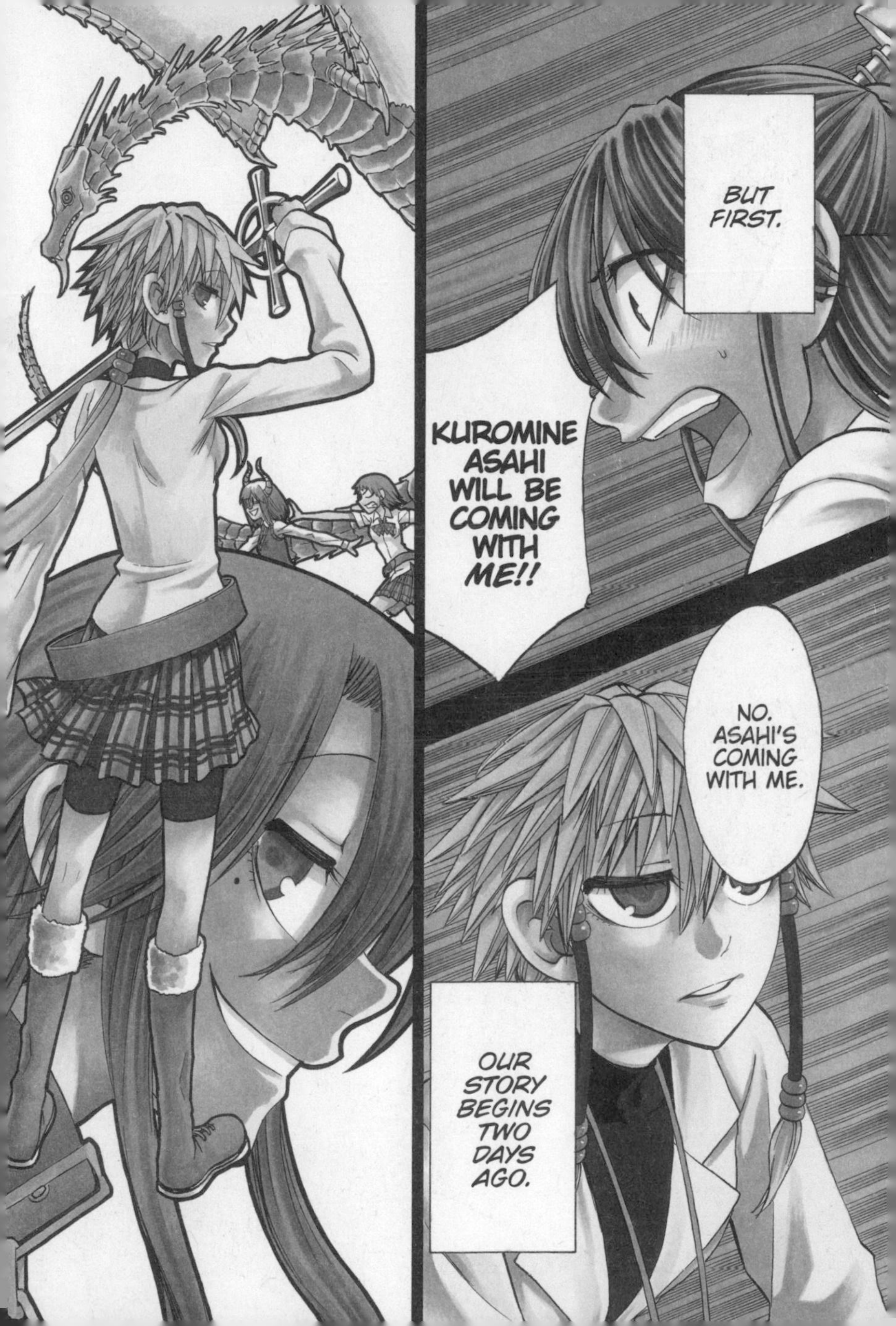
BUT FIRST.
KUROMINE ASAHI WILL BE COMING WITH ME!!
NO. ASAHI'S COMING WITH ME.
OUR STORY BEGINS TWO DAYS AGO.

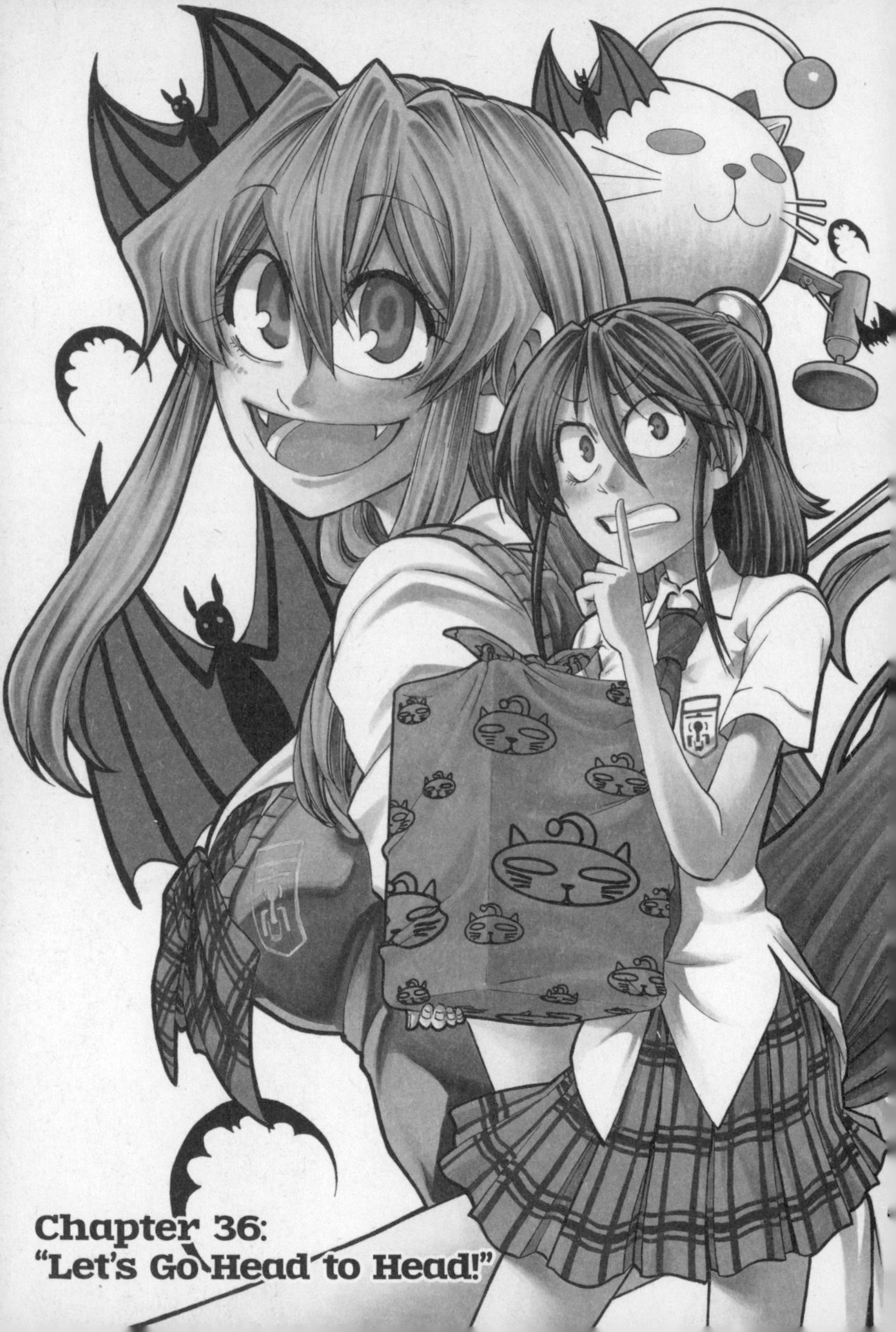

Chapter 36:
"Let's Go Head to Head!"

TOP SECRET

My Monster Secret 5

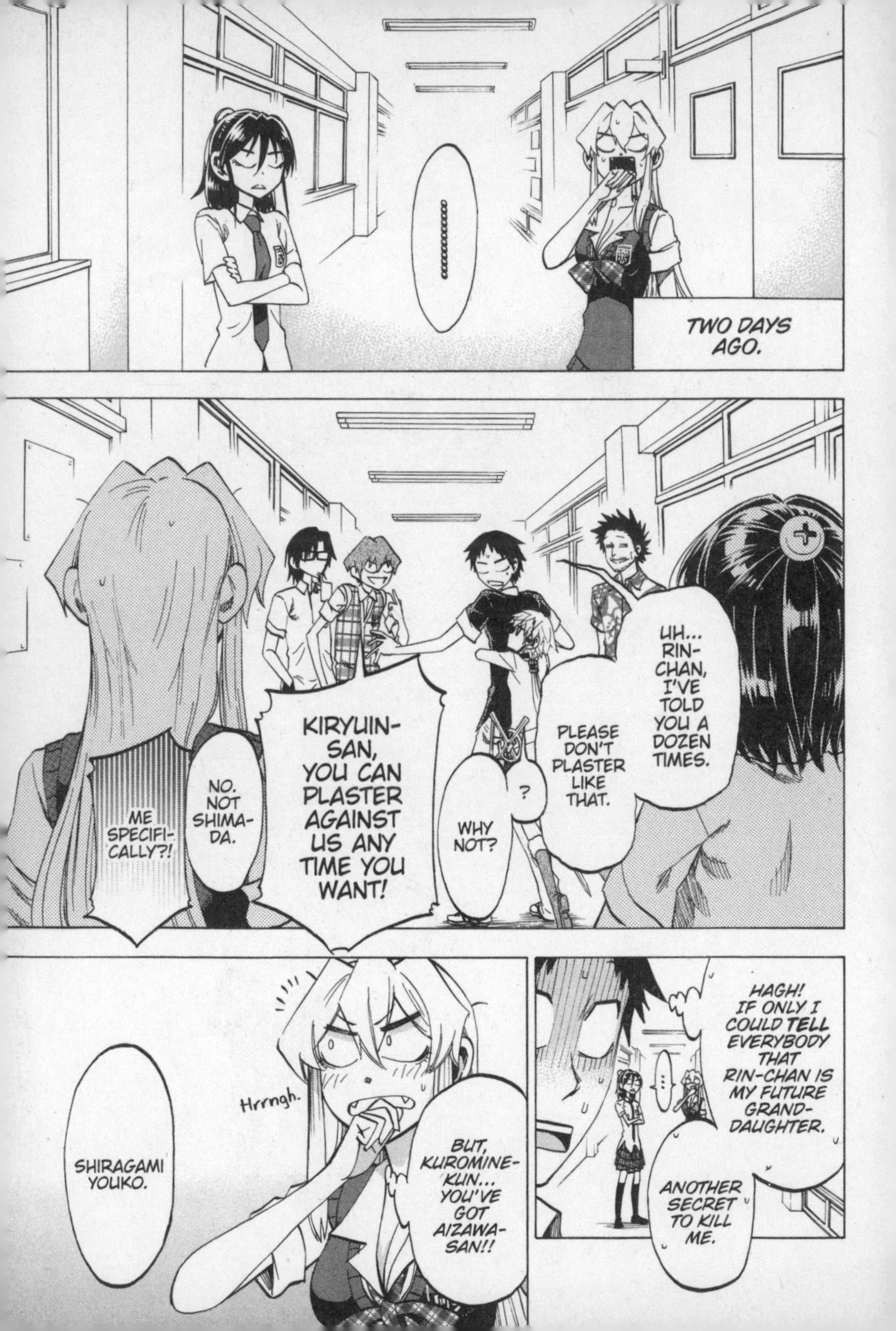
......
TWO DAYS AGO.
UH... RIN-CHAN, I'VE TOLD YOU A DOZEN TIMES.
PLEASE DON'T PLASTER LIKE THAT.
?
WHY NOT?
KIRYUIN-SAN, YOU CAN PLASTER AGAINST US ANY TIME YOU WANT!
NO. NOT SHIMADA.
ME SPECIFICALLY?!
HAGH! IF ONLY I COULD TELL EVERYBODY THAT RIN-CHAN IS MY FUTURE GRAND-DAUGHTER.
...
ANOTHER SECRET TO KILL ME.
BUT, KUROMINE-KUN... YOU'VE GOT AIZAWA-SAN!!
Hrrngh.
SHIRAGAMI YOUKO.

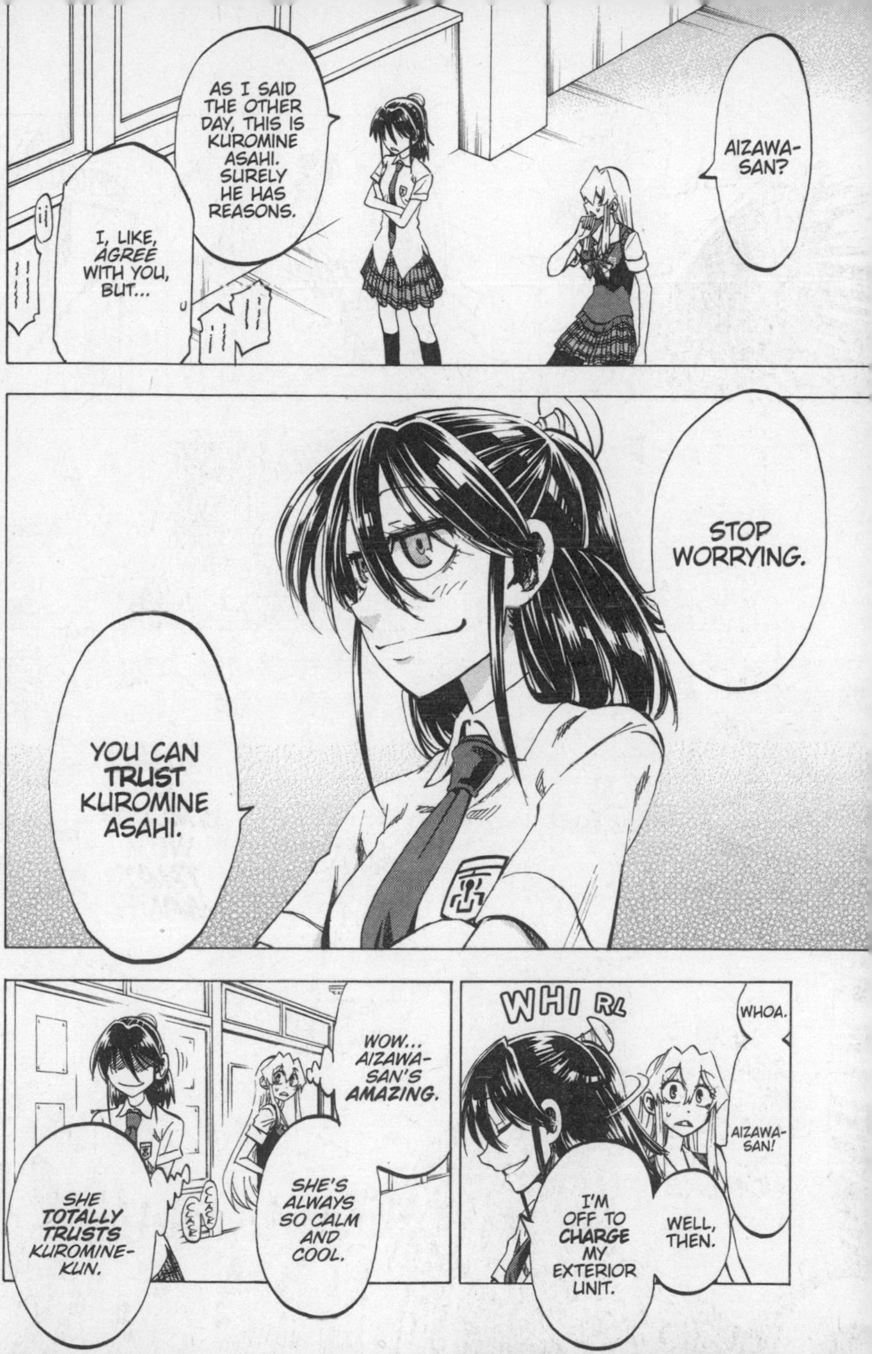
AIZAWA-SAN?
AS I SAID THE OTHER DAY, THIS IS KUROMINE ASAHI. SURELY HE HAS REASONS.
I, LIKE, AGREE WITH YOU, BUT...
STOP WORRYING.
YOU CAN TRUST KUROMINE ASAHI.
WHIRL
WHOA.
AIZAWA-SAN!
WELL, THEN.
I'M OFF TO CHARGE MY EXTERIOR UNIT.
WOW... AIZAWA-SAN'S AMAZING.
SHE'S ALWAYS SO CALM AND COOL.
SHE TOTALLY TRUSTS KUROMINE-KUN.
CLACK CLACK

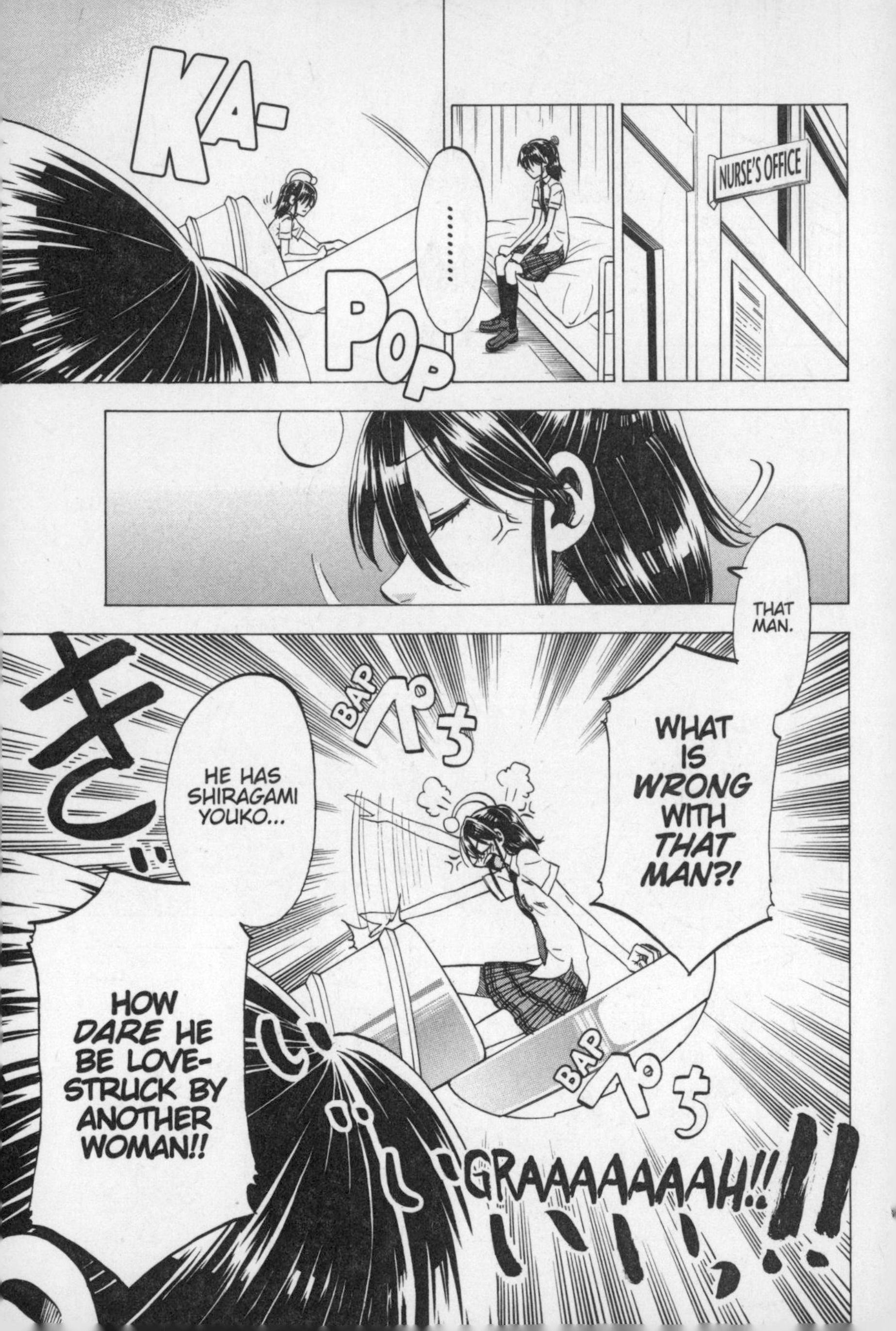
NURSE'S OFFICE
......
KA-POP
THAT MAN.
WHAT IS WRONG WITH THAT MAN?!
BAP ぺち
HE HAS SHIRAGAMI YOUKO...
HOW DARE HE BE LOVE-STRUCK BY ANOTHER WOMAN!!
BAP ぺち
GRAAAAAAAH!!

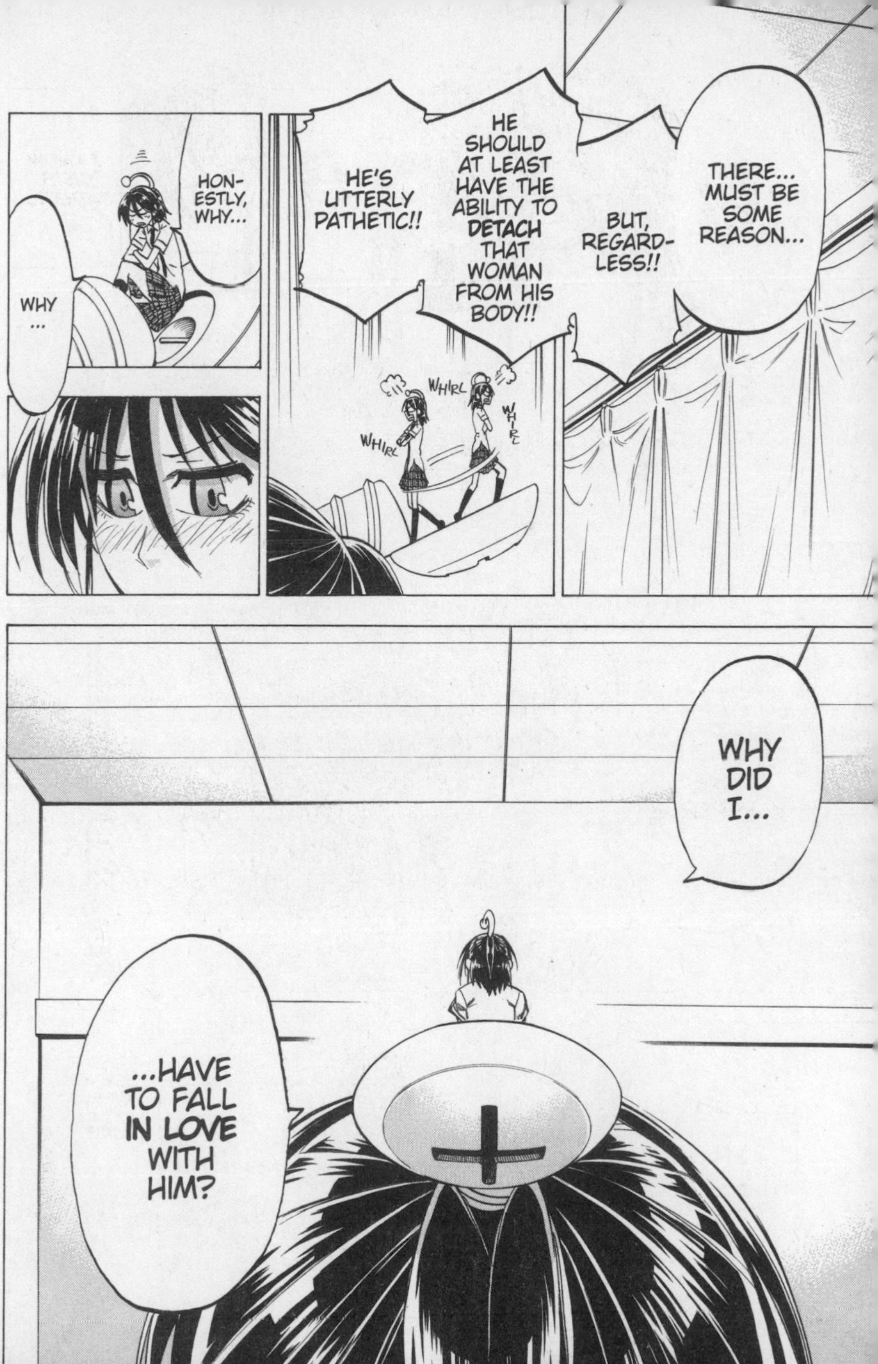
THERE... MUST BE SOME REASON...
BUT, REGARDLESS!!
HE SHOULD AT LEAST HAVE THE ABILITY TO DETACH THAT WOMAN FROM HIS BODY!!
HE'S UTTERLY PATHETIC!!
WHIRL
WHIRL
WHIRL
HON-ESTLY, WHY...
WHY ...
WHY DID I...
...HAVE TO FALL IN LOVE WITH HIM?

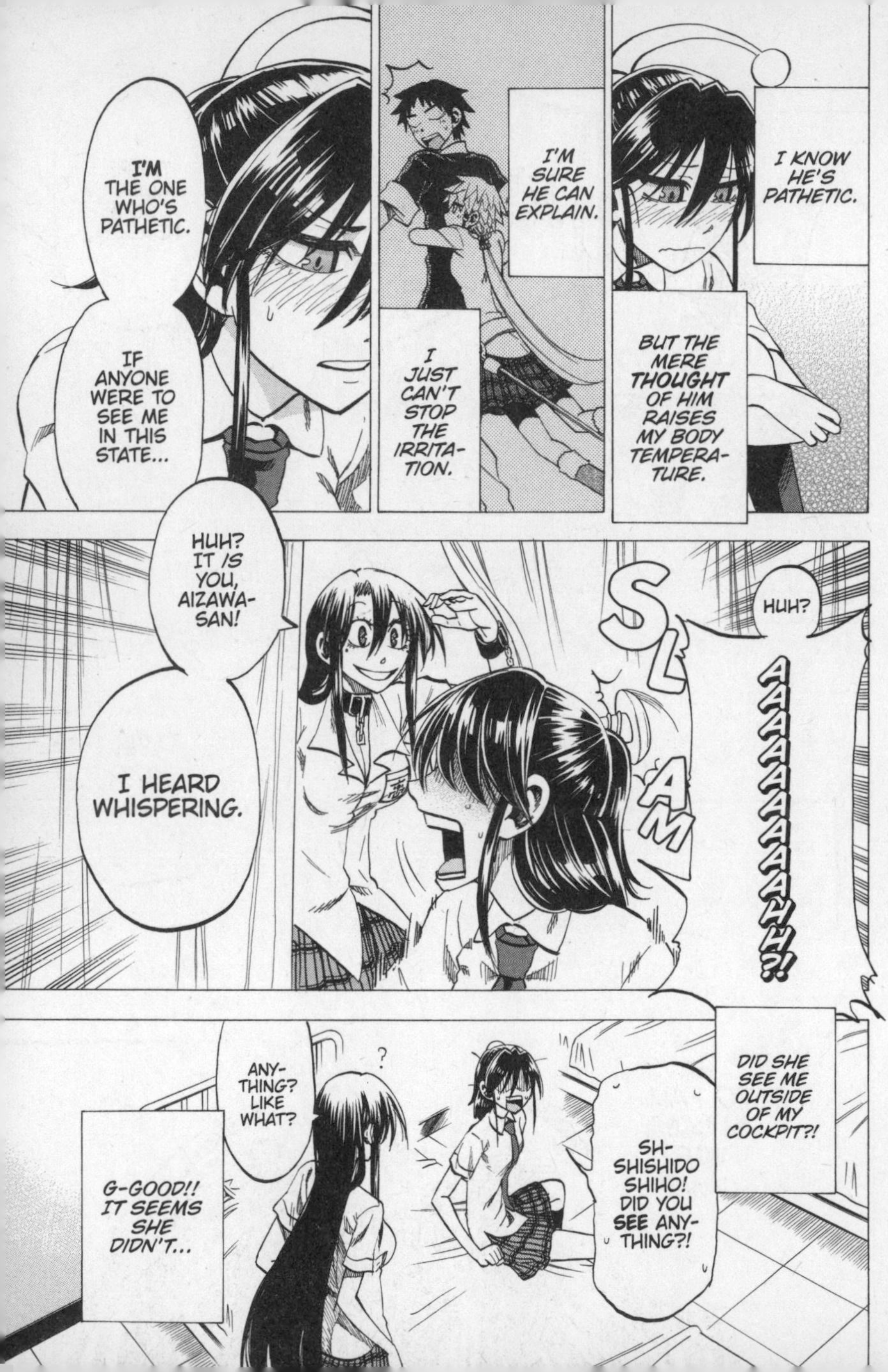
I KNOW HE'S PATHETIC.
BUT THE MERE THOUGHT OF HIM RAISES MY BODY TEMPERATURE.
I'M SURE HE CAN EXPLAIN.
I JUST CAN'T STOP THE IRRITATION.
I'M THE ONE WHO'S PATHETIC.
IF ANYONE WERE TO SEE ME IN THIS STATE...
HUH?
AAAAAAAAAHH?!
SLAM
HUH? IT IS YOU, AIZAWA-SAN!
I HEARD WHISPERING.
DID SHE SEE ME OUTSIDE OF MY COCKPIT?!
SH-SHISHIDO SHIHO! DID YOU SEE ANYTHING?!
?
ANYTHING? LIKE WHAT?
G-GOOD!! IT SEEMS SHE DIDN'T...

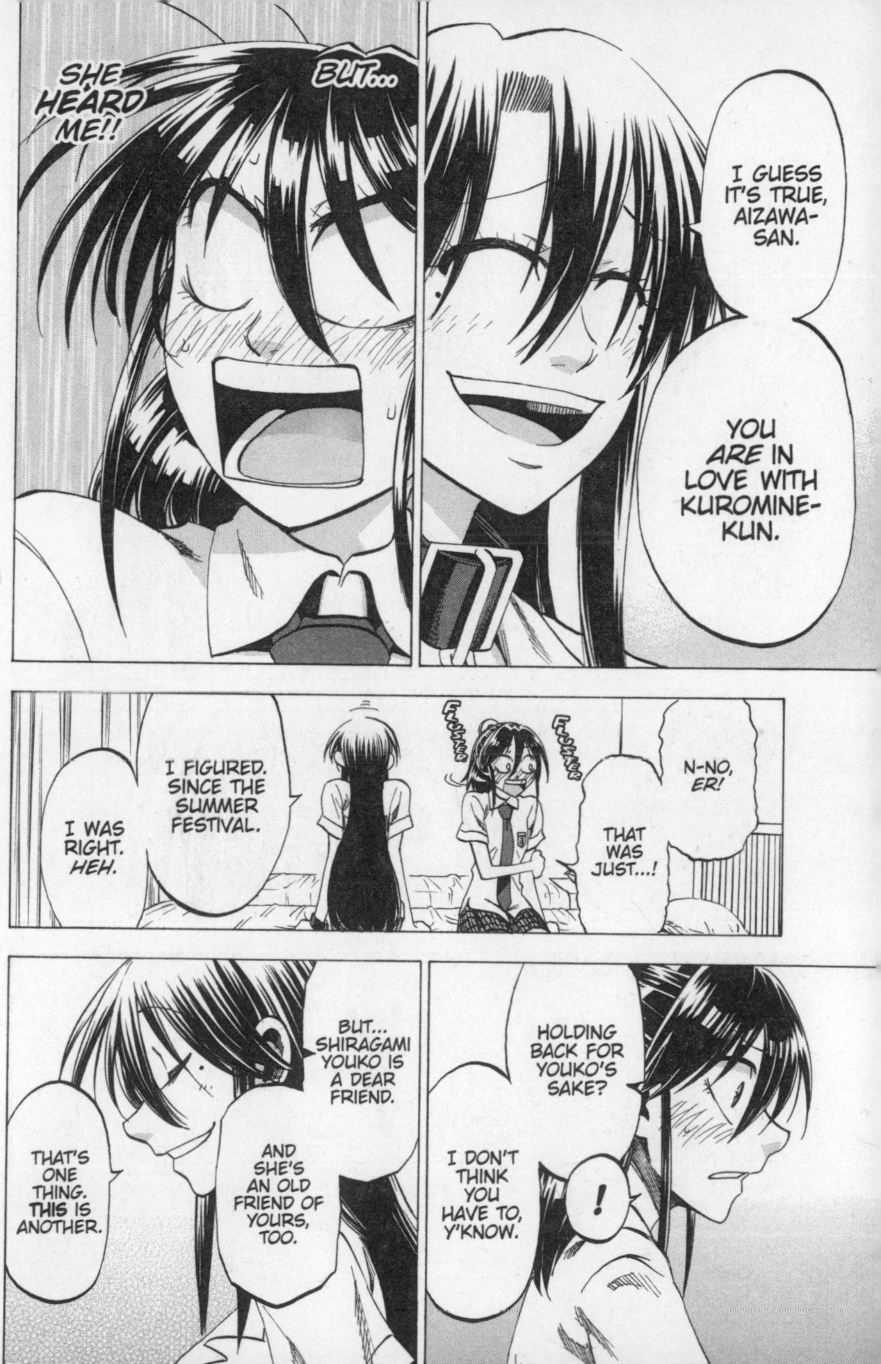

I GUESS IT'S TRUE, AIZAWA-SAN.
YOU *ARE* IN LOVE WITH KUROMINE-KUN.
BUT...
SHE HEARD ME!!
N-NO, ER!
THAT WAS JUST...!
FLUSTER
FLUSTER
I FIGURED. SINCE THE SUMMER FESTIVAL.
I WAS RIGHT. *HEH.*
HOLDING BACK FOR YOUKO'S SAKE?
!
I DON'T THINK YOU HAVE TO, Y'KNOW.
BUT... SHIRAGAMI YOUKO IS A DEAR FRIEND.
AND SHE'S AN OLD FRIEND OF YOURS, TOO.
THAT'S ONE THING. **THIS** IS ANOTHER.

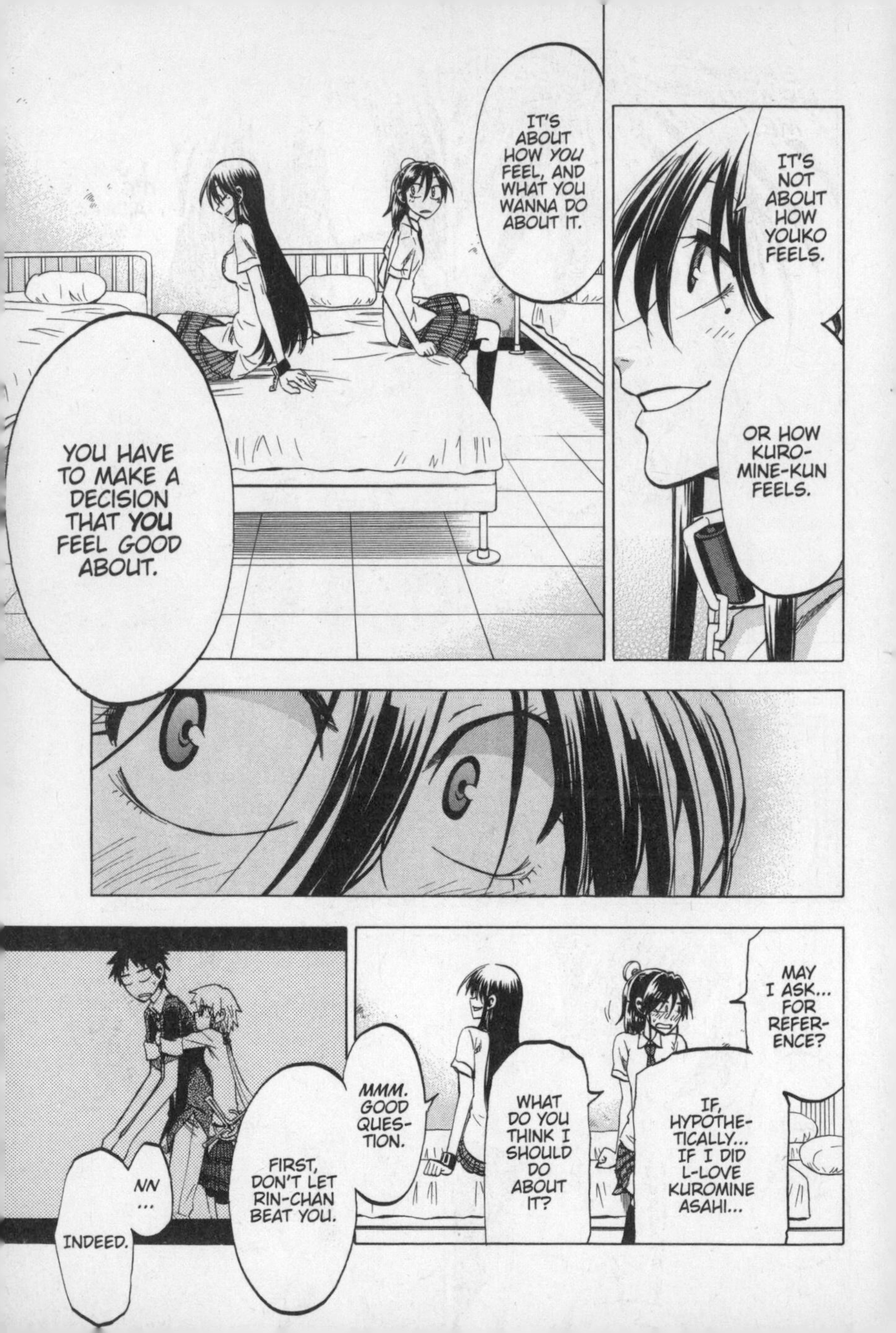
IT'S NOT ABOUT HOW YOUKO FEELS.
OR HOW KURO-MINE-KUN FEELS.
IT'S ABOUT HOW *YOU* FEEL, AND WHAT YOU WANNA DO ABOUT IT.
YOU HAVE TO MAKE A DECISION THAT **YOU** FEEL GOOD ABOUT.
MAY I ASK... FOR REFER-ENCE?
IF, HYPOTHE-TICALLY... IF I DID L-LOVE KUROMINE ASAHI...
WHAT DO YOU THINK I SHOULD DO ABOUT IT?
MMM. GOOD QUES-TION.
FIRST, DON'T LET RIN-CHAN BEAT YOU.
NN ...
INDEED.

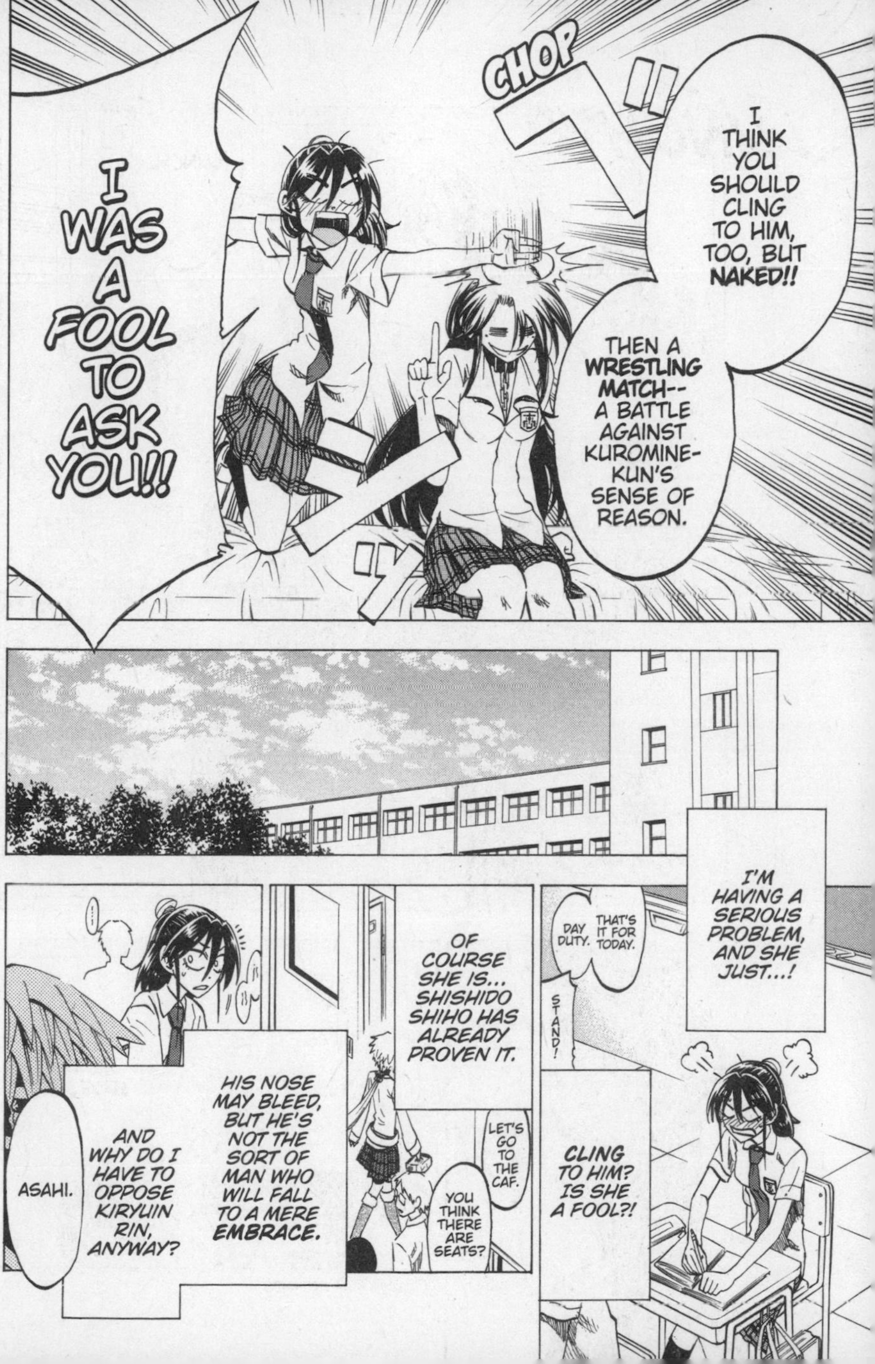
I THINK YOU SHOULD CLING TO HIM, TOO, BUT NAKED!!
THEN A WRESTLING MATCH-- A BATTLE AGAINST KUROMINE-KUN'S SENSE OF REASON.
CHOP
I WAS A FOOL TO ASK YOU!!
I'M HAVING A SERIOUS PROBLEM, AND SHE JUST...!
CLING TO HIM? IS SHE A FOOL?!
THAT'S IT FOR TODAY.
DAY DUTY.
STAND!
OF COURSE SHE IS... SHISHIDO SHIHO HAS ALREADY PROVEN IT.
LET'S GO TO THE CAF.
YOU THINK THERE ARE SEATS?
HIS NOSE MAY BLEED, BUT HE'S NOT THE SORT OF MAN WHO WILL FALL TO A MERE EMBRACE.
!
AND WHY DO I HAVE TO OPPOSE KIRYUIN RIN, ANYWAY?
ASAHI.

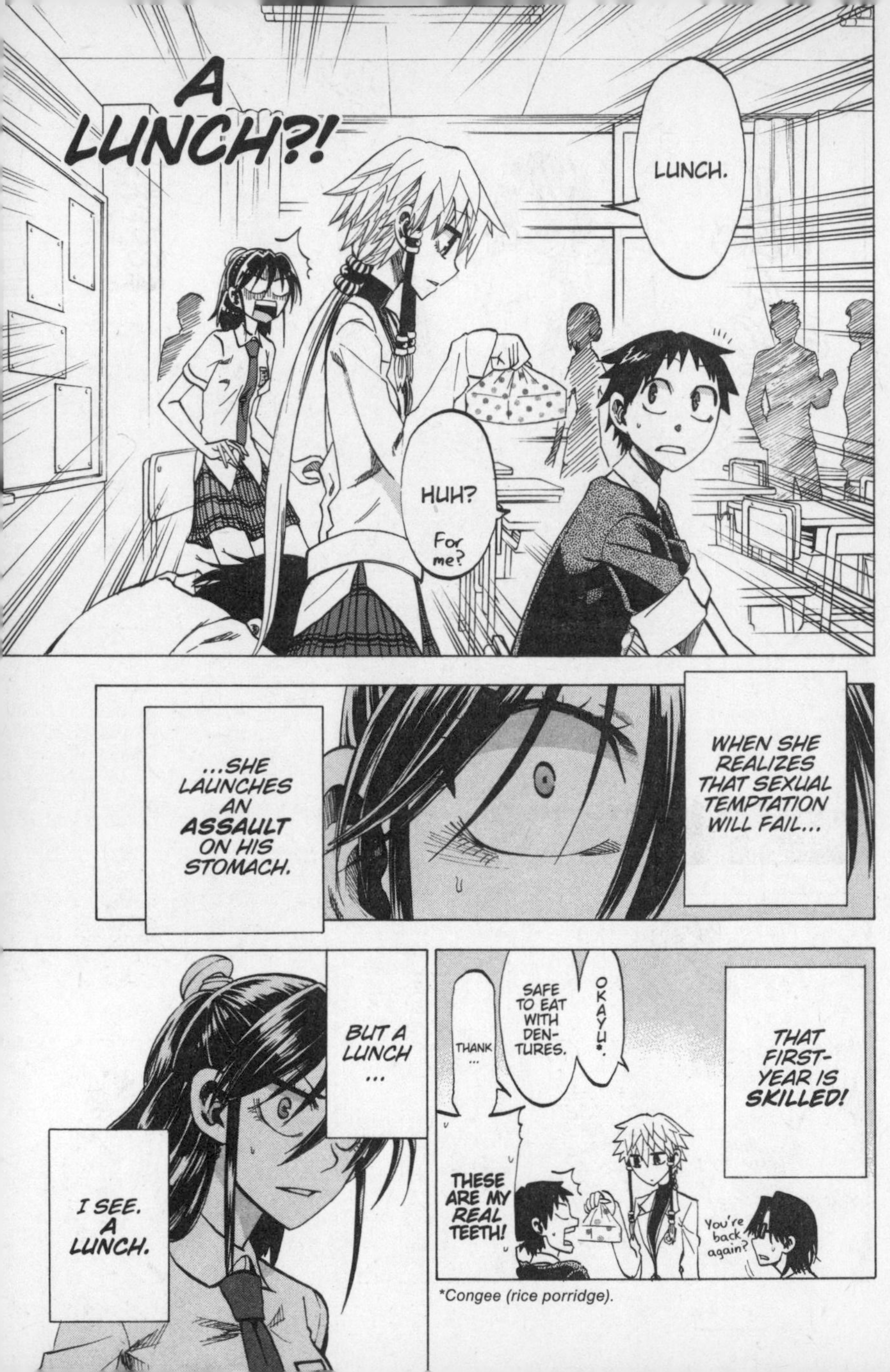
LUNCH.
HUH? For me?
A LUNCH?!
WHEN SHE REALIZES THAT SEXUAL TEMPTATION WILL FAIL...
...SHE LAUNCHES AN ASSAULT ON HIS STOMACH.
THAT FIRST-YEAR IS SKILLED!
OKAYU*.
SAFE TO EAT WITH DENTURES.
THANK...
THESE ARE MY REAL TEETH!
You're back again?
BUT A LUNCH...
I SEE. A LUNCH.
*Congee (rice porridge).

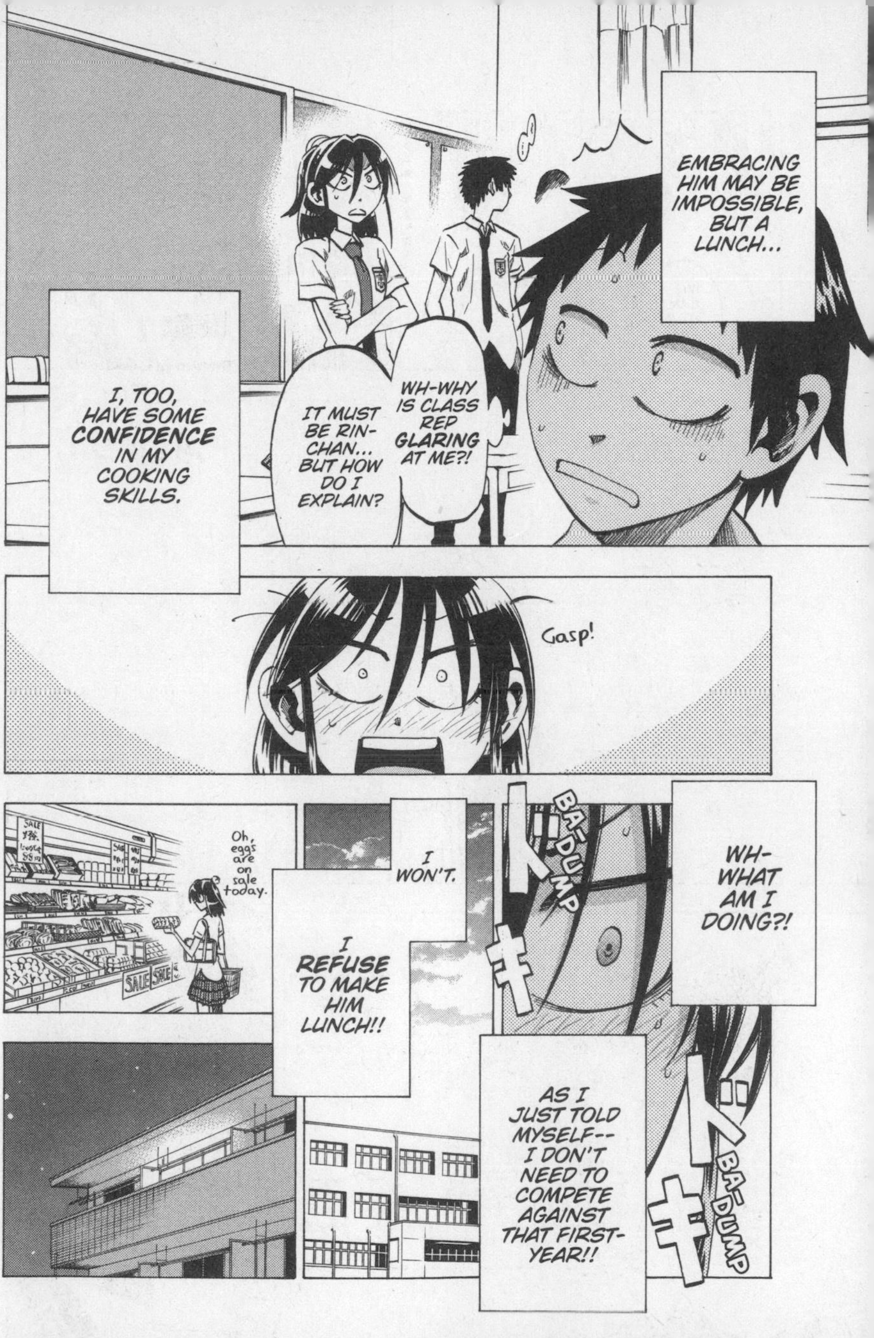
EMBRACING HIM MAY BE IMPOSSIBLE, BUT A LUNCH...
WH-WHY IS CLASS REP GLARING AT ME?!
IT MUST BE RIN-CHAN... BUT HOW DO I EXPLAIN?
I, TOO, HAVE SOME CONFIDENCE IN MY COOKING SKILLS.
Gasp!
WH-WHAT AM I DOING?!
BA-DUMP
I WON'T.
I REFUSE TO MAKE HIM LUNCH!!
Oh, eggs are on sale today.
SALE SALE
AS I JUST TOLD MYSELF-- I DON'T NEED TO COMPETE AGAINST THAT FIRST-YEAR!!
BA-DUMP

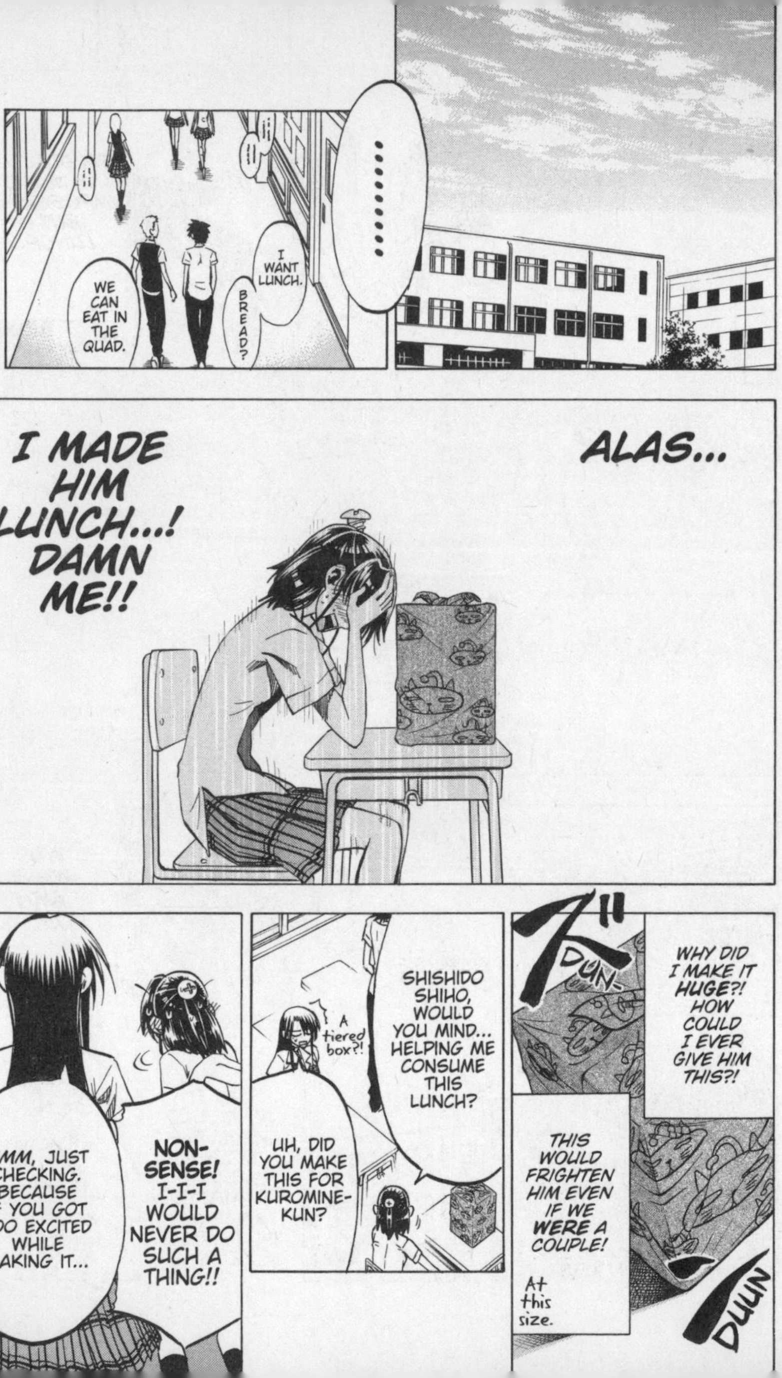
......
I WANT LUNCH.
BREAD?
WE CAN EAT IN THE QUAD.
ALAS...
I MADE HIM LUNCH...! DAMN ME!!
DUN
WHY DID I MAKE IT HUGE?! HOW COULD I EVER GIVE HIM THIS?!
THIS WOULD FRIGHTEN HIM EVEN IF WE WERE A COUPLE!
At this size.
DUUN
SHISHIDO SHIHO, WOULD YOU MIND... HELPING ME CONSUME THIS LUNCH?
A tiered box?!
UH, DID YOU MAKE THIS FOR KUROMINE-KUN?
NON-SENSE! I-I-I WOULD NEVER DO SUCH A THING!!
MMM, JUST CHECKING. BECAUSE IF YOU GOT TOO EXCITED WHILE MAKING IT...

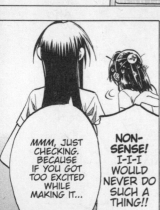

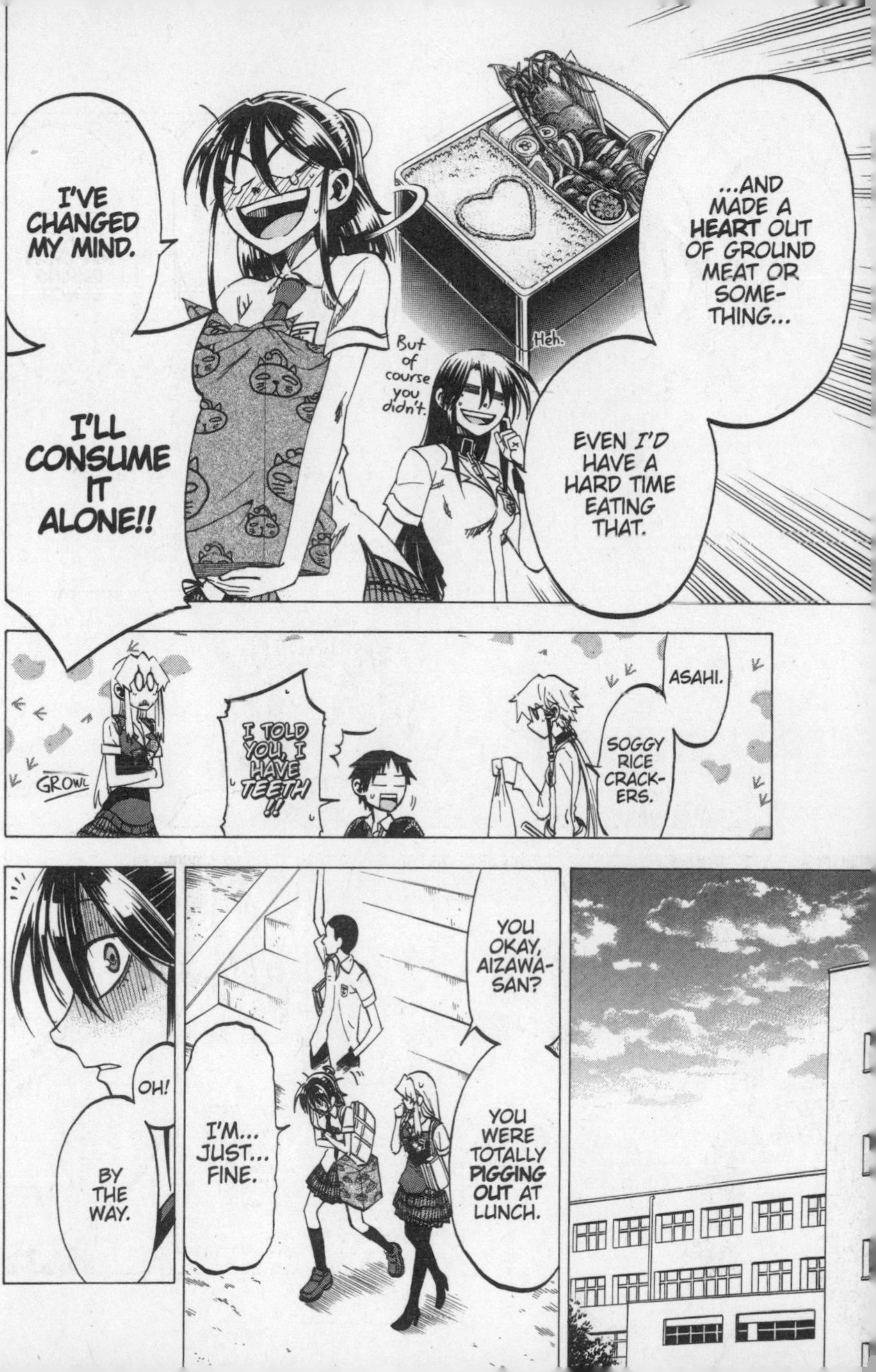
...AND MADE A HEART OUT OF GROUND MEAT OR SOMETHING...
Heh.
EVEN I'D HAVE A HARD TIME EATING THAT.
But of course you didn't.
I'VE CHANGED MY MIND.
I'LL CONSUME IT ALONE!!
ASAHI.
SOGGY RICE CRACKERS.
I TOLD YOU, I HAVE TEETH!!
GROWL
YOU OKAY, AIZAWA-SAN?
YOU WERE TOTALLY PIGGING OUT AT LUNCH.
I'M... JUST... FINE.
OH!
BY THE WAY.

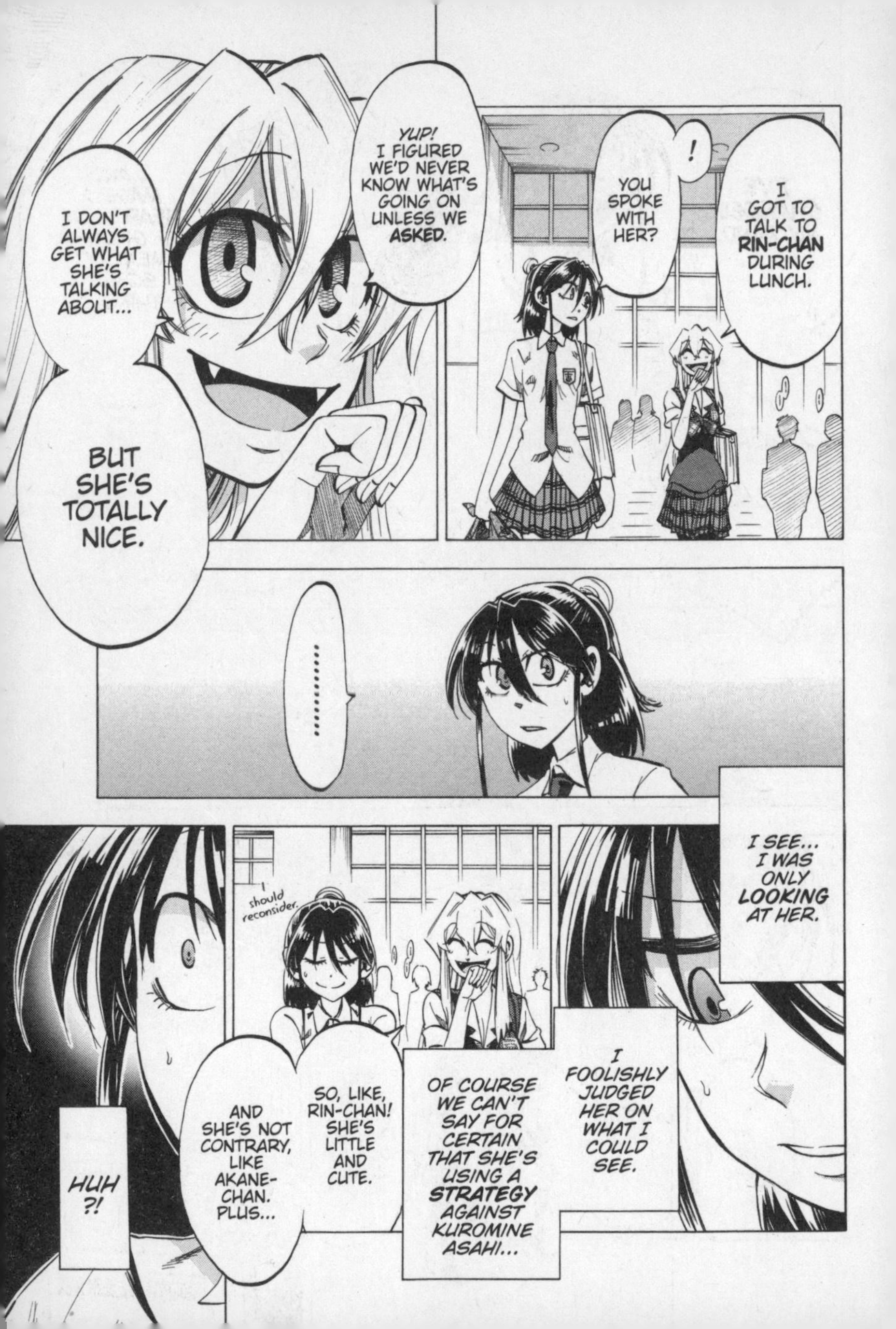
I GOT TO TALK TO RIN-CHAN DURING LUNCH.
!
YOU SPOKE WITH HER?
YUP! I FIGURED WE'D NEVER KNOW WHAT'S GOING ON UNLESS WE ASKED.
I DON'T ALWAYS GET WHAT SHE'S TALKING ABOUT...
BUT SHE'S TOTALLY NICE.
......
I SEE... I WAS ONLY LOOKING AT HER.
I FOOLISHLY JUDGED HER ON WHAT I COULD SEE.
OF COURSE WE CAN'T SAY FOR CERTAIN THAT SHE'S USING A STRATEGY AGAINST KUROMINE ASAHI...
I should reconsider.
SO, LIKE, RIN-CHAN! SHE'S LITTLE AND CUTE.
AND SHE'S NOT CONTRARY, LIKE AKANE-CHAN. PLUS...
HUH?!

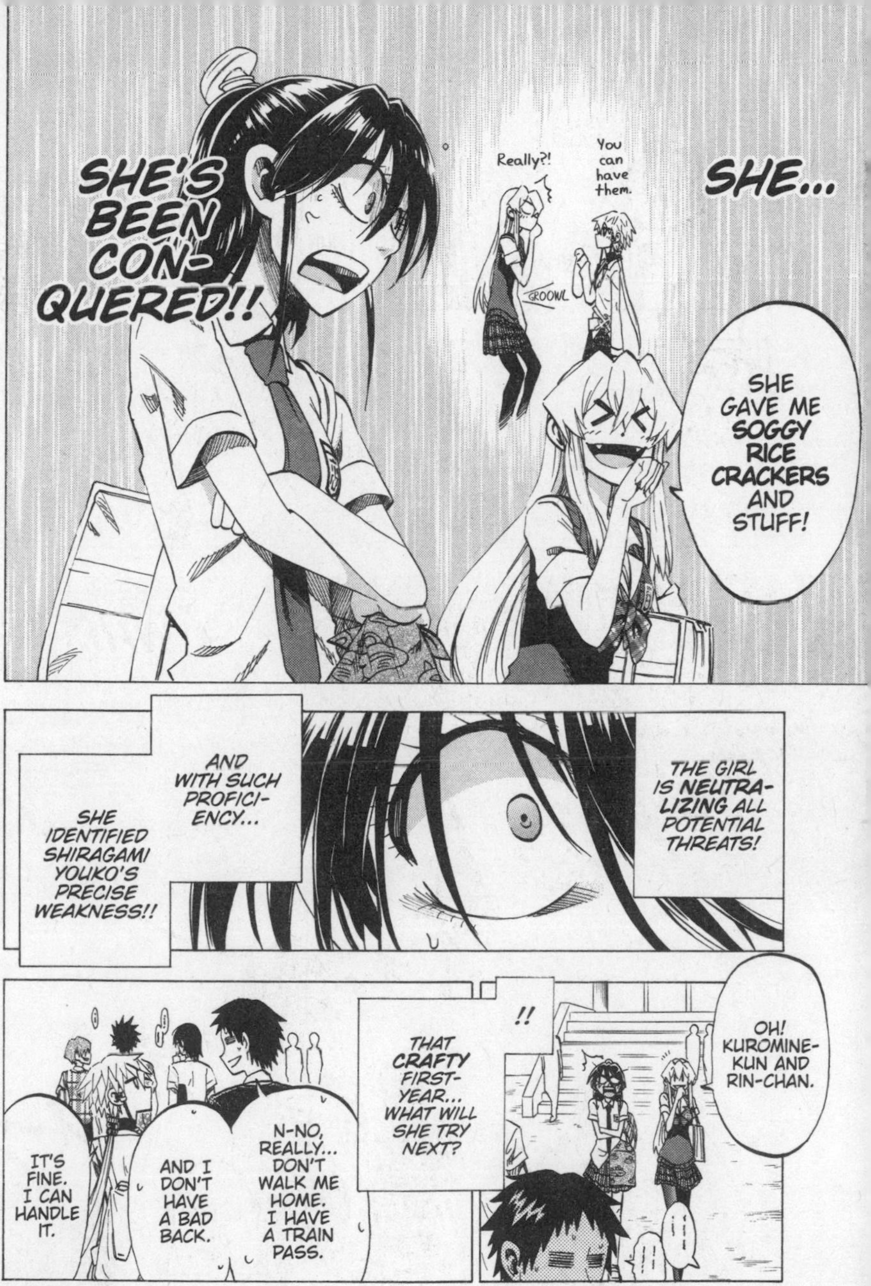
SHE...
You can have them.
Really?!
GROOWL
SHE GAVE ME SOGGY RICE CRACKERS AND STUFF!
SHE'S BEEN CON-QUERED!!
THE GIRL IS NEUTRALIZING ALL POTENTIAL THREATS!
AND WITH SUCH PROFICIENCY...
SHE IDENTIFIED SHIRAGAMI YOUKO'S PRECISE WEAKNESS!!
OH! KUROMINE-KUN AND RIN-CHAN.
!!
THAT CRAFTY FIRST-YEAR... WHAT WILL SHE TRY NEXT?
N-NO, REALLY... DON'T WALK ME HOME. I HAVE A TRAIN PASS.
AND I DON'T HAVE A BAD BACK.
IT'S FINE. I CAN HANDLE IT.

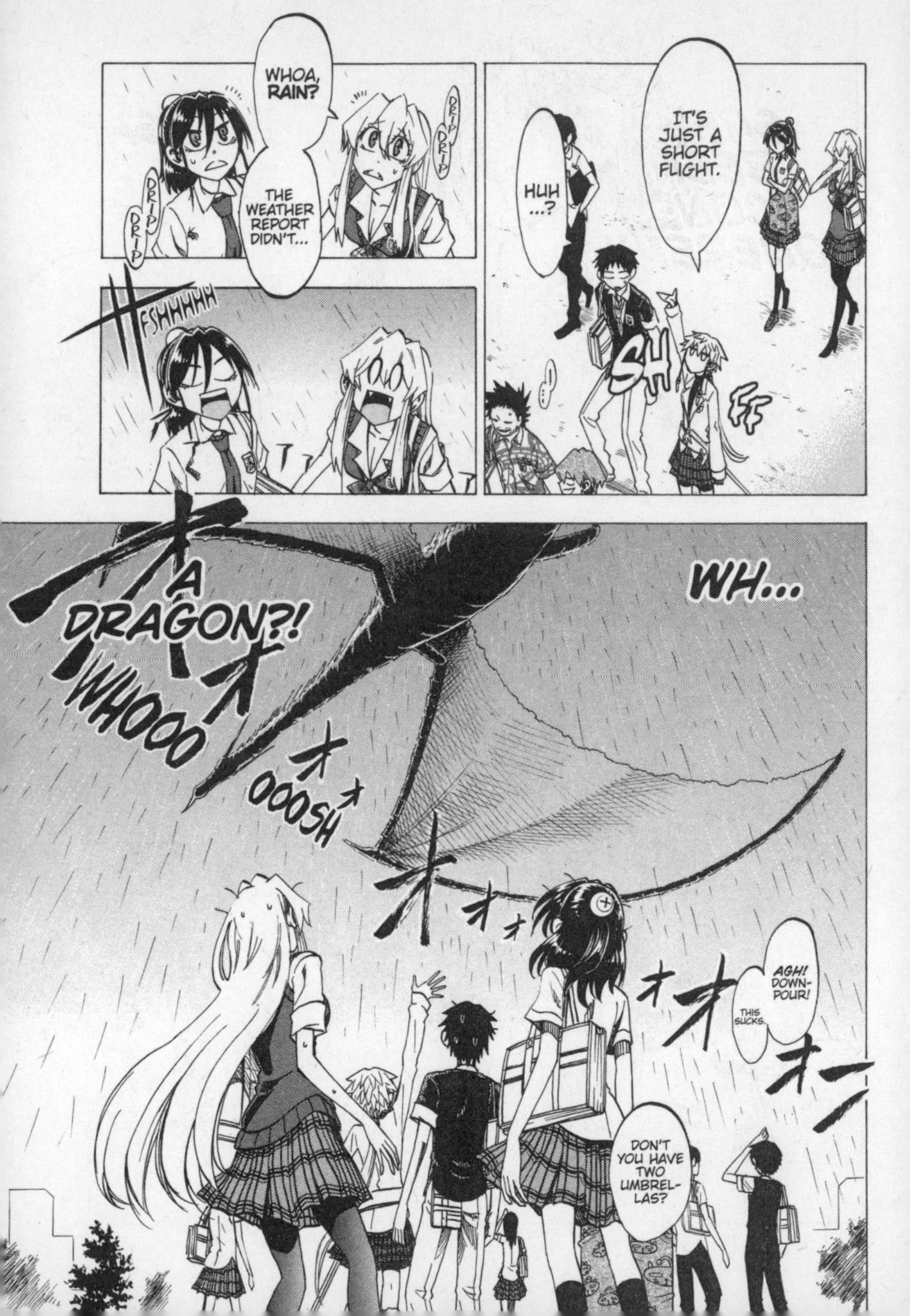
IT'S JUST A SHORT FLIGHT.
HUH ...?
SH
FF
WHOA, RAIN?
DRIP DRIP
THE WEATHER REPORT DIDN'T...
DRIP DRIP
FSHHHHH
WH...
A DRAGON?!
WHOOO
OOOSH
AGH! DOWN-POUR!
THIS SUCKS.
DON'T YOU HAVE TWO UMBREL-LAS?

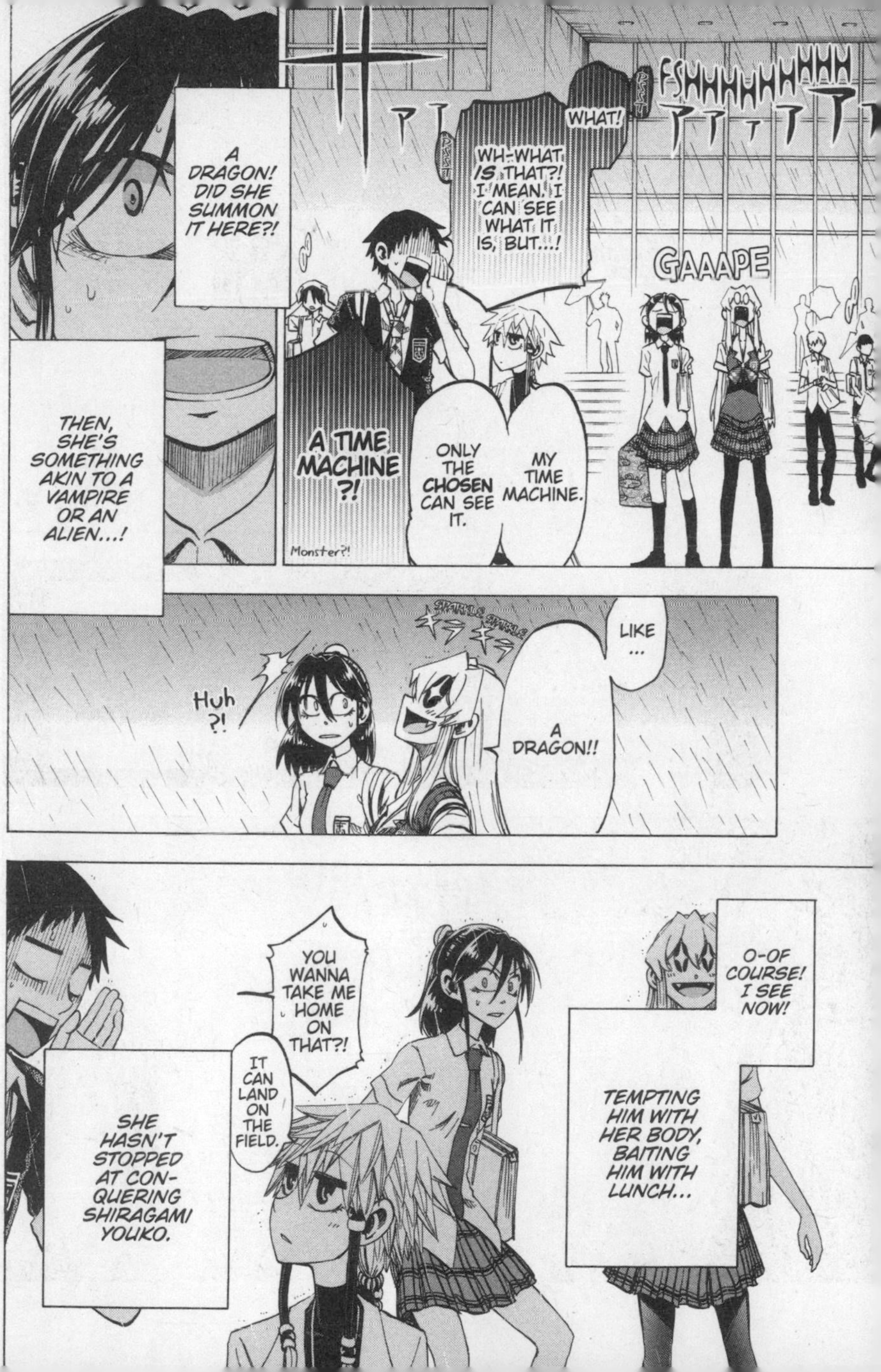
FSHHHHHHHHH
PSST
WHAT!
PSST
WH-WHAT IS THAT?! I MEAN, I CAN SEE WHAT IT IS, BUT...!
GAAAPE
MY TIME MACHINE.
ONLY THE CHOSEN CAN SEE IT.
A TIME MACHINE ?!
Monster?!
A DRAGON! DID SHE SUMMON IT HERE?!
THEN, SHE'S SOMETHING AKIN TO A VAMPIRE OR AN ALIEN...!
SPARKLE SPARKLE
LIKE ...
A DRAGON!!
Huh ?!
O-OF COURSE! I SEE NOW!
TEMPTING HIM WITH HER BODY, BAITING HIM WITH LUNCH...
YOU WANNA TAKE ME HOME ON THAT?!
IT CAN LAND ON THE FIELD.
SHE HASN'T STOPPED AT CON-QUERING SHIRAGAMI YOUKO.

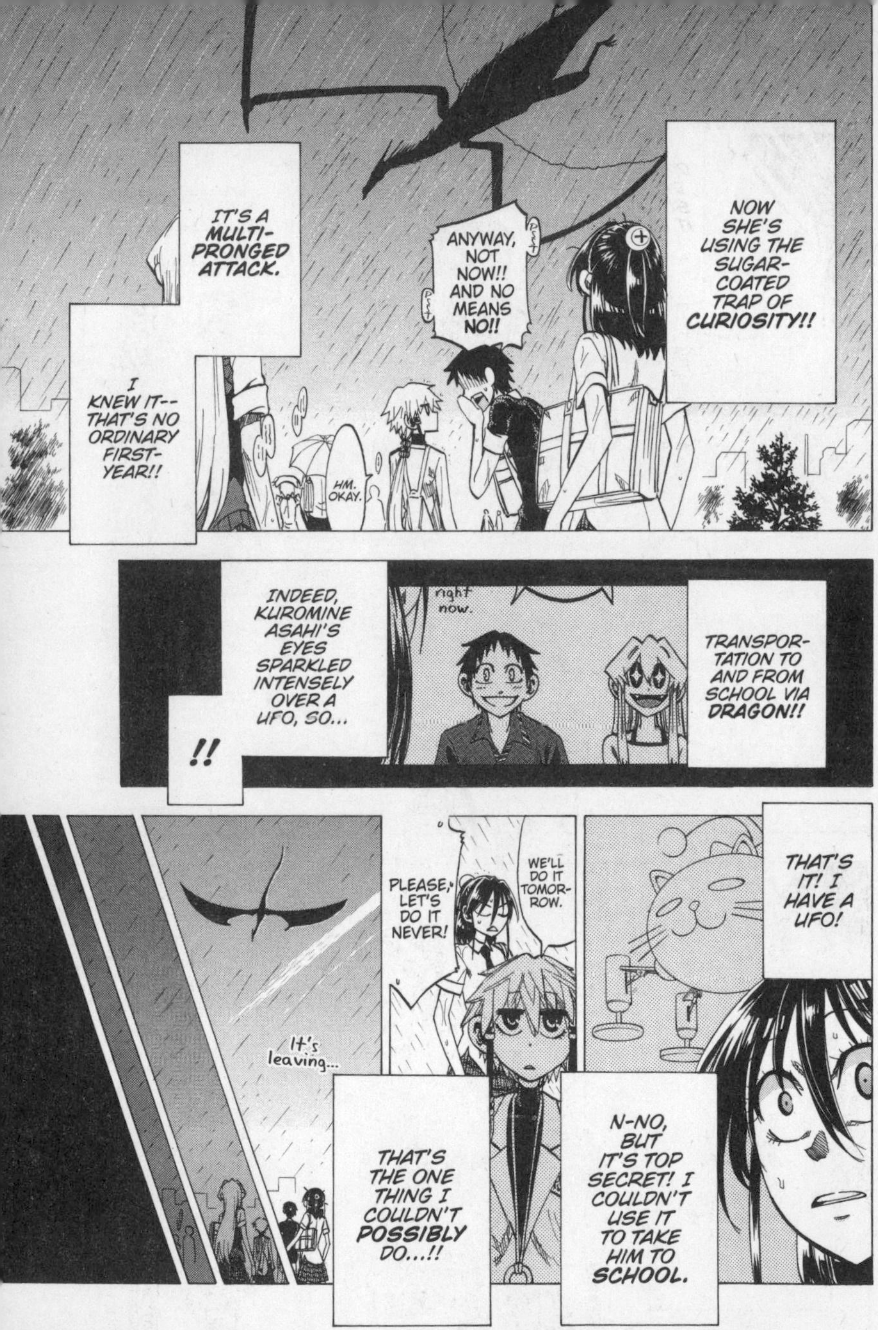
NOW SHE'S USING THE SUGAR-COATED TRAP OF CURIOSITY!!
ANYWAY, NOT NOW!! AND NO MEANS NO!!
IT'S A MULTI-PRONGED ATTACK.
I KNEW IT--THAT'S NO ORDINARY FIRST-YEAR!!
HM. OKAY.
TRANSPORTATION TO AND FROM SCHOOL VIA DRAGON!!
right now.
INDEED, KUROMINE ASAHI'S EYES SPARKLED INTENSELY OVER A UFO, SO...
!!
THAT'S IT! I HAVE A UFO!
N-NO, BUT IT'S TOP SECRET! I COULDN'T USE IT TO TAKE HIM TO SCHOOL.
WE'LL DO IT TOMORROW.
PLEASE, LET'S DO IT NEVER!
THAT'S THE ONE THING I COULDN'T POSSIBLY DO...!!
It's leaving...

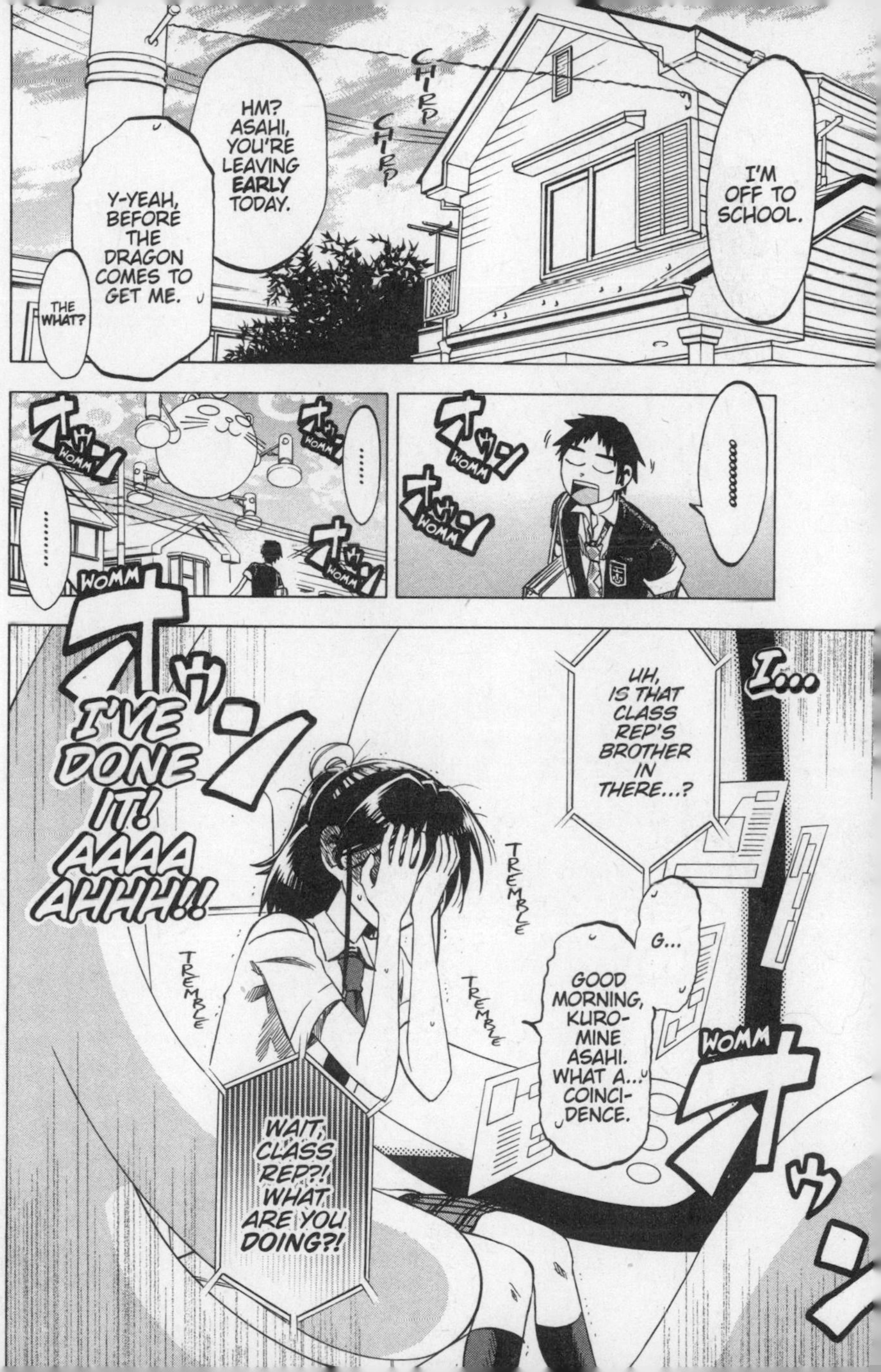
I'M OFF TO SCHOOL.
CHIRP
CHIRP
HM? ASAHI, YOU'RE LEAVING EARLY TODAY.
Y-YEAH, BEFORE THE DRAGON COMES TO GET ME.
THE WHAT?
....
WOMM
WOMM
WOMM
......
WOMM
......
WOMM
I...
UH, IS THAT CLASS REP'S BROTHER IN THERE...?
I'VE DONE IT! AAAA AHHH!!
TREMBLE
TREMBLE
TREMBLE
G...
GOOD MORNING, KUROMINE ASAHI. WHAT A... COINCIDENCE.
WOMM
WAIT, CLASS REP?! WHAT ARE YOU DOING?!

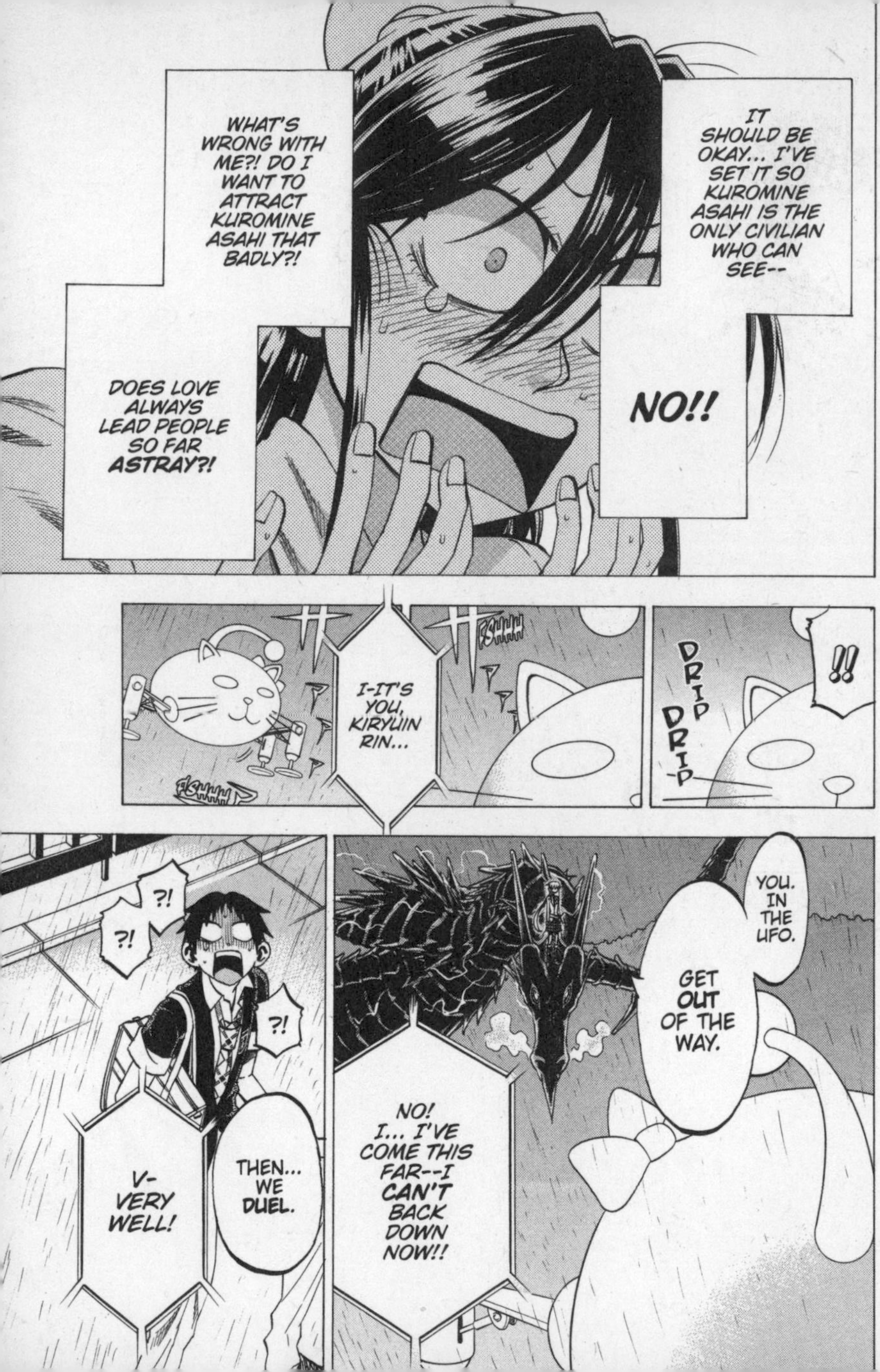
IT SHOULD BE OKAY... I'VE SET IT SO KUROMINE ASAHI IS THE ONLY CIVILIAN WHO CAN SEE--
NO!!
WHAT'S WRONG WITH ME?! DO I WANT TO ATTRACT KUROMINE ASAHI THAT BADLY?!
DOES LOVE ALWAYS LEAD PEOPLE SO FAR ASTRAY?!
!!
DRIP
DRIP
DRIP
FSHHHH
I-IT'S YOU, KIRYUIN RIN...
FSHHHH
YOU. IN THE UFO.
GET OUT OF THE WAY.
NO! I... I'VE COME THIS FAR--I CAN'T BACK DOWN NOW!!
?!
?!
?!
THEN... WE DUEL.
V-VERY WELL!

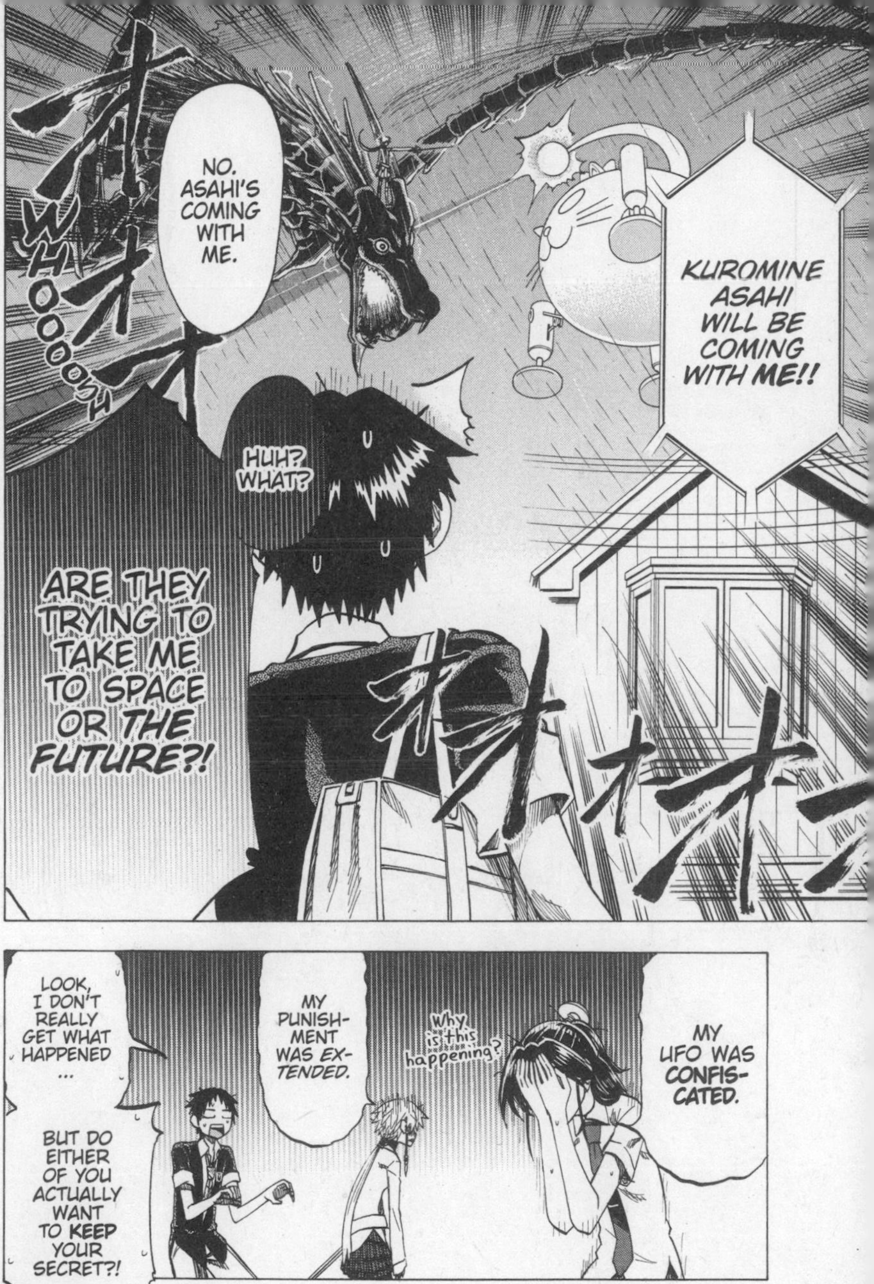
KUROMINE ASAHI WILL BE COMING WITH ME!!
NO. ASAHI'S COMING WITH ME.
WHOOOOOSH
HUH? WHAT?
ARE THEY TRYING TO TAKE ME TO SPACE OR THE FUTURE?!
MY UFO WAS CONFISCATED.
Why is this happening?
MY PUNISHMENT WAS EXTENDED.
LOOK, I DON'T REALLY GET WHAT HAPPENED...
BUT DO EITHER OF YOU ACTUALLY WANT TO KEEP YOUR SECRET?!

Chapter 37: "Let's Compete in the Athletic Meet!"

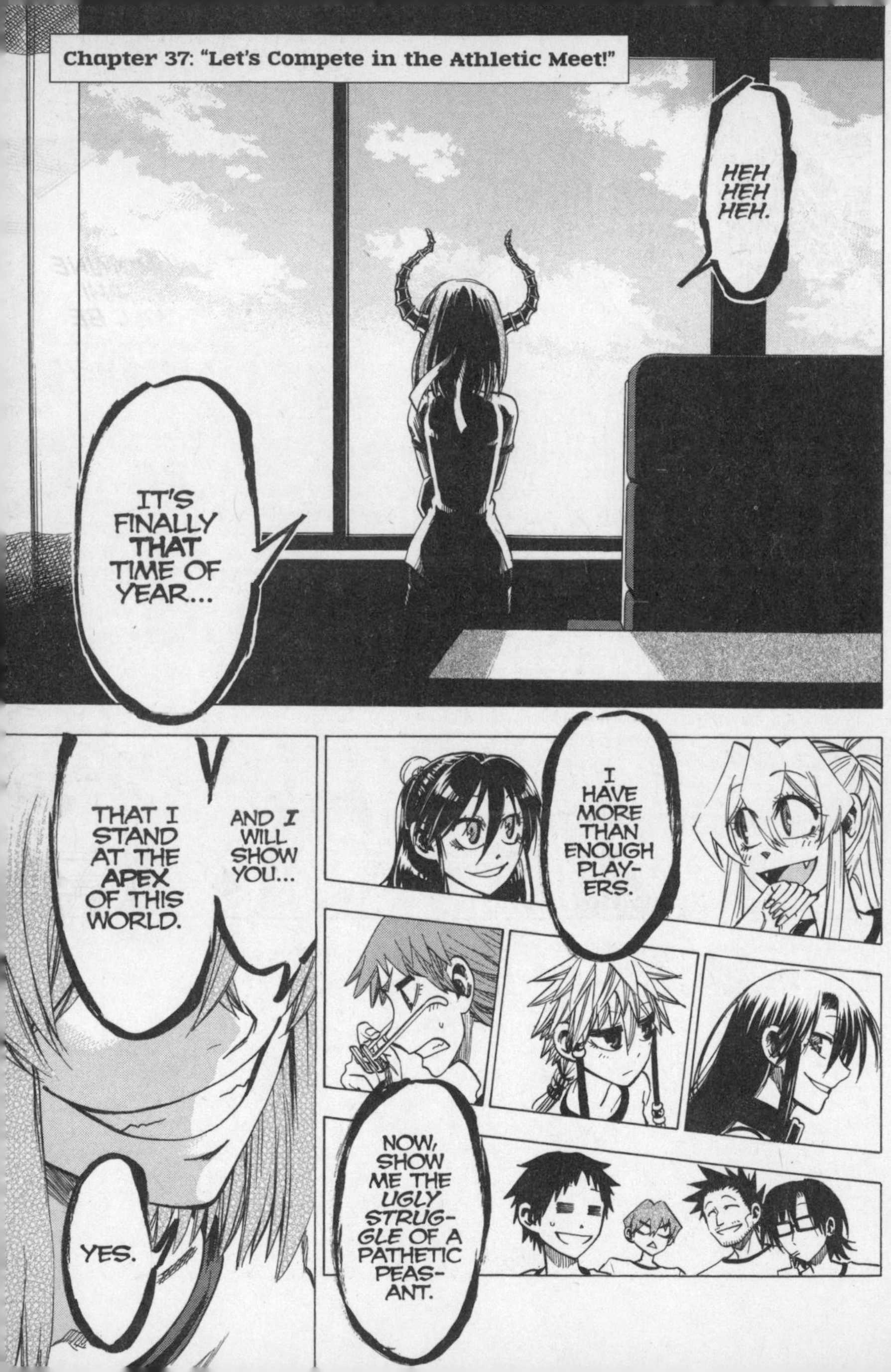
HEH HEH HEH.
IT'S FINALLY THAT TIME OF YEAR...
AND *I* WILL SHOW YOU...
THAT I STAND AT THE APEX OF THIS WORLD.
I HAVE MORE THAN ENOUGH PLAYERS.
NOW, SHOW ME THE *UGLY STRUGGLE* OF A PATHETIC PEASANT.
YES.

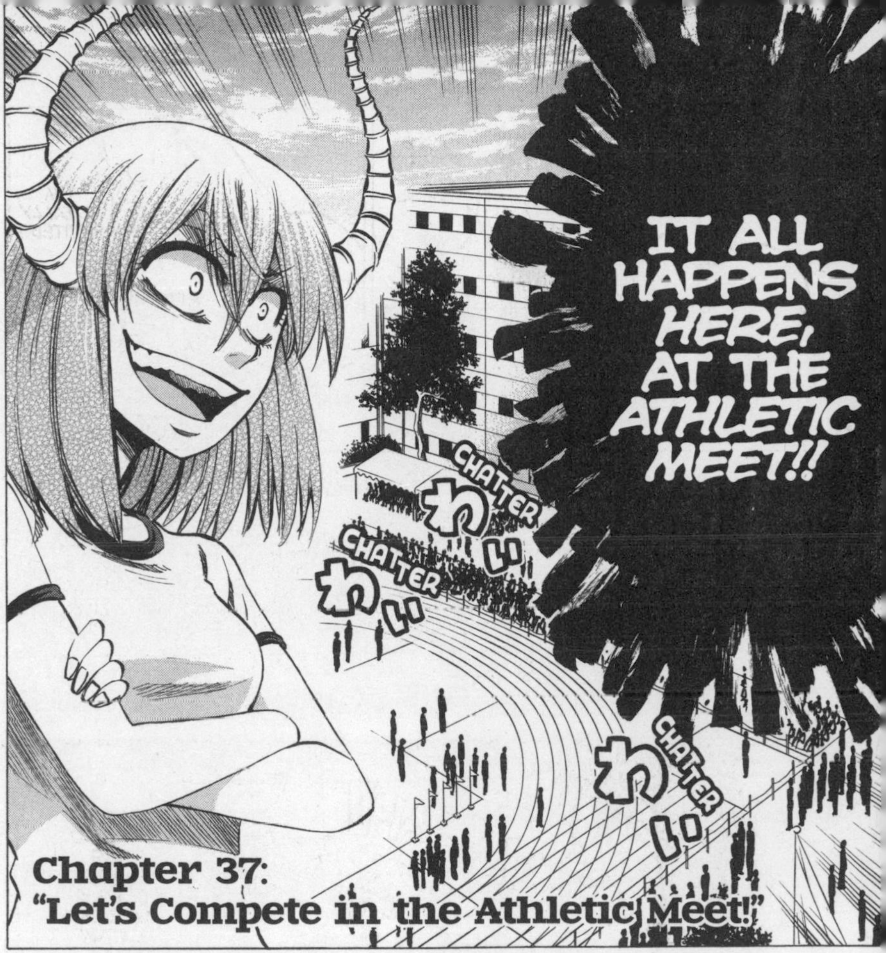
IT ALL HAPPENS HERE, AT THE ATHLETIC MEET!!
CHATTER わい
CHATTER わい
CHATTER わい
Chapter 37: "Let's Compete in the Athletic Meet!"

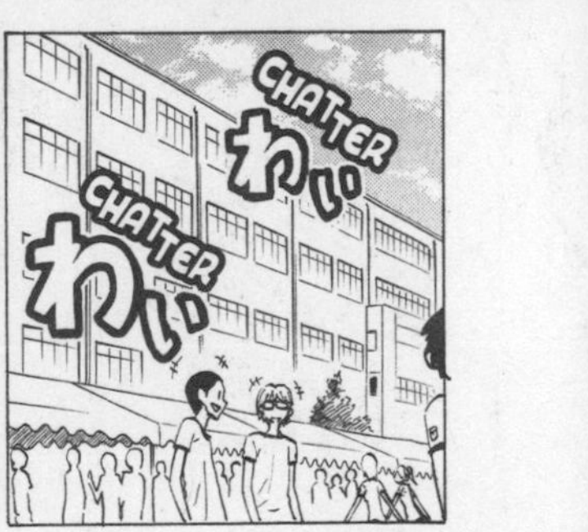
CHATTER わい
CHATTER わい

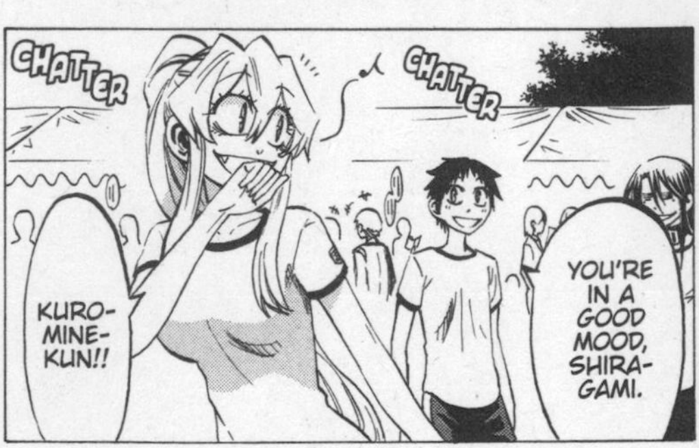
CHATTER
CHATTER
YOU'RE IN A GOOD MOOD, SHIRAGAMI.
KURO-MINE-KUN!!

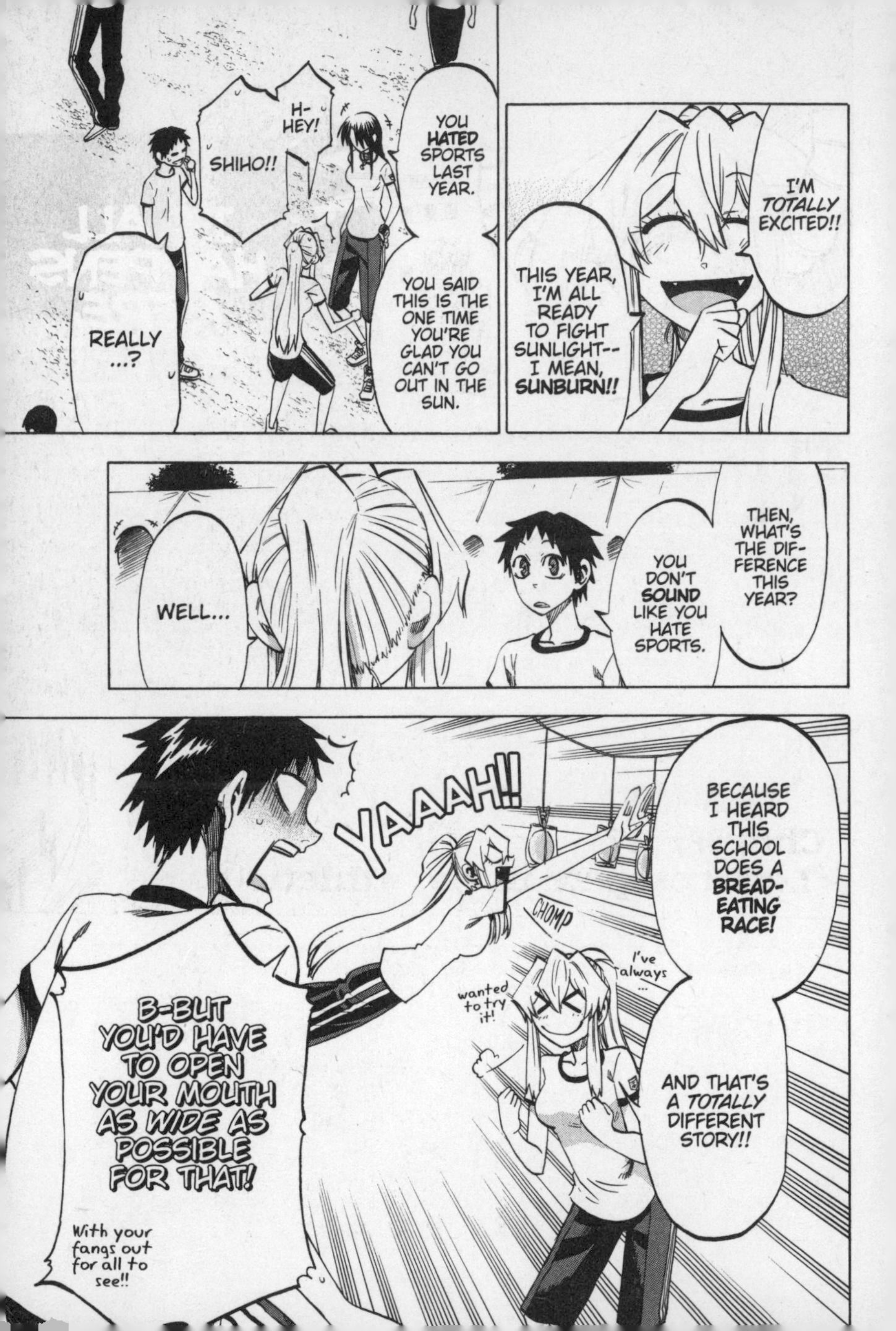
I'M TOTALLY EXCITED!!
THIS YEAR, I'M ALL READY TO FIGHT SUNLIGHT-- I MEAN, SUNBURN!!
YOU HATED SPORTS LAST YEAR.
YOU SAID THIS IS THE ONE TIME YOU'RE GLAD YOU CAN'T GO OUT IN THE SUN.
H-HEY!
SHIHO!!
REALLY ...?
THEN, WHAT'S THE DIF-FERENCE THIS YEAR?
YOU DON'T SOUND LIKE YOU HATE SPORTS.
WELL...
BECAUSE I HEARD THIS SCHOOL DOES A BREAD-EATING RACE!
AND THAT'S A TOTALLY DIFFERENT STORY!!
I've always ...
wanted to try it!
YAAAH!!
CHOMP
B-BUT YOU'D HAVE TO OPEN YOUR MOUTH AS WIDE AS POSSIBLE FOR THAT!
With your fangs out for all to see!!

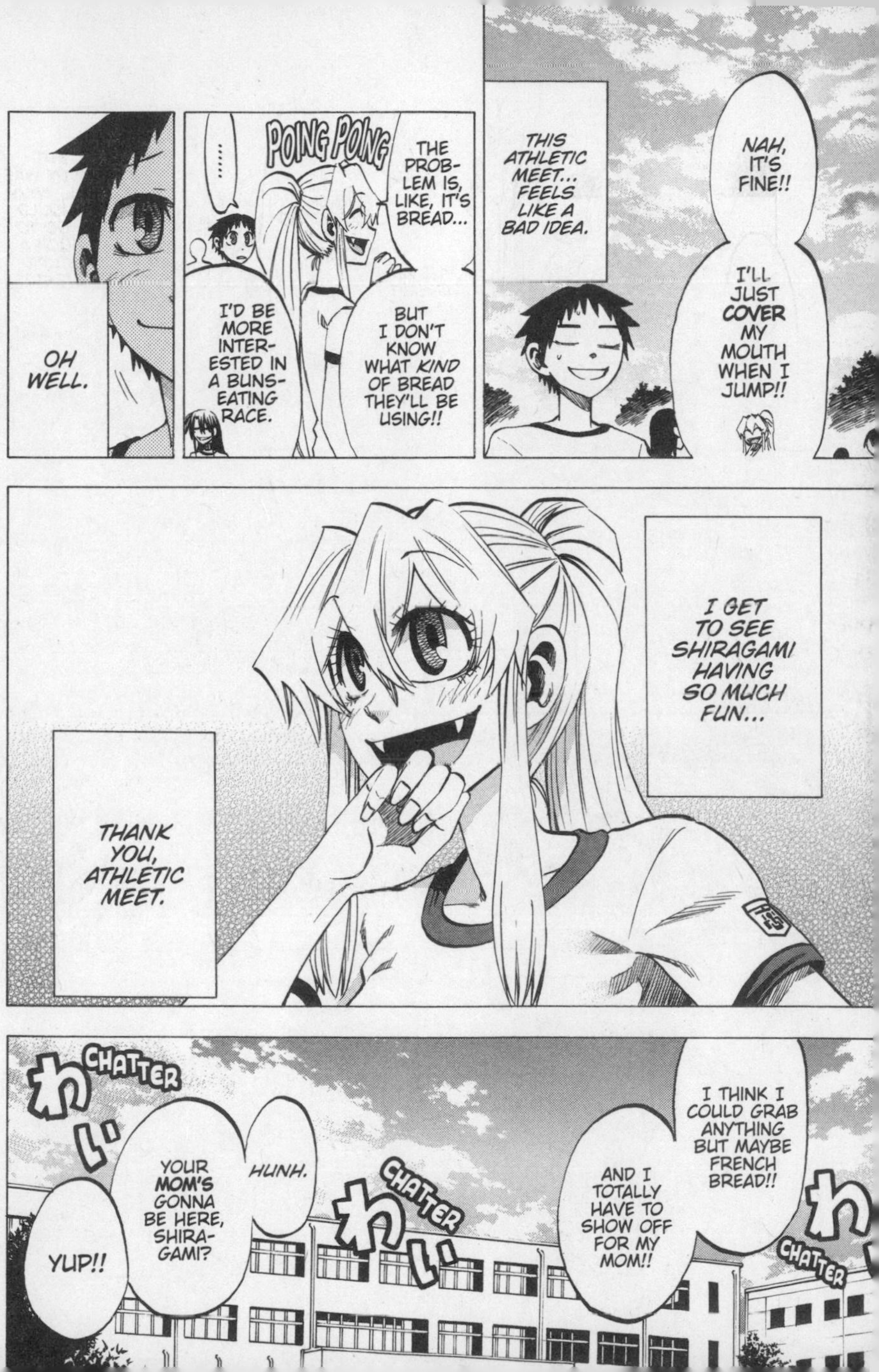
NAH, IT'S FINE!!
I'LL JUST COVER MY MOUTH WHEN I JUMP!!
THIS ATHLETIC MEET... FEELS LIKE A BAD IDEA.
THE PROB-LEM IS, LIKE, IT'S BREAD...
BUT I DON'T KNOW WHAT KIND OF BREAD THEY'LL BE USING!!
POING POING
......
I'D BE MORE INTER-ESTED IN A BUNS-EATING RACE.
OH WELL.
I GET TO SEE SHIRAGAMI HAVING SO MUCH FUN...
THANK YOU, ATHLETIC MEET.
わ CHATTER
I THINK I COULD GRAB ANYTHING BUT MAYBE FRENCH BREAD!!
AND I TOTALLY HAVE TO SHOW OFF FOR MY MOM!!
わい CHATTER
HUNH.
YOUR MOM'S GONNA BE HERE, SHIRA-GAMI?
YUP!!
わい CHATTER

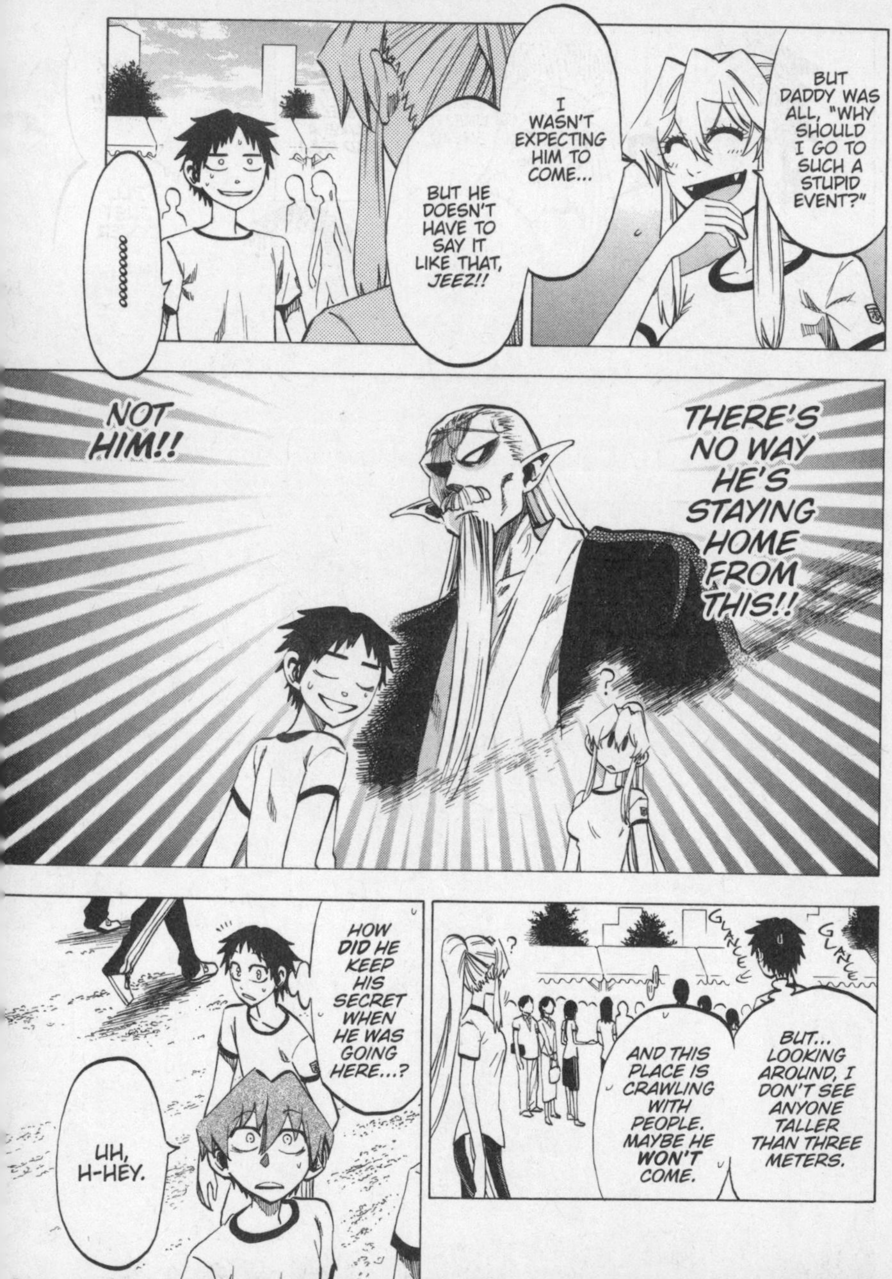
BUT DADDY WAS ALL, "WHY SHOULD I GO TO SUCH A STUPID EVENT?"
I WASN'T EXPECTING HIM TO COME...
BUT HE DOESN'T HAVE TO SAY IT LIKE THAT, JEEZ!!
....
THERE'S NO WAY HE'S STAYING HOME FROM THIS!!
NOT HIM!!
GLANCE
GLANCE
BUT... LOOKING AROUND, I DON'T SEE ANYONE TALLER THAN THREE METERS.
AND THIS PLACE IS CRAWLING WITH PEOPLE. MAYBE HE WON'T COME.
HOW DID HE KEEP HIS SECRET WHEN HE WAS GOING HERE...?
UH, H-HEY.

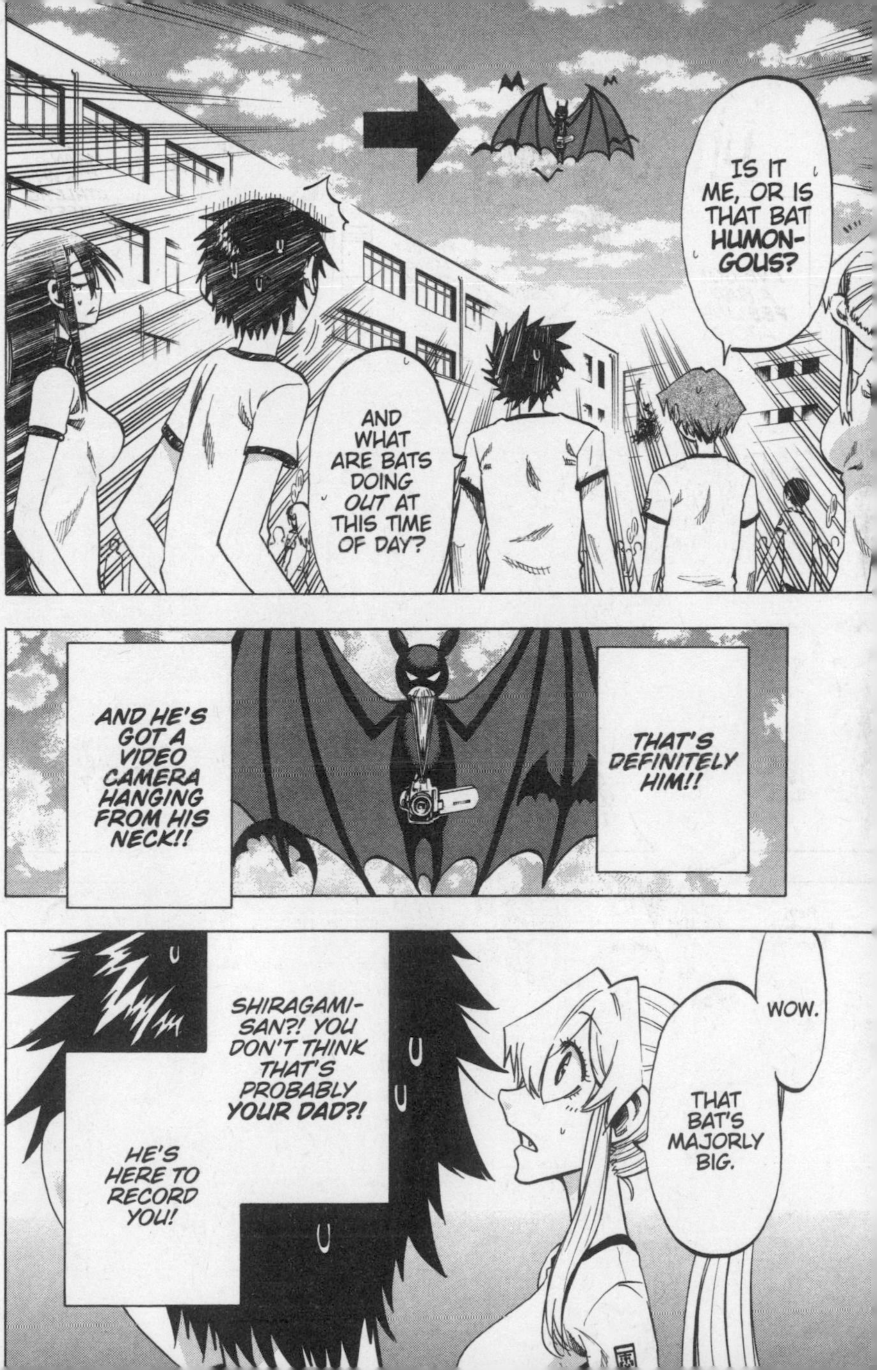
IS IT ME, OR IS THAT BAT HUMONGOUS?
AND WHAT ARE BATS DOING OUT AT THIS TIME OF DAY?
THAT'S DEFINITELY HIM!!
AND HE'S GOT A VIDEO CAMERA HANGING FROM HIS NECK!!
WOW.
THAT BAT'S MAJORLY BIG.
SHIRAGAMI-SAN?! YOU DON'T THINK THAT'S PROBABLY YOUR DAD?!
HE'S HERE TO RECORD YOU!

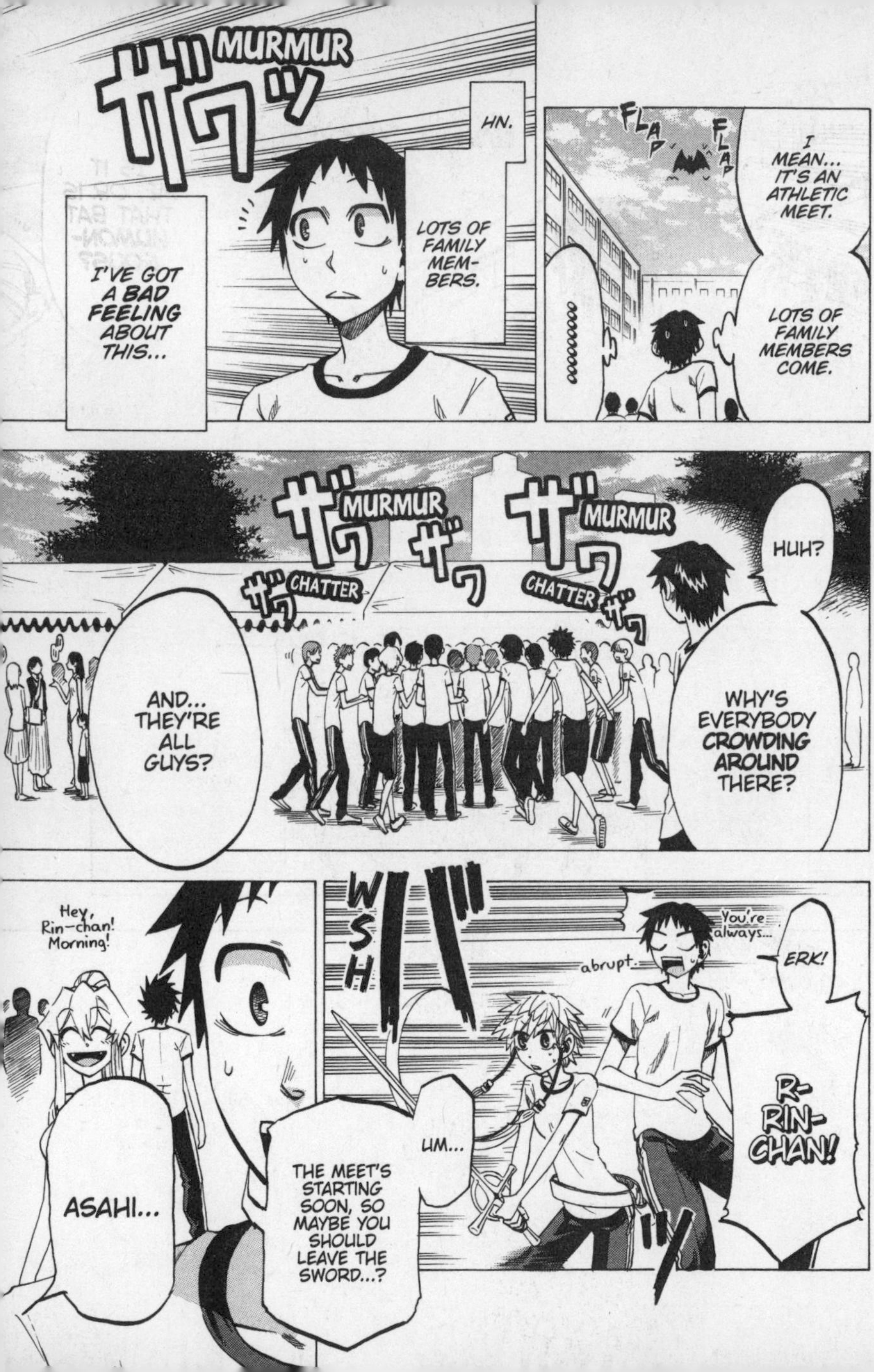
FLAP
FLAP
I MEAN... IT'S AN ATHLETIC MEET.
LOTS OF FAMILY MEMBERS COME.
ザワッ
MURMUR
HN.
LOTS OF FAMILY MEM-BERS.
I'VE GOT A BAD FEELING ABOUT THIS...
HUH?
WHY'S EVERYBODY CROWDING AROUND THERE?
ザワ
MURMUR
ザワ
CHATTER
ザワ
ザワ
MURMUR
ザワ
CHATTER
AND... THEY'RE ALL GUYS?
ERK!
You're always...
abrupt.
WSH
R-RIN-CHAN!
Hey, Rin-chan! Morning!
UM...
THE MEET'S STARTING SOON, SO MAYBE YOU SHOULD LEAVE THE SWORD...?
ASAHI...

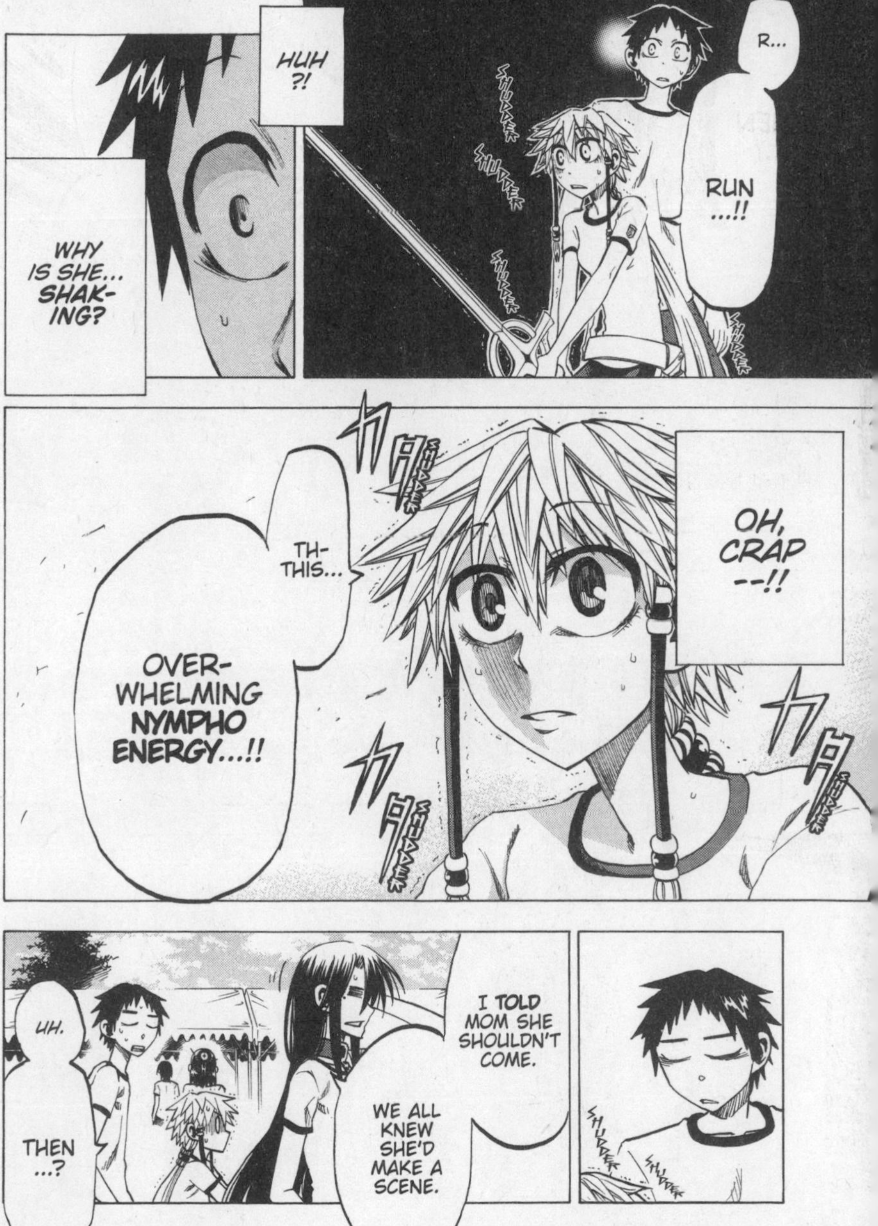
R...
RUN ...!!
SHUDDER
SHUDDER
SHUDDER
SHUDDER
HUH ?!
WHY IS SHE... SHAKING?
OH, CRAP --!!
SHUDDER
TH- THIS...
OVER-WHELMING NYMPHO ENERGY...!!
SHUDDER
SHUDDER
SHUDDER
SHUDDER
I TOLD MOM SHE SHOULDN'T COME.
WE ALL KNEW SHE'D MAKE A SCENE.
UH.
THEN ...?

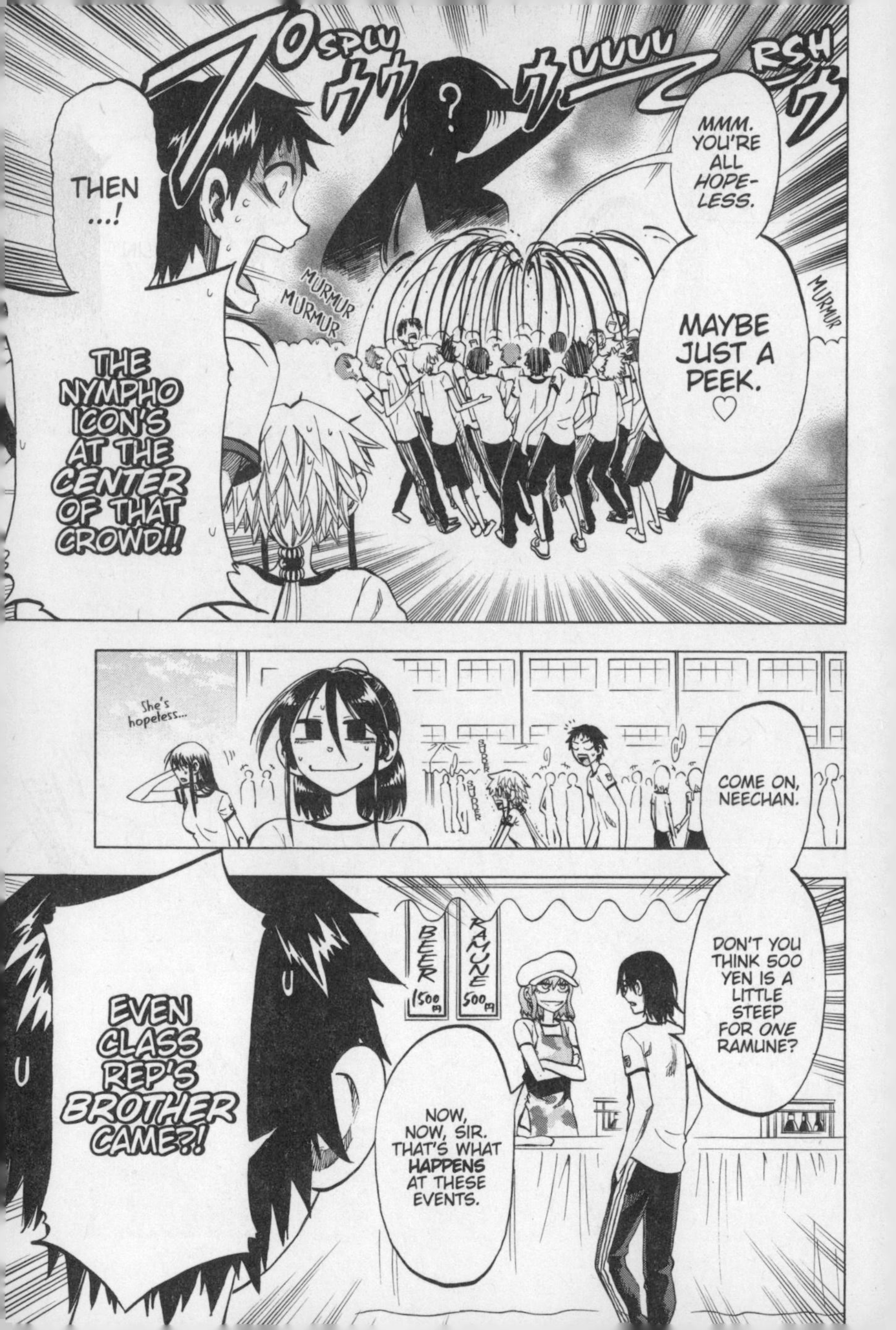

SPLU
UUUU
RSH
MMM. YOU'RE ALL HOPELESS.
MAYBE JUST A PEEK. ♡
MURMUR
MURMUR MURMUR
THEN ...!
THE NYMPHO ICON'S AT THE CENTER OF THAT CROWD!!
COME ON, NEECHAN.
SHUDDER SHUDDER
She's hopeless...
DON'T YOU THINK 500 YEN IS A LITTLE STEEP FOR ONE RAMUNE?
RAMUNE 500円
BEER 1500円
NOW, NOW, SIR. THAT'S WHAT HAPPENS AT THESE EVENTS.
EVEN CLASS REP'S BROTHER CAME?!

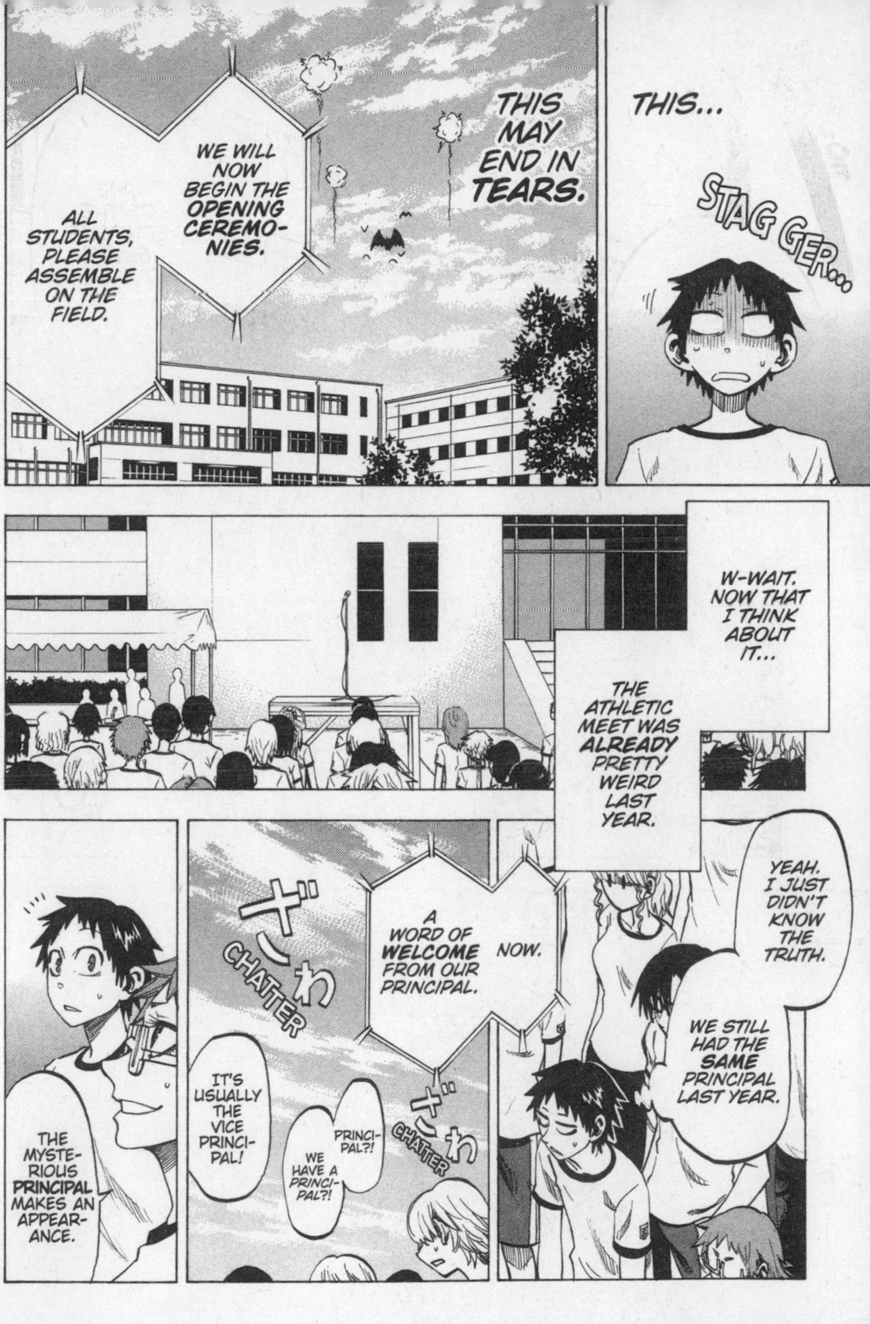
THIS...
STAG GER...
THIS MAY END IN TEARS.
WE WILL NOW BEGIN THE OPENING CEREMONIES.
ALL STUDENTS, PLEASE ASSEMBLE ON THE FIELD.
W-WAIT. NOW THAT I THINK ABOUT IT...
THE ATHLETIC MEET WAS ALREADY PRETTY WEIRD LAST YEAR.
YEAH. I JUST DIDN'T KNOW THE TRUTH.
WE STILL HAD THE SAME PRINCIPAL LAST YEAR.
NOW.
A WORD OF WELCOME FROM OUR PRINCIPAL.
ざわ CHATTER
ざわ CHATTER
PRINCI-PAL?!
WE HAVE A PRINCI-PAL?!
IT'S USUALLY THE VICE PRINCI-PAL!
THE MYSTE-RIOUS PRINCIPAL MAKES AN APPEAR-ANCE.

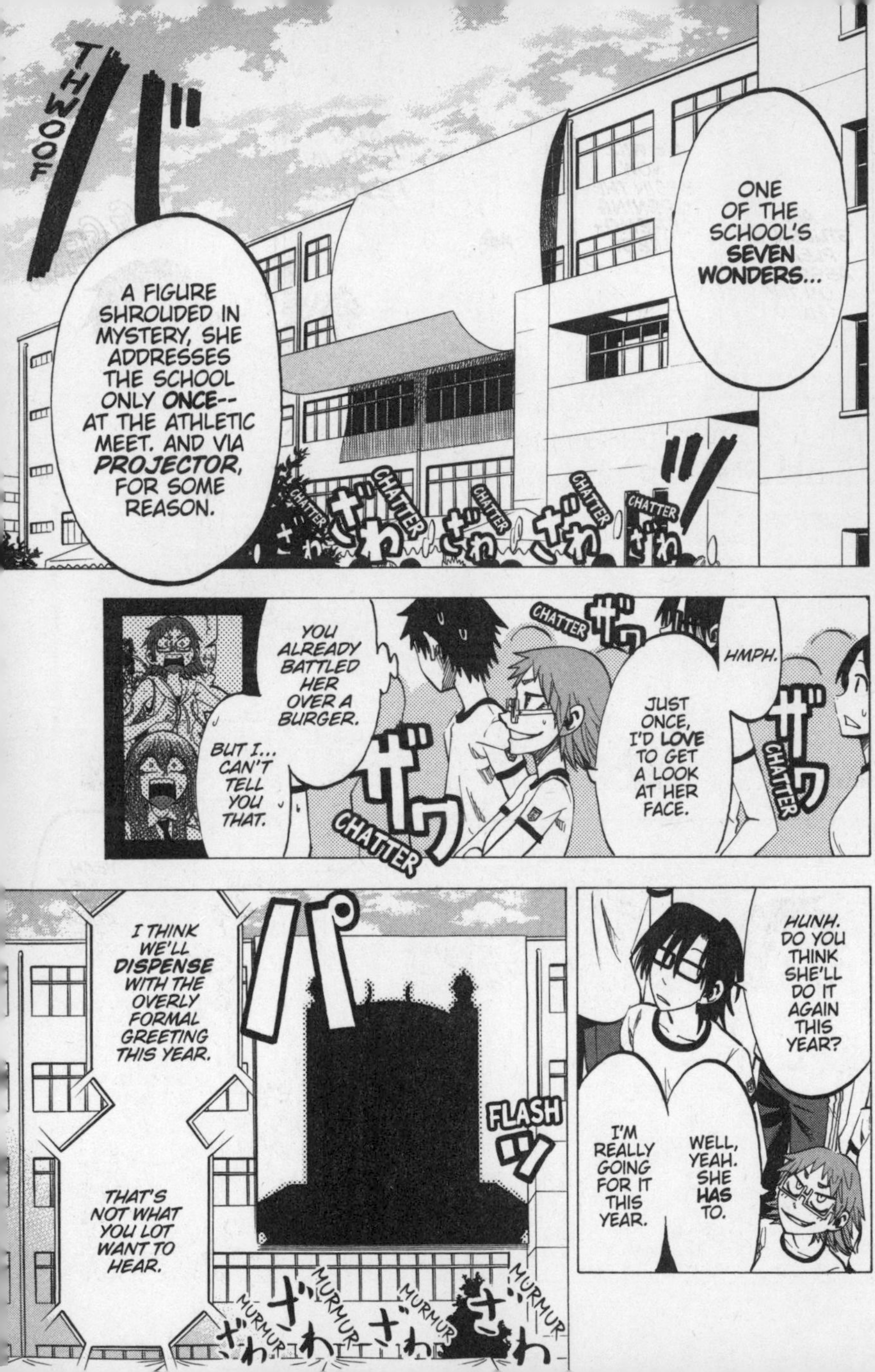
ONE OF THE SCHOOL'S SEVEN WONDERS...
THWOOF
A FIGURE SHROUDED IN MYSTERY, SHE ADDRESSES THE SCHOOL ONLY ONCE-- AT THE ATHLETIC MEET. AND VIA PROJECTOR, FOR SOME REASON.
CHATTER CHATTER CHATTER CHATTER CHATTER
HMPH.
JUST ONCE, I'D LOVE TO GET A LOOK AT HER FACE.
CHATTER
YOU ALREADY BATTLED HER OVER A BURGER.
BUT I... CAN'T TELL YOU THAT.
CHATTER
CHATTER
HUNH. DO YOU THINK SHE'LL DO IT AGAIN THIS YEAR?
WELL, YEAH. SHE HAS TO.
I'M REALLY GOING FOR IT THIS YEAR.
FLASH
I THINK WE'LL DISPENSE WITH THE OVERLY FORMAL GREETING THIS YEAR.
THAT'S NOT WHAT YOU LOT WANT TO HEAR.
MURMUR MURMUR MURMUR MURMUR MURMUR

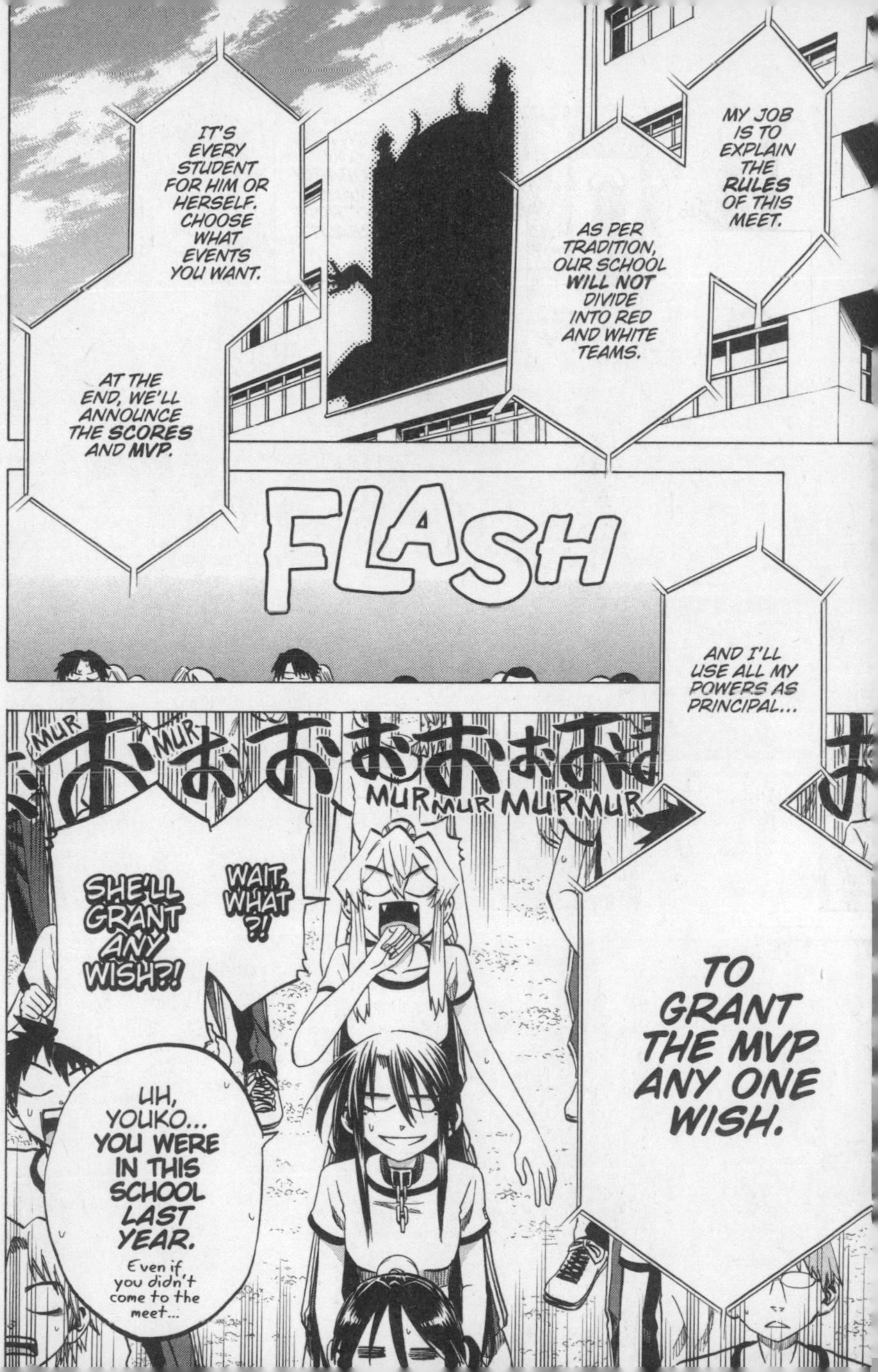
MY JOB IS TO EXPLAIN THE RULES OF THIS MEET.
AS PER TRADITION, OUR SCHOOL WILL NOT DIVIDE INTO RED AND WHITE TEAMS.
IT'S EVERY STUDENT FOR HIM OR HERSELF. CHOOSE WHAT EVENTS YOU WANT.
AT THE END, WE'LL ANNOUNCE THE SCORES AND MVP.
FLASH
AND I'LL USE ALL MY POWERS AS PRINCIPAL...
TO GRANT THE MVP ANY ONE WISH.
MUR MUR
MURMUR MURMUR MURMUR
WAIT, WHAT?!
SHE'LL GRANT ANY WISH?!
UH, YOUKO... YOU WERE IN THIS SCHOOL LAST YEAR.
Even if you didn't come to the meet...

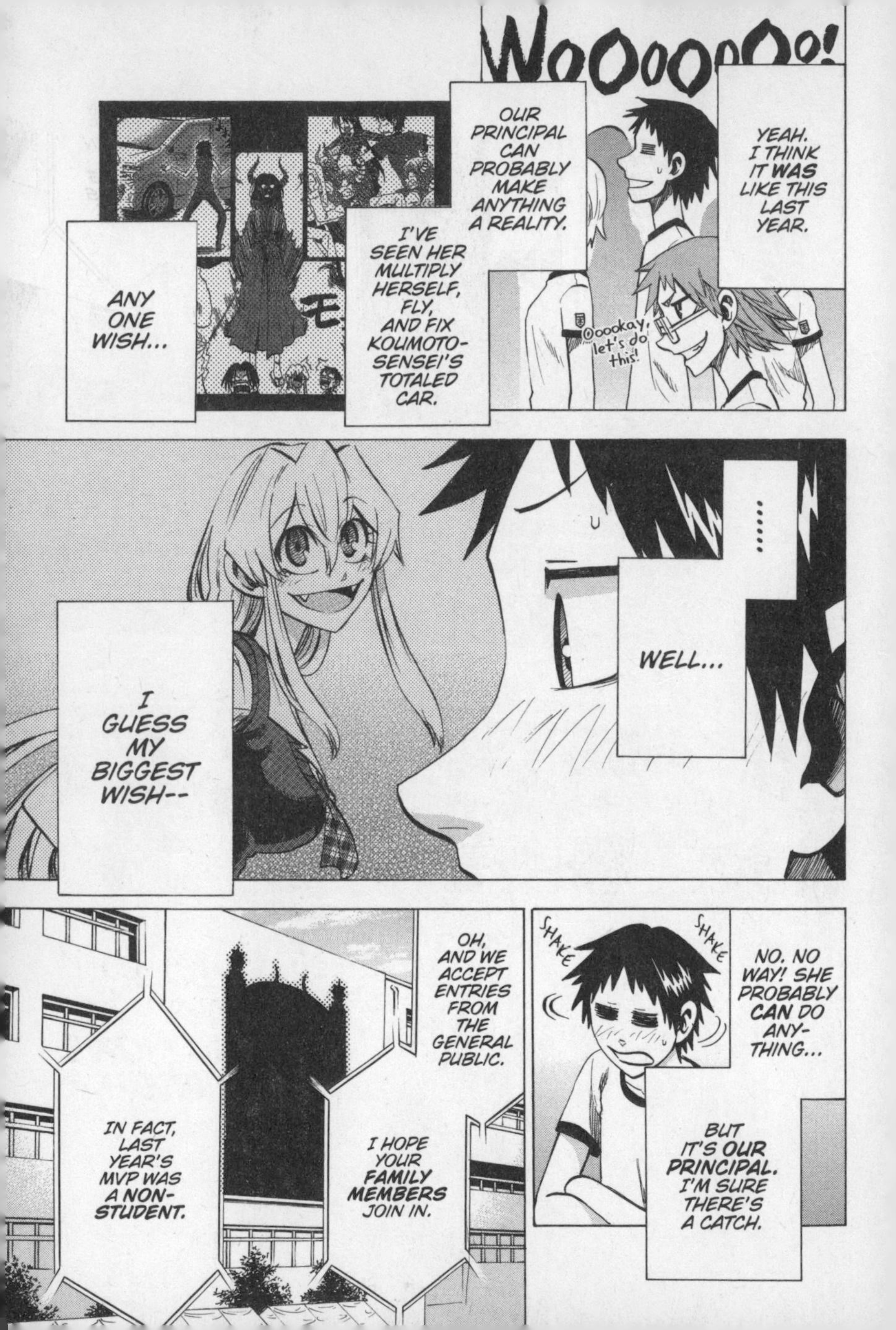
WOOOOOO!
YEAH. I THINK IT WAS LIKE THIS LAST YEAR.
OUR PRINCIPAL CAN PROBABLY MAKE ANYTHING A REALITY.
Oooookay, let's do this!
I'VE SEEN HER MULTIPLY HERSELF, FLY, AND FIX KOUMOTO-SENSEI'S TOTALED CAR.
ANY ONE WISH...
......
WELL...
I GUESS MY BIGGEST WISH--
SHAKE
SHAKE
NO. NO WAY! SHE PROBABLY CAN DO ANY-THING...
BUT IT'S OUR PRINCIPAL. I'M SURE THERE'S A CATCH.
OH, AND WE ACCEPT ENTRIES FROM THE GENERAL PUBLIC.
I HOPE YOUR FAMILY MEMBERS JOIN IN.
IN FACT, LAST YEAR'S MVP WAS A NON-STUDENT.

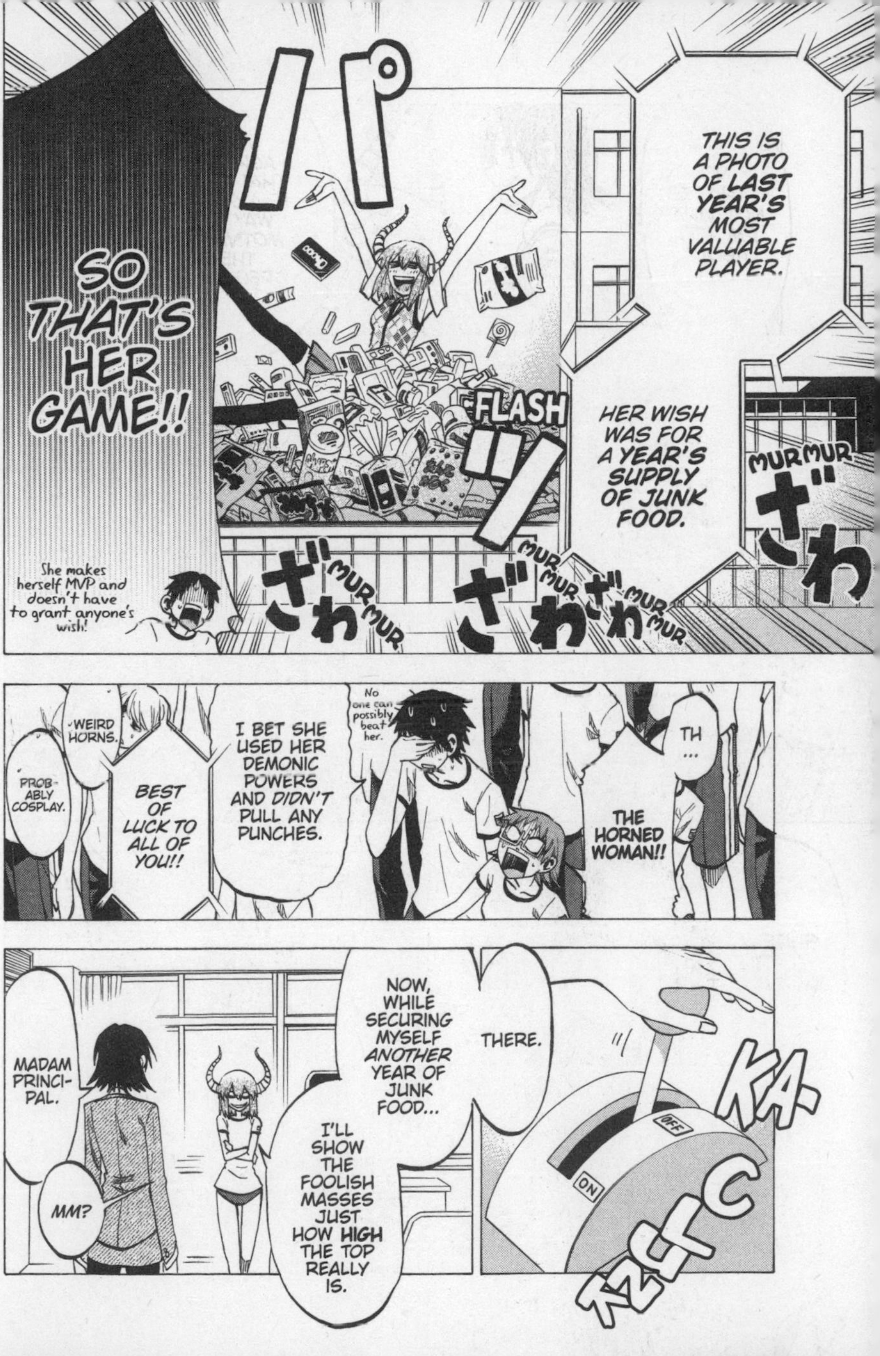

THIS IS A PHOTO OF LAST YEAR'S MOST VALUABLE PLAYER.
HER WISH WAS FOR A YEAR'S SUPPLY OF JUNK FOOD.
MURMUR
ざわ
MUR MUR ざわ MUR MUR ざわ MUR MUR
FLASH
パッ
SO THAT'S HER GAME!!
ざわ MUR MUR
She makes herself MVP and doesn't have to grant anyone's wish!
TH...
THE HORNED WOMAN!!
No one can possibly beat her.
I BET SHE USED HER DEMONIC POWERS AND DIDN'T PULL ANY PUNCHES.
BEST OF LUCK TO ALL OF YOU!!
WEIRD HORNS.
PROBABLY COSPLAY.
KA-
OFF
ON
THERE.
NOW, WHILE SECURING MYSELF ANOTHER YEAR OF JUNK FOOD...
I'LL SHOW THE FOOLISH MASSES JUST HOW HIGH THE TOP REALLY IS.
MADAM PRINCIPAL.
MM?

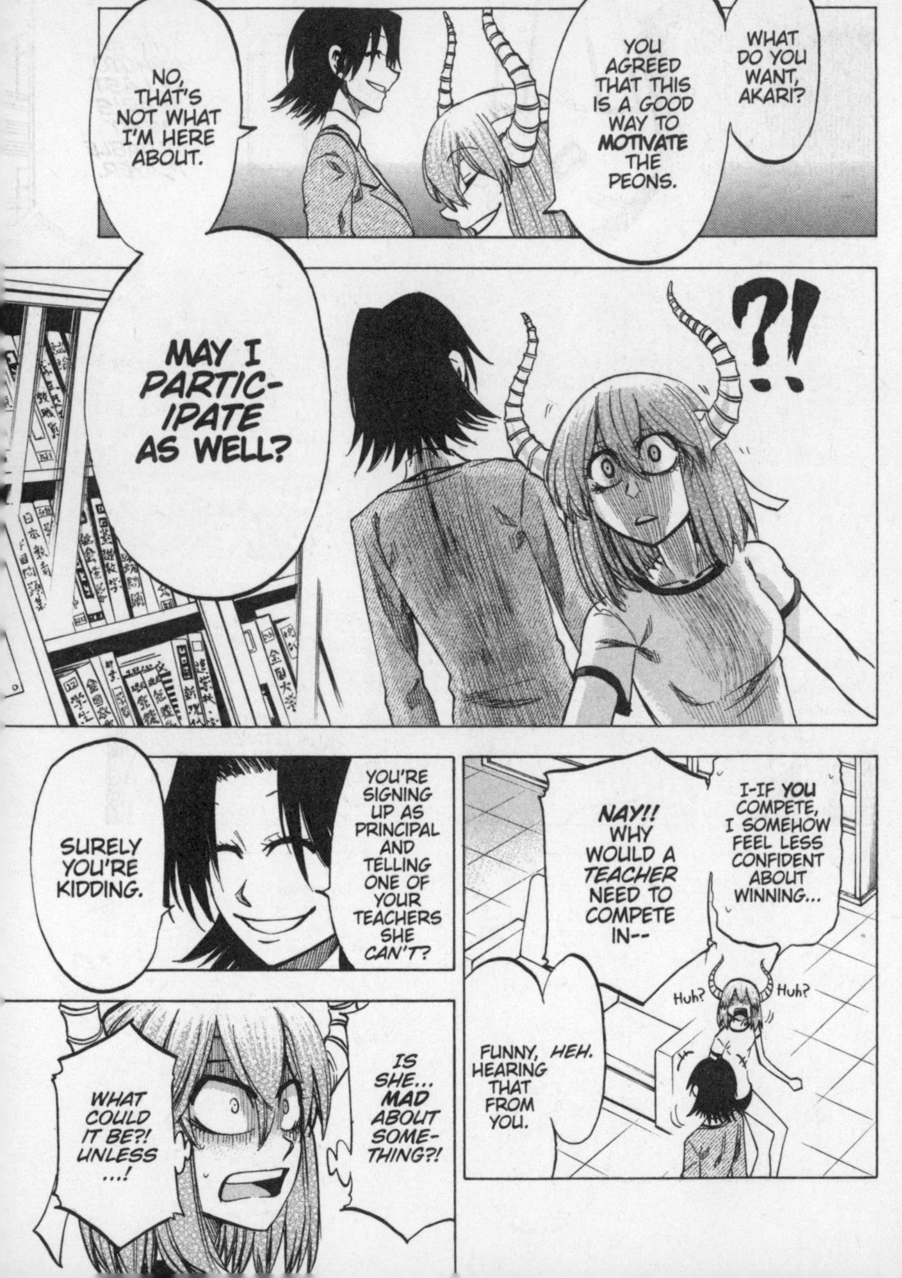
WHAT DO YOU WANT, AKARI?
YOU AGREED THAT THIS IS A GOOD WAY TO MOTIVATE THE PEONS.
NO, THAT'S NOT WHAT I'M HERE ABOUT.
MAY I PARTICIPATE AS WELL?
?!
I-IF YOU COMPETE, I SOMEHOW FEEL LESS CONFIDENT ABOUT WINNING...
NAY!! WHY WOULD A TEACHER NEED TO COMPETE IN--
Huh?
Huh?
FUNNY, HEH. HEARING THAT FROM YOU.
YOU'RE SIGNING UP AS PRINCIPAL AND TELLING ONE OF YOUR TEACHERS SHE CAN'T?
SURELY YOU'RE KIDDING.
IS SHE... MAD ABOUT SOMETHING?!
WHAT COULD IT BE?! UNLESS ...!

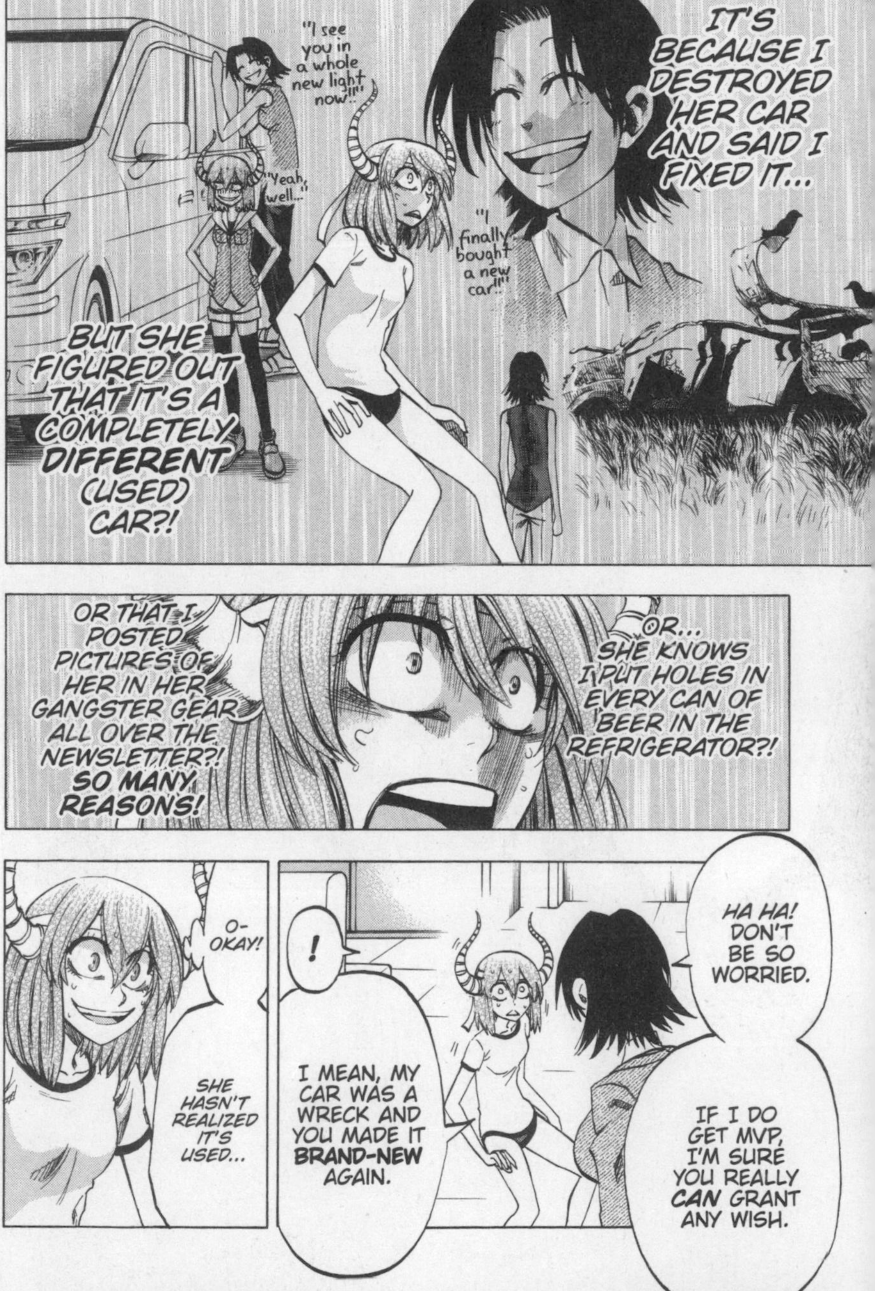
IT'S BECAUSE I DESTROYED HER CAR AND SAID I FIXED IT...
"I see you in a whole new light now!!"
"I finally bought a new car!!"
"Yeah, well.."
BUT SHE FIGURED OUT THAT IT'S A COMPLETELY DIFFERENT (USED) CAR?!
OR... SHE KNOWS I PUT HOLES IN EVERY CAN OF BEER IN THE REFRIGERATOR?!
OR THAT I POSTED PICTURES OF HER IN HER GANGSTER GEAR ALL OVER THE NEWSLETTER?! SO MANY REASONS!
HA HA! DON'T BE SO WORRIED.
IF I DO GET MVP, I'M SURE YOU REALLY CAN GRANT ANY WISH.
!
I MEAN, MY CAR WAS A WRECK AND YOU MADE IT BRAND-NEW AGAIN.
O-OKAY!
SHE HASN'T REALIZED IT'S USED...

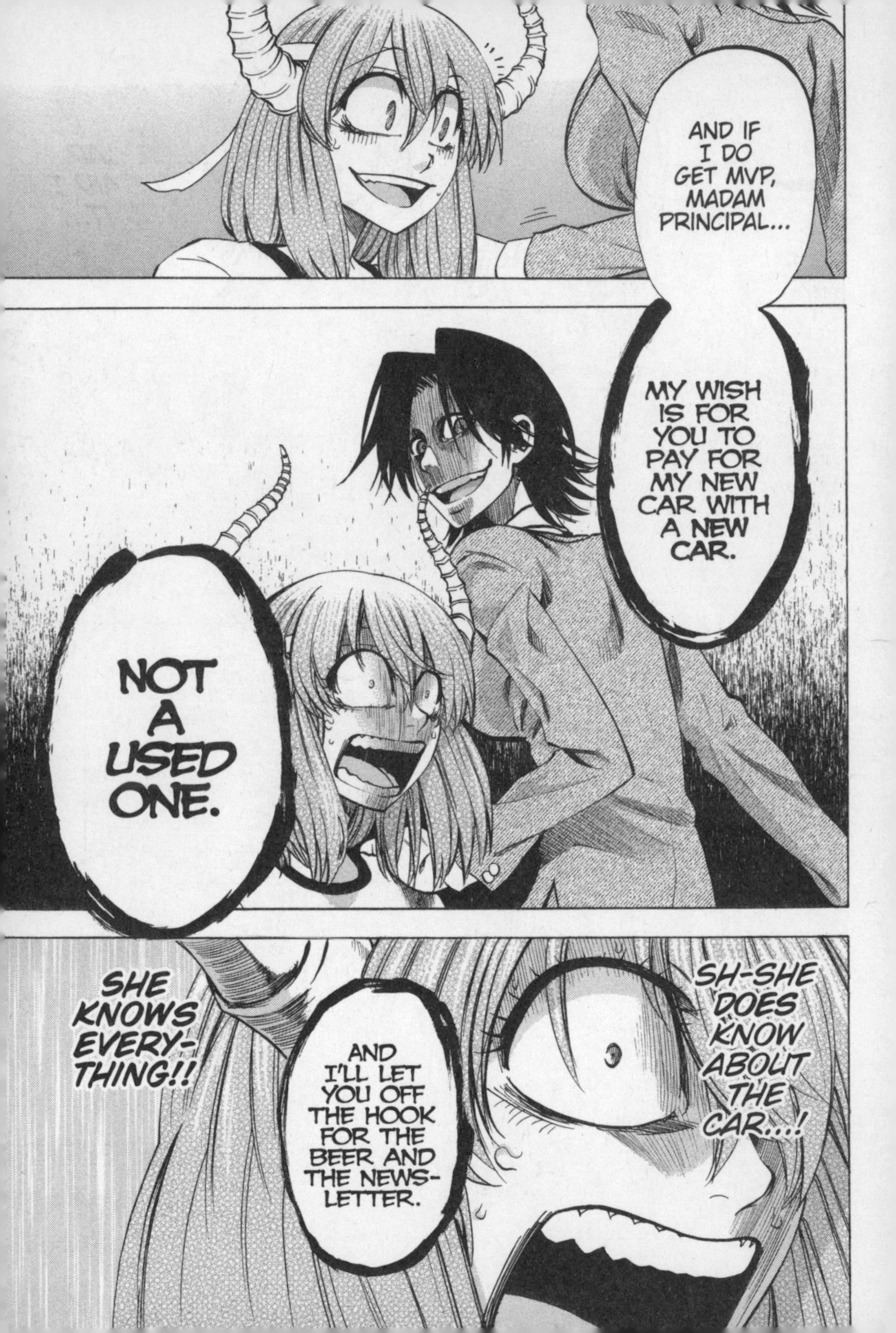
AND IF I DO GET MVP, MADAM PRINCIPAL...
MY WISH IS FOR YOU TO PAY FOR MY NEW CAR WITH A NEW CAR.
NOT A USED ONE.
SH-SHE DOES KNOW ABOUT THE CAR...!
AND I'LL LET YOU OFF THE HOOK FOR THE BEER AND THE NEWS-LETTER.
SHE KNOWS EVERY-THING!!

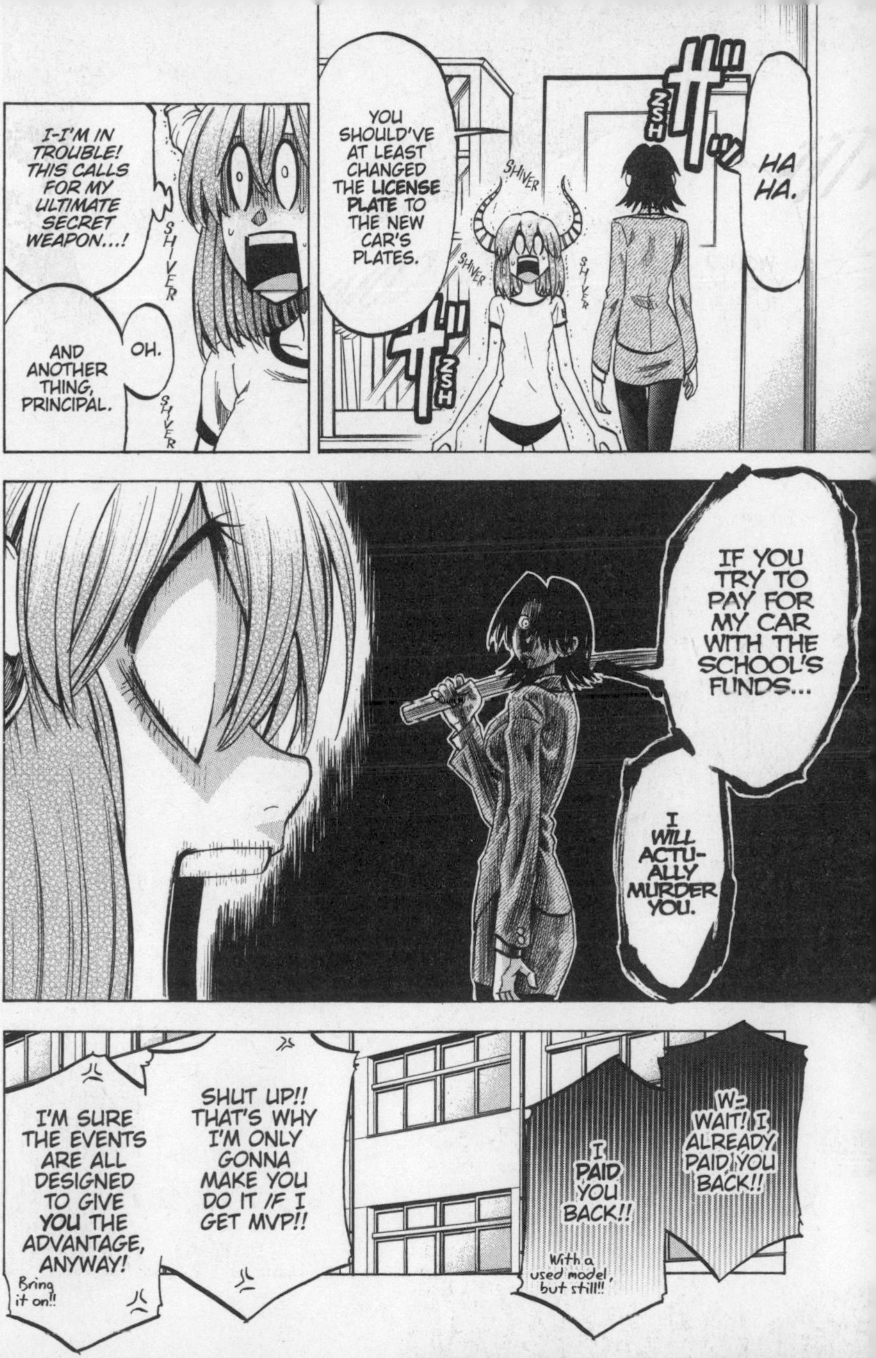
HA HA.
ZSH
YOU SHOULD'VE AT LEAST CHANGED THE **LICENSE PLATE** TO THE NEW CAR'S PLATES.
SHIVER
SHIVER
SHIVER
ZSH
I-I'M IN TROUBLE! THIS CALLS FOR MY ULTIMATE SECRET WEAPON...!
SHIVER
OH.
AND ANOTHER THING, PRINCIPAL.
SHIVER
IF YOU TRY TO PAY FOR MY CAR WITH THE SCHOOL'S FUNDS...
I *WILL* ACTU-ALLY MURDER YOU.
W-WAIT! I ALREADY PAID YOU BACK!!
I **PAID** YOU BACK!!
With a used model, but still!!
SHUT UP!! THAT'S WHY I'M ONLY GONNA MAKE YOU DO IT *IF* I GET MVP!!
I'M SURE THE EVENTS ARE ALL DESIGNED TO GIVE **YOU** THE ADVANTAGE, ANYWAY!
Bring it on!!

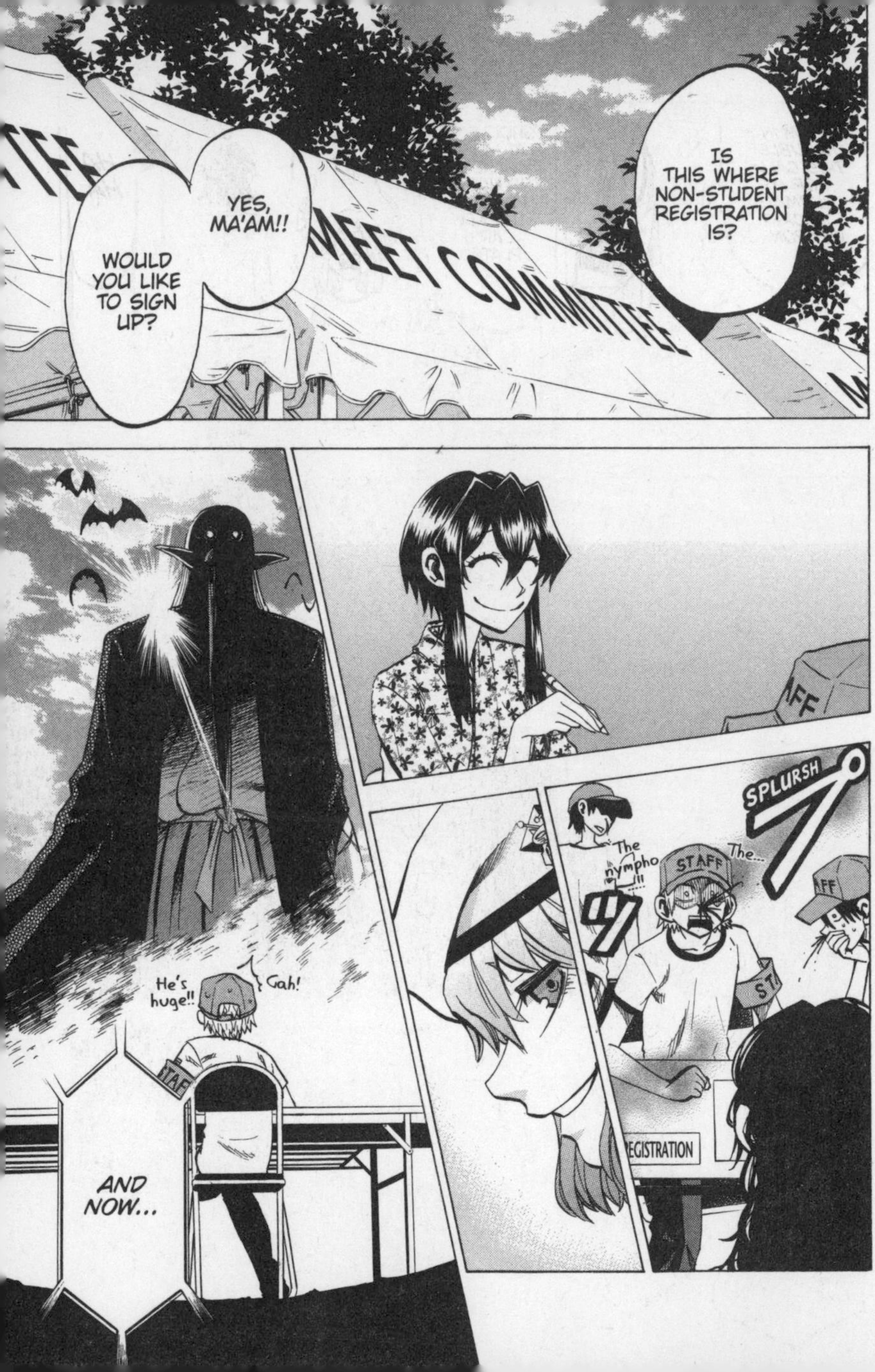

IS THIS WHERE NON-STUDENT REGISTRATION IS?
MEET COMMITTEE
YES, MA'AM!!
WOULD YOU LIKE TO SIGN UP?
SPLURSH
The...
The nympho...!!
REGISTRATION
Gah!
He's huge!!
AND NOW...

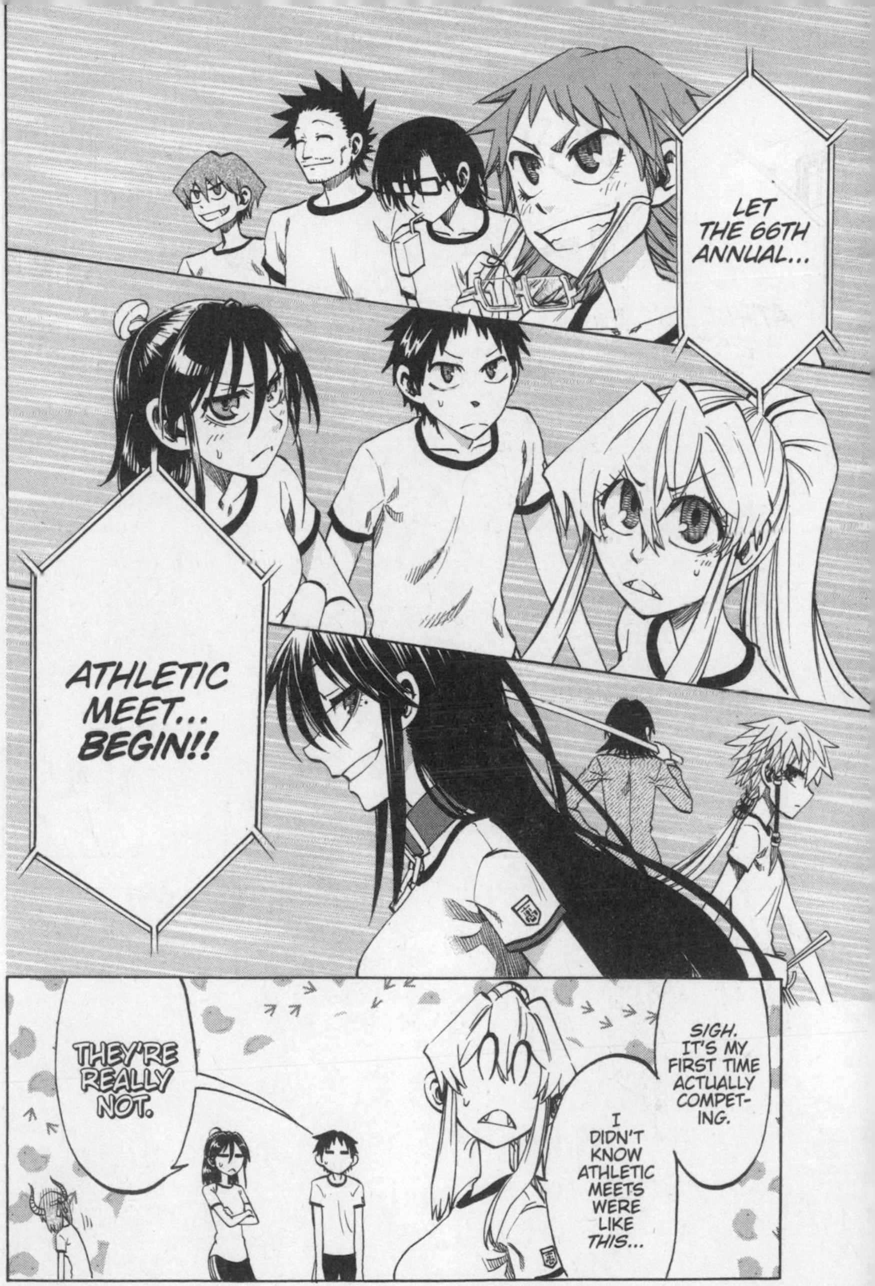
LET THE 66TH ANNUAL...
ATHLETIC MEET... BEGIN!!
SIGH. IT'S MY FIRST TIME ACTUALLY COMPETING.
I DIDN'T KNOW ATHLETIC MEETS WERE LIKE THIS...
THEY'RE REALLY NOT.

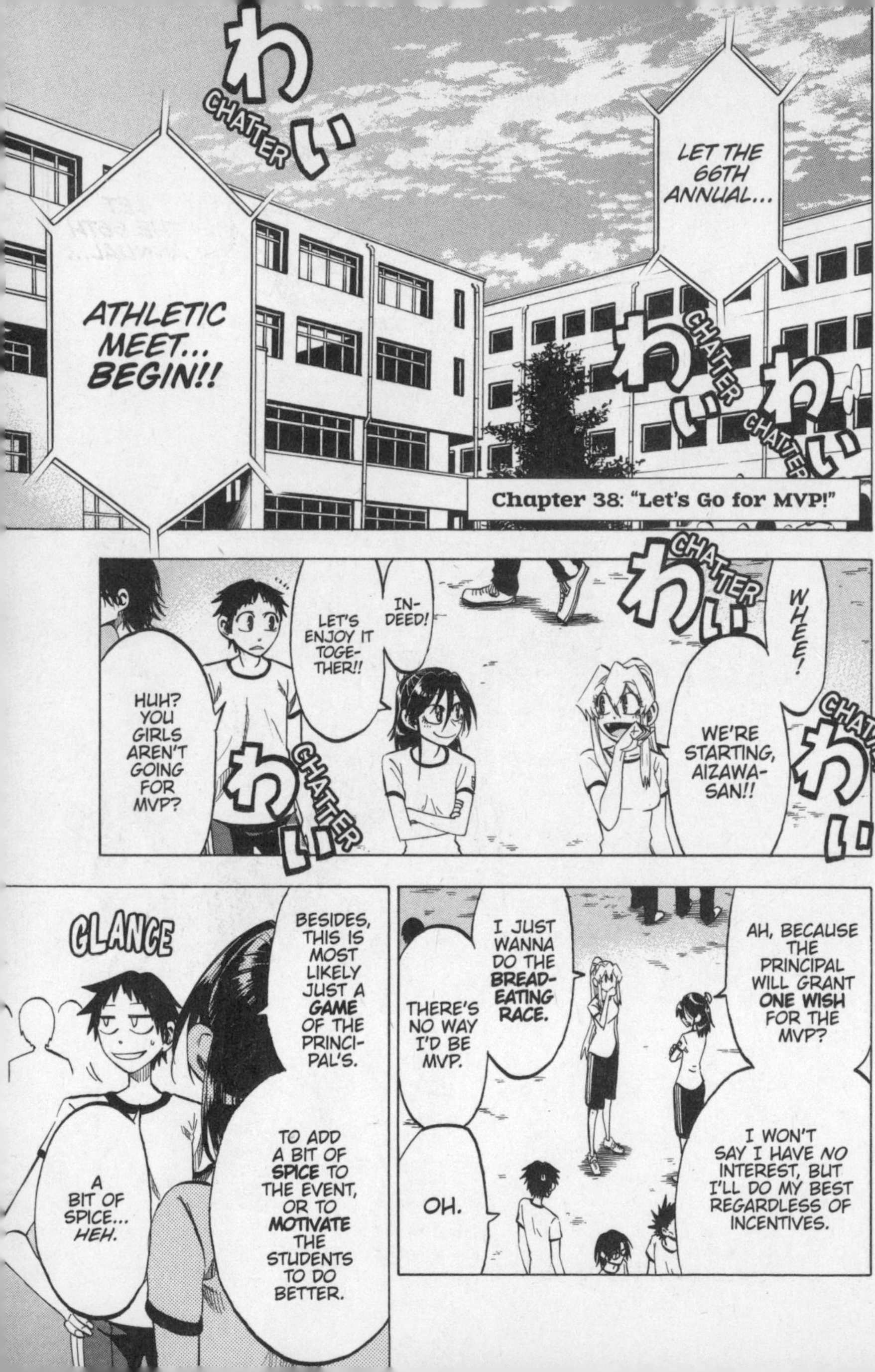
LET THE 66TH ANNUAL...
ATHLETIC MEET... BEGIN!!
わい CHATTER
わい CHATTER
わい CHATTER
Chapter 38: "Let's Go for MVP!"
CHATTER わい
WHEE!
WE'RE STARTING, AIZAWA-SAN!!
CHATTER わい
IN-DEED!
LET'S ENJOY IT TOGE-THER!!
HUH? YOU GIRLS AREN'T GOING FOR MVP?
CHATTER わい
AH, BECAUSE THE PRINCIPAL WILL GRANT ONE WISH FOR THE MVP?
I WON'T SAY I HAVE NO INTEREST, BUT I'LL DO MY BEST REGARDLESS OF INCENTIVES.
I JUST WANNA DO THE BREAD-EATING RACE.
THERE'S NO WAY I'D BE MVP.
OH.
BESIDES, THIS IS MOST LIKELY JUST A GAME OF THE PRINCI-PAL'S.
TO ADD A BIT OF SPICE TO THE EVENT, OR TO MOTIVATE THE STUDENTS TO DO BETTER.
GLANCE
A BIT OF SPICE... HEH.

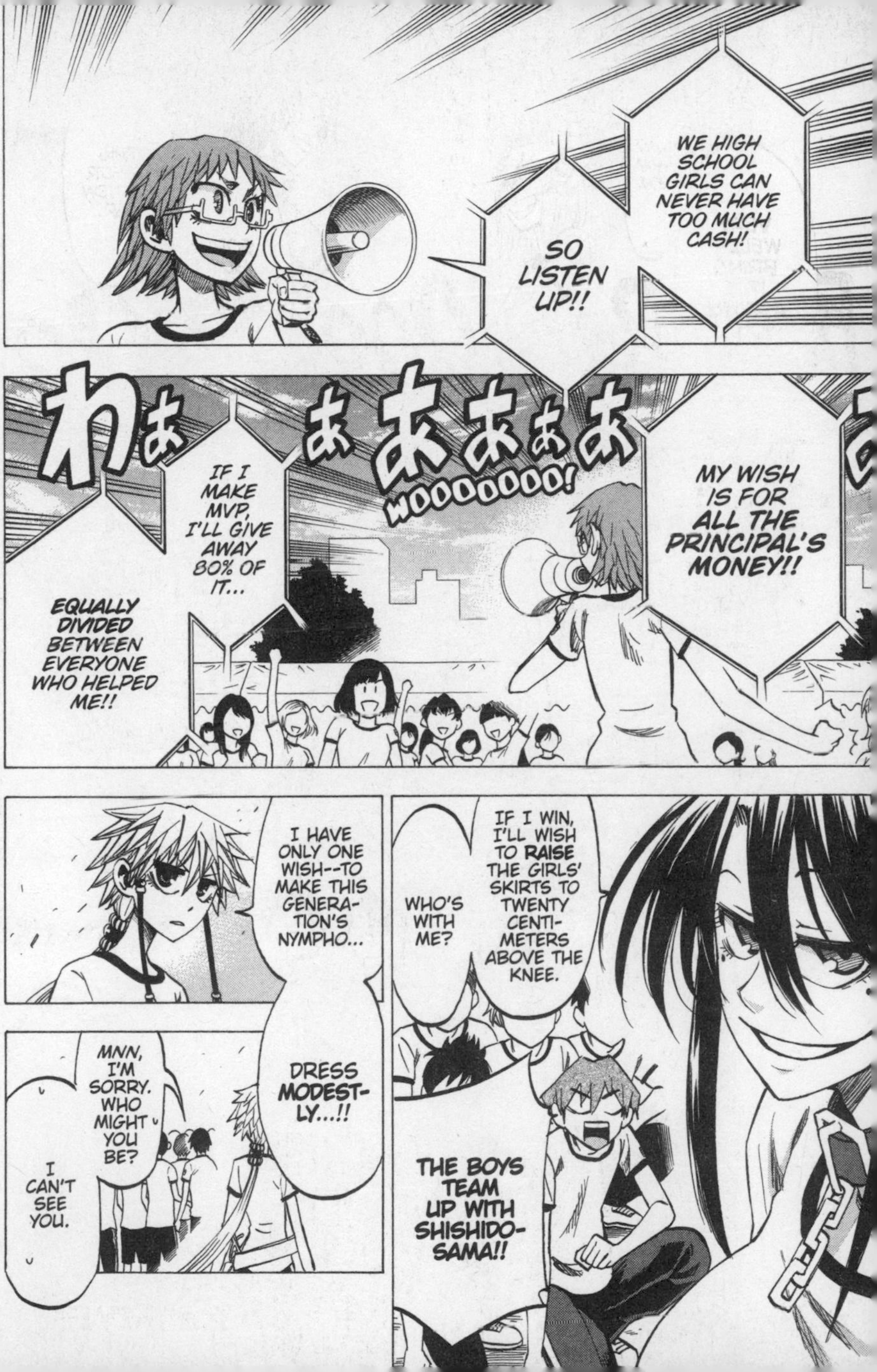
WE HIGH SCHOOL GIRLS CAN NEVER HAVE TOO MUCH CASH!
SO LISTEN UP!!
MY WISH IS FOR ALL THE PRINCIPAL'S MONEY!!
わぁぁあぁぁあ
WOOOOOOOO!
IF I MAKE MVP, I'LL GIVE AWAY 80% OF IT...
EQUALLY DIVIDED BETWEEN EVERYONE WHO HELPED ME!!
IF I WIN, I'LL WISH TO RAISE THE GIRLS' SKIRTS TO TWENTY CENTIMETERS ABOVE THE KNEE.
WHO'S WITH ME?
THE BOYS TEAM UP WITH SHISHIDO-SAMA!!
I HAVE ONLY ONE WISH--TO MAKE THIS GENERATION'S NYMPHO...
DRESS MODESTLY...!!
MNN, I'M SORRY. WHO MIGHT YOU BE?
I CAN'T SEE YOU.

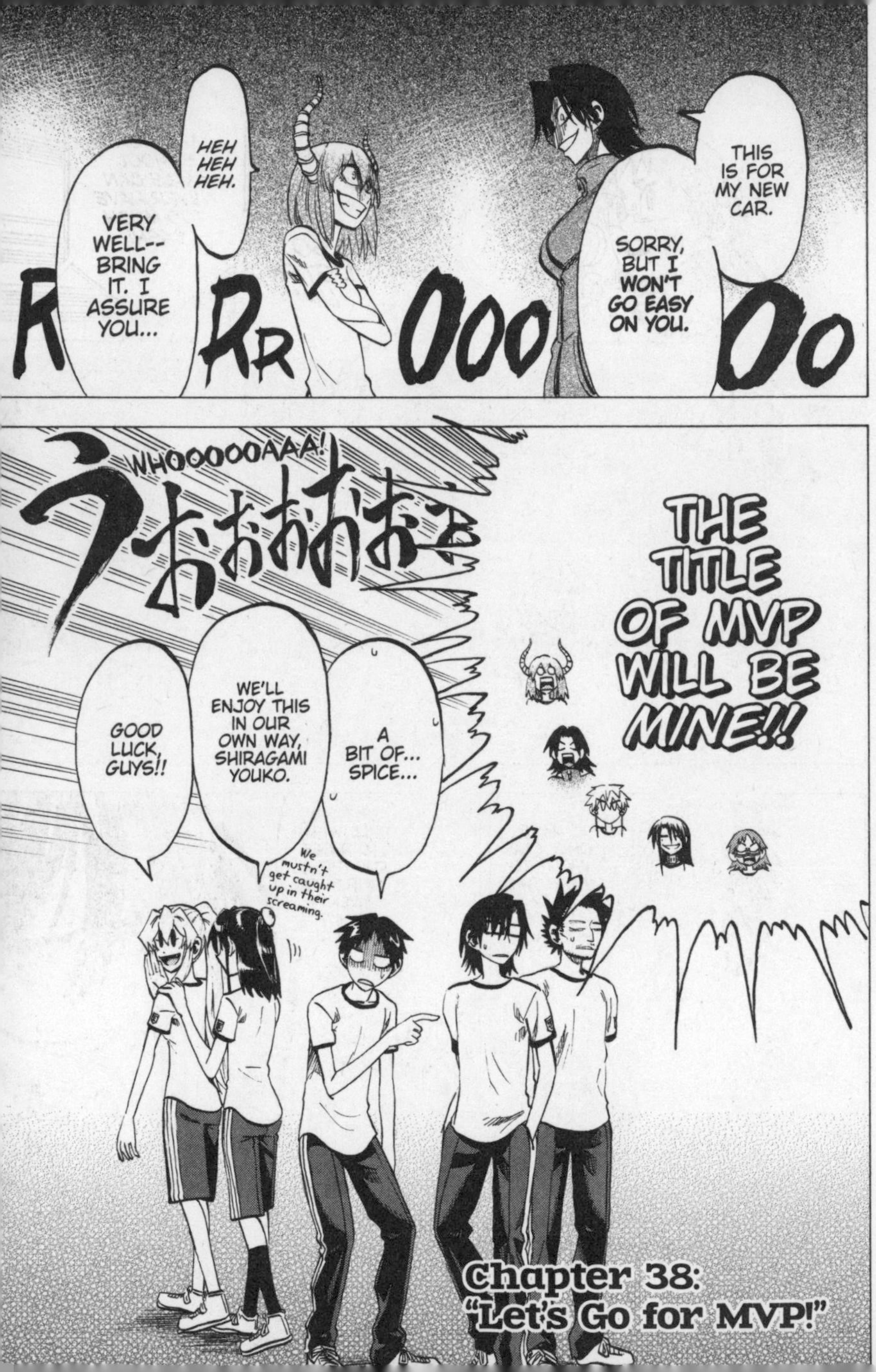
THIS IS FOR MY NEW CAR.
SORRY, BUT I WON'T GO EASY ON YOU.
HEH HEH HEH.
VERY WELL-- BRING IT. I ASSURE YOU...
RRROOOOO
THE TITLE OF MVP WILL BE MINE!!
うおおおおぉ
WHOOOOOAAA!
A BIT OF... SPICE...
WE'LL ENJOY THIS IN OUR OWN WAY, SHIRAGAMI YOUKO.
GOOD LUCK, GUYS!!
We mustn't get caught up in their screaming.

Chapter 38: "Let's Go for MVP!"

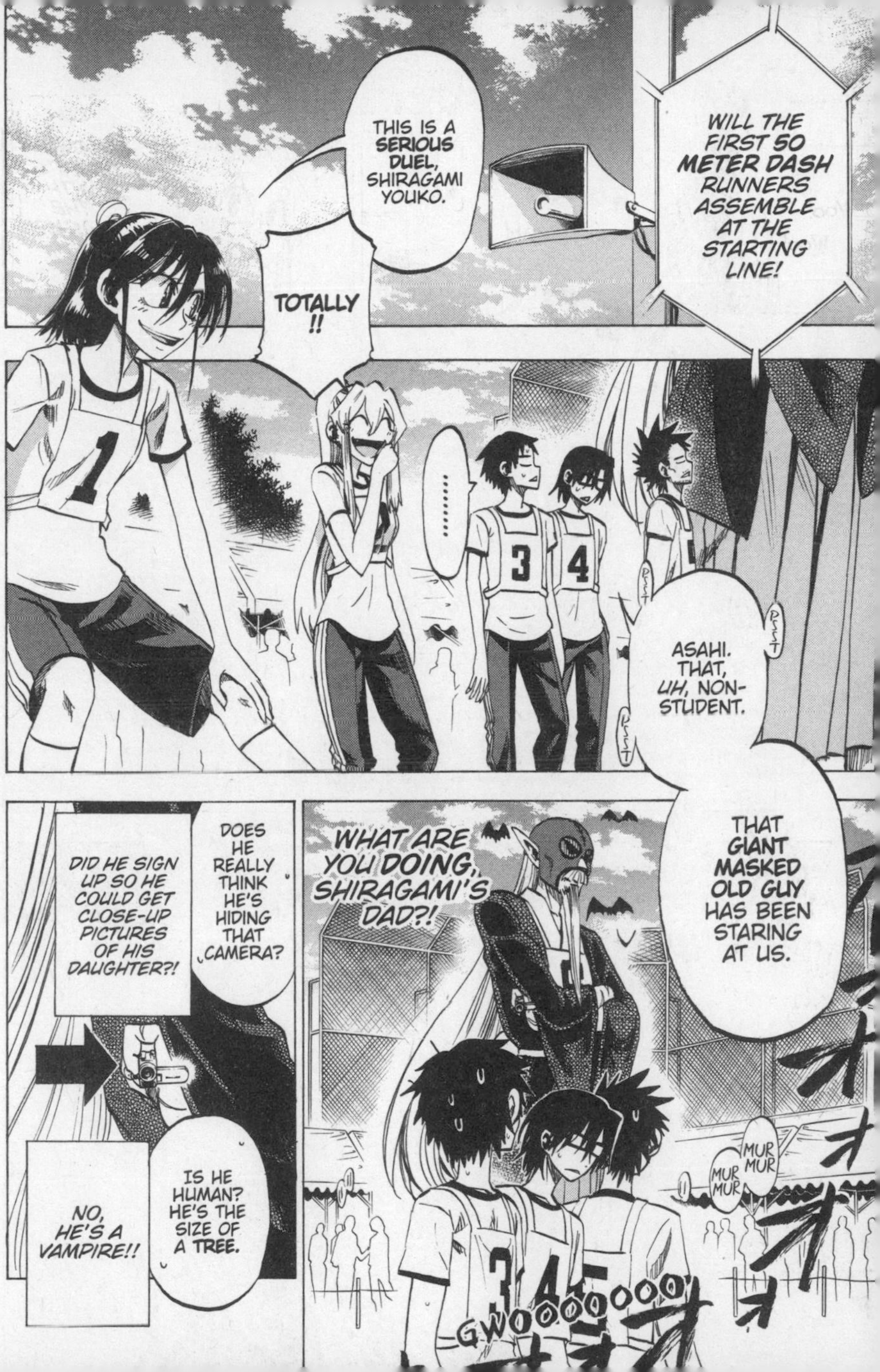
WILL THE FIRST 50 METER DASH RUNNERS ASSEMBLE AT THE STARTING LINE!
THIS IS A SERIOUS DUEL, SHIRAGAMI YOUKO.
TOTALLY !!
......
PSST
PSST
PSST
ASAHI. THAT, UH, NON-STUDENT.
THAT GIANT MASKED OLD GUY HAS BEEN STARING AT US.
WHAT ARE YOU DOING, SHIRAGAMI'S DAD?!
MUR MUR
MUR MUR
GWOOOOOOOO
DOES HE REALLY THINK HE'S HIDING THAT CAMERA?
DID HE SIGN UP SO HE COULD GET CLOSE-UP PICTURES OF HIS DAUGHTER?!
IS HE HUMAN? HE'S THE SIZE OF A TREE.
NO, HE'S A VAMPIRE!!

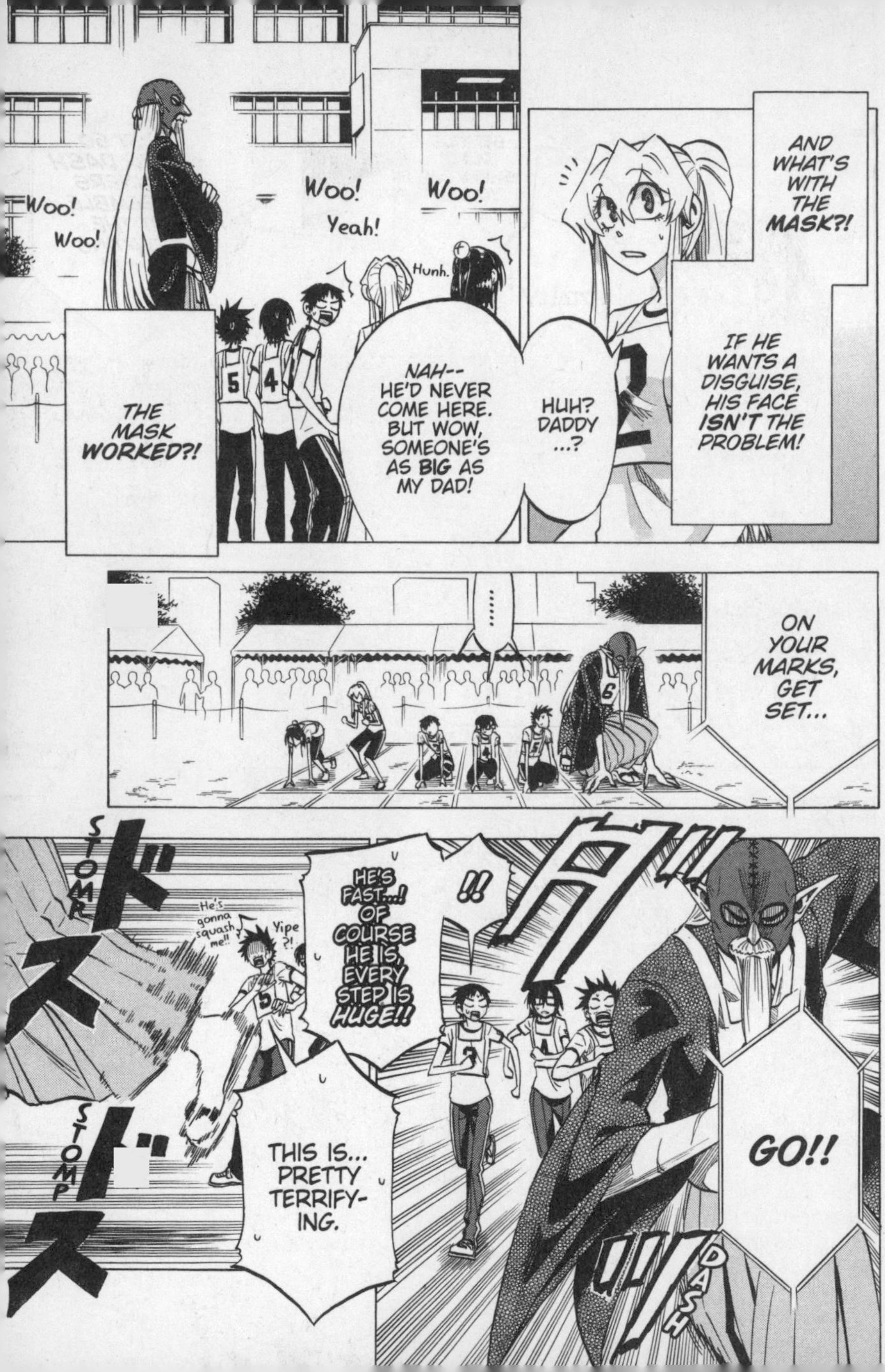
AND WHAT'S WITH THE MASK?!
IF HE WANTS A DISGUISE, HIS FACE ISN'T THE PROBLEM!
Woo!
Woo!
Yeah!
Woo!
Woo!
Hunh.
HUH? DADDY ...?
NAH-- HE'D NEVER COME HERE. BUT WOW, SOMEONE'S AS BIG AS MY DAD!
THE MASK WORKED?!
ON YOUR MARKS, GET SET...
......
GO!!
DASH
!!
HE'S FAST...! OF COURSE HE IS, EVERY STEP IS HUGE!!
THIS IS... PRETTY TERRIFY-ING.
Yipe?!
He's gonna squash me!!
STOMP
STOMP

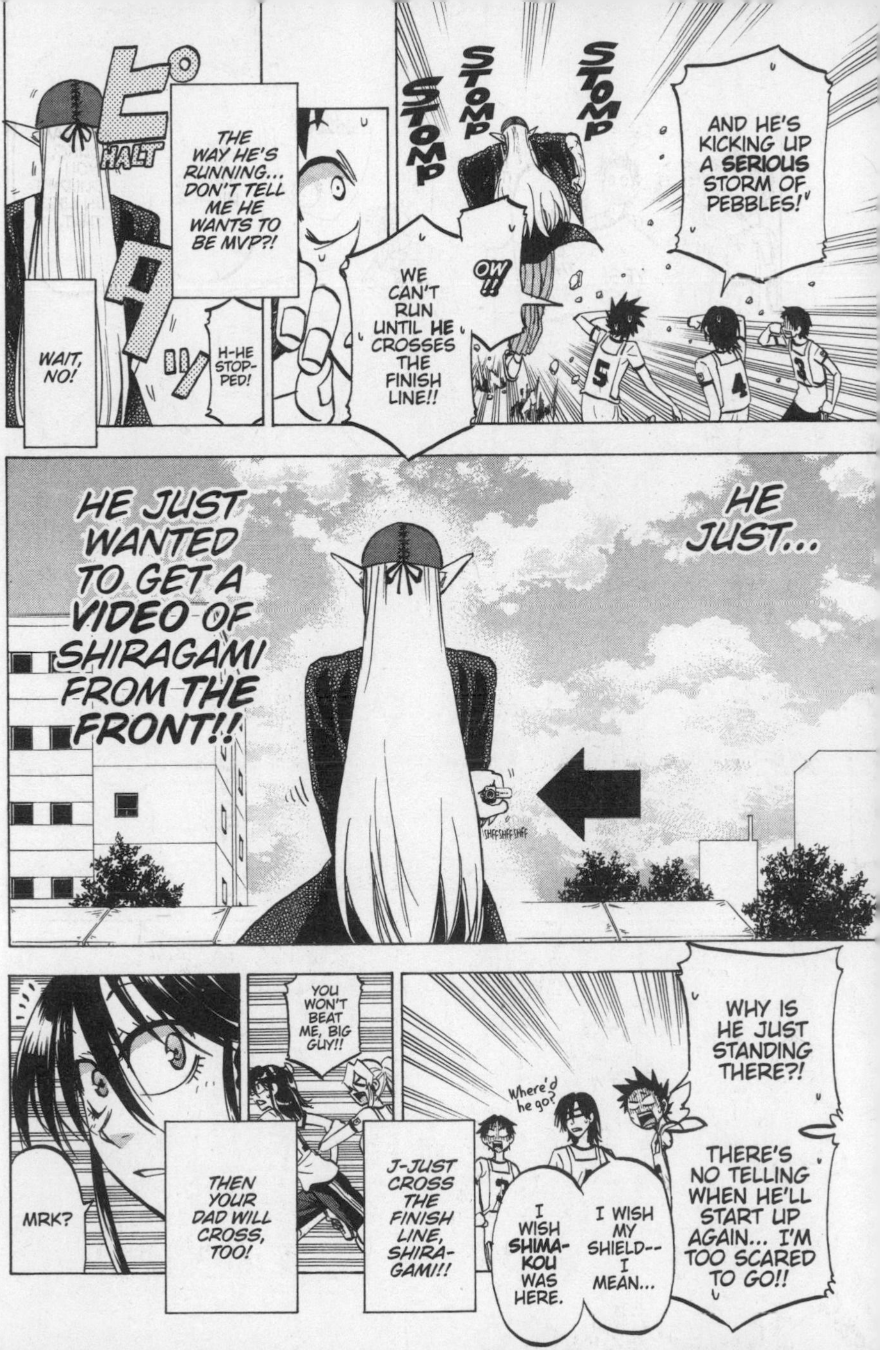
AND HE'S KICKING UP A SERIOUS STORM OF PEBBLES!
STOMP
STOMP
STOMP
OW!!
WE CAN'T RUN UNTIL HE CROSSES THE FINISH LINE!!
THE WAY HE'S RUNNING... DON'T TELL ME HE WANTS TO BE MVP?!
H-HE STOPPED!
HALT
WAIT, NO!
HE JUST...
HE JUST WANTED TO GET A VIDEO OF SHIRAGAMI FROM THE FRONT!!
SHFFSHFFSHFF
WHY IS HE JUST STANDING THERE?!
Where'd he go?
THERE'S NO TELLING WHEN HE'LL START UP AGAIN... I'M TOO SCARED TO GO!!
I WISH MY SHIELD-- I MEAN...
I WISH SHIMA-KOU WAS HERE.
YOU WON'T BEAT ME, BIG GUY!!
J-JUST CROSS THE FINISH LINE, SHIRAGAMI!!
THEN YOUR DAD WILL CROSS, TOO!
MRK?

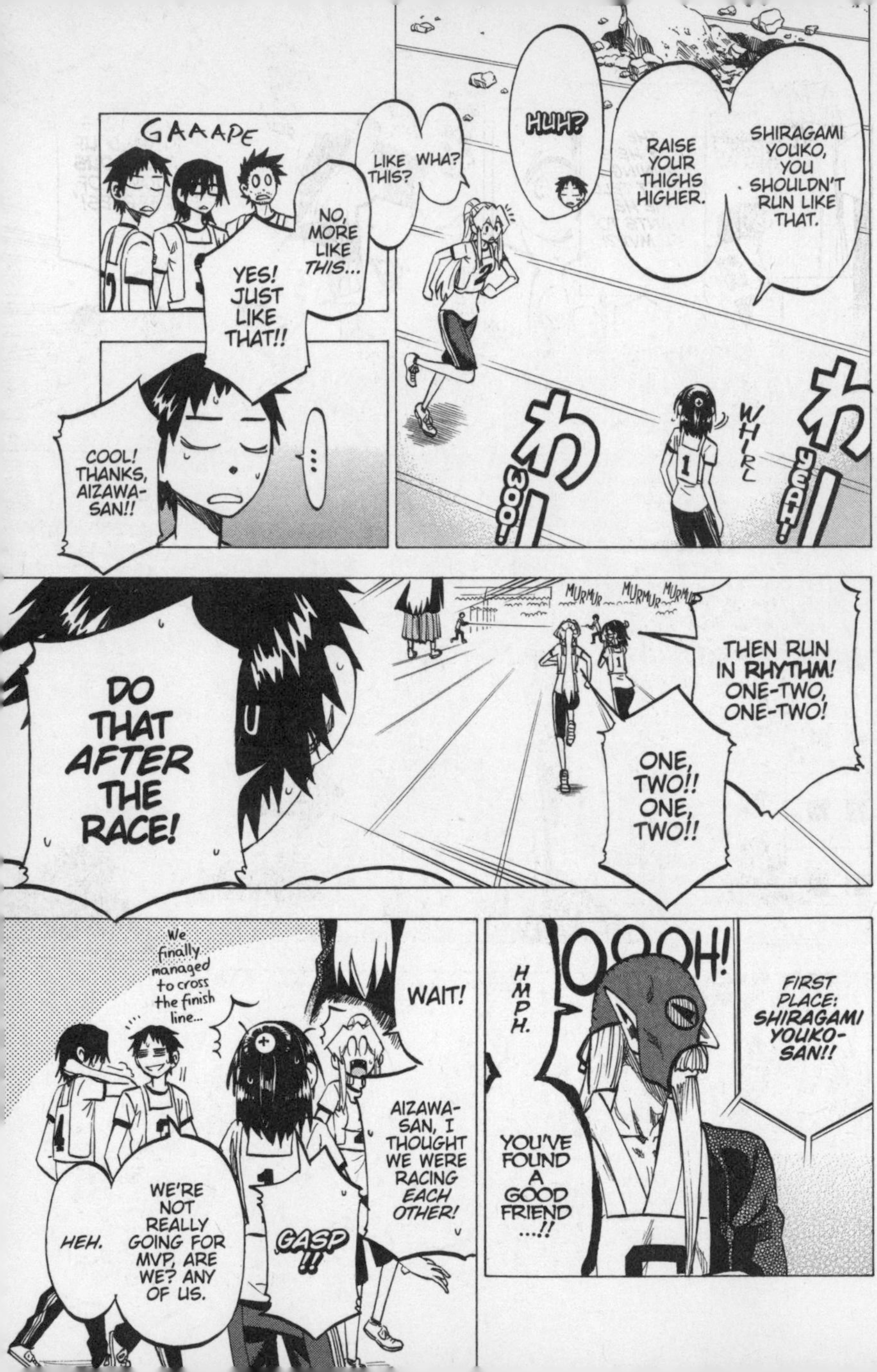
SHIRAGAMI YOUKO, YOU SHOULDN'T RUN LIKE THAT.
RAISE YOUR THIGHS HIGHER.
HUH?
WHA?
LIKE THIS?
NO, MORE LIKE THIS...
わ YEAH!
WHIRL
わ WOO!
GAAAPE
YES! JUST LIKE THAT!!
...
COOL! THANKS, AIZAWA-SAN!!
MURMUR MURMUR MURMUR
THEN RUN IN RHYTHM! ONE-TWO, ONE-TWO!
ONE, TWO!! ONE, TWO!!
DO THAT AFTER THE RACE!
OOOH!
FIRST PLACE: SHIRAGAMI YOUKO-SAN!!
HMPH.
YOU'VE FOUND A GOOD FRIEND...!!
WAIT!
AIZAWA-SAN, I THOUGHT WE WERE RACING EACH OTHER!
GASP!!
We finally managed to cross the finish line...
WE'RE NOT REALLY GOING FOR MVP, ARE WE? ANY OF US.
HEH.

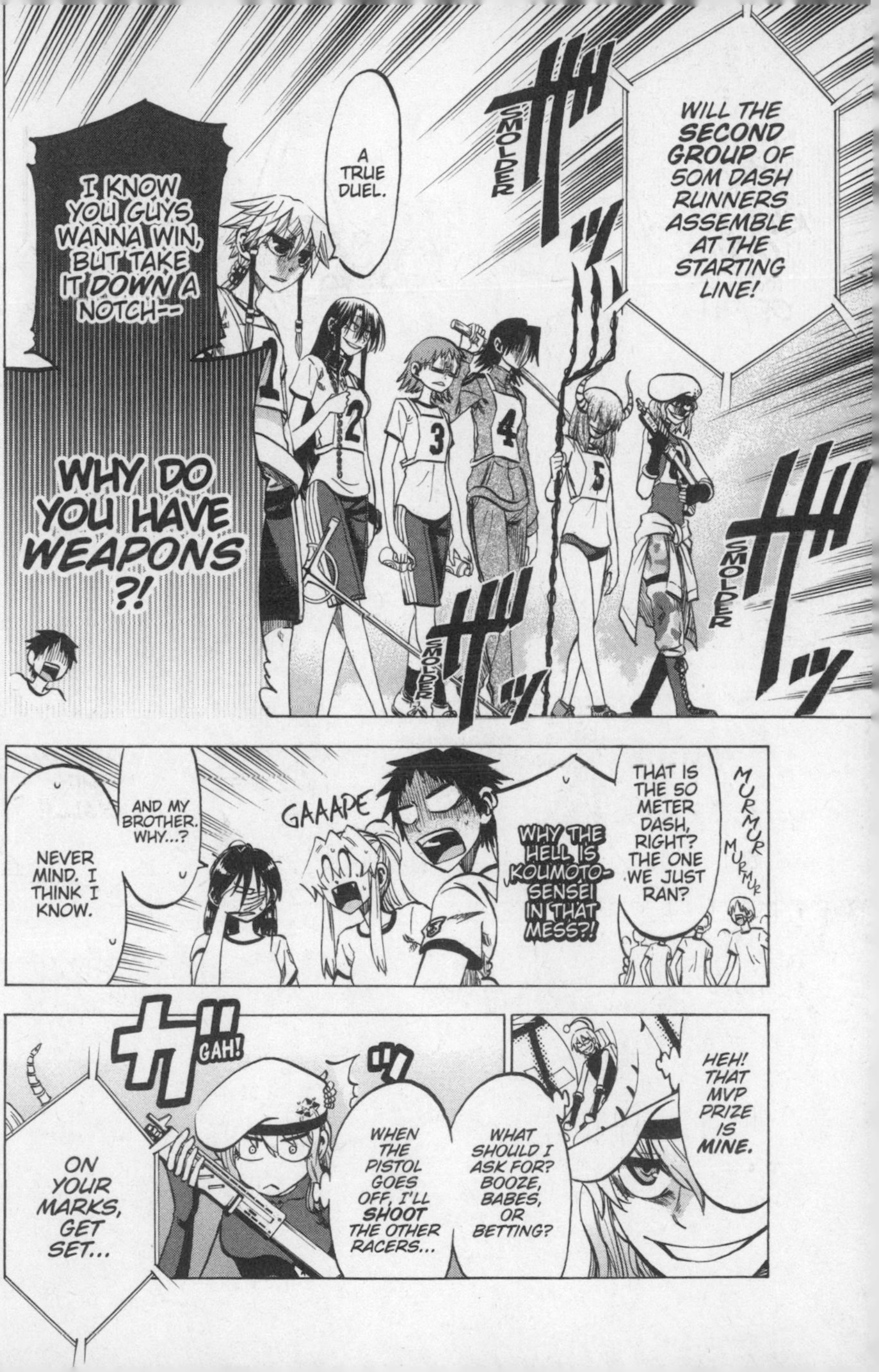
WILL THE SECOND GROUP OF 50M DASH RUNNERS ASSEMBLE AT THE STARTING LINE!
SMOLDER
A TRUE DUEL.
I KNOW YOU GUYS WANNA WIN, BUT TAKE IT DOWN A NOTCH--
SMOLDER
SMOLDER
WHY DO YOU HAVE WEAPONS ?!
MURMUR MURMUR
THAT IS THE 50 METER DASH, RIGHT? THE ONE WE JUST RAN?
WHY THE HELL IS KOUMOTO-SENSEI IN THAT MESS?!
GAAAPE
AND MY BROTHER. WHY...?
NEVER MIND. I THINK I KNOW.
HEH! THAT MVP PRIZE IS MINE.
WHAT SHOULD I ASK FOR? BOOZE, BABES, OR BETTING?
WHEN THE PISTOL GOES OFF, I'LL SHOOT THE OTHER RACERS...
GAH!
ON YOUR MARKS, GET SET...

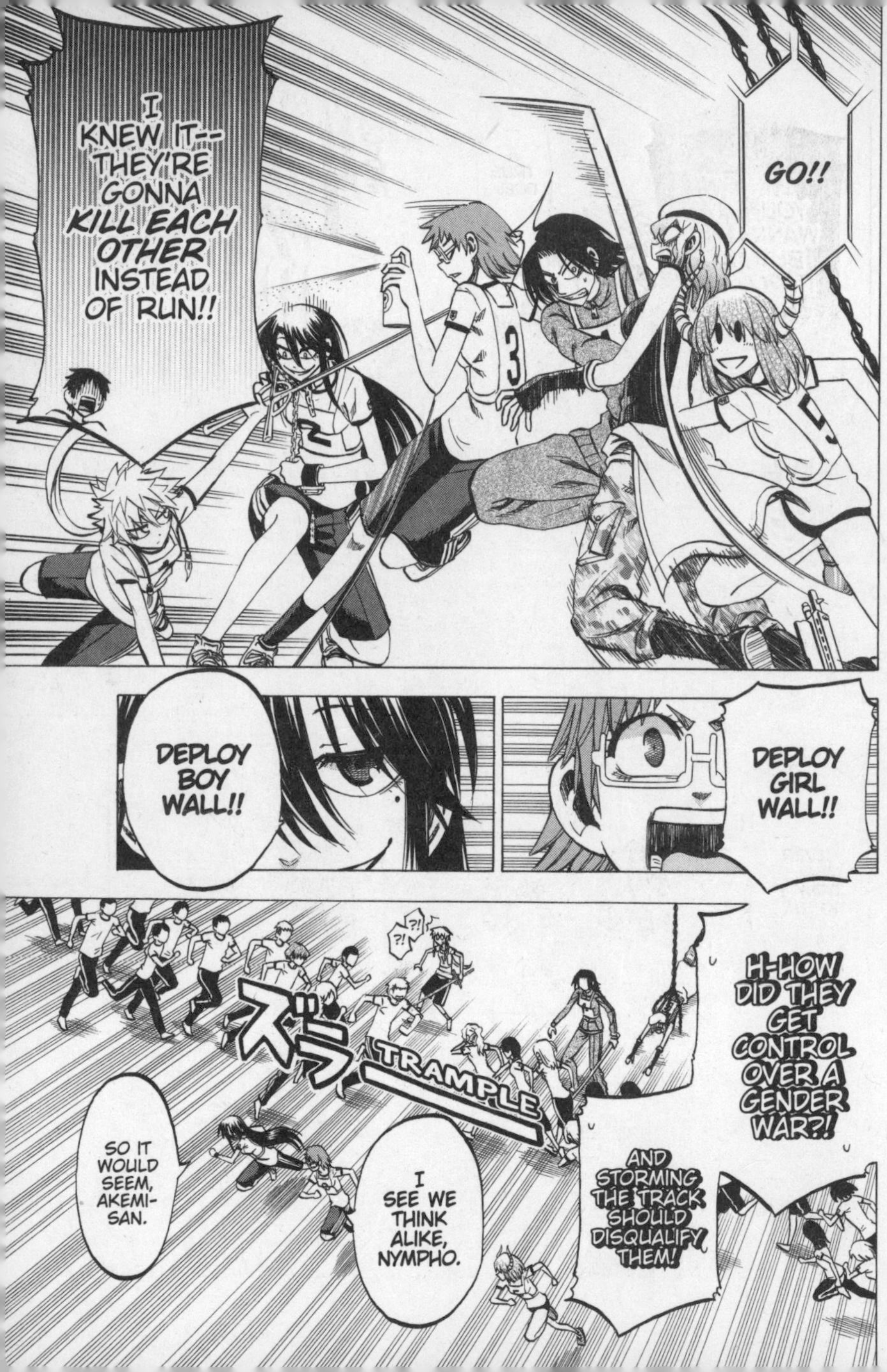
GO!!
I KNEW IT-- THEY'RE GONNA KILL EACH OTHER INSTEAD OF RUN!!
DEPLOY GIRL WALL!!
DEPLOY BOY WALL!!
H-HOW DID THEY GET CONTROL OVER A GENDER WAR?!
AND STORMING THE TRACK SHOULD DISQUALIFY THEM!
?!
?!
ズラ
TRAMPLE
I SEE WE THINK ALIKE, NYMPHO.
SO IT WOULD SEEM, AKEMI-SAN.

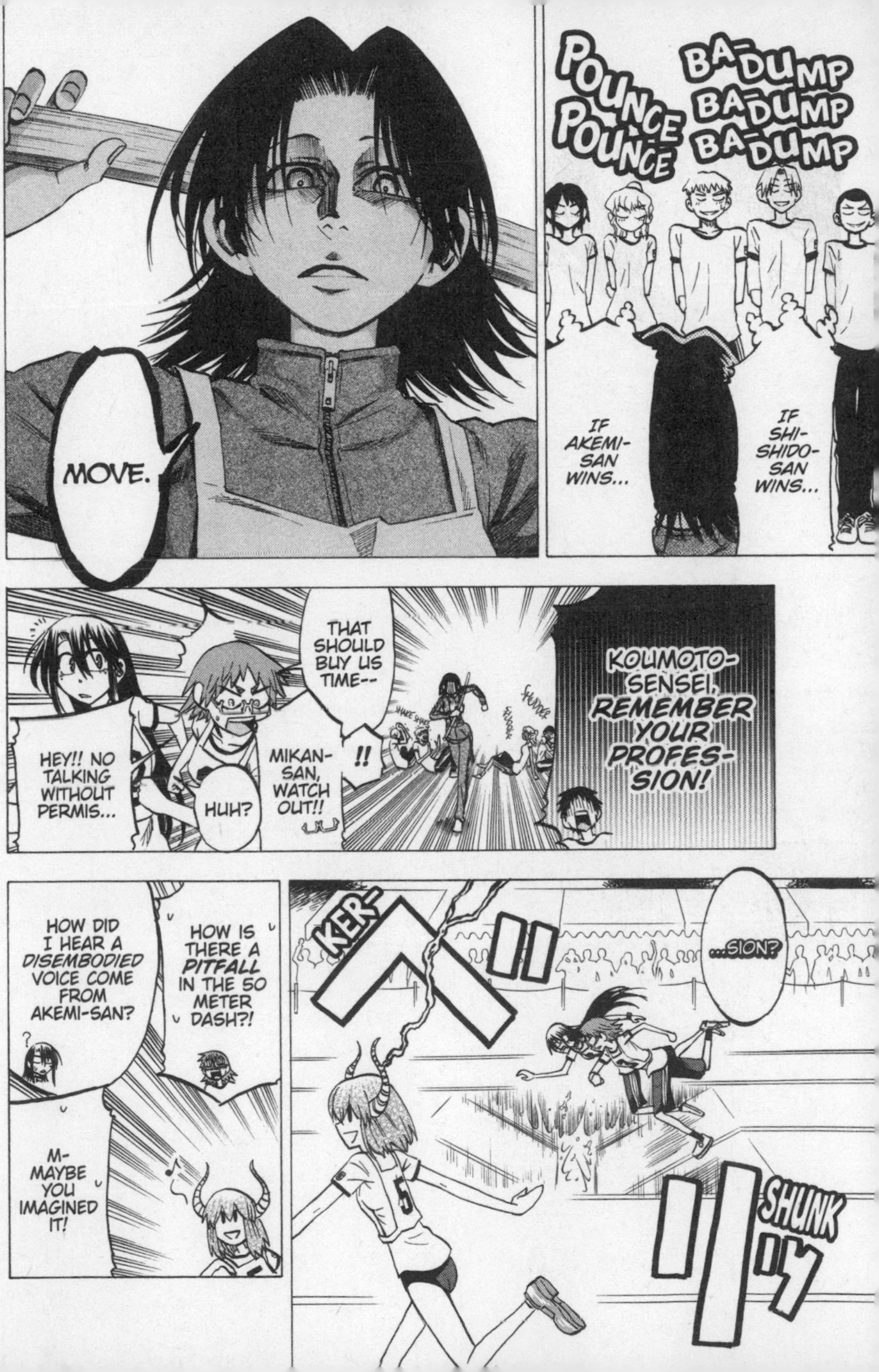
BA-DUMP BA-DUMP BA-DUMP
POUNCE POUNCE
IF SHI-SHIDO-SAN WINS...
IF AKEMI-SAN WINS...
MOVE.
KOUMOTO-SENSEI, REMEMBER YOUR PROFES-SION!
SHUDDER
THAT SHOULD BUY US TIME--
MIKAN-SAN, WATCH OUT!!
!!
HUH?
HEY!! NO TALKING WITHOUT PERMIS...
...SION?
KER-
SHUNK
HOW IS THERE A PITFALL IN THE 50 METER DASH?!
HOW DID I HEAR A DISEMBODIED VOICE COME FROM AKEMI-SAN?
M-MAYBE YOU IMAGINED IT!

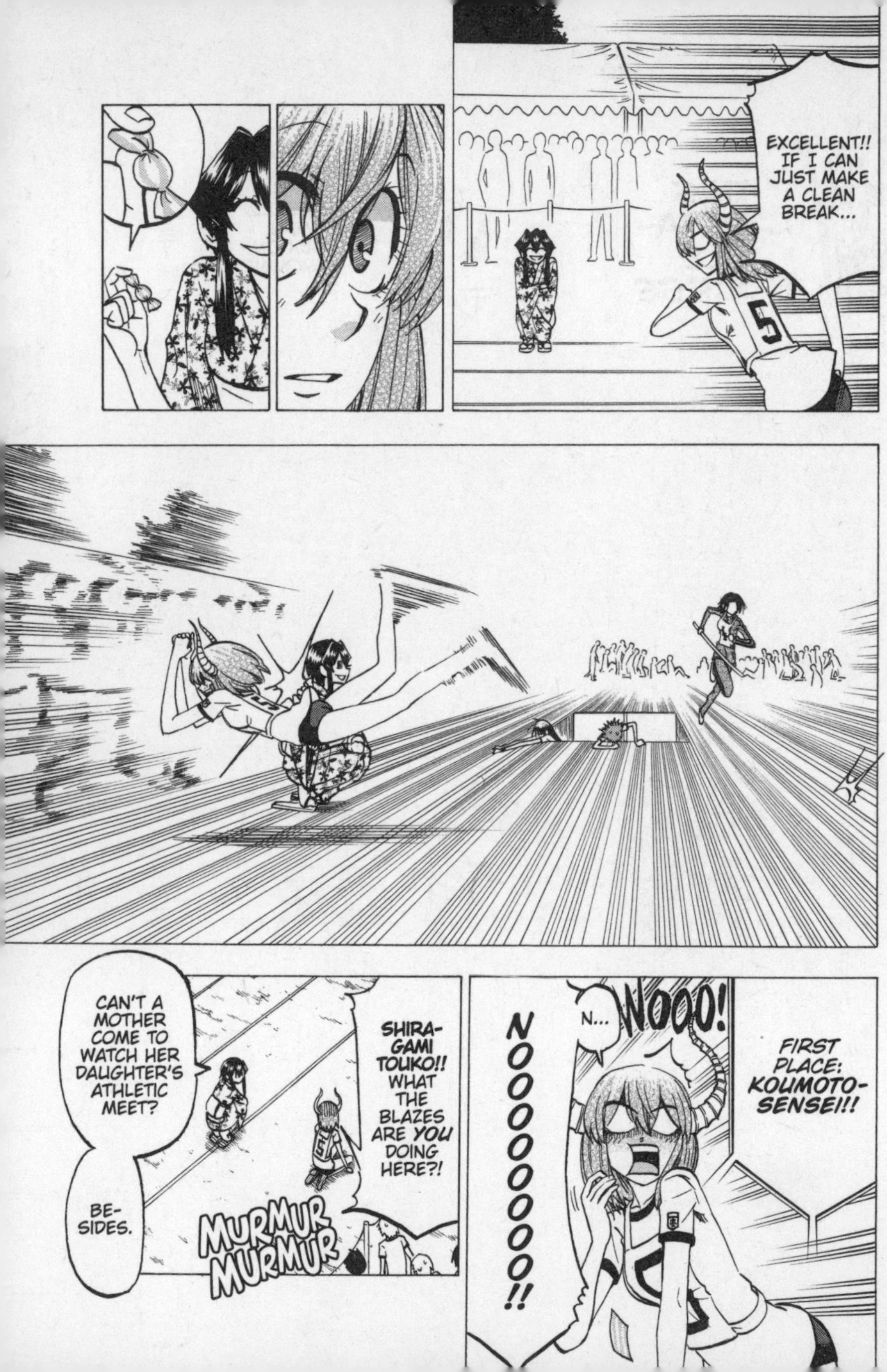
EXCELLENT!! IF I CAN JUST MAKE A CLEAN BREAK...
FIRST PLACE: KOUMOTO-SENSEI!!!
N...
NOOO!
NOOOOOOOOOO!!
SHIRA-GAMI TOUKO!! WHAT THE BLAZES ARE *YOU* DOING HERE?!
CAN'T A MOTHER COME TO WATCH HER DAUGHTER'S ATHLETIC MEET?
BE-SIDES.
MURMUR MURMUR

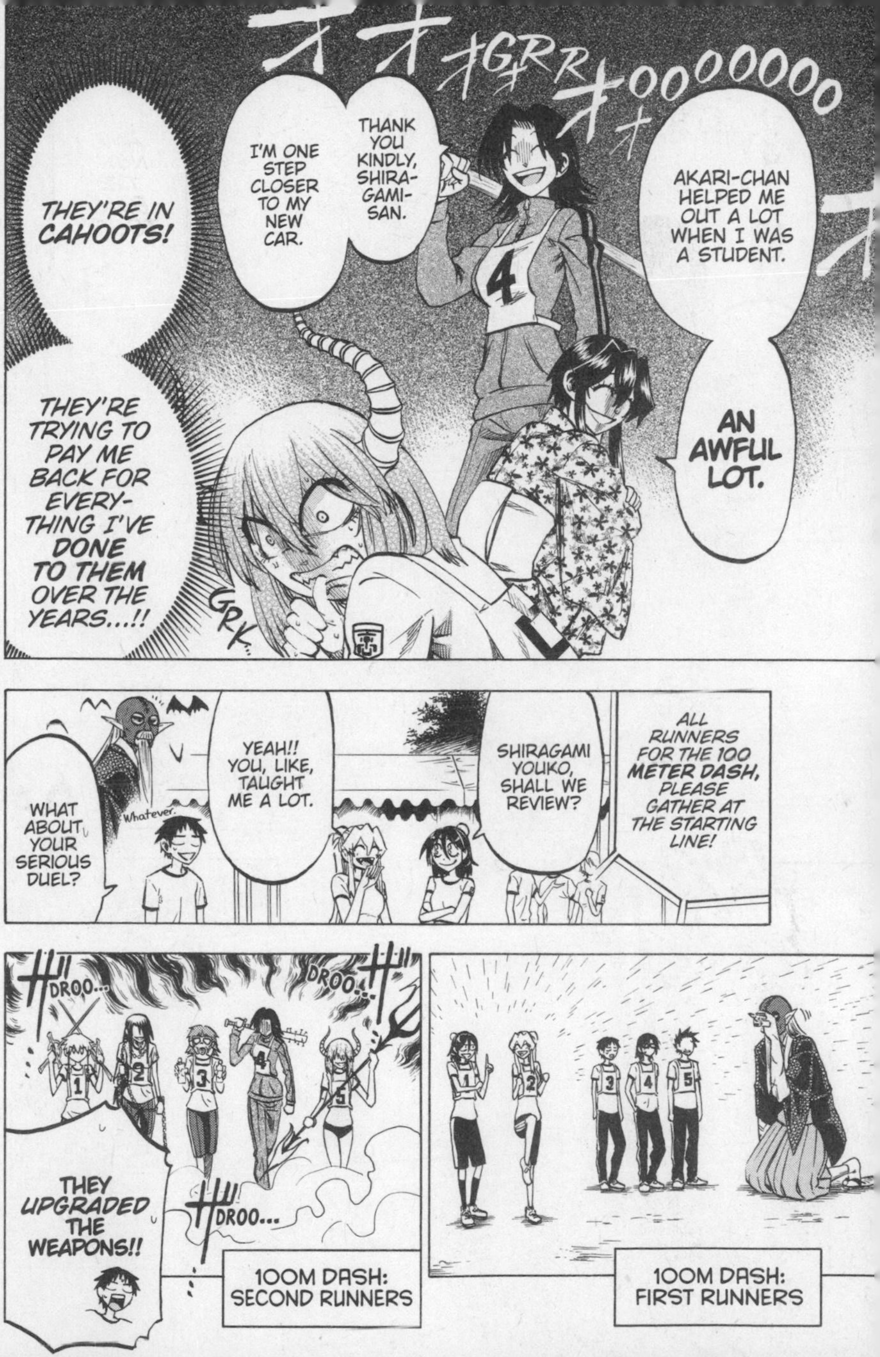
GRRR OOOOOOO
AKARI-CHAN HELPED ME OUT A LOT WHEN I WAS A STUDENT.
AN AWFUL LOT.
THANK YOU KINDLY, SHIRAGAMI-SAN.
I'M ONE STEP CLOSER TO MY NEW CAR.
THEY'RE IN CAHOOTS!
THEY'RE TRYING TO PAY ME BACK FOR EVERYTHING I'VE DONE TO THEM OVER THE YEARS...!!
GRK...
ALL RUNNERS FOR THE 100 METER DASH, PLEASE GATHER AT THE STARTING LINE!
SHIRAGAMI YOUKO, SHALL WE REVIEW?
YEAH!! YOU, LIKE, TAUGHT ME A LOT.
Whatever.
WHAT ABOUT YOUR SERIOUS DUEL?
100M DASH: FIRST RUNNERS
DROO...
DROO...
DROO...
THEY UPGRADED THE WEAPONS!!
100M DASH: SECOND RUNNERS

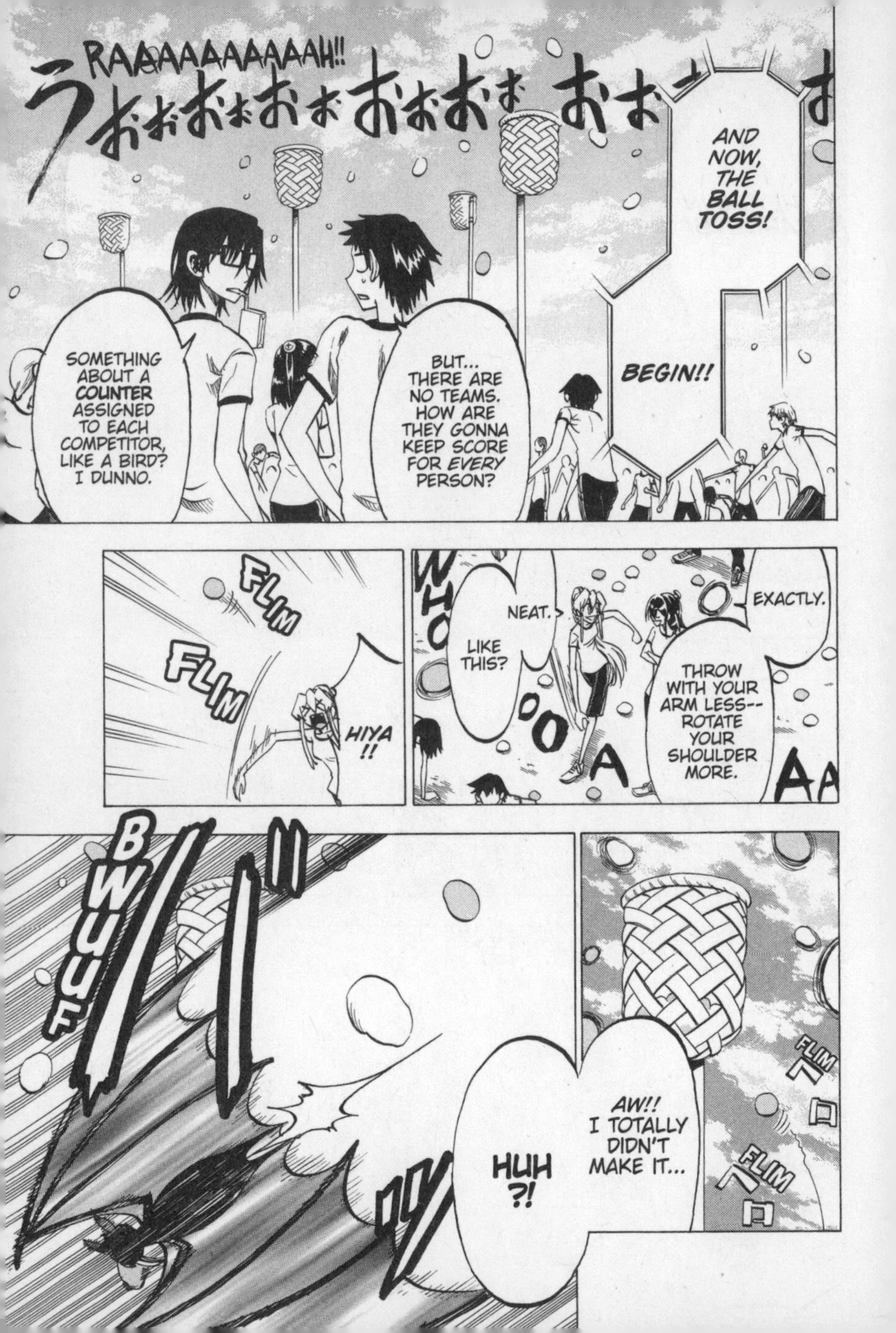
RAAAAAAAAAAH!!
AND NOW, THE BALL TOSS!
BEGIN!!
BUT... THERE ARE NO TEAMS. HOW ARE THEY GONNA KEEP SCORE FOR *EVERY* PERSON?
SOMETHING ABOUT A **COUNTER** ASSIGNED TO EACH COMPETITOR, LIKE A BIRD? I DUNNO.
EXACTLY.
THROW WITH YOUR ARM LESS-- ROTATE YOUR SHOULDER MORE.
NEAT.
LIKE THIS?
FLIM
FLIM
HIYA!!
FLIM
FLIM
AW!! I TOTALLY DIDN'T MAKE IT...
HUH?!
BWUUF

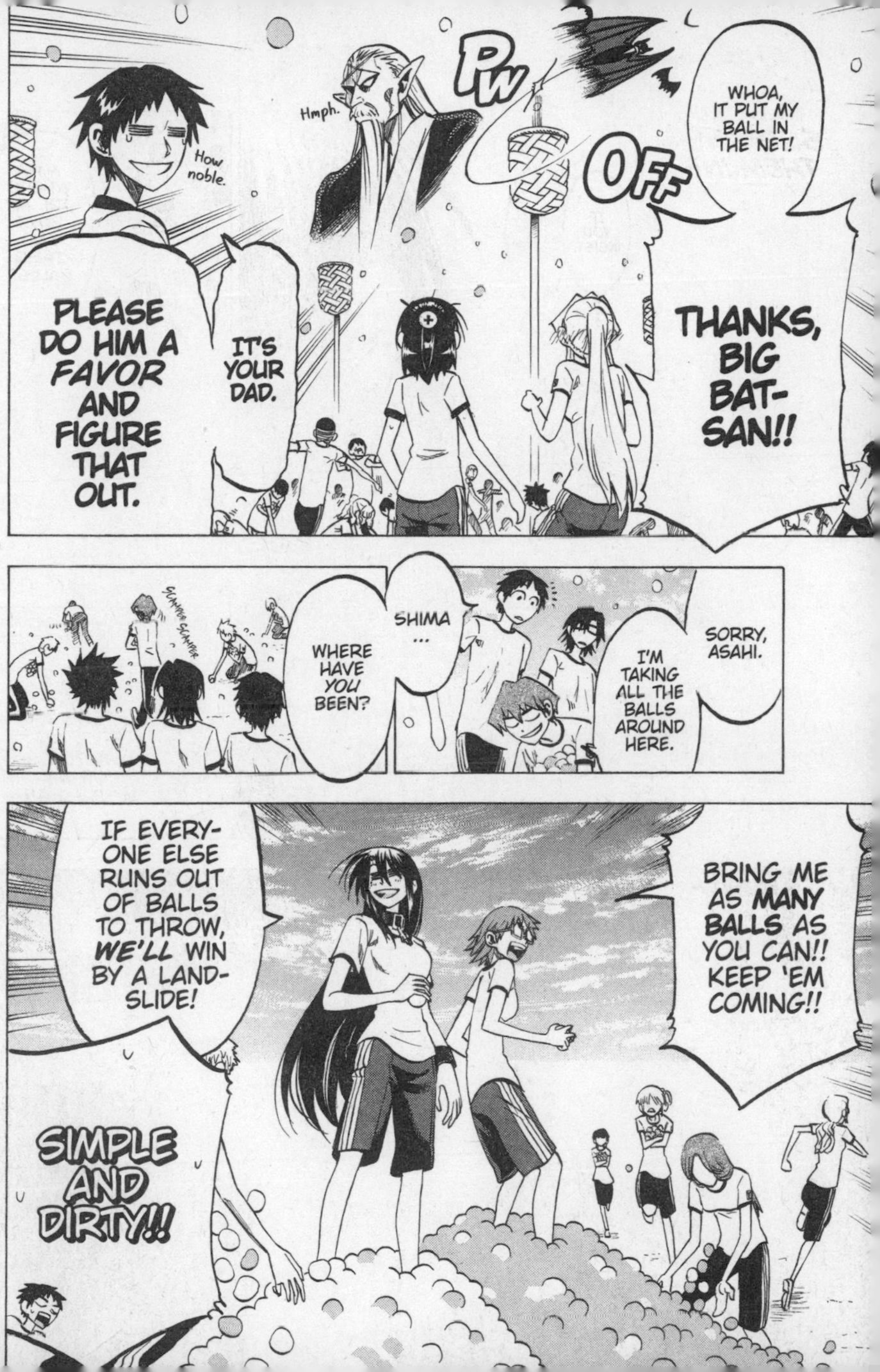
WHOA, IT PUT MY BALL IN THE NET!
PW
OFF
THANKS, BIG BAT-SAN!!
Hmph.
How noble.
IT'S YOUR DAD.
PLEASE DO HIM A *FAVOR* AND FIGURE THAT OUT.
SORRY, ASAHI.
I'M TAKING ALL THE BALLS AROUND HERE.
SHIMA ...
WHERE HAVE *YOU* BEEN?
SCAMPER SCAMPER
BRING ME AS **MANY BALLS** AS YOU CAN!! KEEP 'EM COMING!!
IF EVERY-ONE ELSE RUNS OUT OF BALLS TO THROW, ***WE'LL*** WIN BY A LAND-SLIDE!
SIMPLE AND DIRTY!!

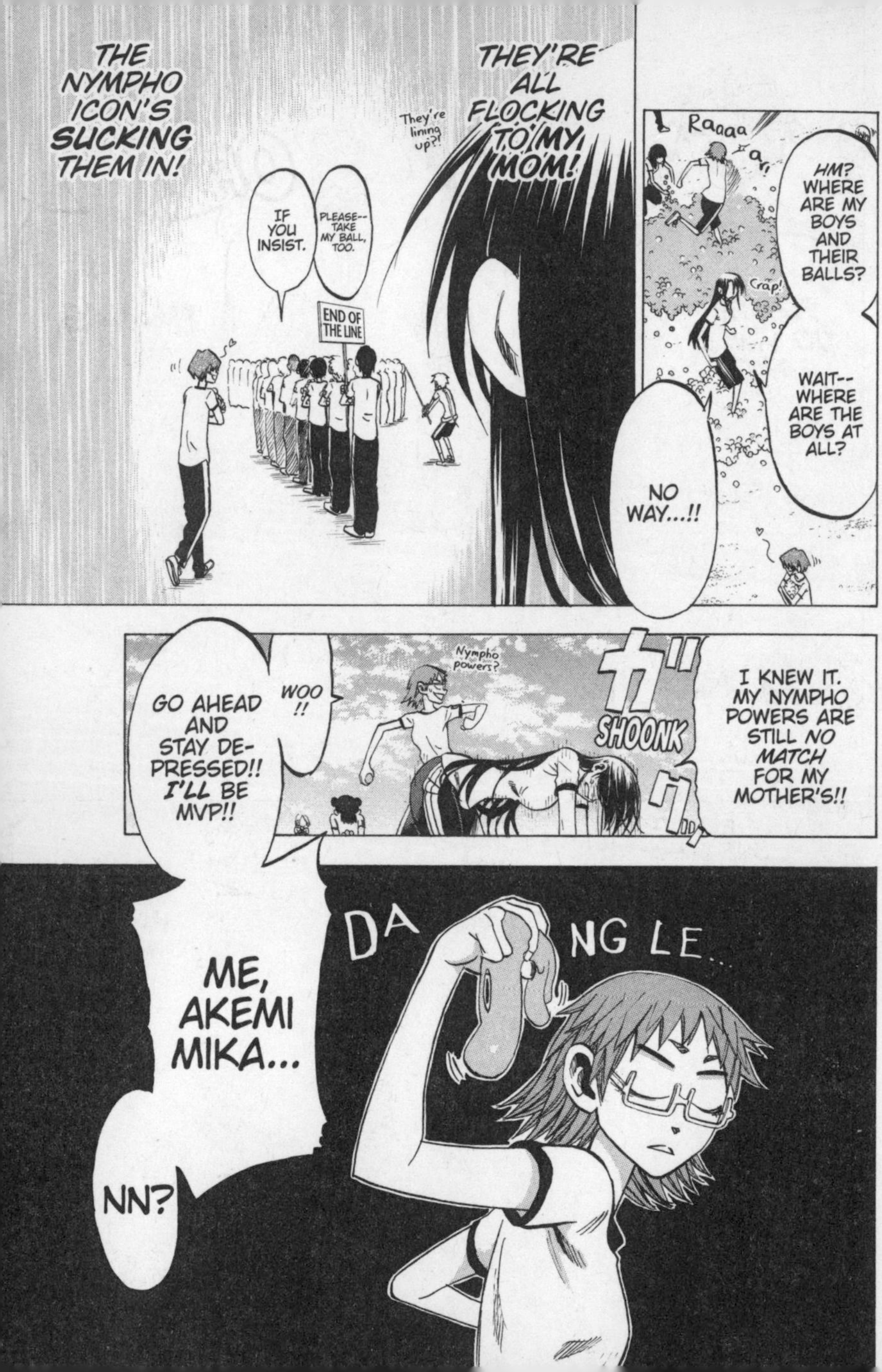
Raaaa
ar!
HM? WHERE ARE MY BOYS AND THEIR BALLS?
Crap!
WAIT--WHERE ARE THE BOYS AT ALL?
NO WAY...!!
THEY'RE ALL FLOCKING TO MY MOM!
They're lining up?!
THE NYMPHO ICON'S SUCKING THEM IN!
PLEASE--TAKE MY BALL, TOO.
IF YOU INSIST.
END OF THE LINE
I KNEW IT. MY NYMPHO POWERS ARE STILL *NO MATCH* FOR MY MOTHER'S!!
SHOONK
Nympho powers?
WOO!!
GO AHEAD AND STAY DE-PRESSED!! *I'LL* BE MVP!!
DA NG LE...
ME, AKEMI MIKA...
NN?

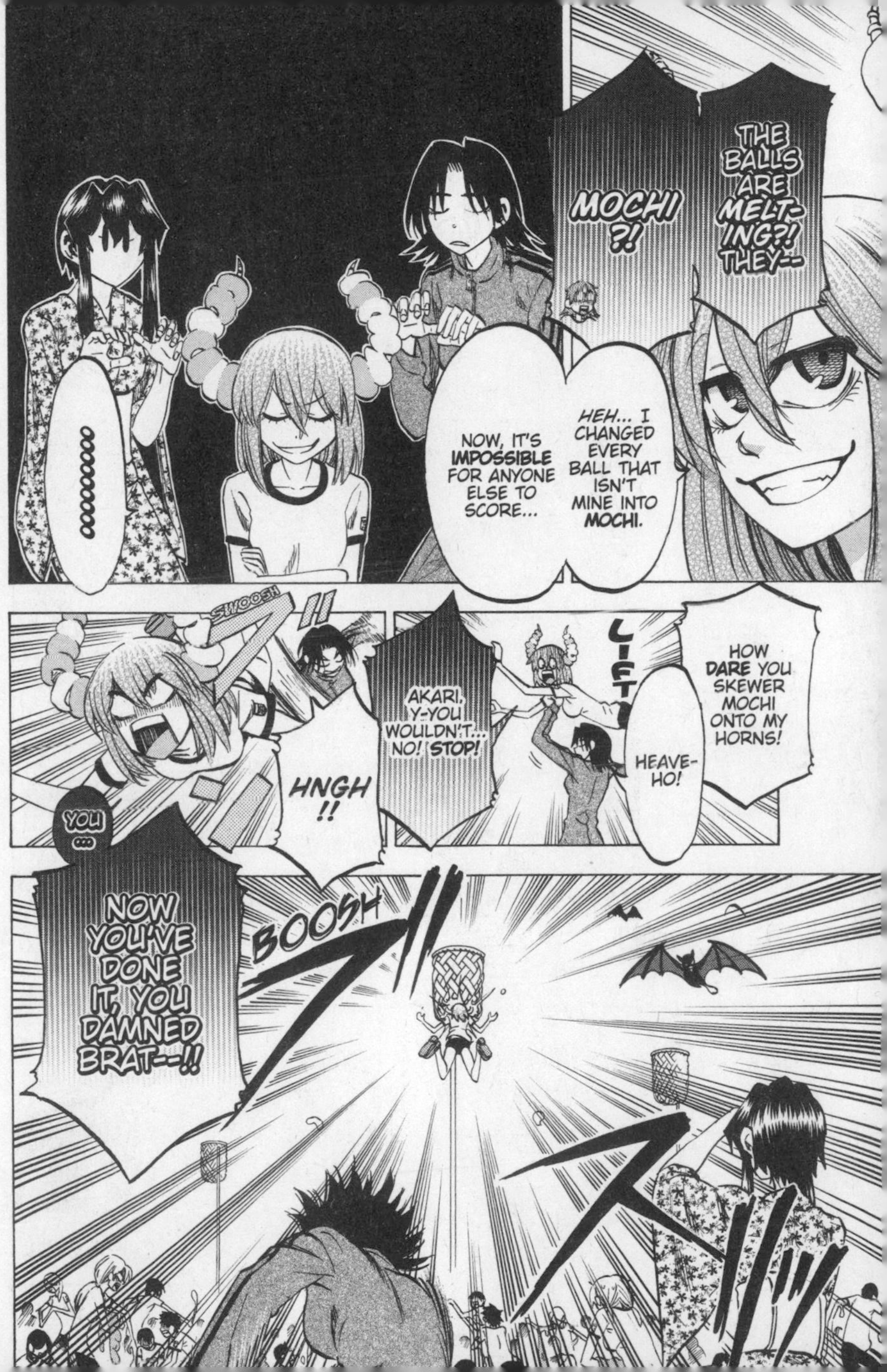
THE BALLS ARE MELTING?! THEY--
MOCHI ?!
HEH... I CHANGED EVERY BALL THAT ISN'T MINE INTO **MOCHI.**
NOW, IT'S **IMPOSSIBLE** FOR ANYONE ELSE TO SCORE...
....
HOW **DARE** YOU SKEWER MOCHI ONTO MY HORNS!
LIFT
HEAVE-HO!
AKARI, Y-YOU WOULDN'T... NO! **STOP!**
SWOOSH
HNGH !!
YOU ...
BOOSH
NOW YOU'VE DONE IT, YOU DAMNED BRAT--!!

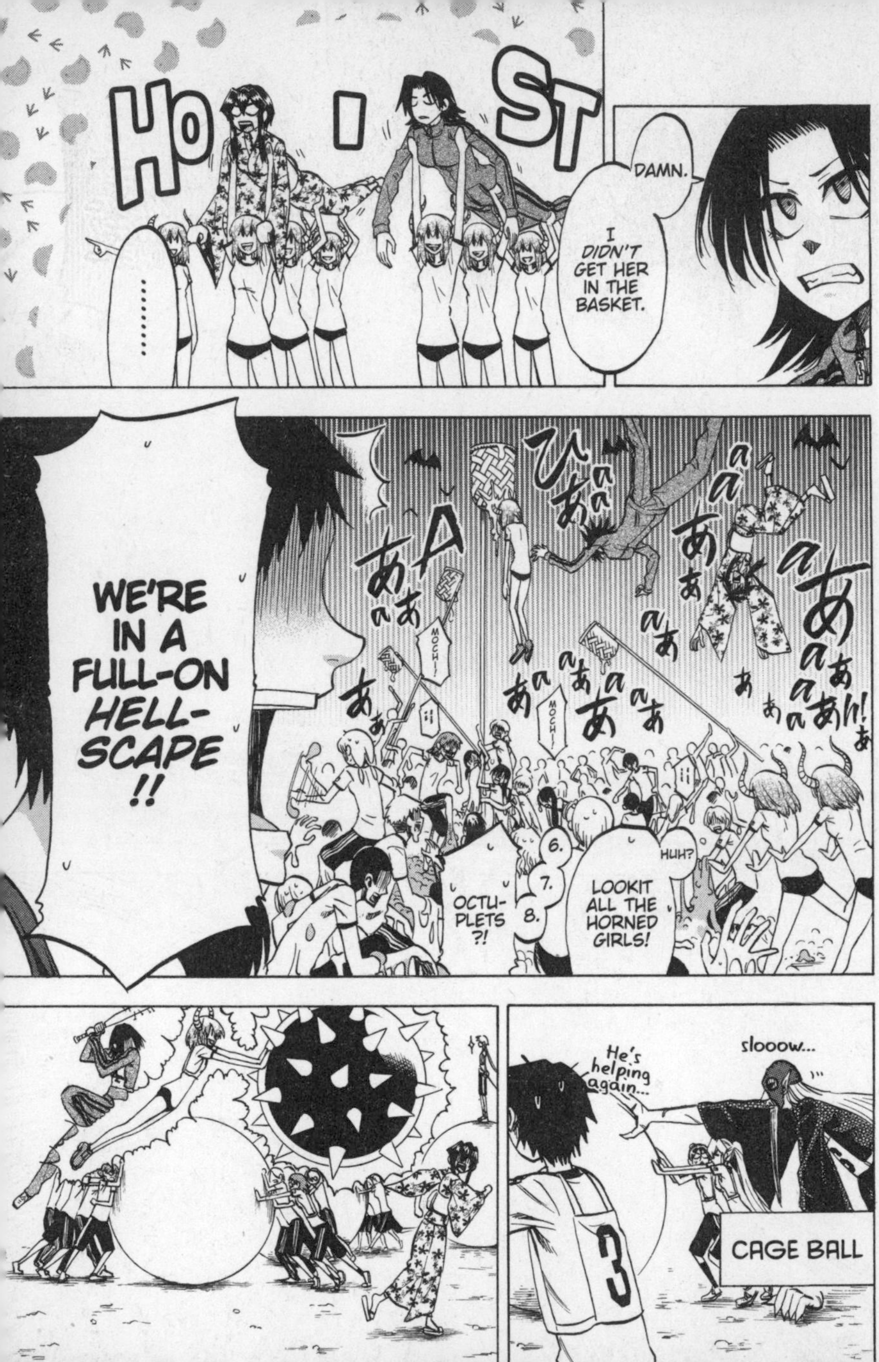
DAMN.
I DIDN'T GET HER IN THE BASKET.
HOIST
......
ひあaa
A
あaあ
MOCHI!
MOCHI!
LOOKIT ALL THE HORNED GIRLS!
HUH?
6.
7.
8.
OCTU-PLETS?!
WE'RE IN A FULL-ON HELL-SCAPE!!
sloooow...
He's helping again...
CAGE BALL

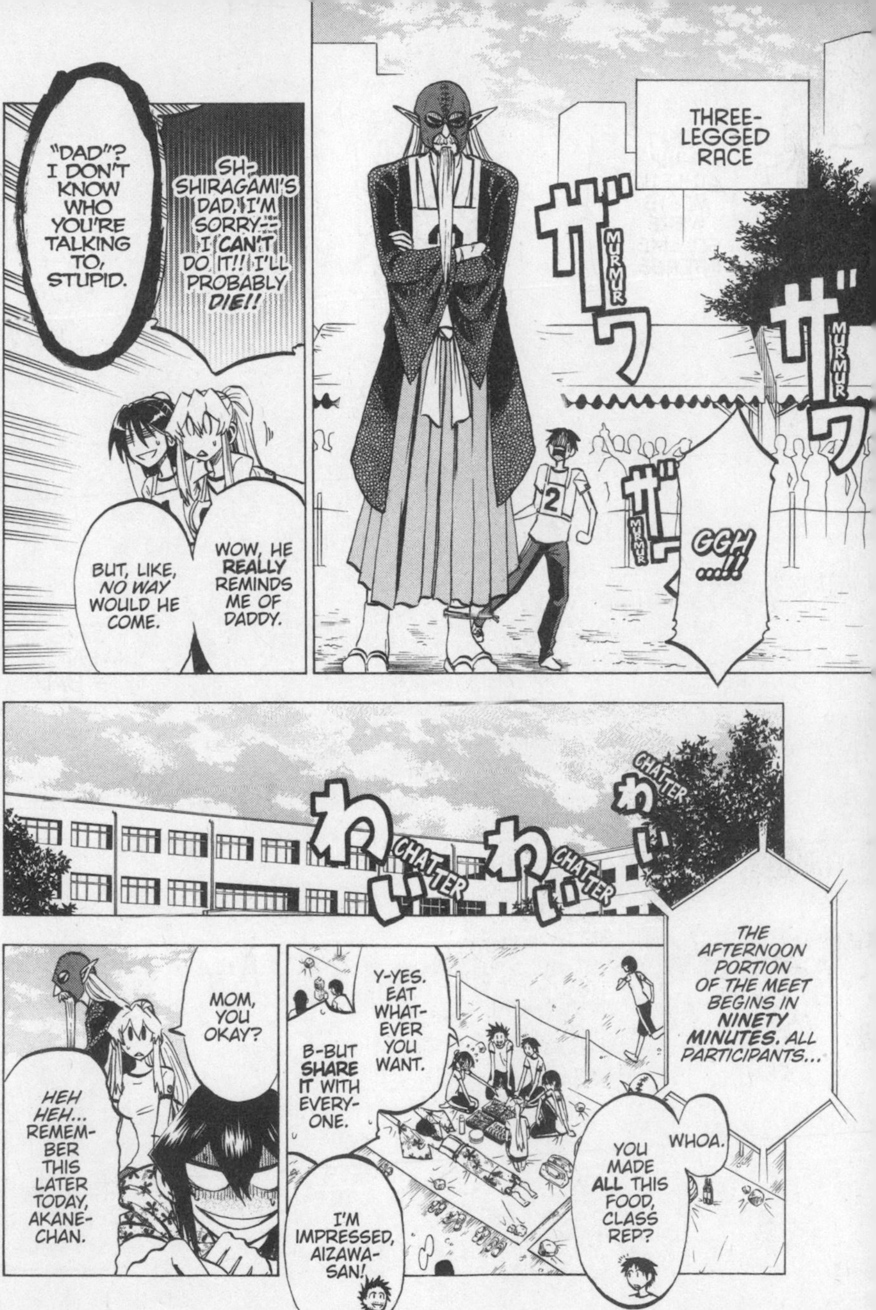
THREE-LEGGED RACE
ザワ MURMUR
ザワ MURMUR
ザワ MURMUR
GGH ...!!
SH-SHIRAGAMI'S DAD, I'M SORRY-- I CAN'T DO IT!! I'LL PROBABLY DIE!!
"DAD"? I DON'T KNOW WHO YOU'RE TALKING TO, STUPID.
WOW, HE REALLY REMINDS ME OF DADDY.
BUT, LIKE, NO WAY WOULD HE COME.
わい CHATTER
わい CHATTER
わい CHATTER
THE AFTERNOON PORTION OF THE MEET BEGINS IN NINETY MINUTES. ALL PARTICIPANTS...
WHOA.
YOU MADE ALL THIS FOOD, CLASS REP?
I'M IMPRESSED, AIZAWA-SAN!
Y-YES. EAT WHATEVER YOU WANT.
B-BUT SHARE IT WITH EVERYONE.
MOM, YOU OKAY?
HEH HEH... REMEMBER THIS LATER TODAY, AKANE-CHAN.

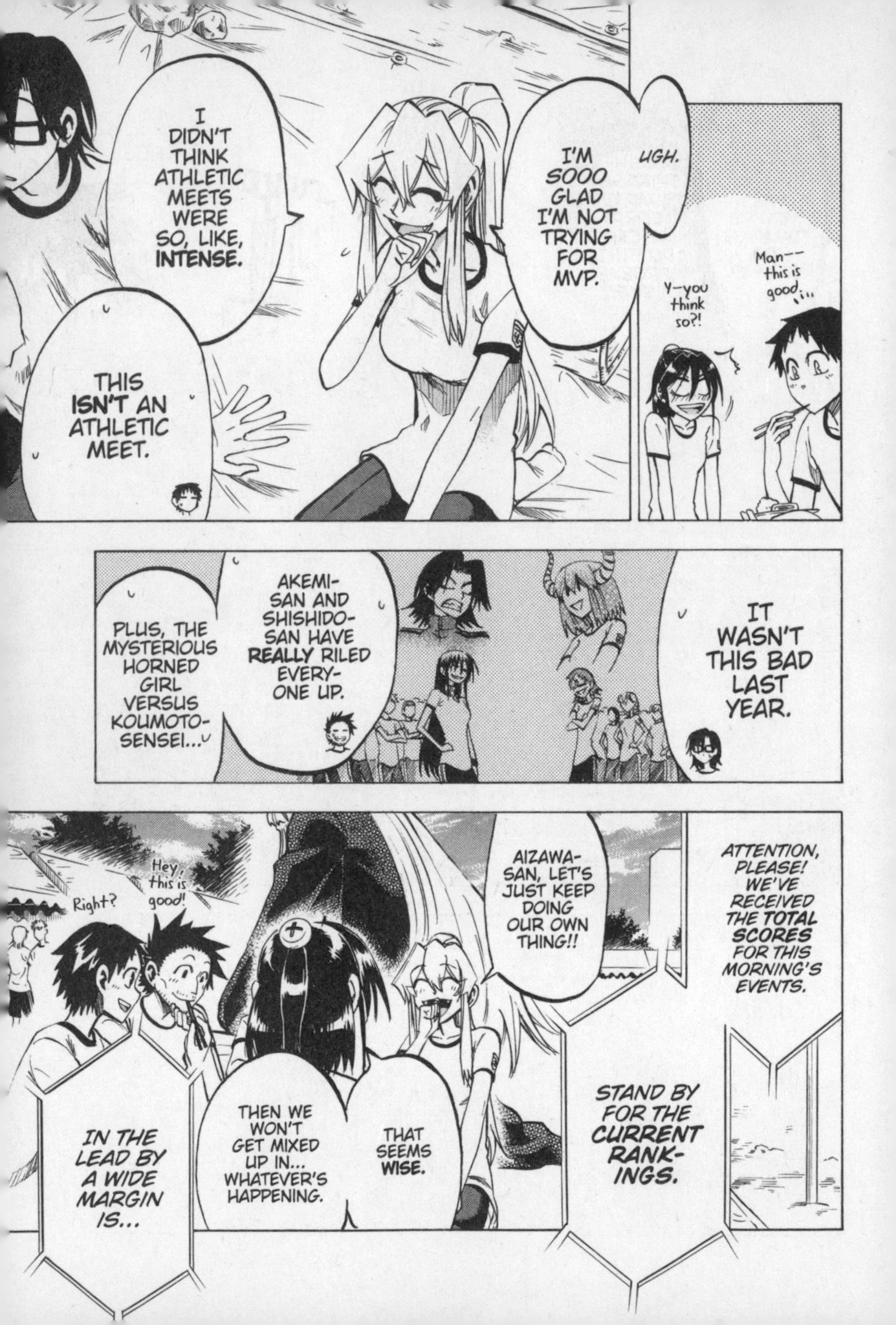

UGH.
Man-- this is good...
Y-you think so?!
I'M SOOO GLAD I'M NOT TRYING FOR MVP.
I DIDN'T THINK ATHLETIC MEETS WERE SO, LIKE, INTENSE.
THIS ISN'T AN ATHLETIC MEET.
IT WASN'T THIS BAD LAST YEAR.
AKEMI-SAN AND SHISHIDO-SAN HAVE REALLY RILED EVERY-ONE UP.
PLUS, THE MYSTERIOUS HORNED GIRL VERSUS KOUMOTO-SENSEI...
ATTENTION, PLEASE! WE'VE RECEIVED THE TOTAL SCORES FOR THIS MORNING'S EVENTS.
AIZAWA-SAN, LET'S JUST KEEP DOING OUR OWN THING!!
Hey, this is good!
Right?
STAND BY FOR THE CURRENT RANK-INGS.
THAT SEEMS WISE.
THEN WE WON'T GET MIXED UP IN... WHATEVER'S HAPPENING.
IN THE LEAD BY A WIDE MARGIN IS...

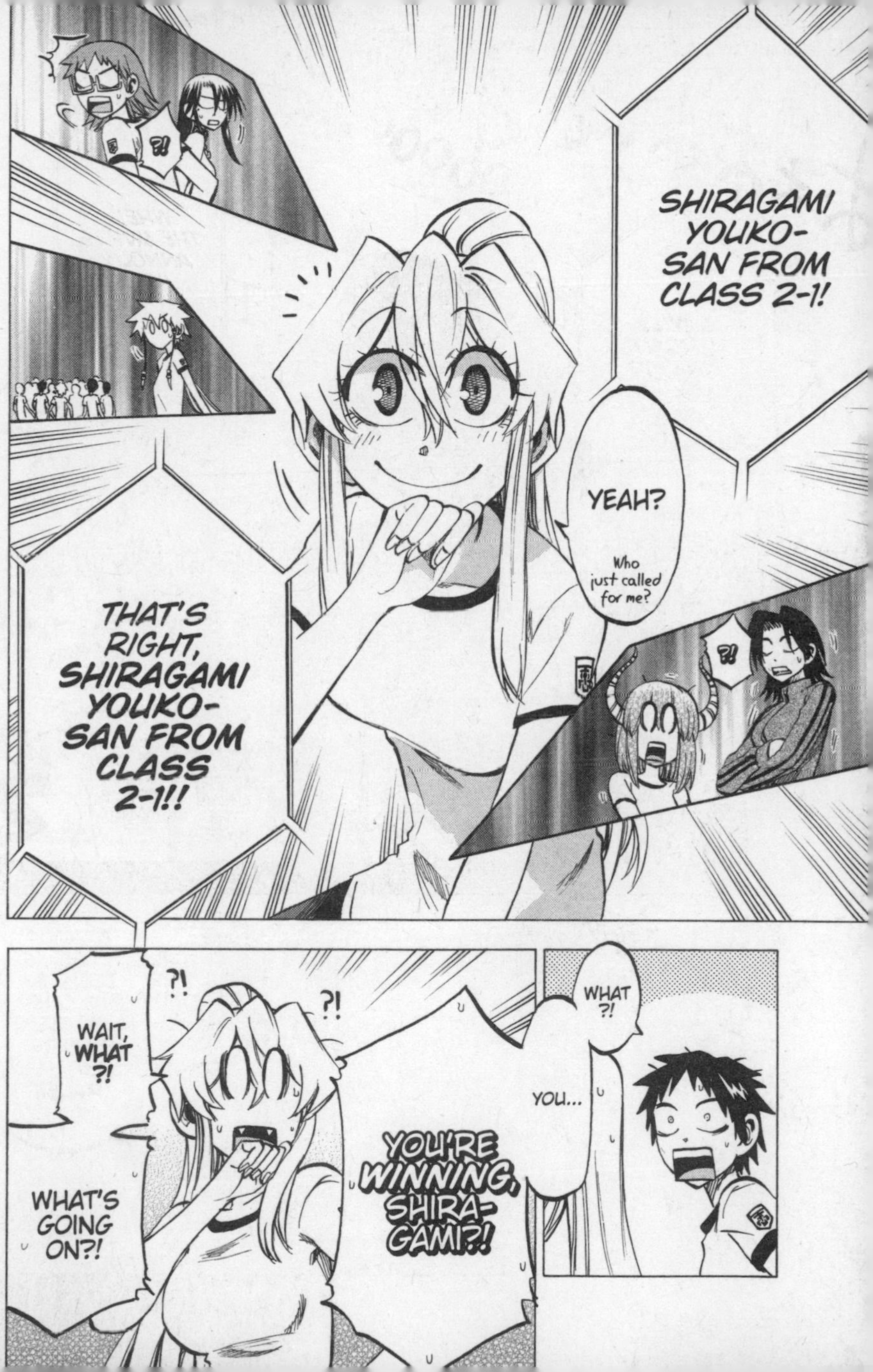

SHIRAGAMI YOUKO-SAN FROM CLASS 2-1!
?!
YEAH?
Who just called for me?
?!
THAT'S RIGHT, SHIRAGAMI YOUKO-SAN FROM CLASS 2-1!!
WHAT ?!
YOU...
YOU'RE WINNING, SHIRA-GAMI?!
?!
?!
WAIT, WHAT ?!
WHAT'S GOING ON?!

Chapter 39: "Let's Go for MVP!!"

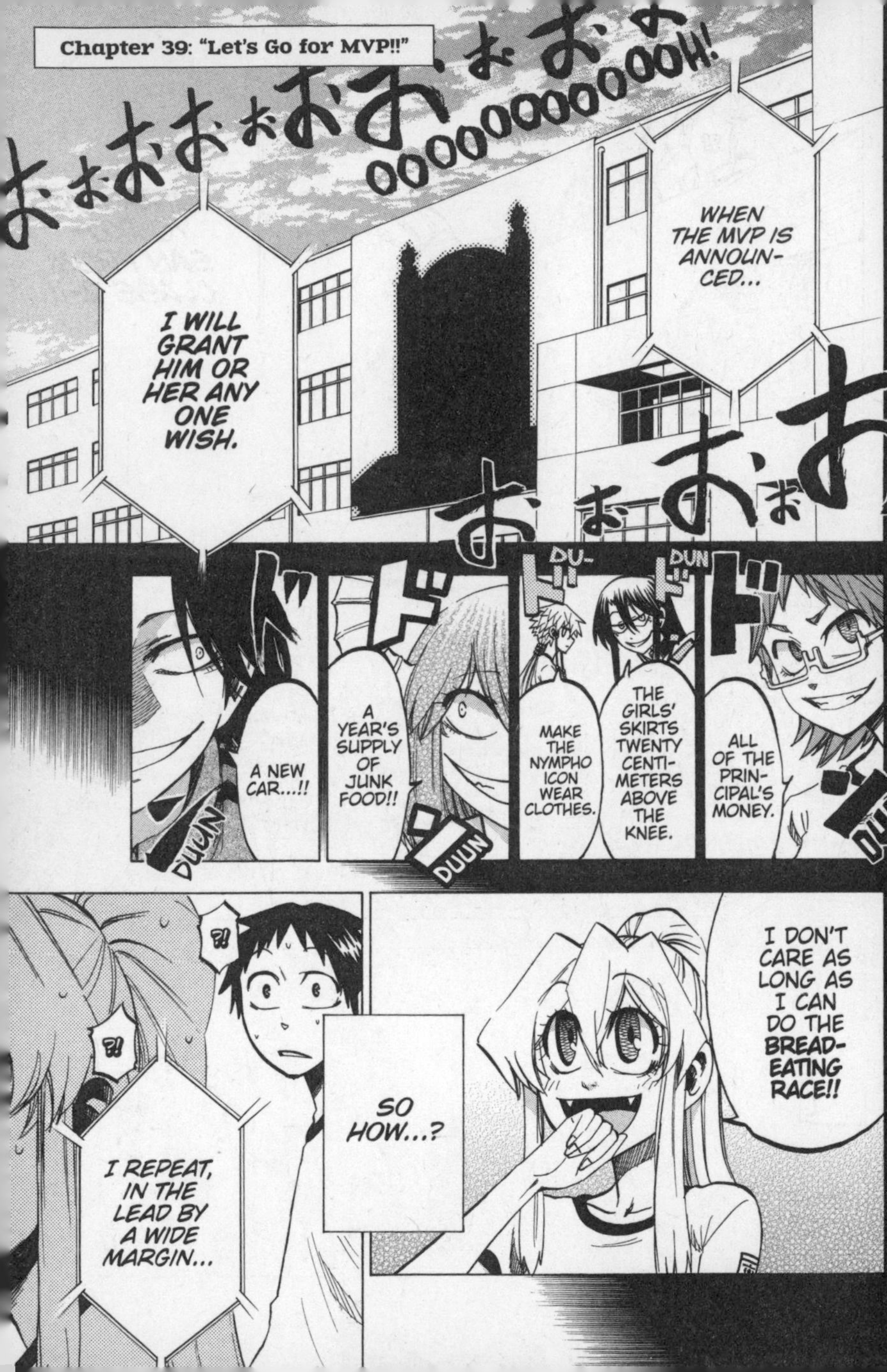
おぉおぉおおぉお
OOOOOOOOOOOOH!
WHEN THE MVP IS ANNOUN-CED...
I WILL GRANT HIM OR HER ANY ONE WISH.
おぉおぉお
DUN
ALL OF THE PRIN-CIPAL'S MONEY.
DUN
THE GIRLS' SKIRTS TWENTY CENTI-METERS ABOVE THE KNEE.
DU-
MAKE THE NYMPHO ICON WEAR CLOTHES.
DUUN
A YEAR'S SUPPLY OF JUNK FOOD!!
DUUN
A NEW CAR...!!
I DON'T CARE AS LONG AS I CAN DO THE BREAD-EATING RACE!!
?!
SO HOW...?
?!
I REPEAT, IN THE LEAD BY A WIDE MARGIN...

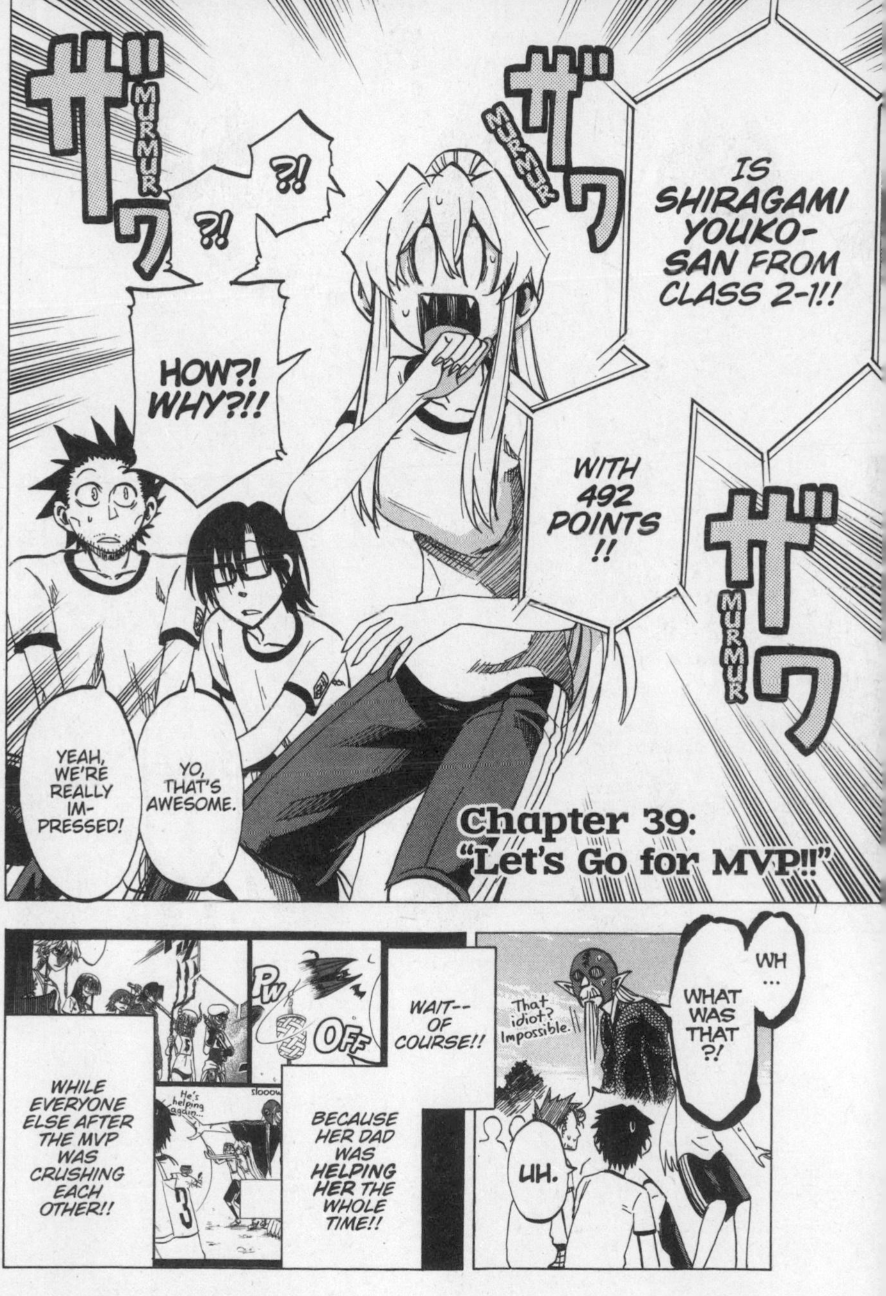
IS SHIRAGAMI YOUKO-SAN FROM CLASS 2-1!!
ザワ MURMUR
WITH 492 POINTS !!
ザワ MURMUR
?!
?!
ザワ MURMUR
HOW?! WHY?!!
YO, THAT'S AWESOME.
YEAH, WE'RE REALLY IM-PRESSED!
Chapter 39: "Let's Go for MVP!!"
WH ...
WHAT WAS THAT?!
That idiot? Impossible.
UH.
WAIT-- OF COURSE!!
BECAUSE HER DAD WAS HELPING HER THE WHOLE TIME!!
PW
OFF
He's helping again...
slooow
WHILE EVERYONE ELSE AFTER THE MVP WAS CRUSHING EACH OTHER!!

CONGRATS ON YOUR **BIG LEAD**, SHIRAGAMI-SAN.

GOOD WORK, YOUKO.

NOPE.

BUT YOU UNDER-STAND THAT WE CAN'T LET YOU **WIN**.

EVEN RIN-CHAN?!

AKEMI-SAN, SHIHO...

NONE OF THEM ARE KIDDING!

SHE CAUGHT THE ATTENTION OF THE **WRONG** CROWD!

WRONG... IT WILL BE MINE.

NO-- MINE.

WILL BE MINE.

THE TITLE OF MVP...

WINCE

H-HEY, MIKAN!

I KNOW YOU WANNA WIN, BUT YOU WOULDN'T REALLY ATTACK SHIRAGAMI?

OH, PLEASE. I WOULDN'T DO ANYTHING TO SHIRAGAMI-SAN. I MEAN...

WE'VE STILL GOT A CHANCE AT MVP.

I WON'T LOSE.

THE LAST EVENT'S COMING UP--THE OBSTACLE COURSE. FIRST PLACE GETS **300** POINTS!!

RIN	SHIHO	MIKAN
202	238	272

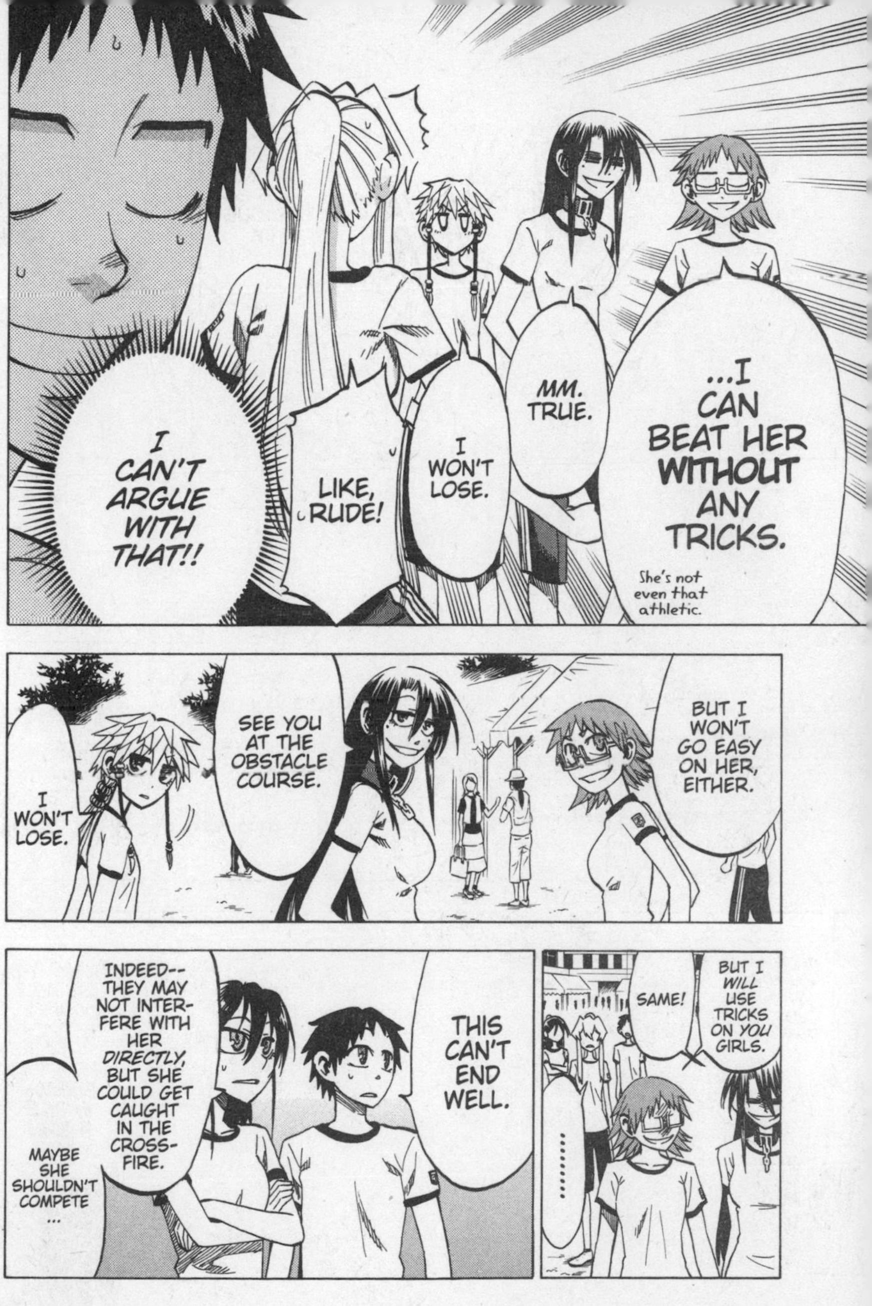
...I CAN BEAT HER WITHOUT ANY TRICKS.
She's not even that athletic.
MM. TRUE.
I WON'T LOSE.
LIKE, RUDE!
I CAN'T ARGUE WITH THAT!!
BUT I WON'T GO EASY ON HER, EITHER.
SEE YOU AT THE OBSTACLE COURSE.
I WON'T LOSE.
BUT I *WILL* USE TRICKS ON *YOU* GIRLS.
SAME!
......
THIS CAN'T END WELL.
INDEED-- THEY MAY NOT INTER-FERE WITH HER *DIRECTLY*, BUT SHE COULD GET CAUGHT IN THE CROSS-FIRE.
MAYBE SHE SHOULDN'T COMPETE ...

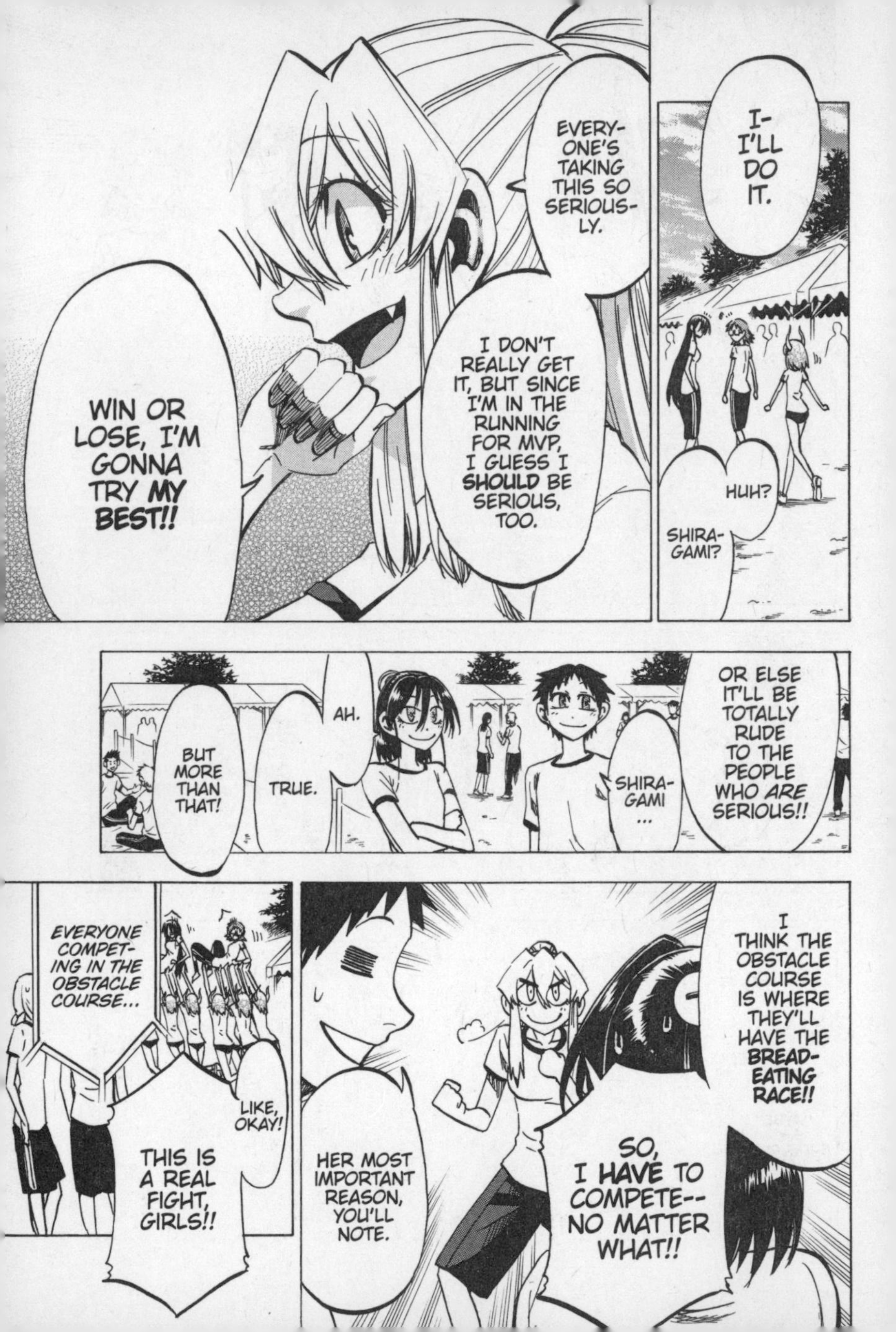

I- I'LL DO IT.
HUH?
SHIRAGAMI?
EVERYONE'S TAKING THIS SO SERIOUSLY.
I DON'T REALLY GET IT, BUT SINCE I'M IN THE RUNNING FOR MVP, I GUESS I SHOULD BE SERIOUS, TOO.
WIN OR LOSE, I'M GONNA TRY MY BEST!!
OR ELSE IT'LL BE TOTALLY RUDE TO THE PEOPLE WHO ARE SERIOUS!!
SHIRAGAMI ...
AH.
TRUE.
BUT MORE THAN THAT!
I THINK THE OBSTACLE COURSE IS WHERE THEY'LL HAVE THE BREAD-EATING RACE!!
SO, I HAVE TO COMPETE-- NO MATTER WHAT!!
HER MOST IMPORTANT REASON, YOU'LL NOTE.
EVERYONE COMPETING IN THE OBSTACLE COURSE...
LIKE, OKAY!
THIS IS A REAL FIGHT, GIRLS!!

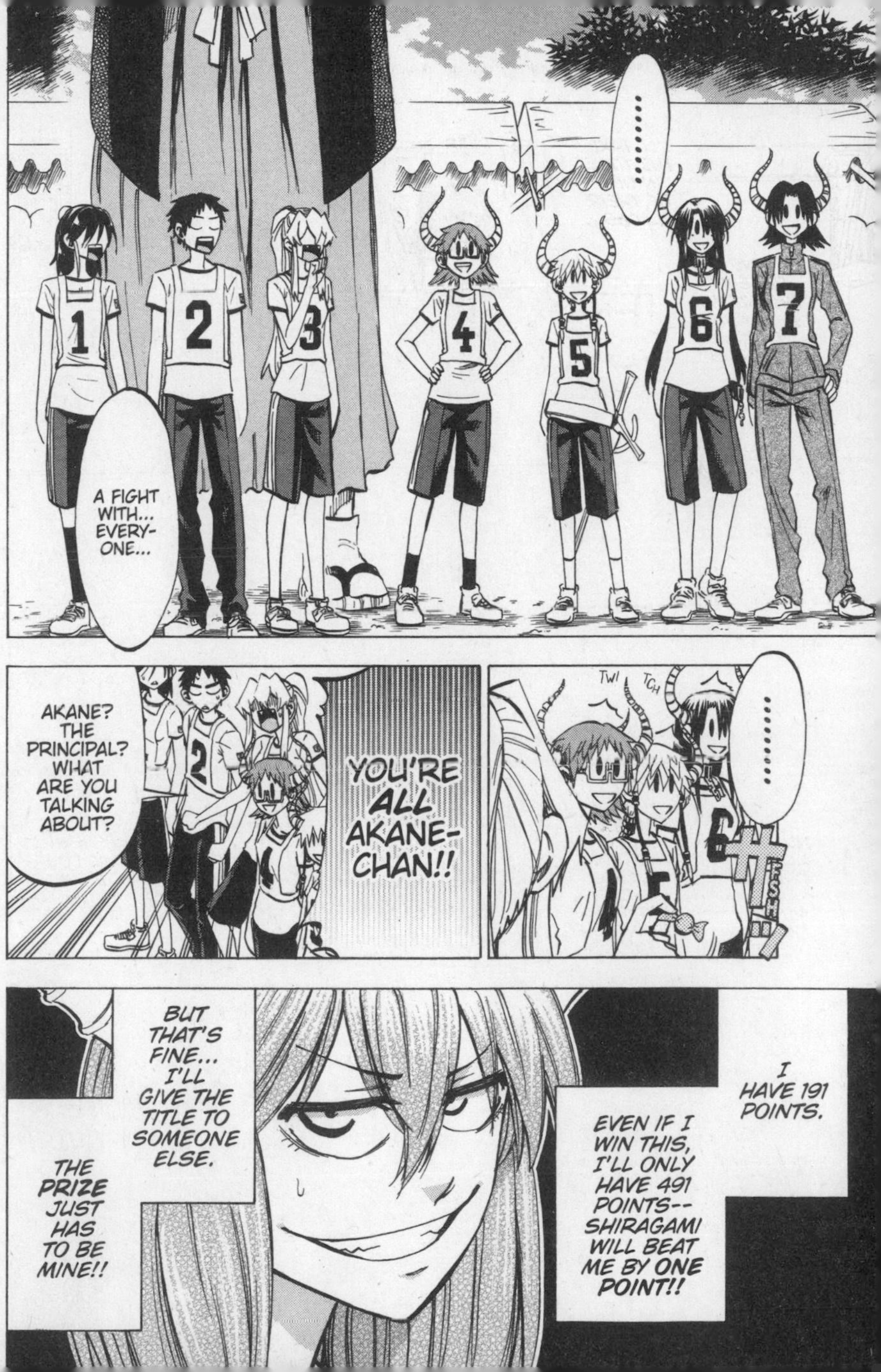
......
A FIGHT WITH... EVERY-ONE...
TWI TCH
......
YOU'RE ALL AKANE-CHAN!!
AKANE? THE PRINCIPAL? WHAT ARE YOU TALKING ABOUT?
I HAVE 191 POINTS.
EVEN IF I WIN THIS, I'LL ONLY HAVE 491 POINTS-- SHIRAGAMI WILL BEAT ME BY ONE POINT!!
BUT THAT'S FINE... I'LL GIVE THE TITLE TO SOMEONE ELSE.
THE PRIZE JUST HAS TO BE MINE!!

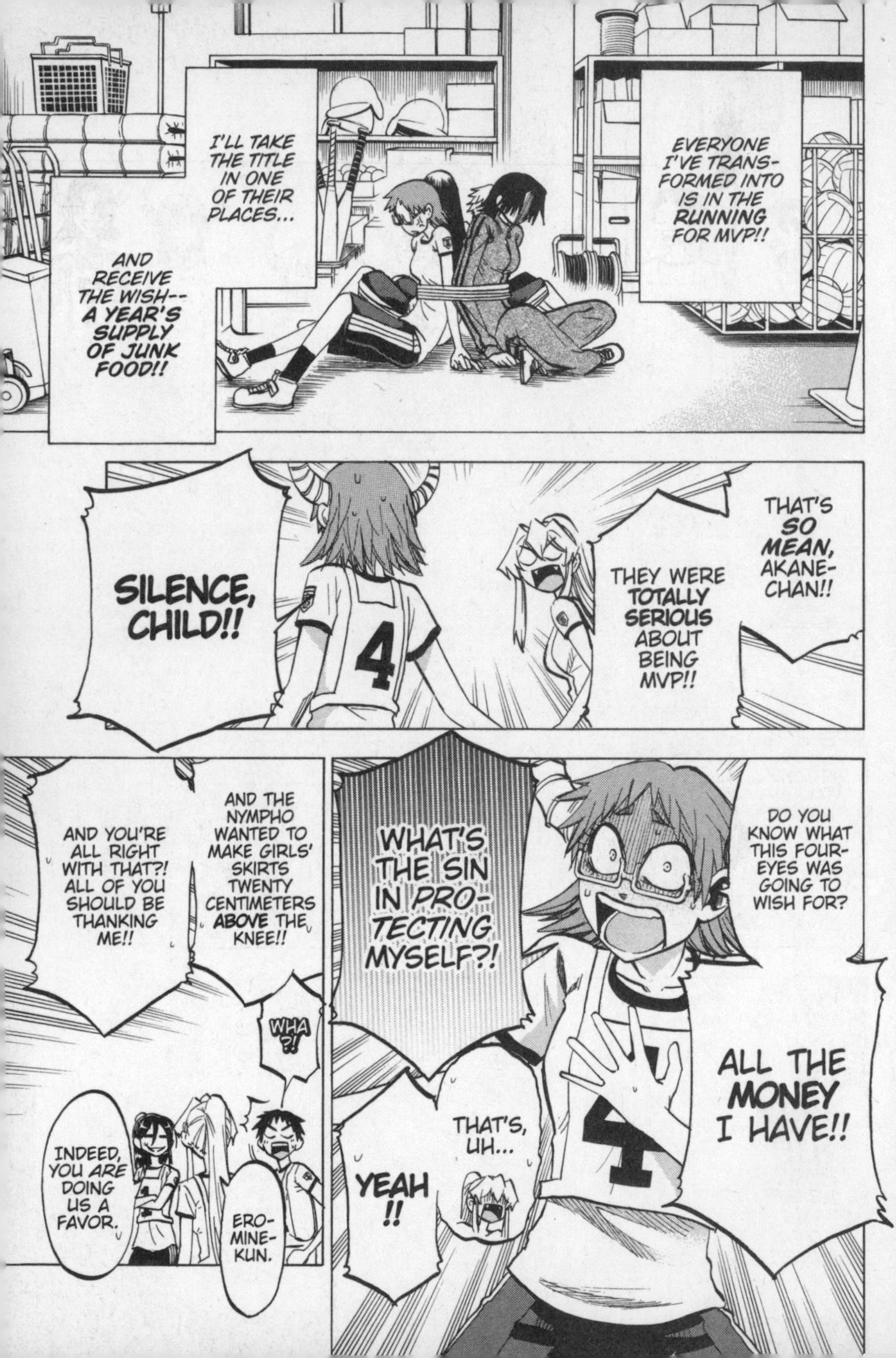
EVERYONE I'VE TRANS-FORMED INTO IS IN THE RUNNING FOR MVP!!
I'LL TAKE THE TITLE IN ONE OF THEIR PLACES...
AND RECEIVE THE WISH-- A YEAR'S SUPPLY OF JUNK FOOD!!
THAT'S SO MEAN, AKANE-CHAN!!
THEY WERE TOTALLY SERIOUS ABOUT BEING MVP!!
SILENCE, CHILD!!
DO YOU KNOW WHAT THIS FOUR-EYES WAS GOING TO WISH FOR?
WHAT'S THE SIN IN PRO-TECTING MYSELF?!
ALL THE MONEY I HAVE!!
THAT'S, UH...
YEAH!!
AND THE NYMPHO WANTED TO MAKE GIRLS' SKIRTS TWENTY CENTIMETERS ABOVE THE KNEE!!
AND YOU'RE ALL RIGHT WITH THAT?! ALL OF YOU SHOULD BE THANKING ME!!
WHA?!
INDEED, YOU ARE DOING US A FAVOR.
ERO-MINE-KUN.

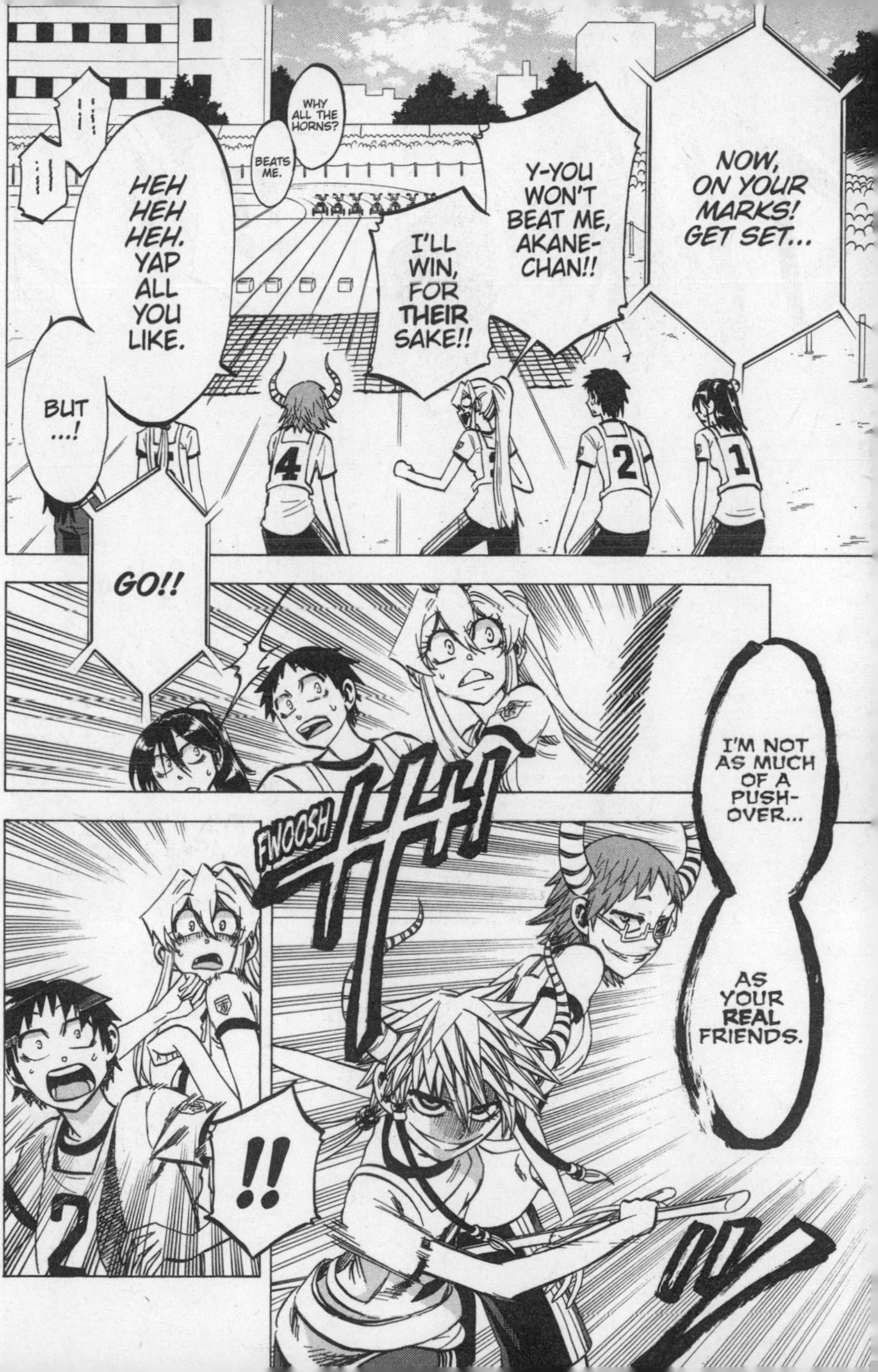
NOW, ON YOUR MARKS! GET SET...
Y-YOU WON'T BEAT ME, AKANE-CHAN!!
I'LL WIN, FOR THEIR SAKE!!
WHY ALL THE HORNS?
BEATS ME.
HEH HEH HEH. YAP ALL YOU LIKE.
BUT ...!
GO!!
I'M NOT AS MUCH OF A PUSH-OVER...
AS YOUR REAL FRIENDS.
FWOOSH
!!

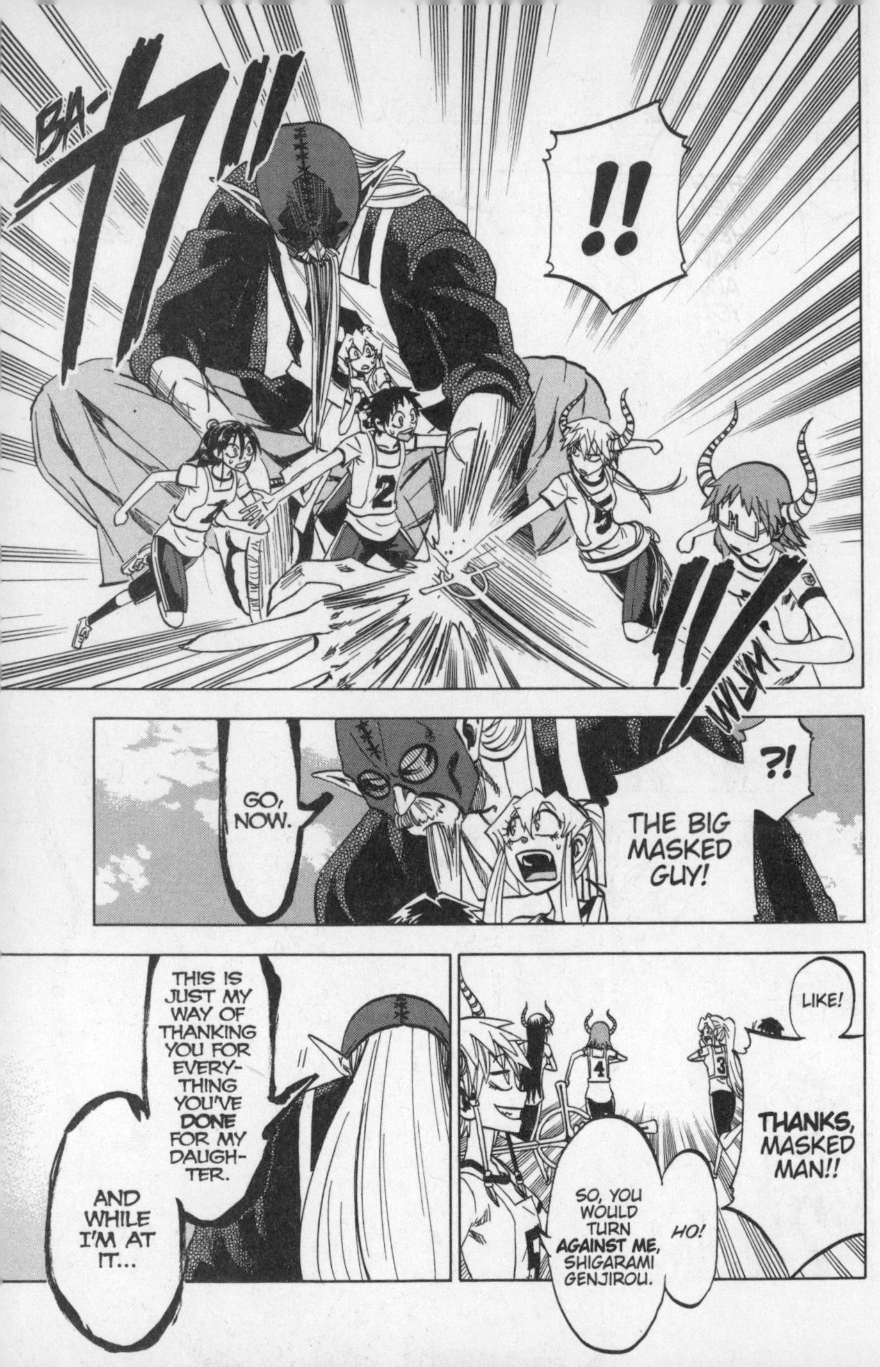
BA-
!!
?!
THE BIG MASKED GUY!
GO, NOW.
LIKE!
THANKS, MASKED MAN!!
HO!
SO, YOU WOULD TURN **AGAINST ME**, SHIGARAMI GENJIROU.
THIS IS JUST MY WAY OF THANKING YOU FOR EVERY-THING YOU'VE **DONE** FOR MY DAUGH-TER.
AND WHILE I'M AT IT...

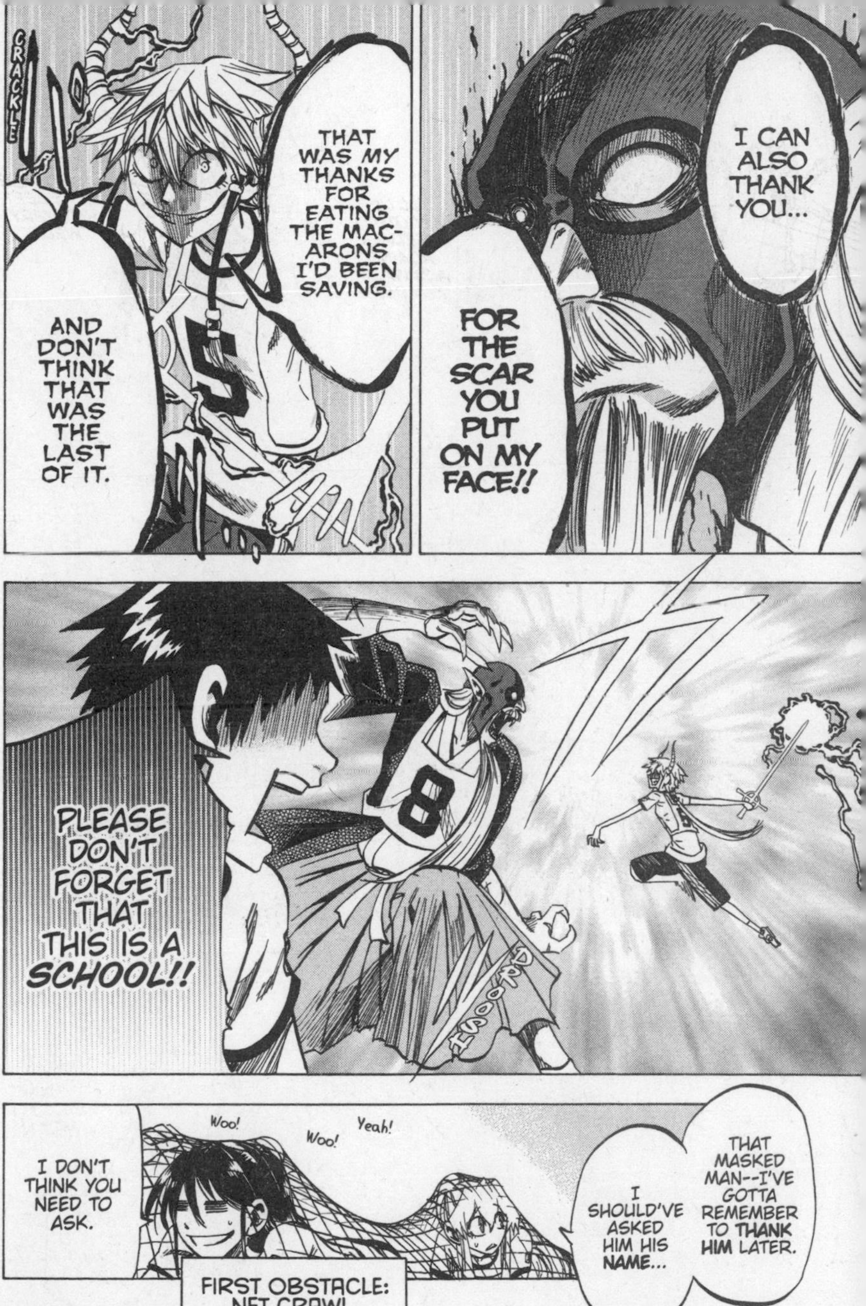
I CAN ALSO THANK YOU...
FOR THE SCAR YOU PUT ON MY FACE!!
THAT WAS MY THANKS FOR EATING THE MACARONS I'D BEEN SAVING.
CRACKLE
AND DON'T THINK THAT WAS THE LAST OF IT.
DROOSH
PLEASE DON'T FORGET THAT THIS IS A SCHOOL!!
THAT MASKED MAN--I'VE GOTTA REMEMBER TO THANK HIM LATER.
I SHOULD'VE ASKED HIM HIS NAME...
Yeah!
Woo!
Woo!
I DON'T THINK YOU NEED TO ASK.
FIRST OBSTACLE: NET CRAWL.

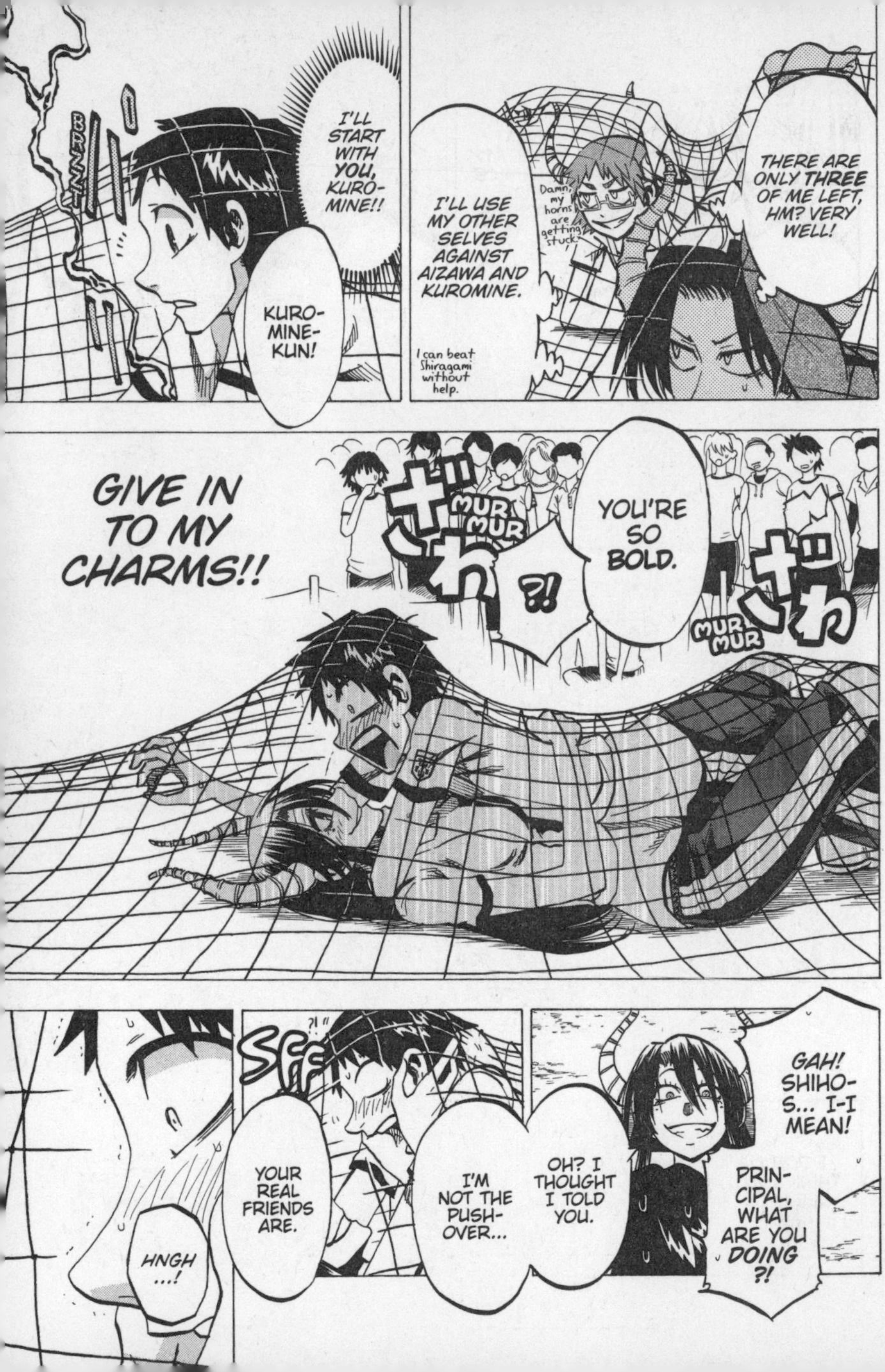
THERE ARE ONLY THREE OF ME LEFT, HM? VERY WELL!
Damn, my horns are getting stuck!
I'LL USE MY OTHER SELVES AGAINST AIZAWA AND KUROMINE.
I can beat Shiragami without help.
I'LL START WITH YOU, KUROMINE!!
KUROMINE-KUN!
ざわ MUR MUR
YOU'RE SO BOLD.
?!
ざわ MUR MUR
GIVE IN TO MY CHARMS!!
GAH! SHIHOS... I-I MEAN!
PRINCIPAL, WHAT ARE YOU DOING?!
OH? I THOUGHT I TOLD YOU.
I'M NOT THE PUSHOVER...
YOUR REAL FRIENDS ARE.
SFF
?!
HNGH...!

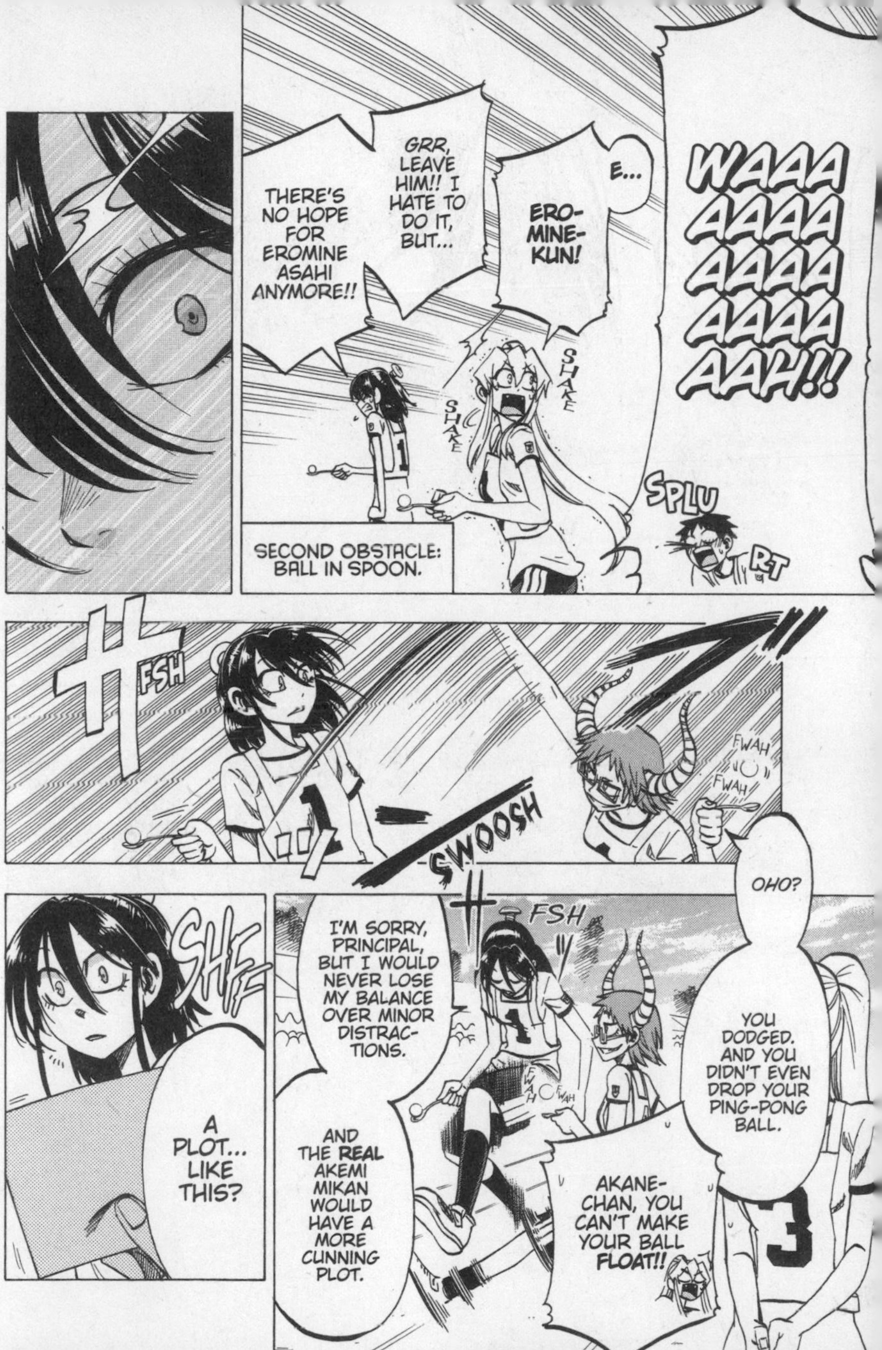
WAAAAAAAAAAAAAAAAAAAAH!!
SPLURT
E...
ERO-MINE-KUN!
SHAKE
SHAKE
GRR, LEAVE HIM!! I HATE TO DO IT, BUT...
THERE'S NO HOPE FOR EROMINE ASAHI ANYMORE!!
SECOND OBSTACLE: BALL IN SPOON.
FWAH FWAH
SWOOSH
FSH
OHO?
YOU DODGED. AND YOU DIDN'T EVEN DROP YOUR PING-PONG BALL.
FSH
I'M SORRY, PRINCIPAL, BUT I WOULD NEVER LOSE MY BALANCE OVER MINOR DISTRAC-TIONS.
FWAH FWAH
AKANE-CHAN, YOU CAN'T MAKE YOUR BALL FLOAT!!
AND THE REAL AKEMI MIKAN WOULD HAVE A MORE CUNNING PLOT.
SHE
A PLOT... LIKE THIS?

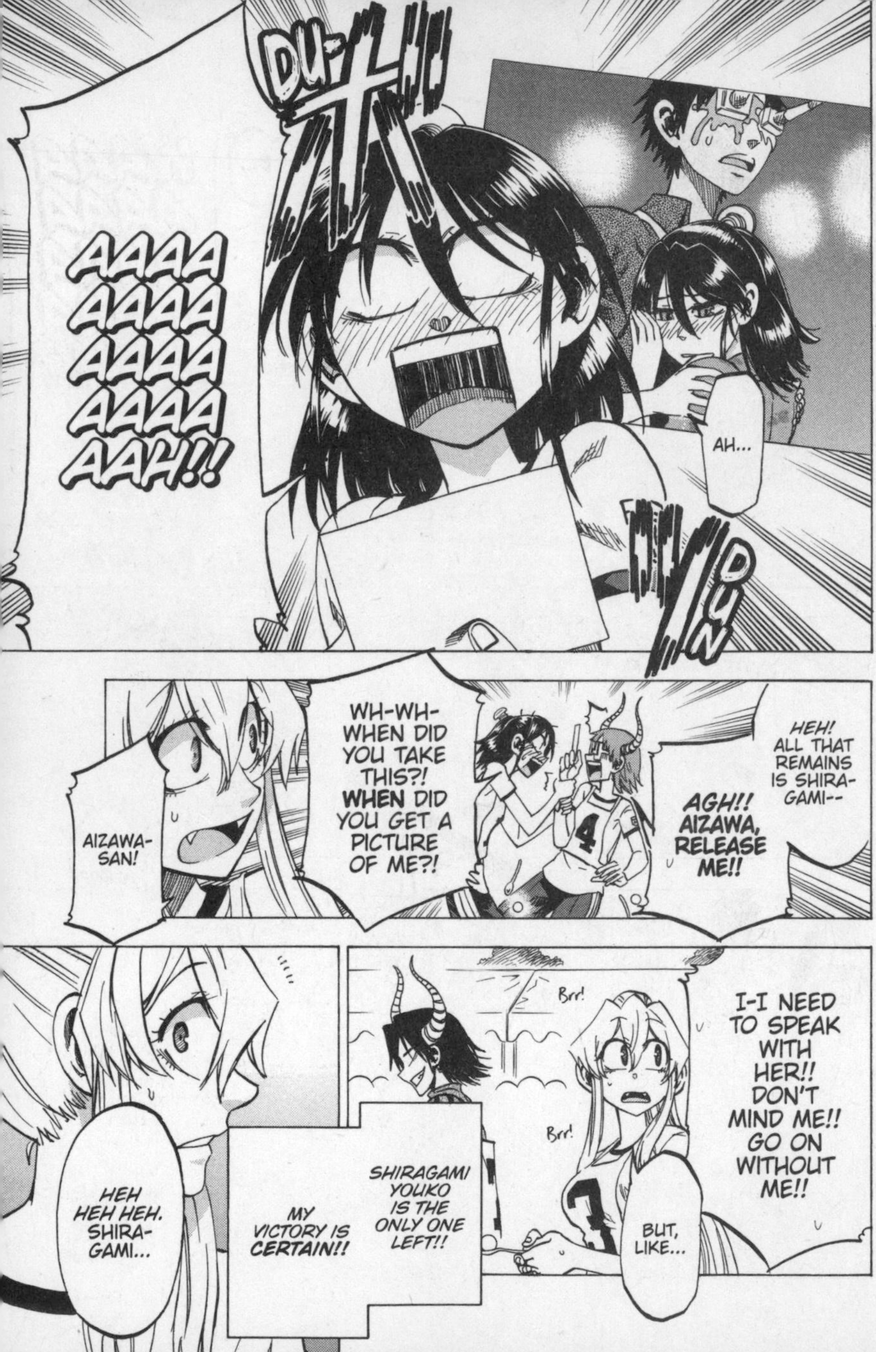
DU-
AH...
DUN
AAAA AAAA AAAA AAAA AAH!!
HEH! ALL THAT REMAINS IS SHIRA-GAMI--
AGH!! AIZAWA, RELEASE ME!!
WH-WH-WHEN DID YOU TAKE THIS?! WHEN DID YOU GET A PICTURE OF ME?!
AIZAWA-SAN!
I-I NEED TO SPEAK WITH HER!! DON'T MIND ME!! GO ON WITHOUT ME!!
Brr!
Brr!
BUT, LIKE...
SHIRAGAMI YOUKO IS THE ONLY ONE LEFT!!
MY VICTORY IS CERTAIN!!
HEH HEH HEH. SHIRA-GAMI...

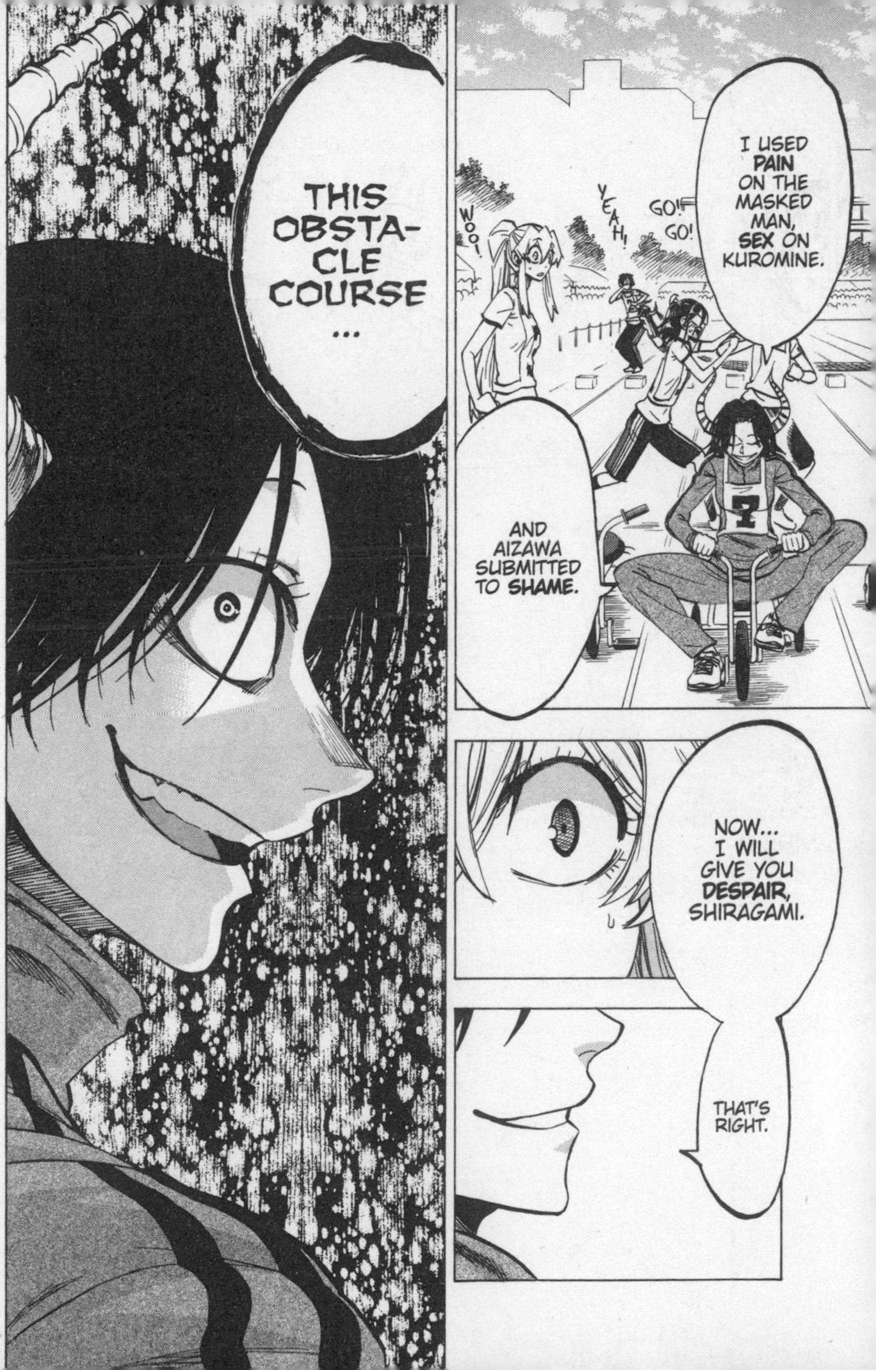
I USED PAIN ON THE MASKED MAN, SEX ON KUROMINE.
GO! GO!
YEAH!
WOO!
AND AIZAWA SUBMITTED TO SHAME.
NOW... I WILL GIVE YOU DESPAIR, SHIRAGAMI.
THAT'S RIGHT.
THIS OBSTACLE COURSE ...

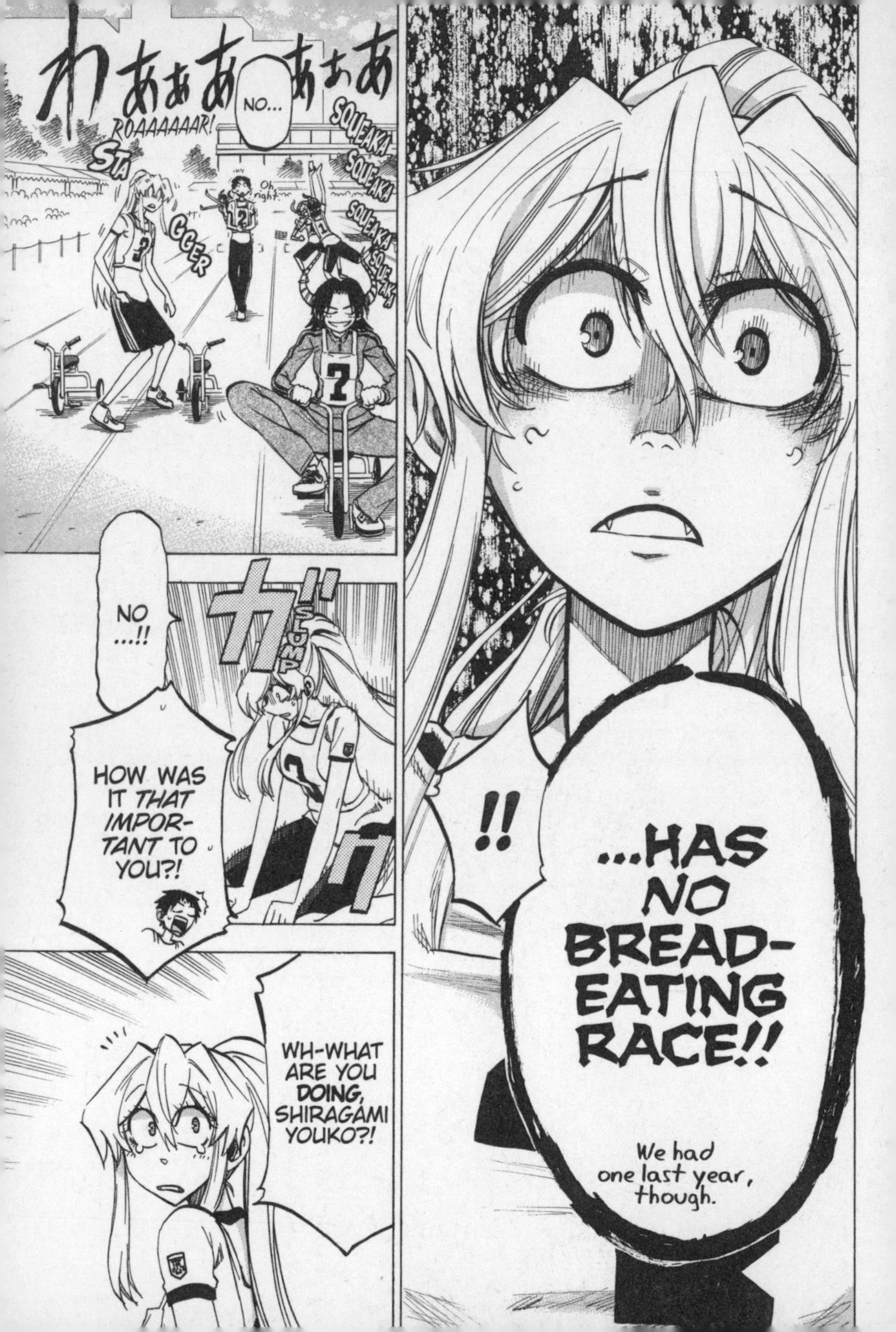
!!
...HAS NO BREAD-EATING RACE!!
We had one last year, though.
ROAAAAAAR!
NO...
STAGGER
Oh, right.
SQUEAKA SQUEAKA SQUEAKA SQUEAK
NO ...!!
HOW WAS IT THAT IMPORTANT TO YOU?!
SLUMP
WH-WHAT ARE YOU DOING, SHIRAGAMI YOUKO?!

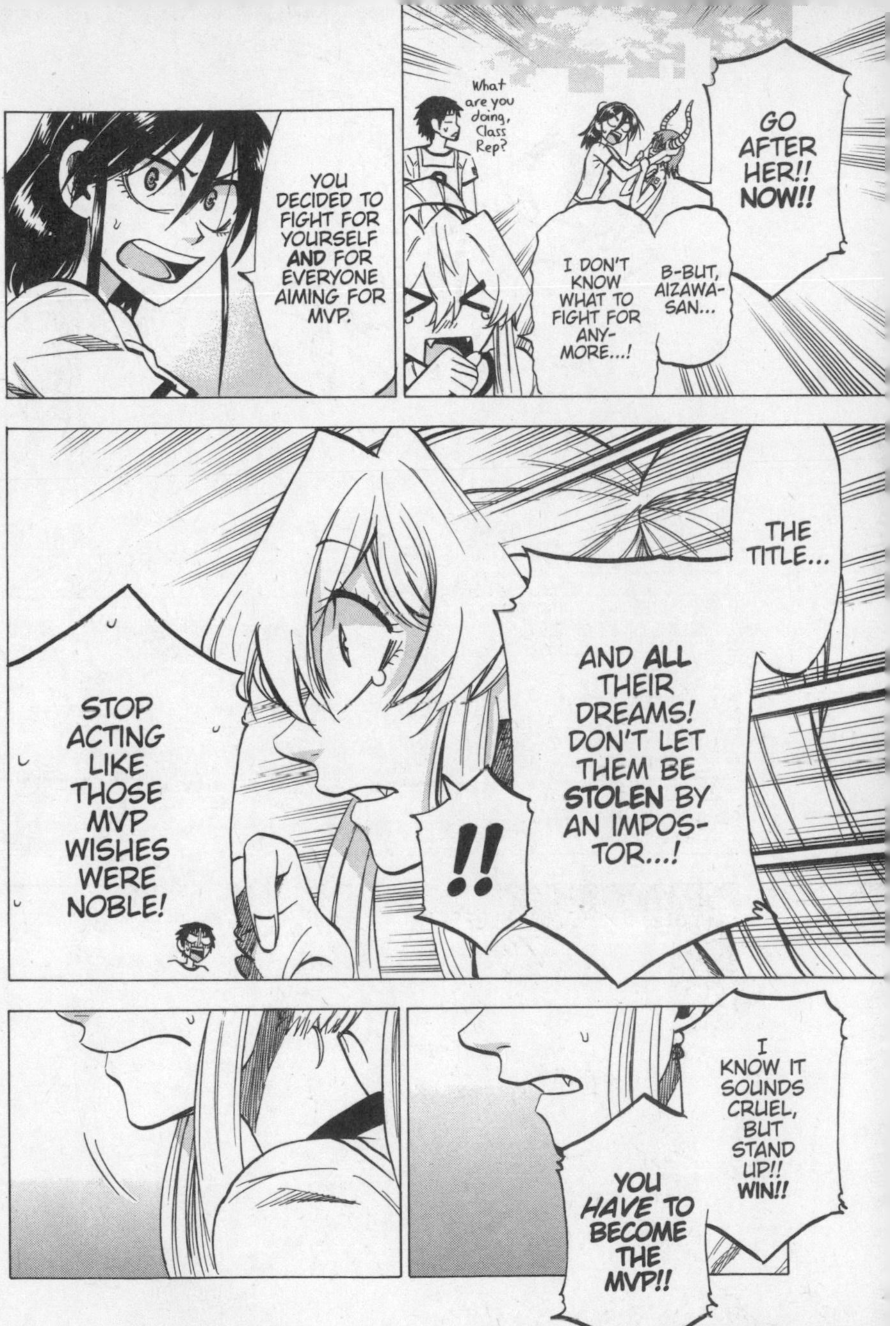
GO AFTER HER!! NOW!!
What are you doing, Class Rep?
B-BUT, AIZAWA-SAN...
I DON'T KNOW WHAT TO FIGHT FOR ANY-MORE...!
YOU DECIDED TO FIGHT FOR YOURSELF AND FOR EVERYONE AIMING FOR MVP.
THE TITLE...
AND ALL THEIR DREAMS! DON'T LET THEM BE STOLEN BY AN IMPOS-TOR...!
!!
STOP ACTING LIKE THOSE MVP WISHES WERE NOBLE!
I KNOW IT SOUNDS CRUEL, BUT STAND UP!! WIN!!
YOU HAVE TO BECOME THE MVP!!

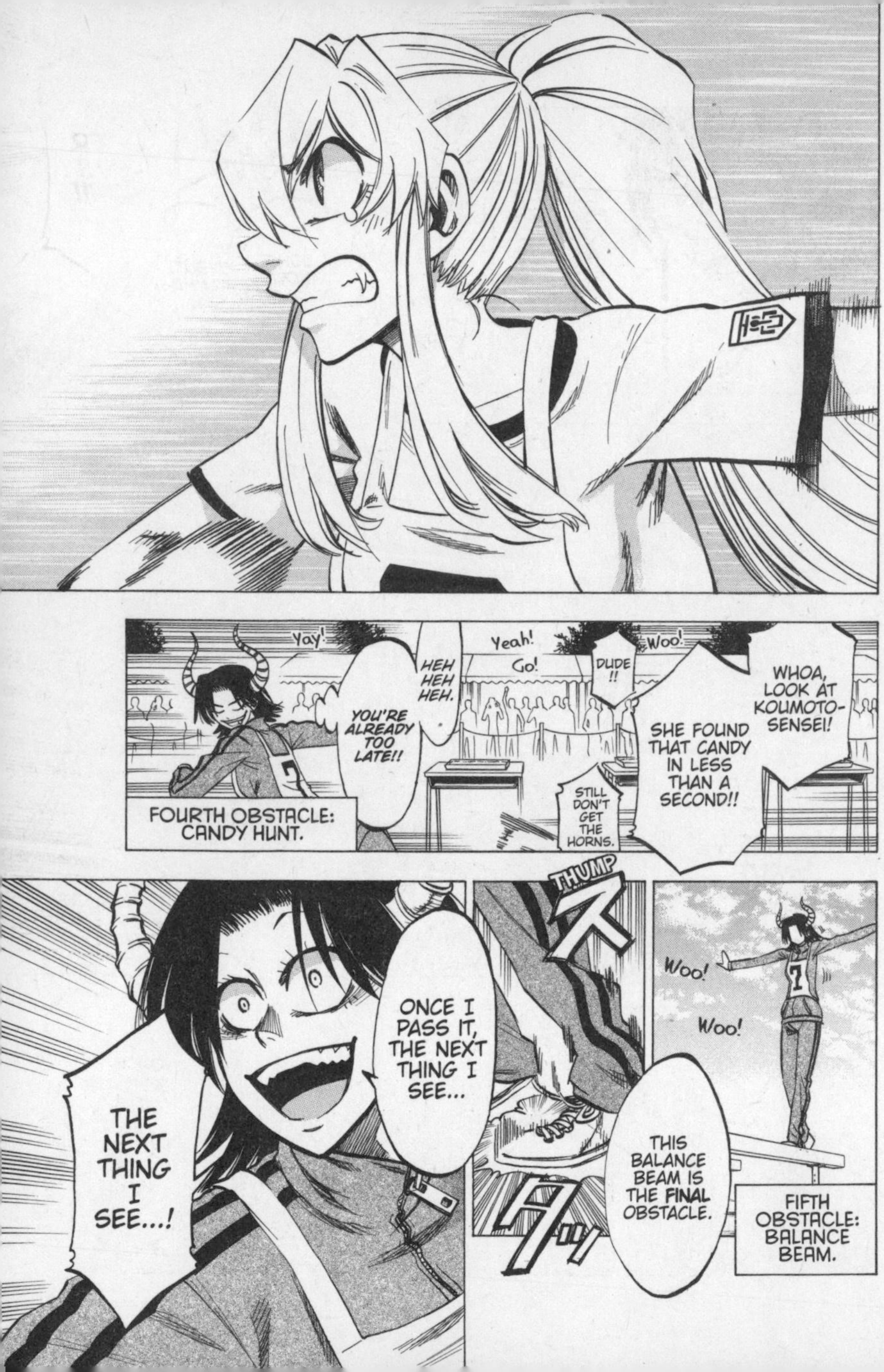
WHOA, LOOK AT KOUMOTO-SENSEI!
Woo!
SHE FOUND THAT CANDY IN LESS THAN A SECOND!!
DUDE!!
Yeah!
Go!
STILL DON'T GET THE HORNS.
HEH HEH HEH.
Yay!
YOU'RE ALREADY TOO LATE!!
FOURTH OBSTACLE: CANDY HUNT.
Woo!
Woo!
FIFTH OBSTACLE: BALANCE BEAM.
THUMP
THIS BALANCE BEAM IS THE FINAL OBSTACLE.
ONCE I PASS IT, THE NEXT THING I SEE...
THE NEXT THING I SEE...!

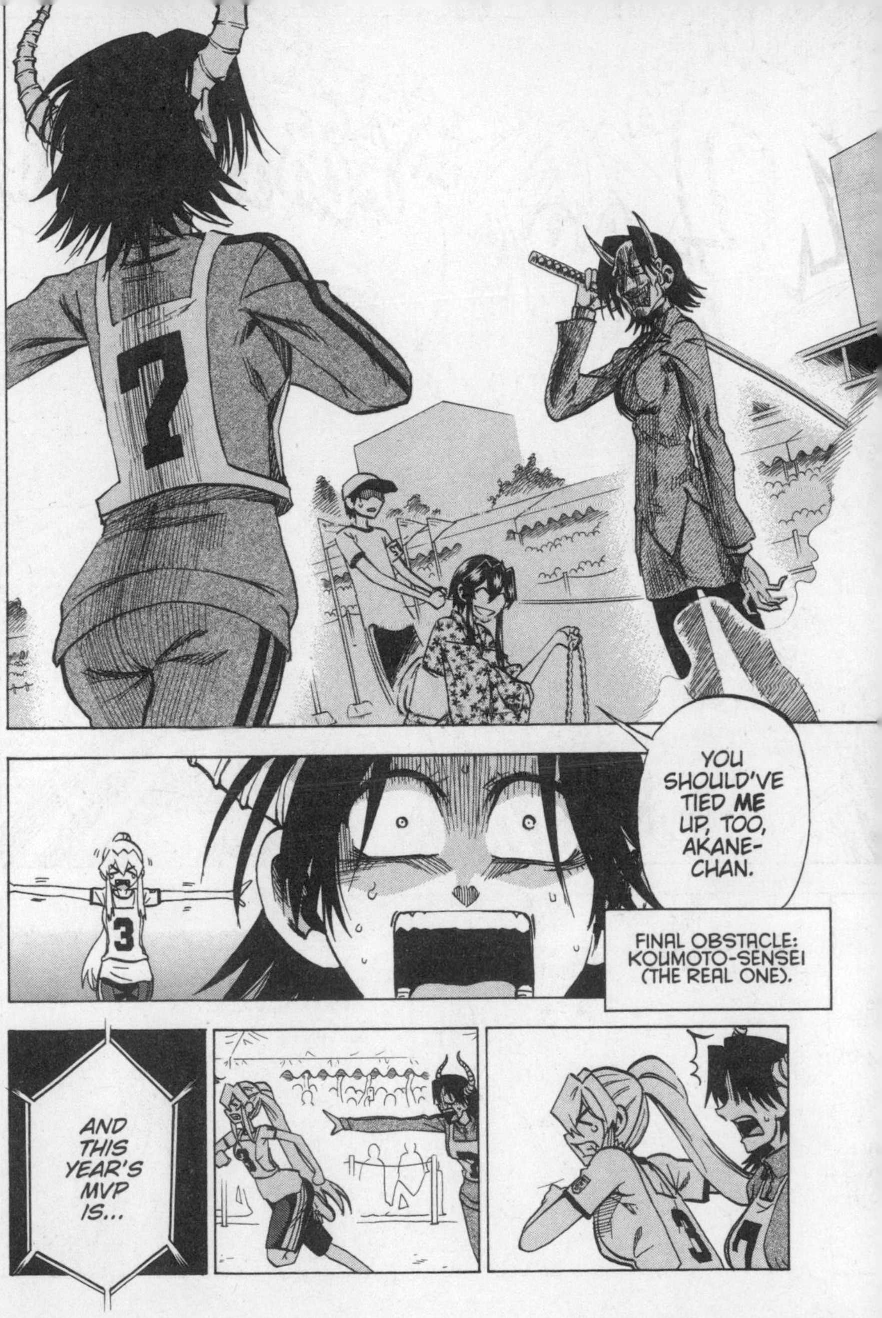
YOU SHOULD'VE TIED ME UP, TOO, AKANE-CHAN.
FINAL OBSTACLE: KOUMOTO-SENSEI (THE REAL ONE).
AND THIS YEAR'S MVP IS...

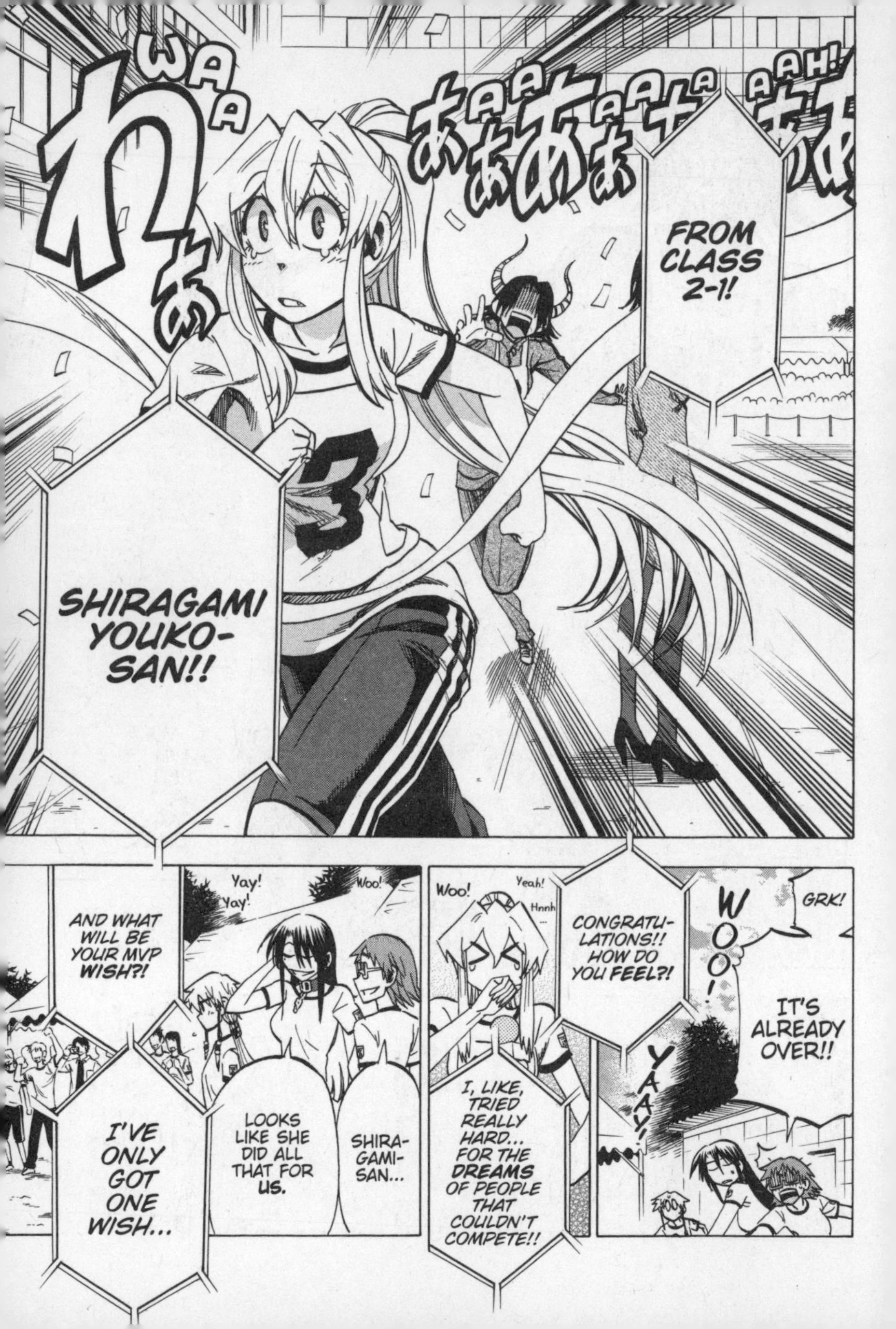
わあああああああ
WAAAAAAAAAAH!
FROM CLASS 2-1!
SHIRAGAMI YOUKO-SAN!!
GRK!
WOO!
IT'S ALREADY OVER!!
YAAY!
CONGRATULATIONS!! HOW DO YOU FEEL?!
Woo!
Yeah!
Hnnh...
I, LIKE, TRIED REALLY HARD... FOR THE DREAMS OF PEOPLE THAT COULDN'T COMPETE!!
Woo!
Yay!
Yay!
SHIRAGAMI-SAN...
LOOKS LIKE SHE DID ALL THAT FOR US.
AND WHAT WILL BE YOUR MVP WISH?!
I'VE ONLY GOT ONE WISH...

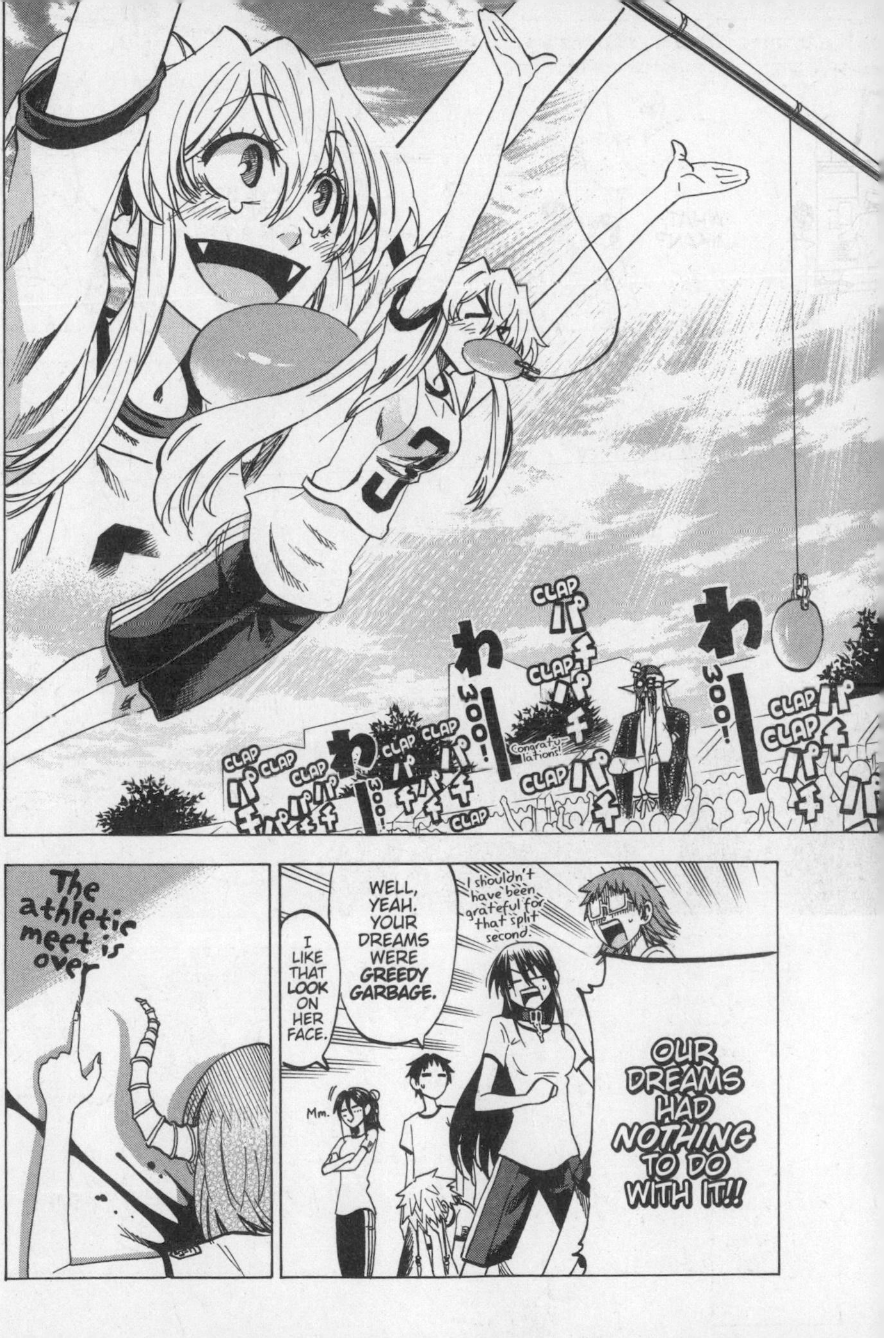
CLAP パ CLAP チ
わー WOO!
CLAP パ CLAP チ
CLAP パチ
Congratulations!
CLAP パチ CLAP パチ
わー WOO!
CLAP パチ CLAP パチ CLAP
わー WOO!
CLAP パチ CLAP パチ CLAP パチ
OUR DREAMS HAD NOTHING TO DO WITH IT!!
I shouldn't have been grateful for that split second.
WELL, YEAH. YOUR DREAMS WERE GREEDY GARBAGE.
I LIKE THAT LOOK ON HER FACE.
Mm.
The athletic meet is over

Chapter 40: "Let's Investigate the Seven Wonders!"

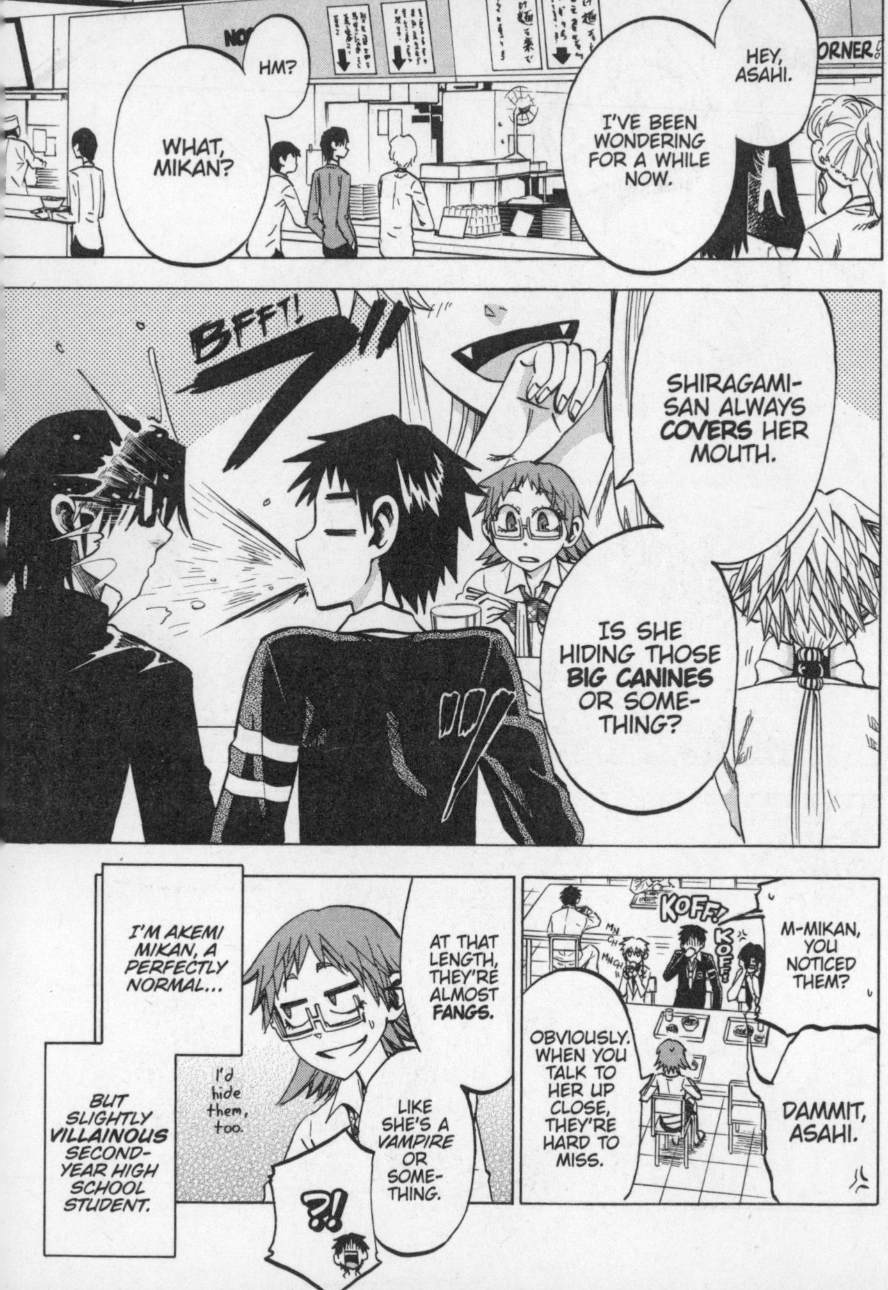
HEY, ASAHI.
I'VE BEEN WONDERING FOR A WHILE NOW.
HM?
WHAT, MIKAN?
SHIRAGAMI-SAN ALWAYS **COVERS** HER MOUTH.
IS SHE HIDING THOSE **BIG CANINES** OR SOME-THING?
BFFT!
KOFF!
KOFF
M-MIKAN, YOU NOTICED THEM?
OBVIOUSLY. WHEN YOU TALK TO HER UP CLOSE, THEY'RE HARD TO MISS.
DAMMIT, ASAHI.
AT THAT LENGTH, THEY'RE ALMOST **FANGS.**
LIKE SHE'S A *VAMPIRE* OR SOME-THING.
I'd hide them, too.
?!
I'M AKEMI MIKAN, A PERFECTLY NORMAL...
*BUT SLIGHTLY **VILLAINOUS** SECOND-YEAR HIGH SCHOOL STUDENT.*

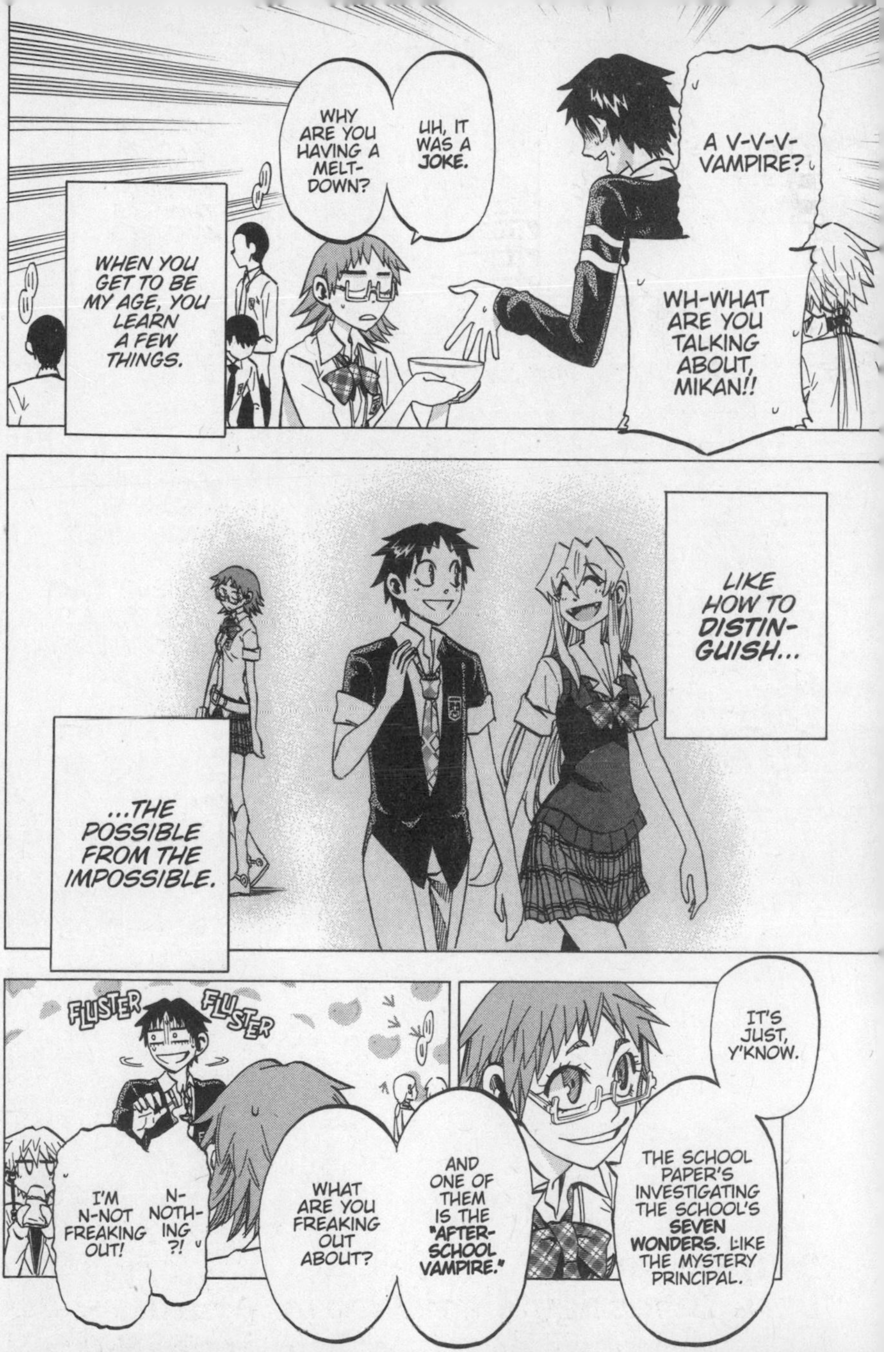
A V-V-V-VAMPIRE?
WH-WHAT ARE YOU TALKING ABOUT, MIKAN!!
UH, IT WAS A JOKE.
WHY ARE YOU HAVING A MELT-DOWN?
WHEN YOU GET TO BE MY AGE, YOU LEARN A FEW THINGS.
LIKE HOW TO DISTIN-GUISH...
...THE POSSIBLE FROM THE IMPOSSIBLE.
IT'S JUST, Y'KNOW.
THE SCHOOL PAPER'S INVESTIGATING THE SCHOOL'S SEVEN WONDERS. LIKE THE MYSTERY PRINCIPAL.
AND ONE OF THEM IS THE "AFTER-SCHOOL VAMPIRE."
WHAT ARE YOU FREAKING OUT ABOUT?
FLUSTER
FLUSTER
N-NOTHING?!
I'M N-NOT FREAKING OUT!

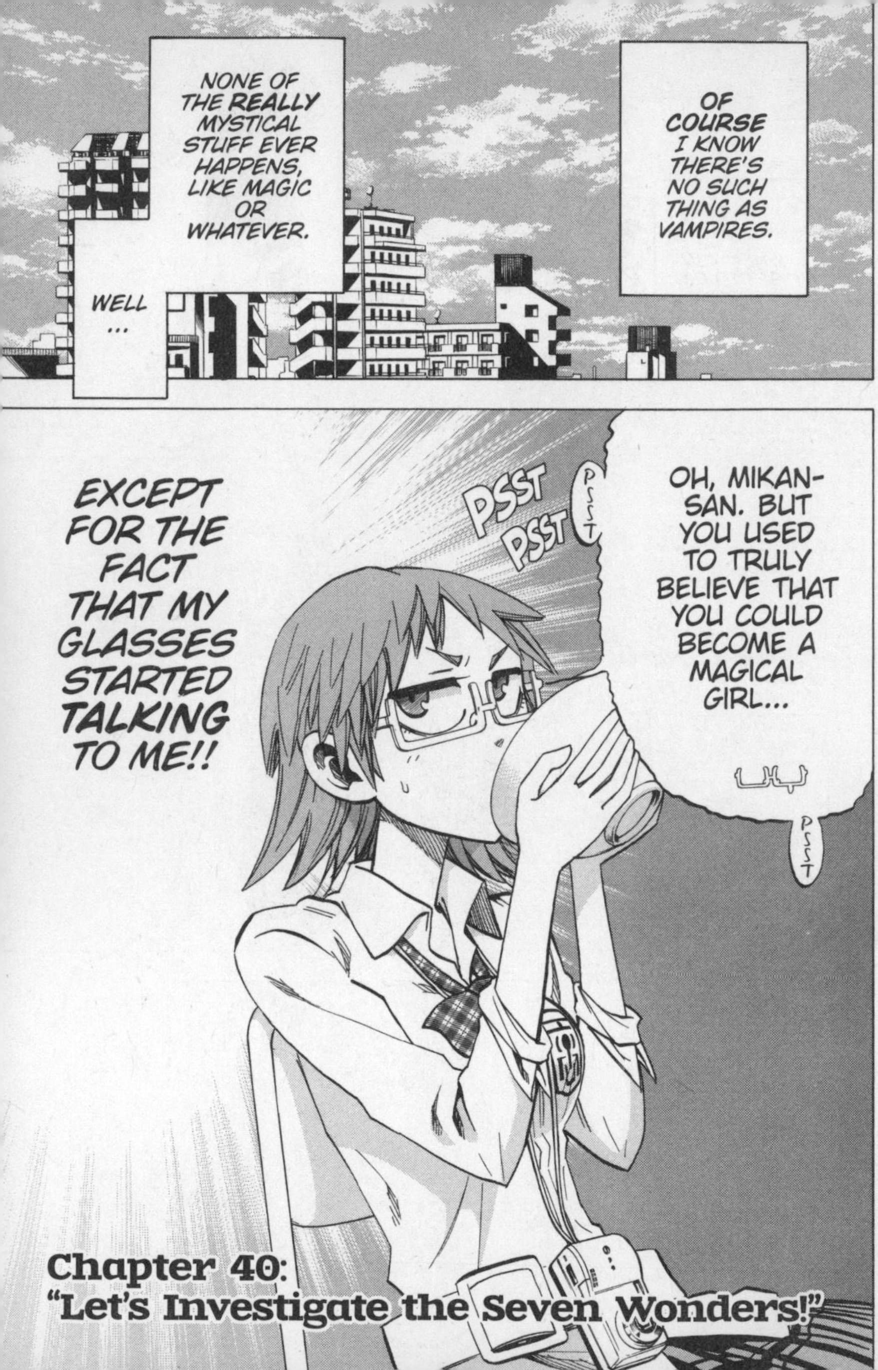
OF COURSE I KNOW THERE'S NO SUCH THING AS VAMPIRES.
NONE OF THE REALLY MYSTICAL STUFF EVER HAPPENS, LIKE MAGIC OR WHATEVER.
WELL ...
PSST
PSST PSST
OH, MIKAN-SAN. BUT YOU USED TO TRULY BELIEVE THAT YOU COULD BECOME A MAGICAL GIRL...
PSST
EXCEPT FOR THE FACT THAT MY GLASSES STARTED TALKING TO ME!!

Chapter 40: "Let's Investigate the Seven Wonders!"

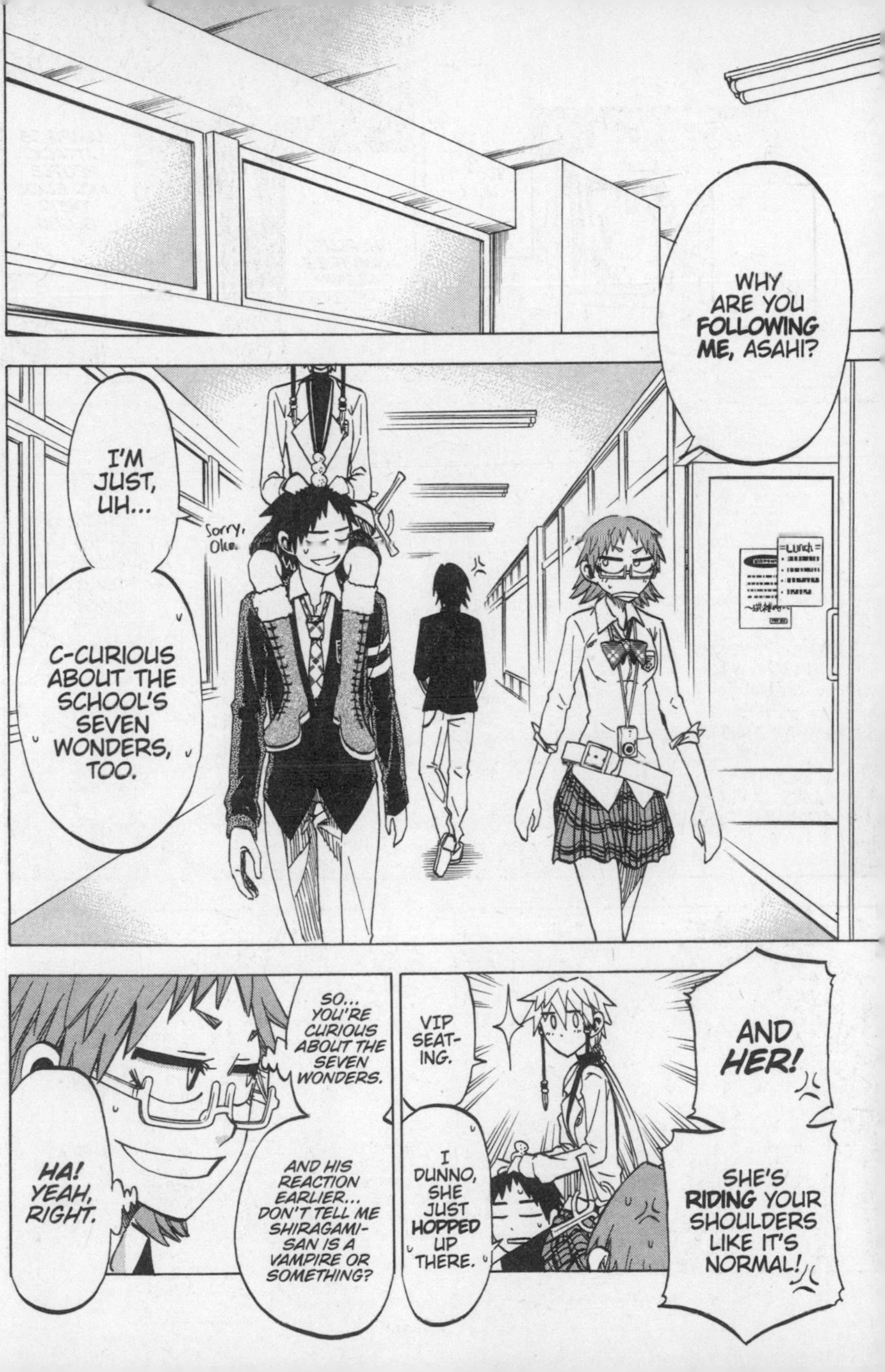
WHY ARE YOU FOLLOWING ME, ASAHI?
I'M JUST, UH...
Sorry, Oka.
C-CURIOUS ABOUT THE SCHOOL'S SEVEN WONDERS, TOO.
AND HER!
VIP SEATING.
SHE'S RIDING YOUR SHOULDERS LIKE IT'S NORMAL!
I DUNNO, SHE JUST HOPPED UP THERE.
SO... YOU'RE CURIOUS ABOUT THE SEVEN WONDERS.
AND HIS REACTION EARLIER... DON'T TELL ME SHIRAGAMI-SAN IS A VAMPIRE OR SOMETHING?
HA! YEAH, RIGHT.

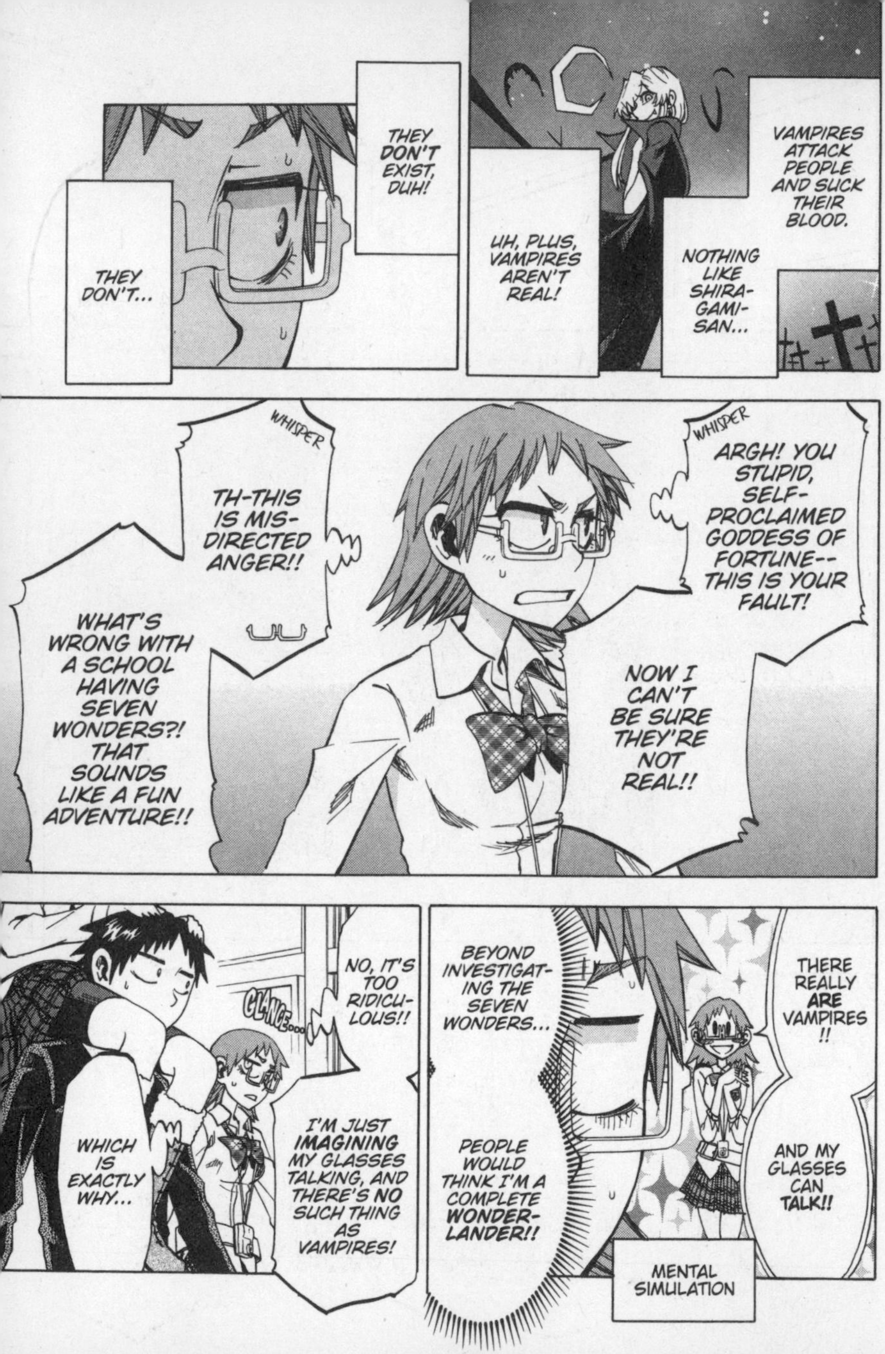
VAMPIRES ATTACK PEOPLE AND SUCK THEIR BLOOD.
NOTHING LIKE SHIRA-GAMI-SAN...
UH, PLUS, VAMPIRES AREN'T REAL!
THEY DON'T EXIST, DUH!
THEY DON'T...
WHISPER
ARGH! YOU STUPID, SELF-PROCLAIMED GODDESS OF FORTUNE-- THIS IS YOUR FAULT!
NOW I CAN'T BE SURE THEY'RE NOT REAL!!
WHISPER
TH-THIS IS MIS-DIRECTED ANGER!!
WHAT'S WRONG WITH A SCHOOL HAVING SEVEN WONDERS?! THAT SOUNDS LIKE A FUN ADVENTURE!!
THERE REALLY ARE VAMPIRES!!
AND MY GLASSES CAN TALK!!
BEYOND INVESTIGAT-ING THE SEVEN WONDERS...
PEOPLE WOULD THINK I'M A COMPLETE WONDER-LANDER!!
MENTAL SIMULATION
NO, IT'S TOO RIDICU-LOUS!!
GLANCE...
I'M JUST IMAGINING MY GLASSES TALKING, AND THERE'S NO SUCH THING AS VAMPIRES!
WHICH IS EXACTLY WHY...

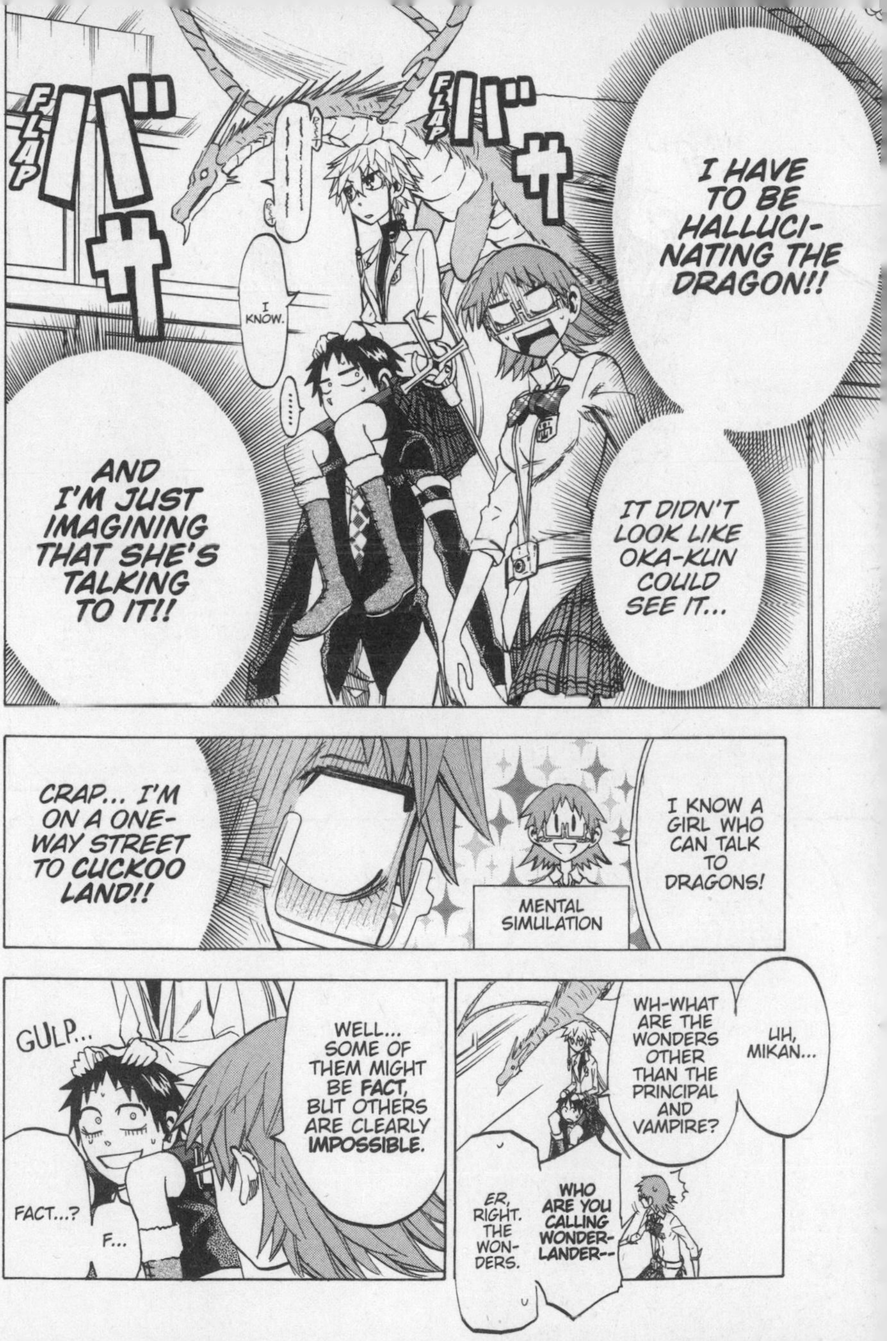
I HAVE TO BE HALLUCINATING THE DRAGON!!
IT DIDN'T LOOK LIKE OKA-KUN COULD SEE IT...
FLAP
I KNOW.
...
AND I'M JUST IMAGINING THAT SHE'S TALKING TO IT!!
FLAP
I KNOW A GIRL WHO CAN TALK TO DRAGONS!
MENTAL SIMULATION
CRAP... I'M ON A ONE-WAY STREET TO CUCKOO LAND!!
UH, MIKAN...
WH-WHAT ARE THE WONDERS OTHER THAN THE PRINCIPAL AND VAMPIRE?
WHO ARE YOU CALLING WONDERLANDER--
ER, RIGHT. THE WONDERS.
WELL... SOME OF THEM MIGHT BE FACT, BUT OTHERS ARE CLEARLY IMPOSSIBLE.
GULP...
FACT...?
F...

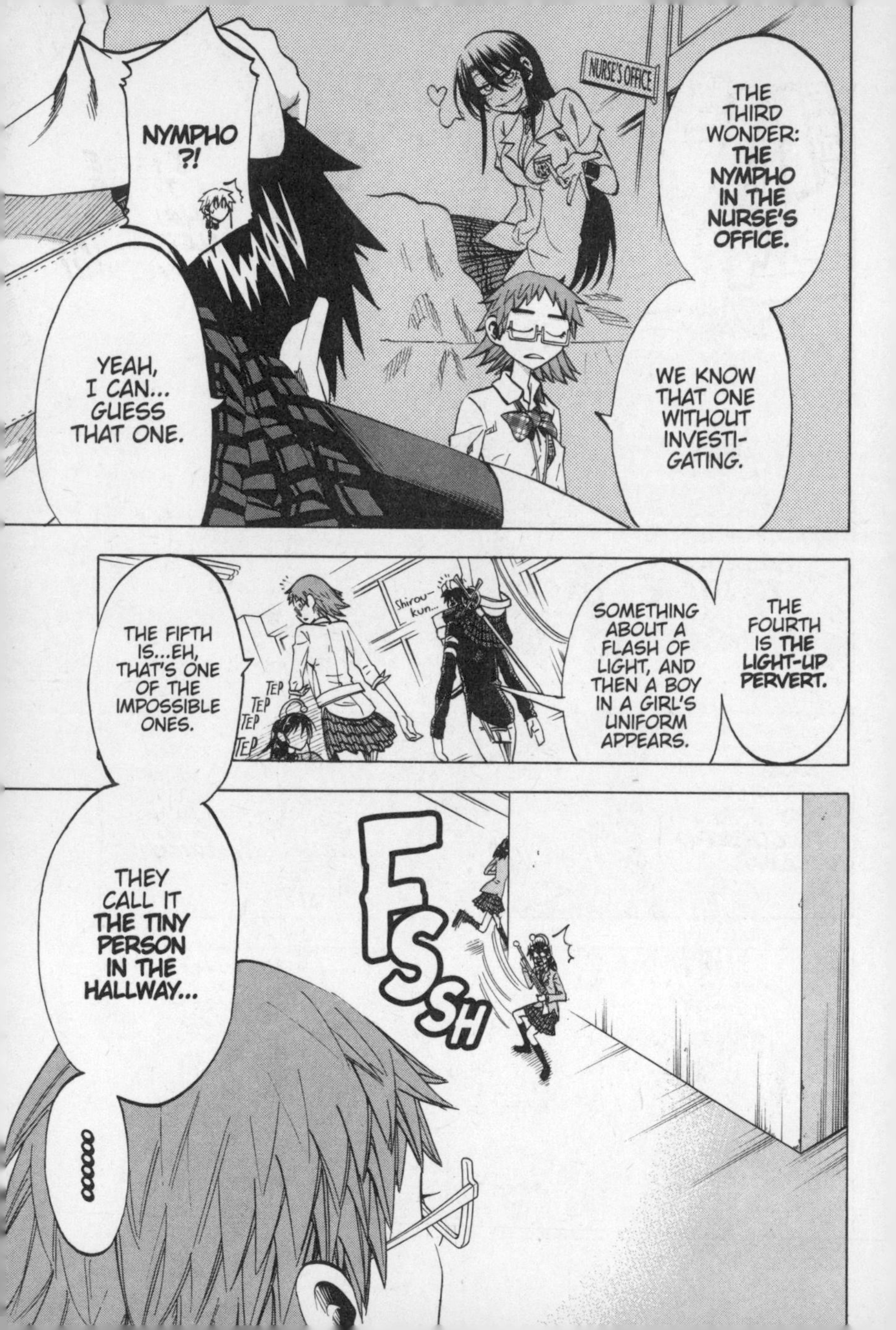
NURSE'S OFFICE
THE THIRD WONDER: THE NYMPHO IN THE NURSE'S OFFICE.
WE KNOW THAT ONE WITHOUT INVESTI-GATING.
NYMPHO ?!
YEAH, I CAN... GUESS THAT ONE.
THE FOURTH IS THE LIGHT-UP PERVERT.
SOMETHING ABOUT A FLASH OF LIGHT, AND THEN A BOY IN A GIRL'S UNIFORM APPEARS.
Shirou-kun...
THE FIFTH IS...EH, THAT'S ONE OF THE IMPOSSIBLE ONES.
TEP TEP TEP TEP
FSSH
THEY CALL IT THE TINY PERSON IN THE HALLWAY...
OOOOOO

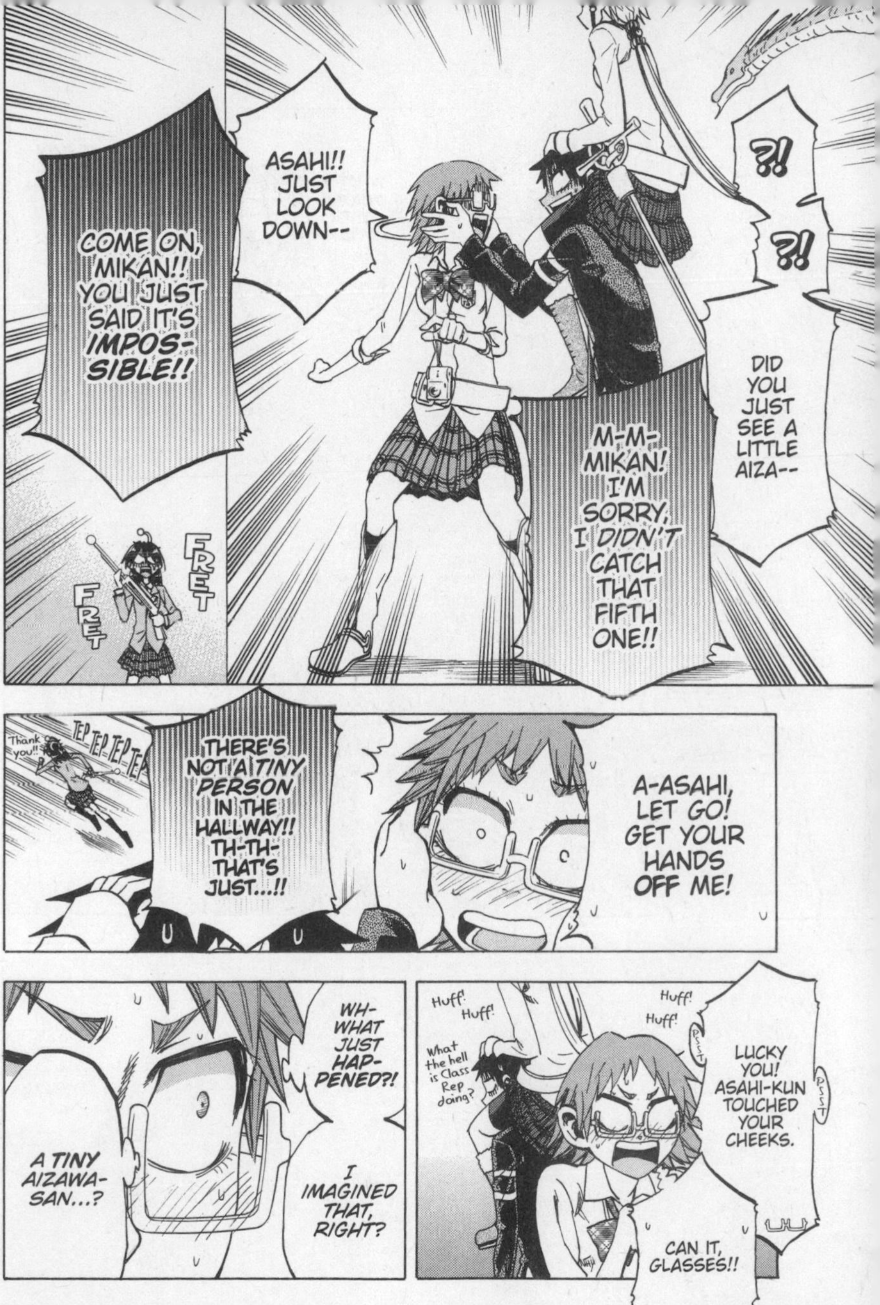
?!
?!
DID YOU JUST SEE A LITTLE AIZA--
M-M-MIKAN! I'M SORRY, I DIDN'T CATCH THAT FIFTH ONE!!
ASAHI!! JUST LOOK DOWN--
COME ON, MIKAN!! YOU JUST SAID IT'S IMPOSSIBLE!!
FRET
FRET
A-ASAHI, LET GO! GET YOUR HANDS OFF ME!
THERE'S NOT A TINY PERSON IN THE HALLWAY!! TH-TH-THAT'S JUST...!!
TEP TEP TEP TEP
Thank you!!
Huff! Huff!
Huff! Huff!
LUCKY YOU! ASAHI-KUN TOUCHED YOUR CHEEKS.
PSST
PSST
What the hell is Class Rep doing?
CAN IT, GLASSES!!
WH-WHAT JUST HAPPENED?!
I IMAGINED THAT, RIGHT?
A TINY AIZAWA-SAN...?

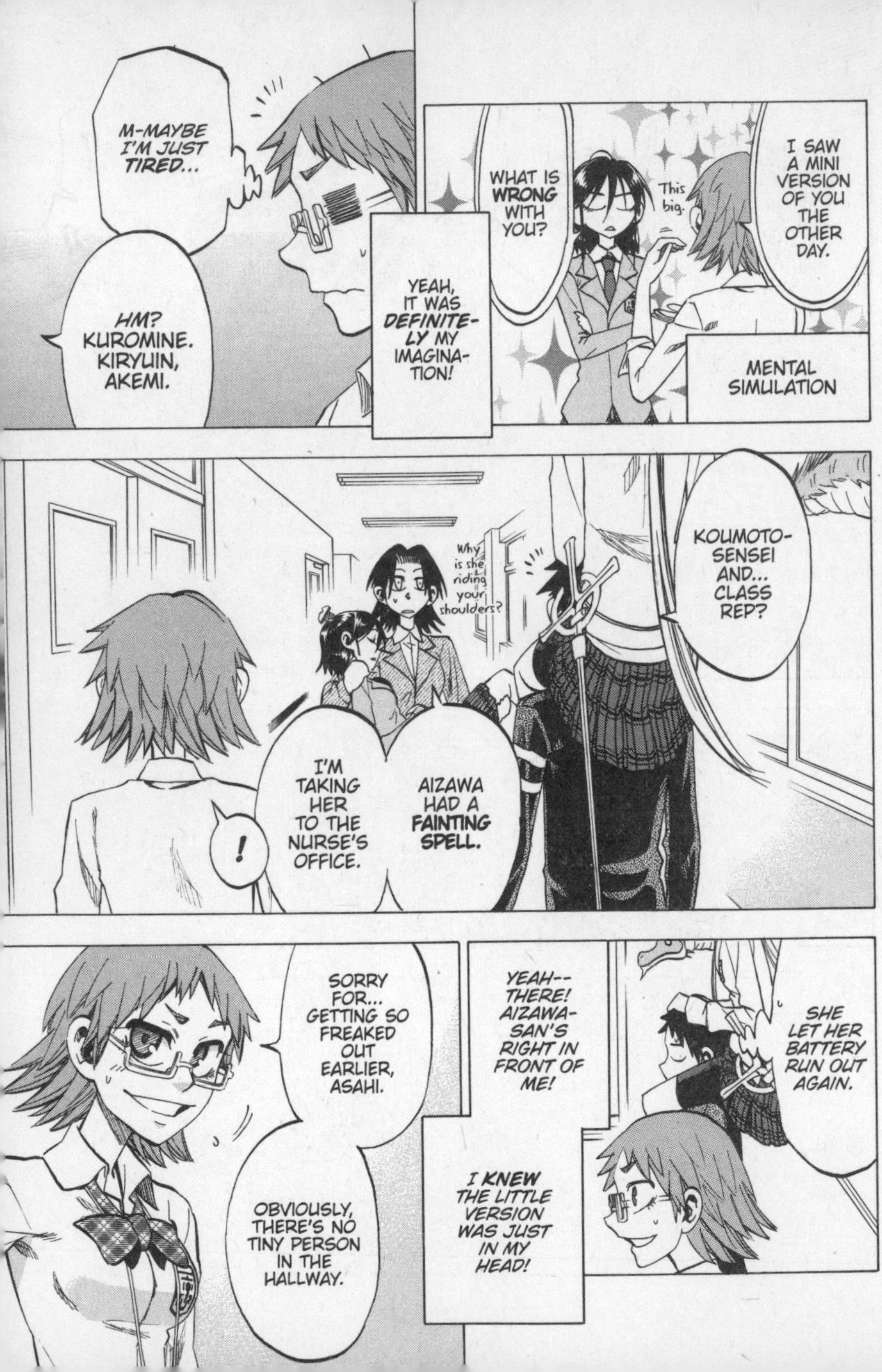
I SAW A MINI VERSION OF YOU THE OTHER DAY.
This big.
WHAT IS WRONG WITH YOU?
MENTAL SIMULATION
M-MAYBE I'M JUST TIRED...
YEAH, IT WAS DEFINITE-LY MY IMAGINA-TION!
HM? KUROMINE. KIRYUIN, AKEMI.
KOUMOTO-SENSEI AND... CLASS REP?
Why is she riding your shoulders?
AIZAWA HAD A FAINTING SPELL.
I'M TAKING HER TO THE NURSE'S OFFICE.
!
SHE LET HER BATTERY RUN OUT AGAIN.
YEAH-- THERE! AIZAWA-SAN'S RIGHT IN FRONT OF ME!
I KNEW THE LITTLE VERSION WAS JUST IN MY HEAD!
SORRY FOR... GETTING SO FREAKED OUT EARLIER, ASAHI.
OBVIOUSLY, THERE'S NO TINY PERSON IN THE HALLWAY.

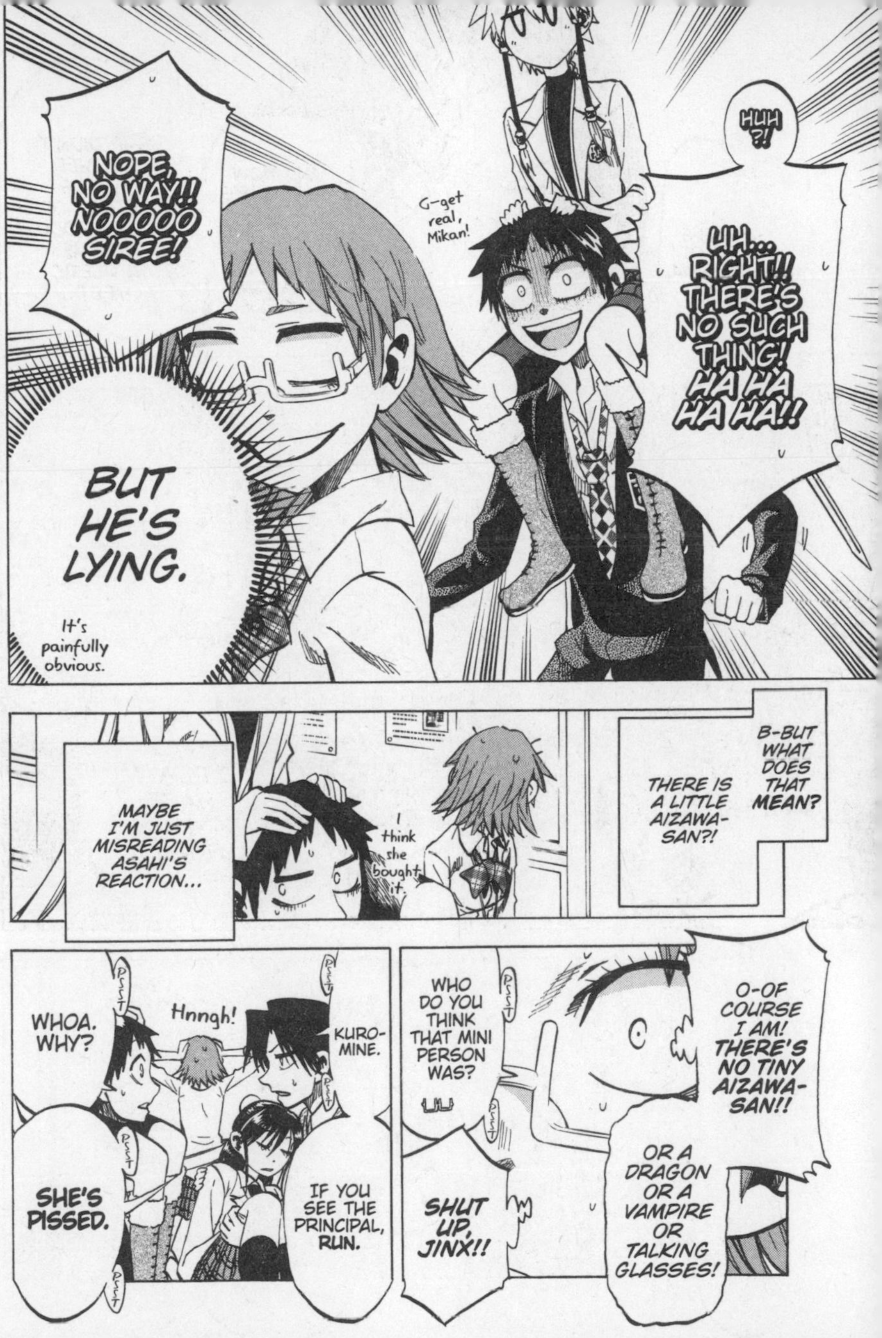
HUH ?!
UH... RIGHT!! THERE'S NO SUCH THING! HA HA HA HA!!
G-get real, Mikan!
NOPE, NO WAY!! NOOOOO SIREE!
BUT HE'S LYING.
It's painfully obvious.
B-BUT WHAT DOES THAT MEAN?
THERE IS A LITTLE AIZAWA-SAN?!
I think she bought it.
MAYBE I'M JUST MISREADING ASAHI'S REACTION...
O-OF COURSE I AM! THERE'S NO TINY AIZAWA-SAN!!
OR A DRAGON OR A VAMPIRE OR TALKING GLASSES!
WHO DO YOU THINK THAT MINI PERSON WAS?
PSST
SHUT UP, JINX!!
KURO-MINE.
PSST
Hnngh!
WHOA. WHY?
PSST
IF YOU SEE THE PRINCIPAL, RUN.
SHE'S PISSED.
PSST

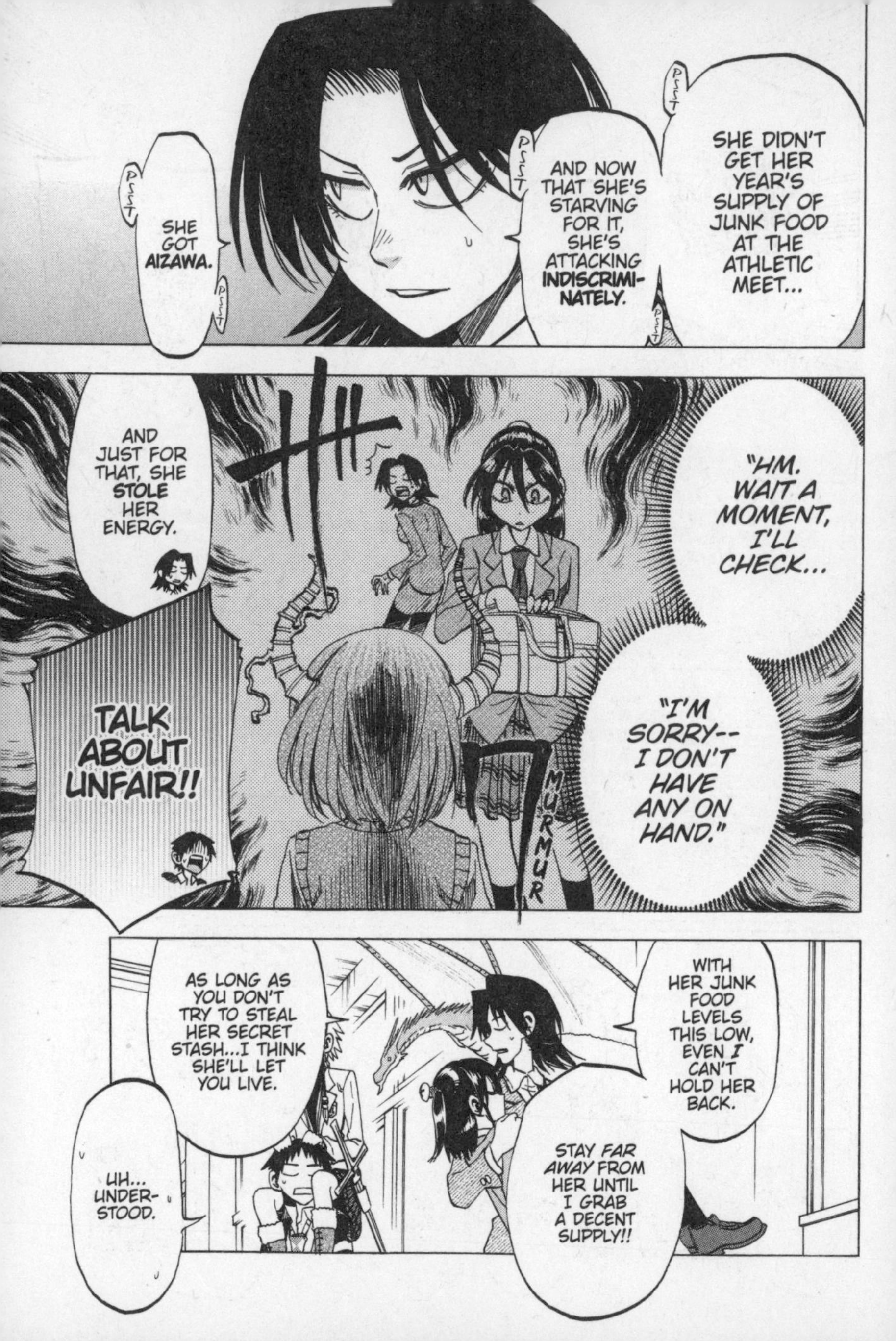
PSST
SHE DIDN'T GET HER YEAR'S SUPPLY OF JUNK FOOD AT THE ATHLETIC MEET...
PSST
AND NOW THAT SHE'S STARVING FOR IT, SHE'S ATTACKING **INDISCRIMINATELY.**
PSST
SHE GOT **AIZAWA.**
PSST
"HM. WAIT A MOMENT, I'LL CHECK...
"I'M SORRY-- I DON'T HAVE ANY ON HAND."
MURMUR
AND JUST FOR THAT, SHE **STOLE** HER ENERGY.
TALK ABOUT UNFAIR!!
WITH HER JUNK FOOD LEVELS THIS LOW, EVEN *I* CAN'T HOLD HER BACK.
STAY *FAR* AWAY FROM HER UNTIL I GRAB A DECENT SUPPLY!!
AS LONG AS YOU DON'T TRY TO STEAL HER SECRET STASH...I THINK SHE'LL LET YOU LIVE.
UH... UNDER-STOOD.

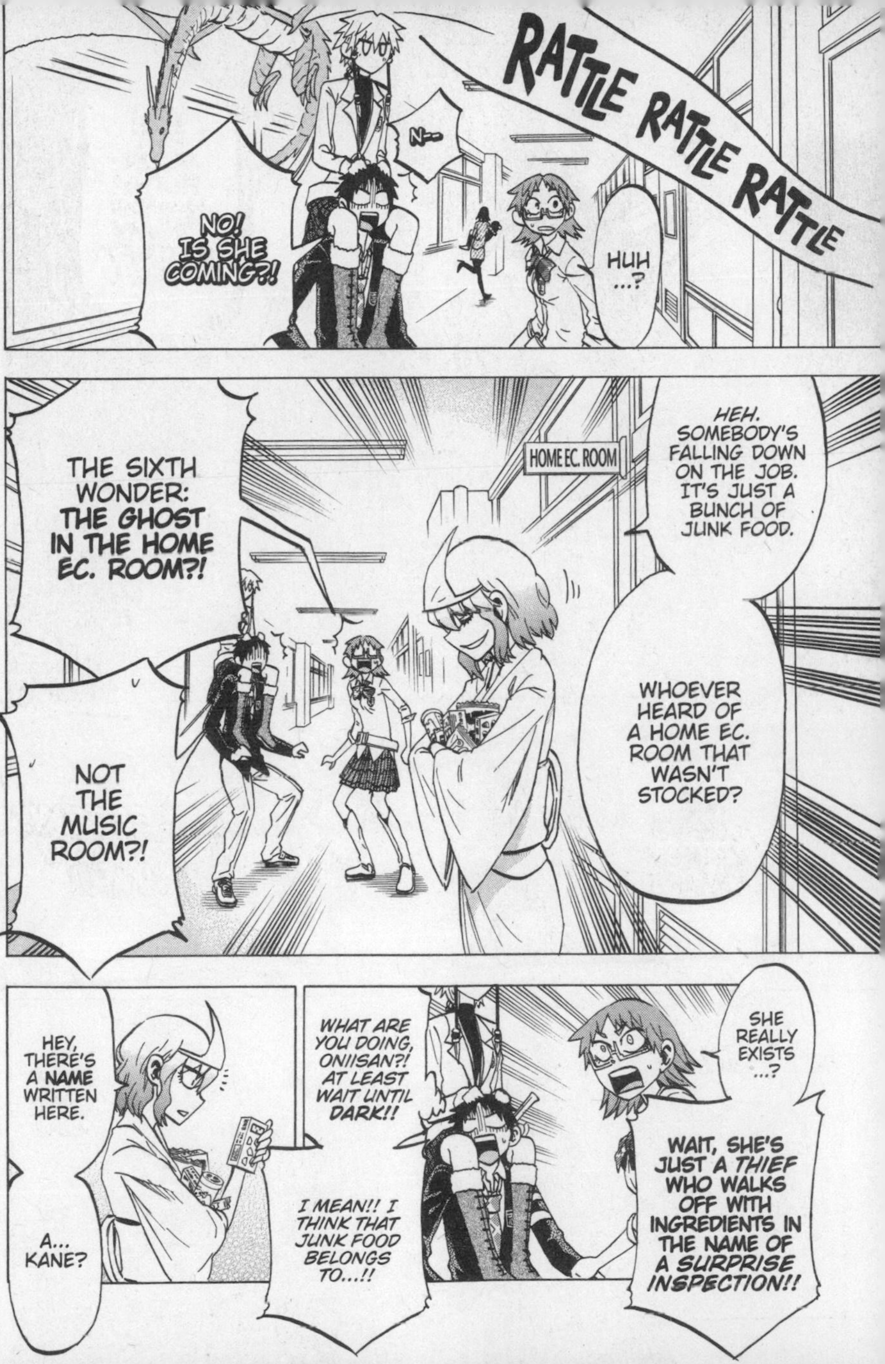
RATTLE RATTLE RATTLE
HUH ...?
N--
NO! IS SHE COMING?!
HEH. SOMEBODY'S FALLING DOWN ON THE JOB. IT'S JUST A BUNCH OF JUNK FOOD.
HOME EC. ROOM
WHOEVER HEARD OF A HOME EC. ROOM THAT WASN'T STOCKED?
THE SIXTH WONDER: THE GHOST IN THE HOME EC. ROOM?!
NOT THE MUSIC ROOM?!
SHE REALLY EXISTS ...?
WHAT ARE YOU DOING, ONIISAN?! AT LEAST WAIT UNTIL DARK!!
WAIT, SHE'S JUST A THIEF WHO WALKS OFF WITH INGREDIENTS IN THE NAME OF A SURPRISE INSPECTION!!
I MEAN!! I THINK THAT JUNK FOOD BELONGS TO...!!
HEY, THERE'S A NAME WRITTEN HERE.
A... KANE?

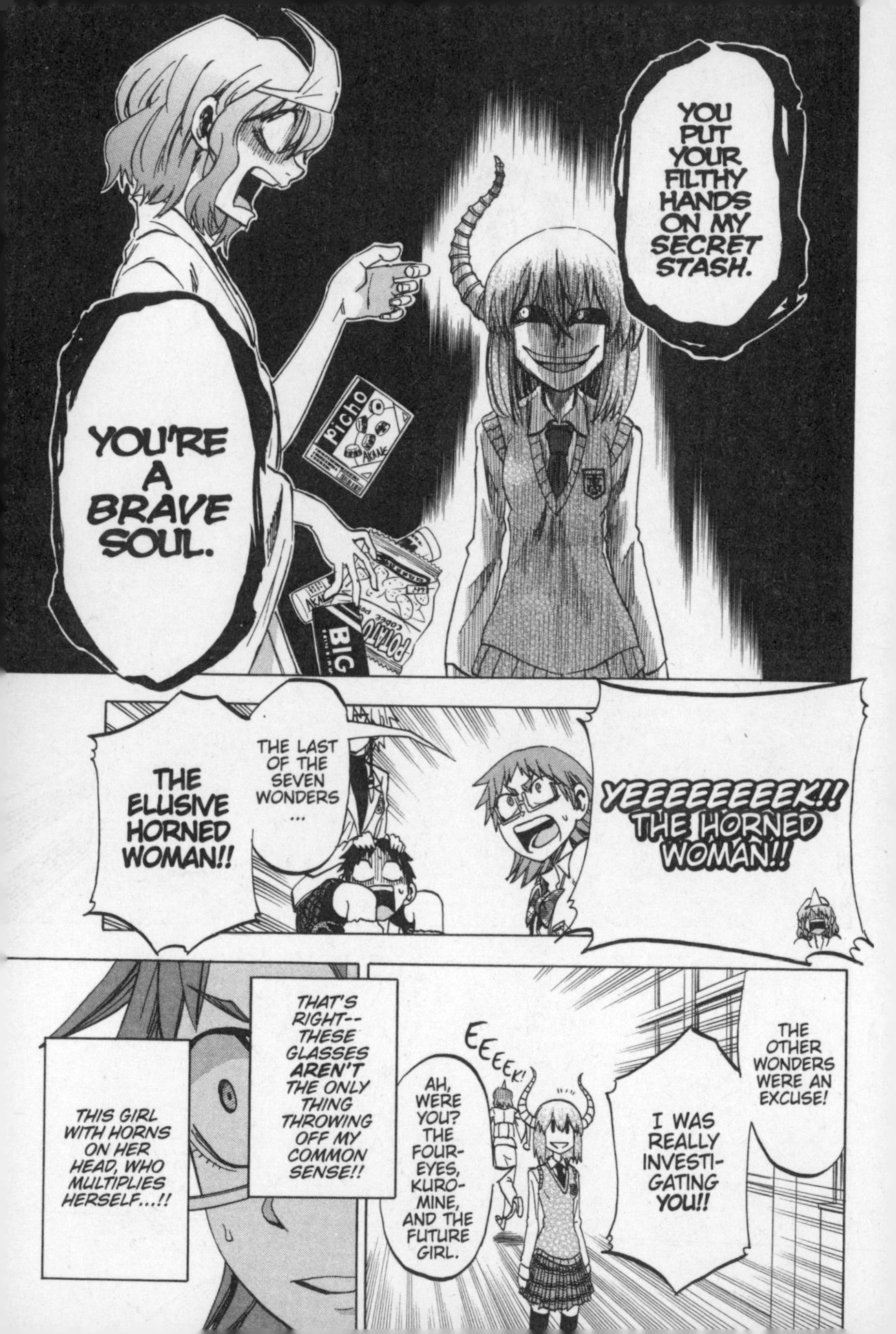
YOU PUT YOUR FILTHY HANDS ON MY SECRET STASH.
YOU'RE A BRAVE SOUL.
YEEEEEEEEEK!! THE HORNED WOMAN!!
THE LAST OF THE SEVEN WONDERS ...
THE ELUSIVE HORNED WOMAN!!
THE OTHER WONDERS WERE AN EXCUSE!
I WAS REALLY INVESTI-GATING YOU!!
EEEEK!
AH, WERE YOU? THE FOUR-EYES, KURO-MINE, AND THE FUTURE GIRL.
THAT'S RIGHT-- THESE GLASSES AREN'T THE ONLY THING THROWING OFF MY COMMON SENSE!!
THIS GIRL WITH HORNS ON HER HEAD, WHO MULTIPLIES HERSELF...!!

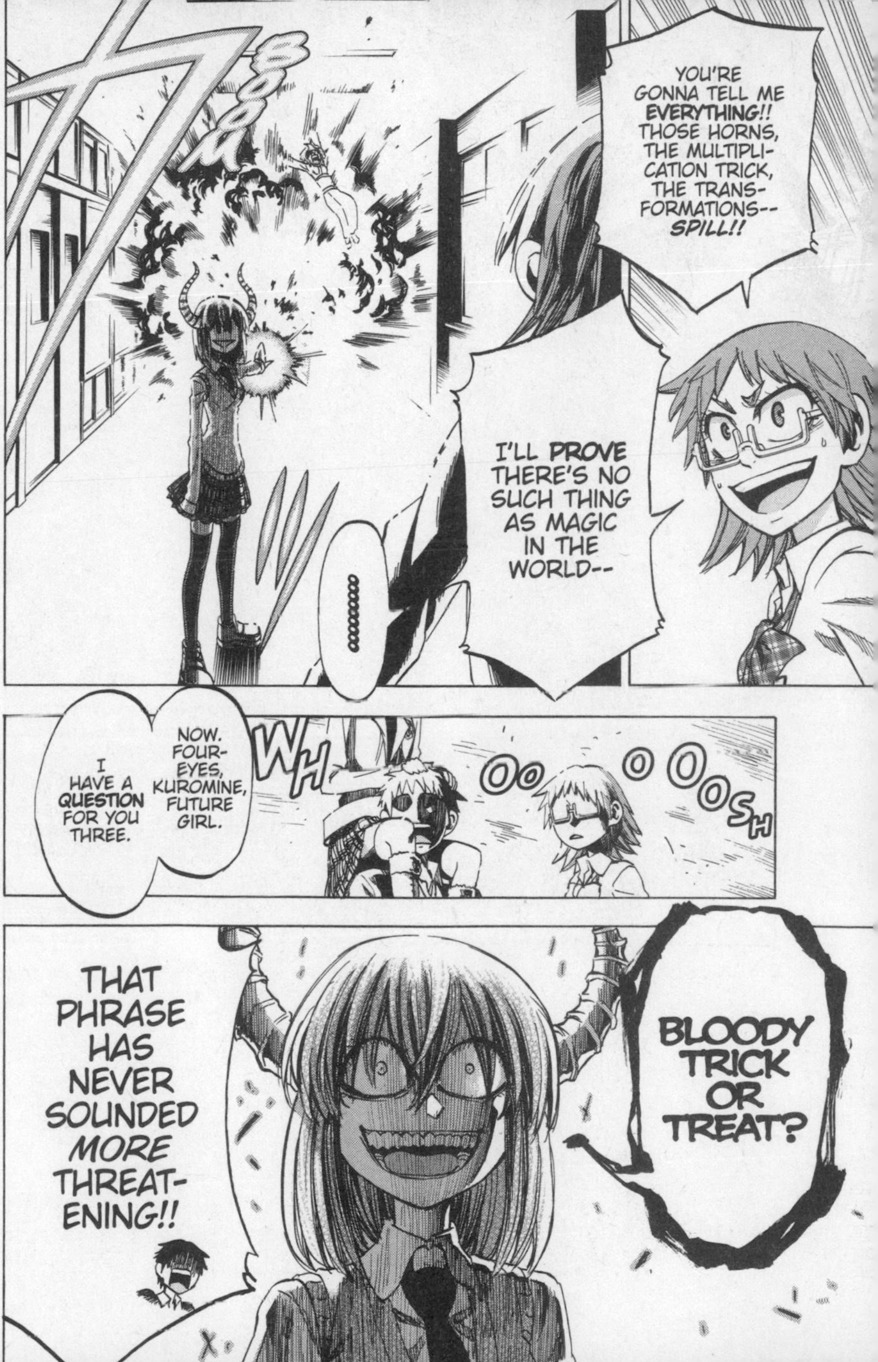
YOU'RE GONNA TELL ME EVERYTHING!! THOSE HORNS, THE MULTIPLICATION TRICK, THE TRANSFORMATIONS-- SPILL!!
I'LL PROVE THERE'S NO SUCH THING AS MAGIC IN THE WORLD--
....
BOOM
NOW. FOUR-EYES, KUROMINE, FUTURE GIRL.
I HAVE A QUESTION FOR YOU THREE.
WHOOOOOOSH
BLOODY TRICK OR TREAT?
THAT PHRASE HAS NEVER SOUNDED MORE THREATENING!!

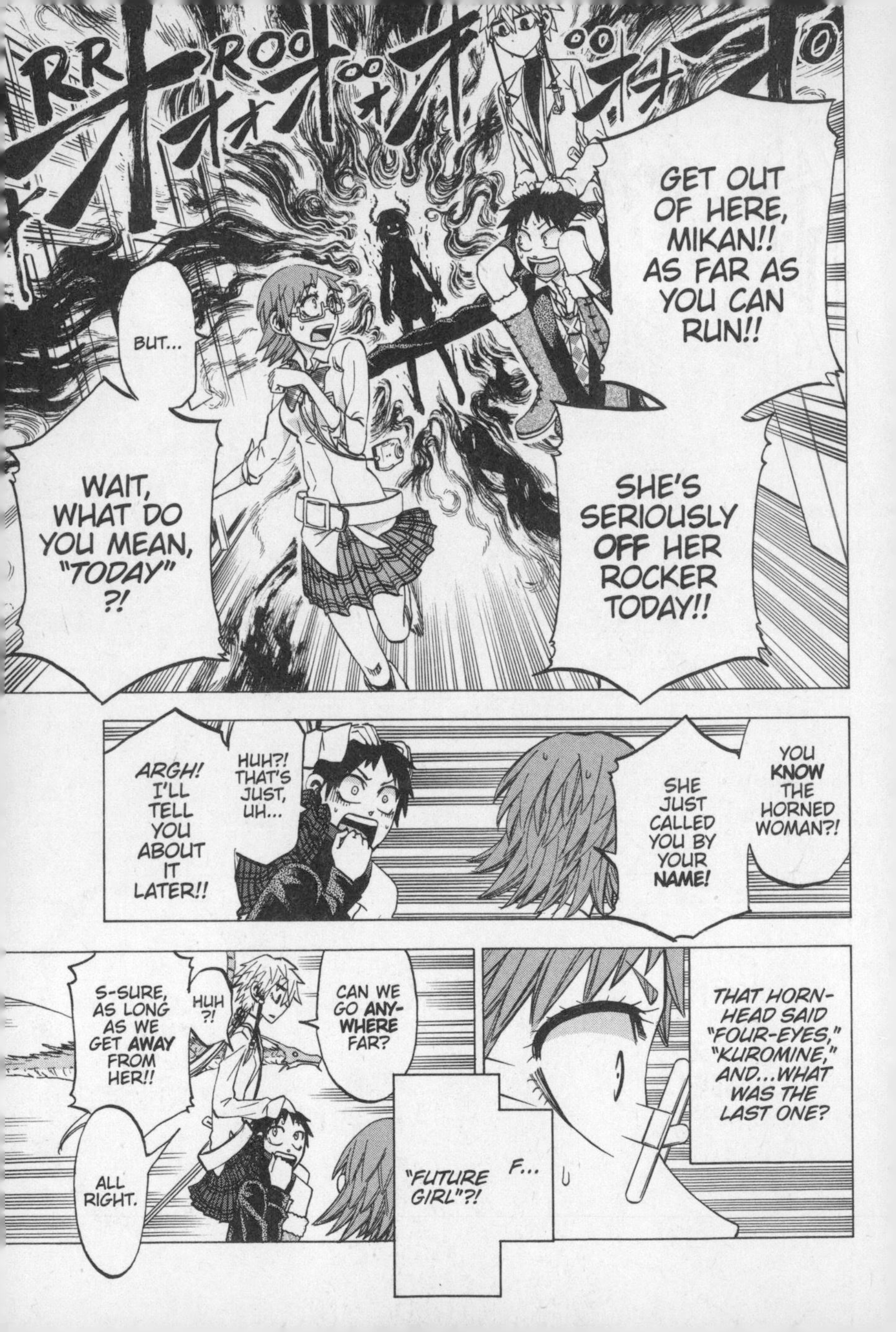
RR ROO OO OO O
GET OUT OF HERE, MIKAN!! AS FAR AS YOU CAN RUN!!
BUT...
SHE'S SERIOUSLY OFF HER ROCKER TODAY!!
WAIT, WHAT DO YOU MEAN, "TODAY"?!
YOU KNOW THE HORNED WOMAN?!
SHE JUST CALLED YOU BY YOUR NAME!
HUH?! THAT'S JUST, UH...
ARGH! I'LL TELL YOU ABOUT IT LATER!!
THAT HORN-HEAD SAID "FOUR-EYES," "KUROMINE," AND...WHAT WAS THE LAST ONE?
F...
"FUTURE GIRL"?!
CAN WE GO ANYWHERE FAR?
HUH?!
S-SURE, AS LONG AS WE GET AWAY FROM HER!!
ALL RIGHT.

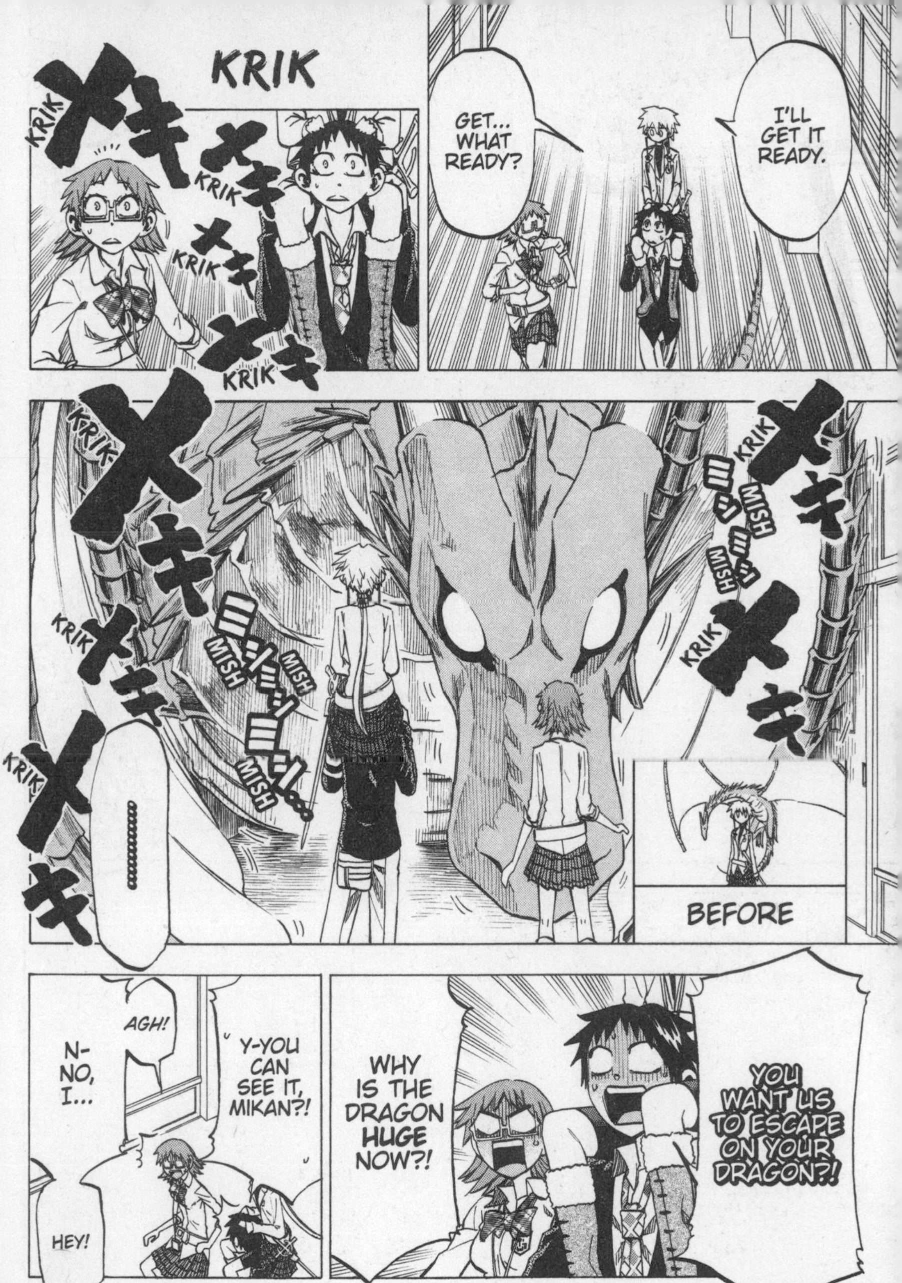
I'LL GET IT READY.
GET... WHAT READY?
KRIK
KRIK
KRIK
KRIK
KRIK
KRIK
MISH
MISH
KRIK
KRIK
MISH
MISH
MISH
KRIK
KRIK
....
BEFORE
YOU WANT US TO ESCAPE ON YOUR DRAGON?!
WHY IS THE DRAGON HUGE NOW?!
Y-YOU CAN SEE IT, MIKAN?!
AGH!
N-NO, I...
HEY!

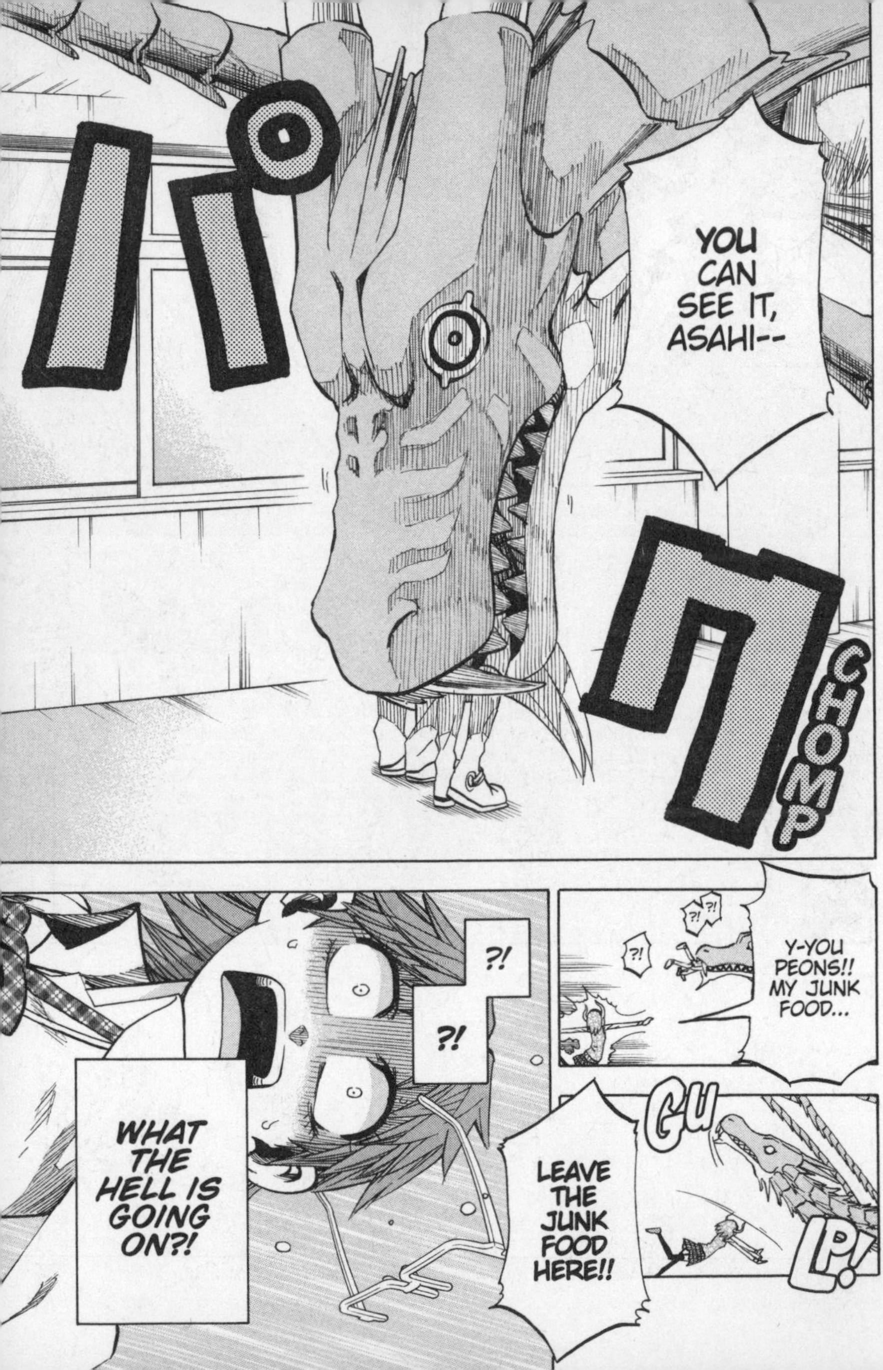
YOU CAN SEE IT, ASAHI--
CHOMP
Y-YOU PEONS!! MY JUNK FOOD...
?!
?!
?!
?!
?!
?!
WHAT THE HELL IS GOING ON?!
GULP!
LEAVE THE JUNK FOOD HERE!!

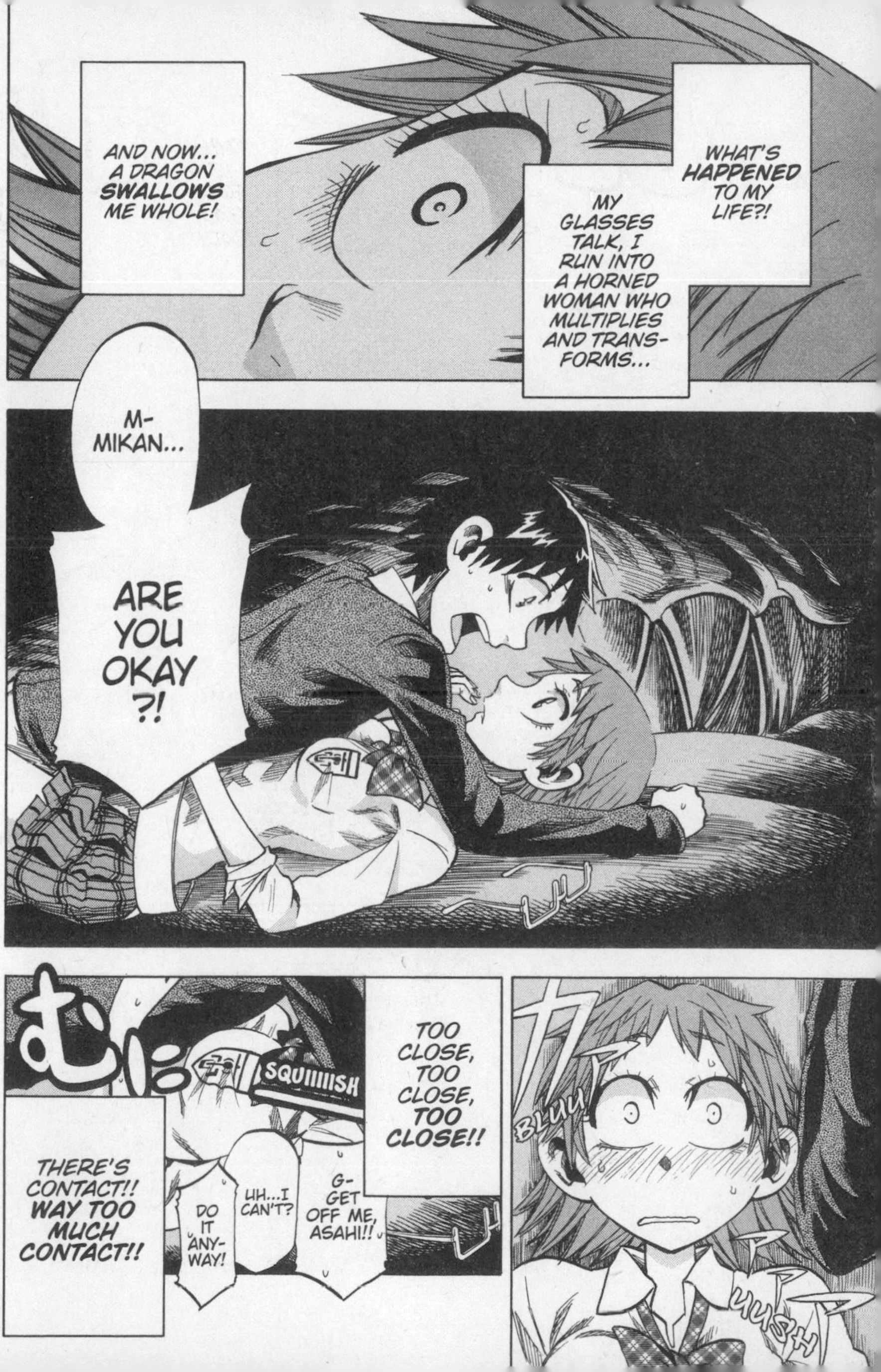
WHAT'S HAPPENED TO MY LIFE?!
MY GLASSES TALK, I RUN INTO A HORNED WOMAN WHO MULTIPLIES AND TRANS-FORMS...
AND NOW... A DRAGON SWALLOWS ME WHOLE!
M-MIKAN...
ARE YOU OKAY?!
BLUU
PUUSH
TOO CLOSE, TOO CLOSE, TOO CLOSE!!
G-GET OFF ME, ASAHI!!
UH...I CAN'T?
DO IT ANY-WAY!
SQUIIIIISH
THERE'S CONTACT!! WAY TOO MUCH CONTACT!!

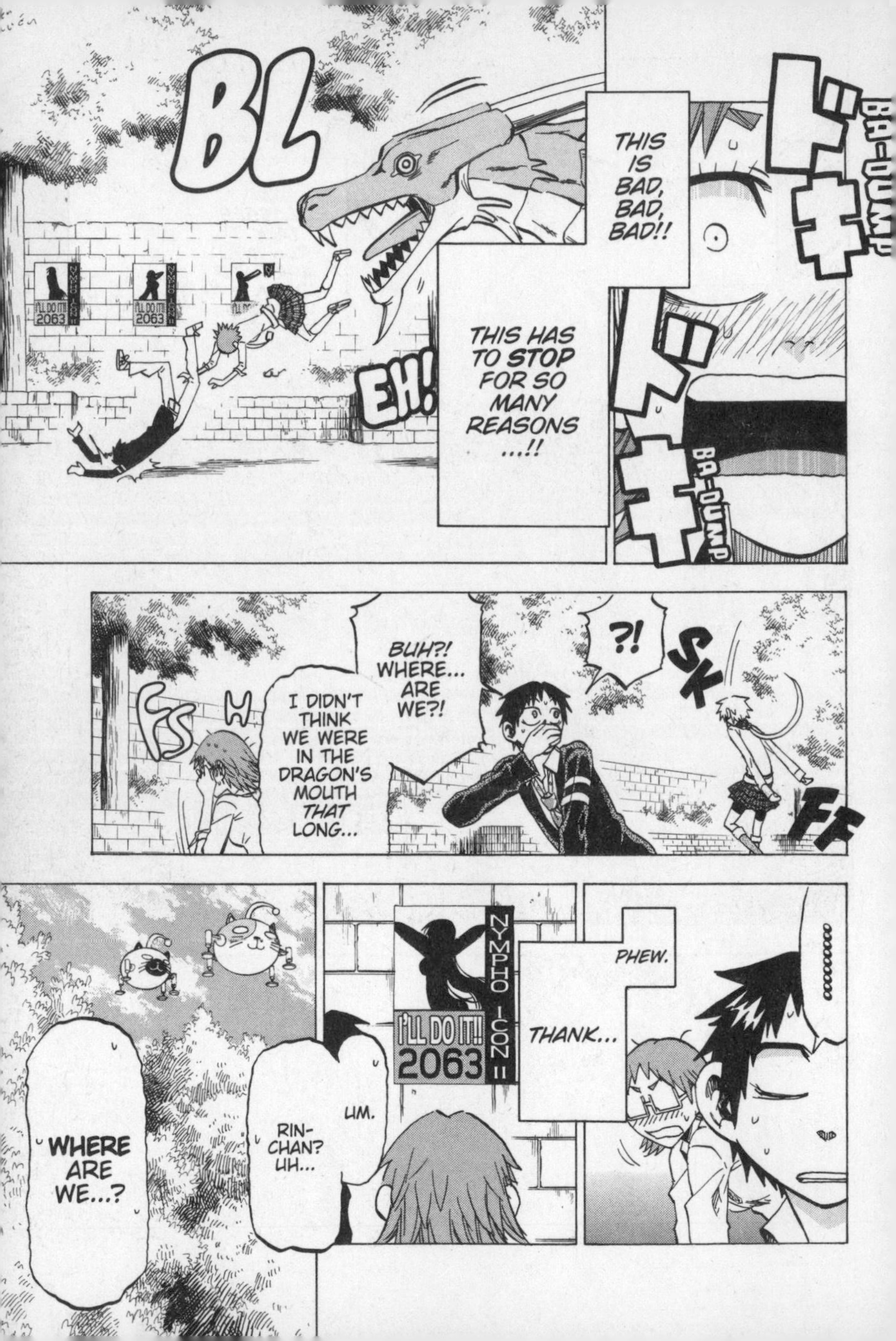

BA-DUMP
THIS IS BAD, BAD, BAD!!
THIS HAS TO STOP FOR SO MANY REASONS ...!!
BA-DUMP
BL
EH!
?!
SK
FF
BUH?! WHERE... ARE WE?!
I DIDN'T THINK WE WERE IN THE DRAGON'S MOUTH THAT LONG...
FSH
......
PHEW.
THANK...
NYMPHO ICON II
I'LL DO IT!! 2063
UM.
RIN-CHAN? UH...
WHERE ARE WE...?

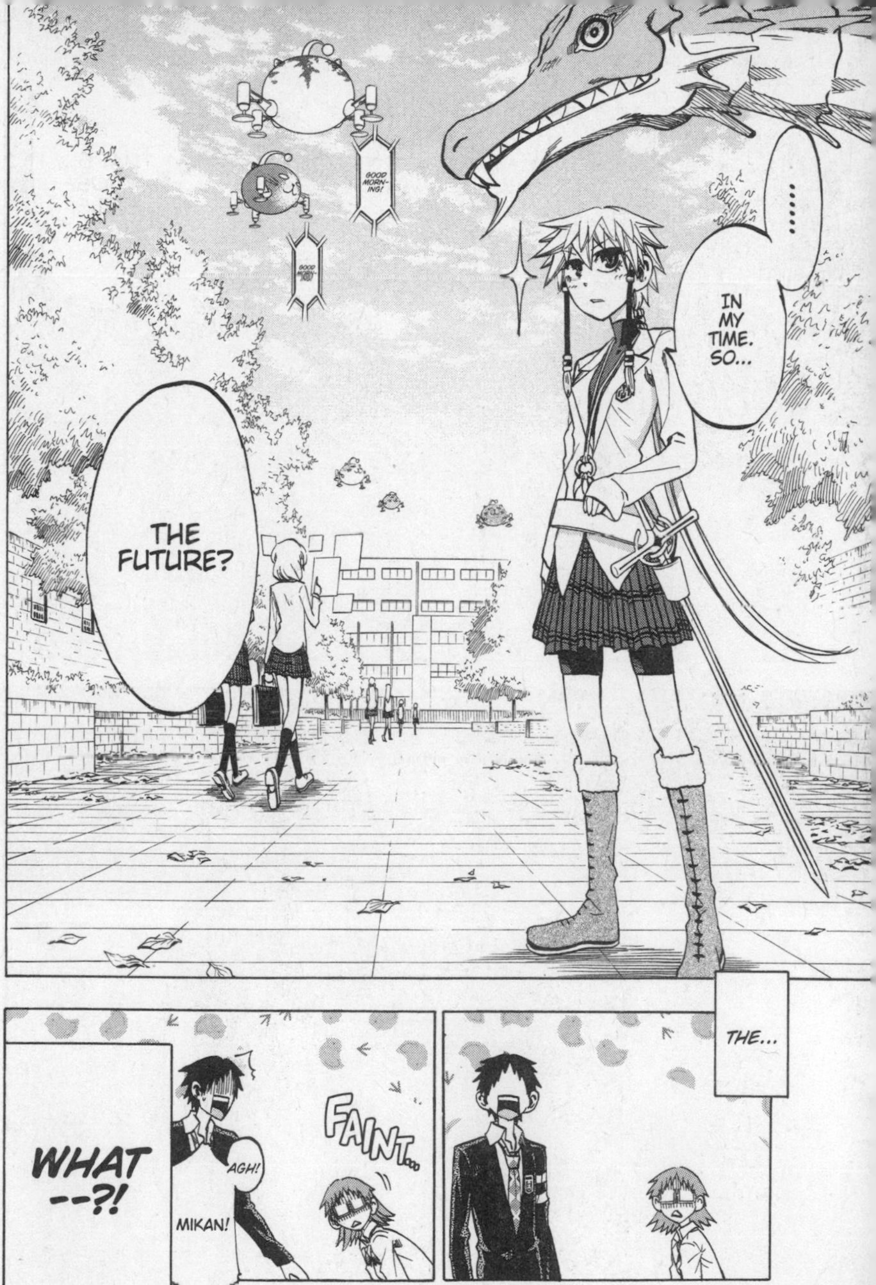
......
IN MY TIME. SO...
GOOD MORN-ING!
THE FUTURE?
THE...
FAINT...
AGH!
MIKAN!
WHAT--?!

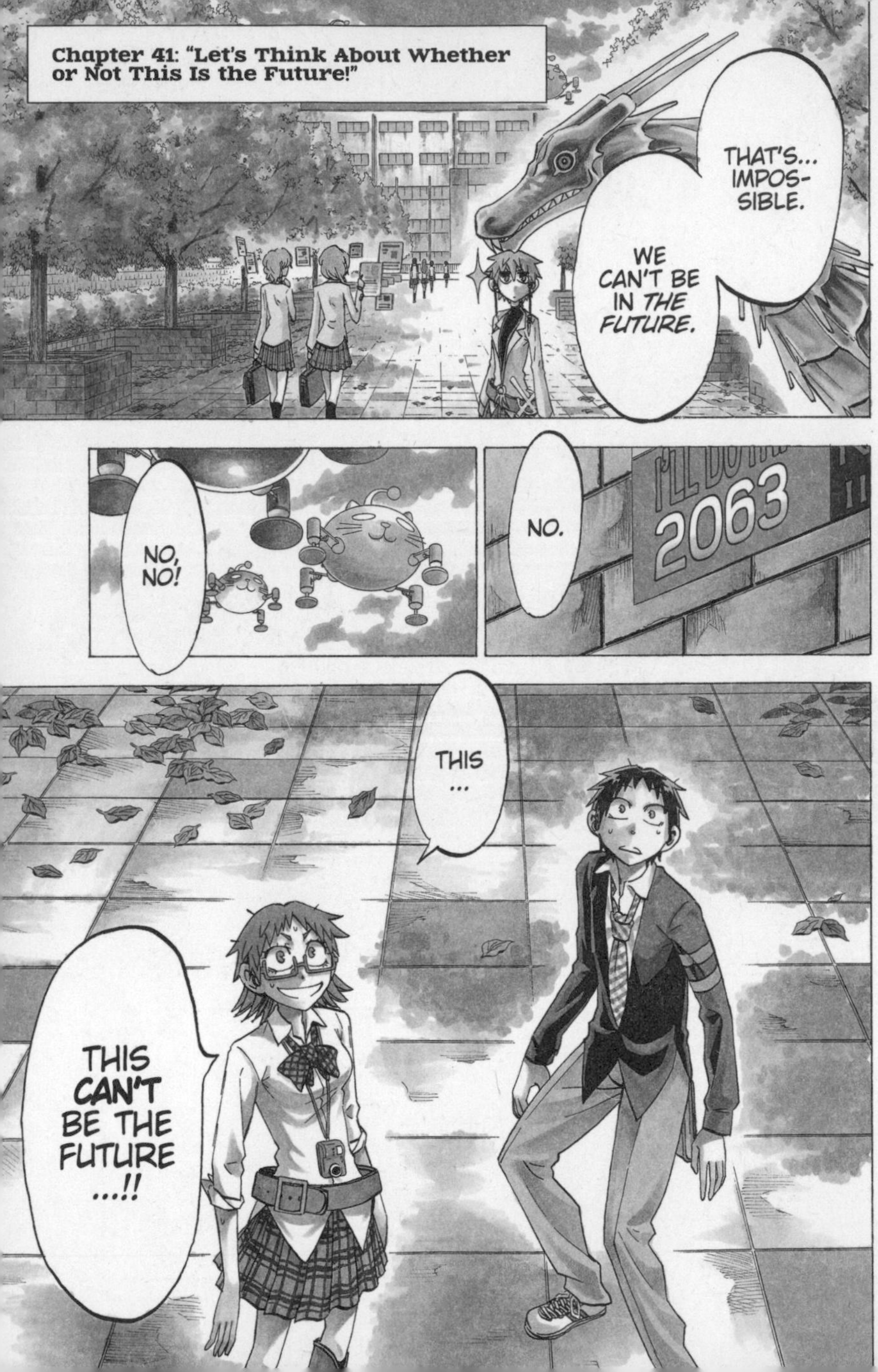
Chapter 41: "Let's Think About Whether or Not This Is the Future!"
THAT'S... IMPOS-SIBLE.
WE CAN'T BE IN *THE FUTURE.*
NO.
2063
NO, NO!
THIS ...
THIS **CAN'T** BE THE FUTURE ...!!

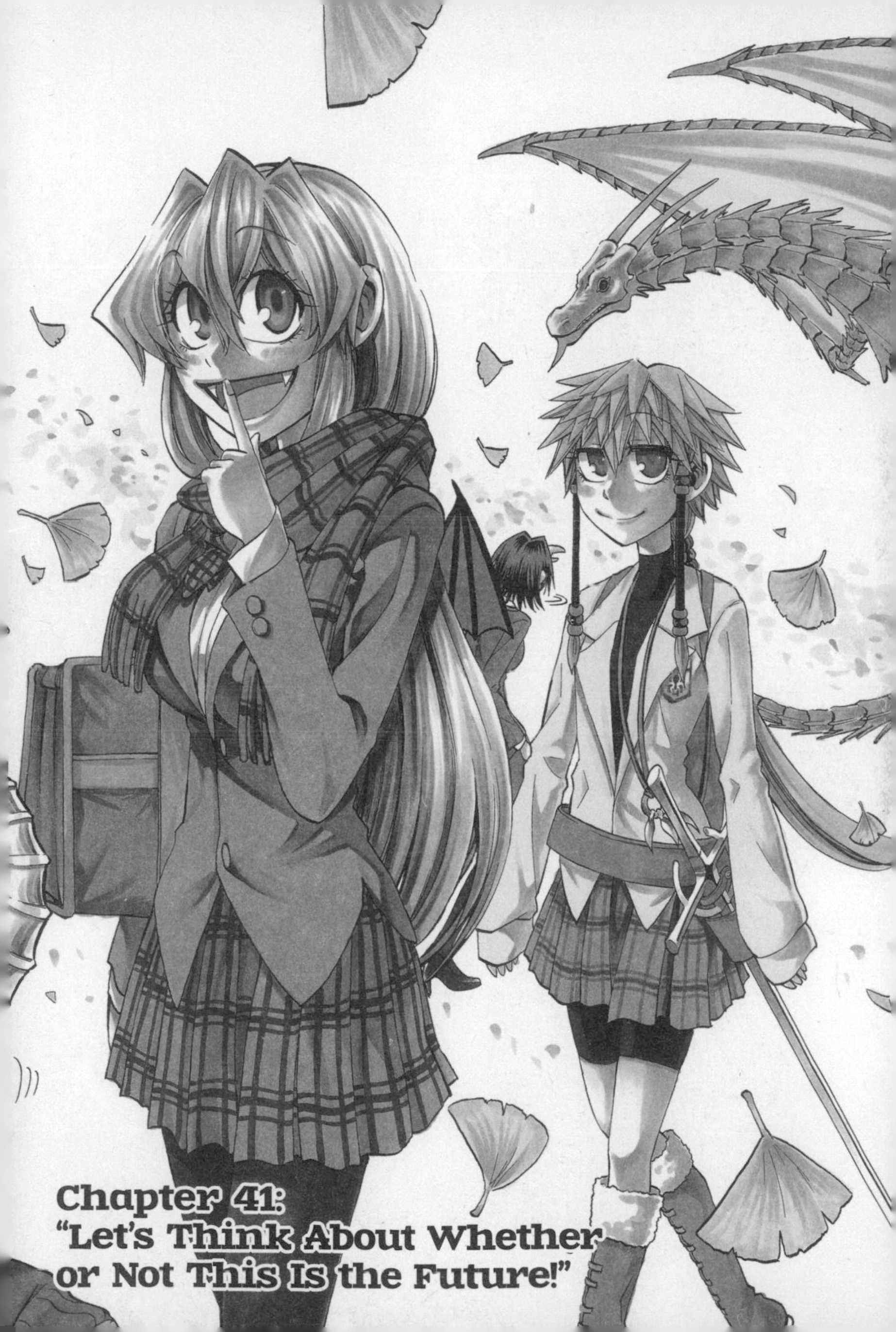
Chapter 41:
"Let's Think About Whether or Not This Is the Future!"

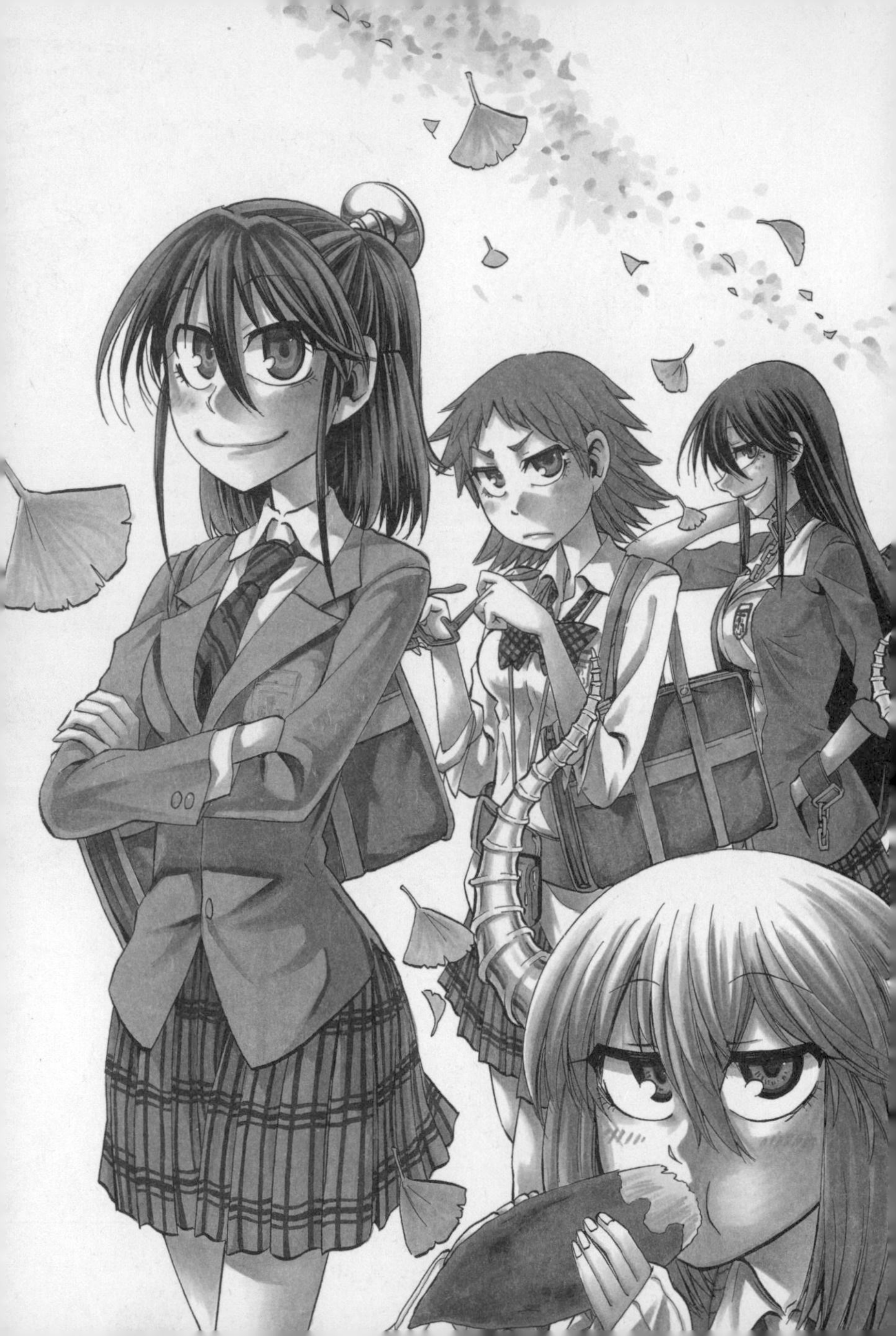

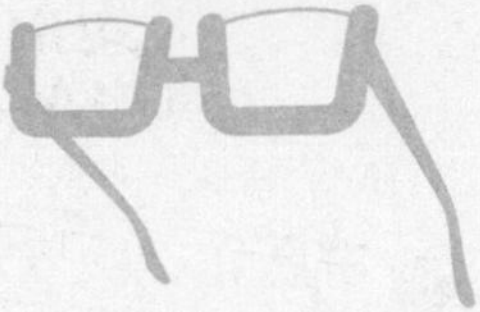

TOP SECRET

My Monster Secret 5

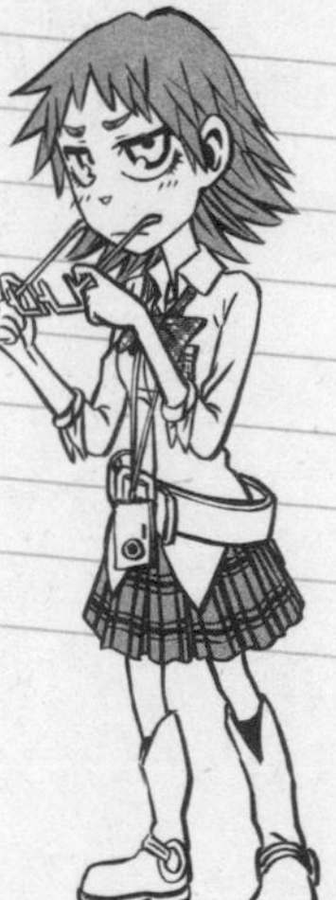

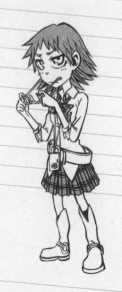

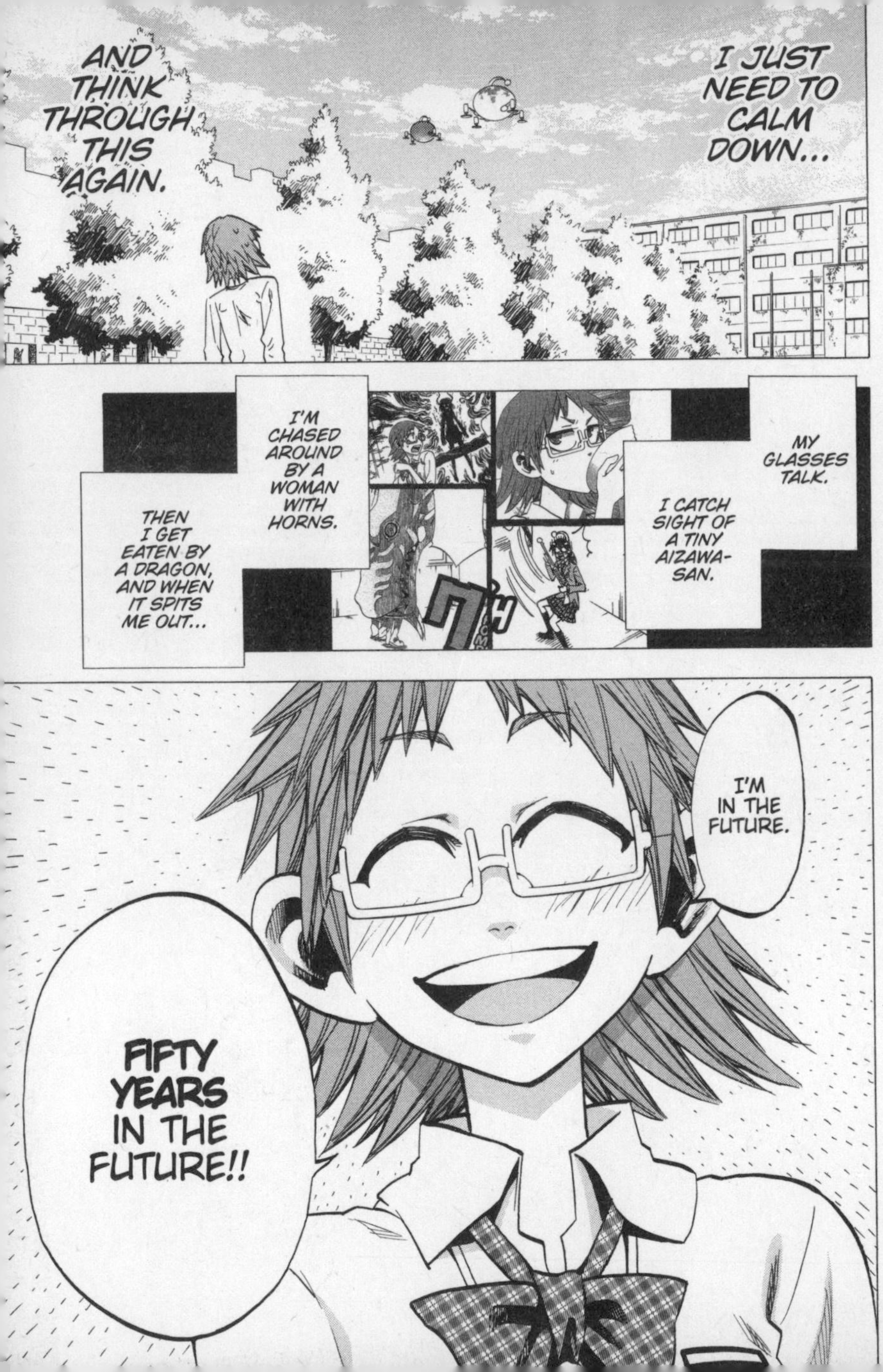
I JUST NEED TO CALM DOWN...
AND THINK THROUGH THIS AGAIN.
MY GLASSES TALK.
I CATCH SIGHT OF A TINY AIZAWA-SAN.
I'M CHASED AROUND BY A WOMAN WITH HORNS.
THEN I GET EATEN BY A DRAGON, AND WHEN IT SPITS ME OUT...
I'M IN THE FUTURE.
FIFTY YEARS IN THE FUTURE!!

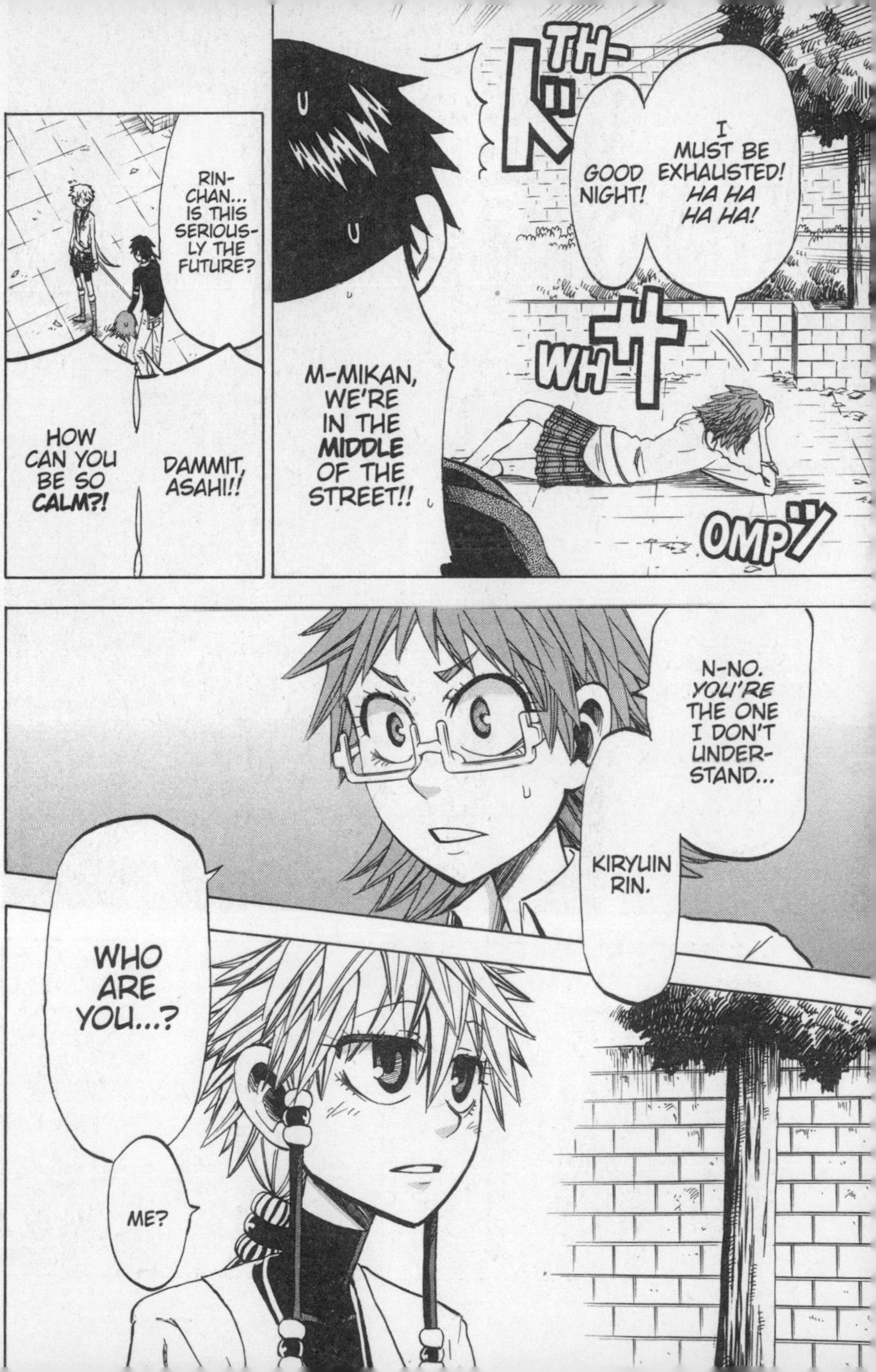
TH-
I MUST BE EXHAUSTED! HA HA HA HA!
GOOD NIGHT!
WH
OMP
M-MIKAN, WE'RE IN THE MIDDLE OF THE STREET!!
RIN-CHAN... IS THIS SERIOUSLY THE FUTURE?
DAMMIT, ASAHI!!
HOW CAN YOU BE SO CALM?!
N-NO. YOU'RE THE ONE I DON'T UNDERSTAND...
KIRYUIN RIN.
WHO ARE YOU...?
ME?

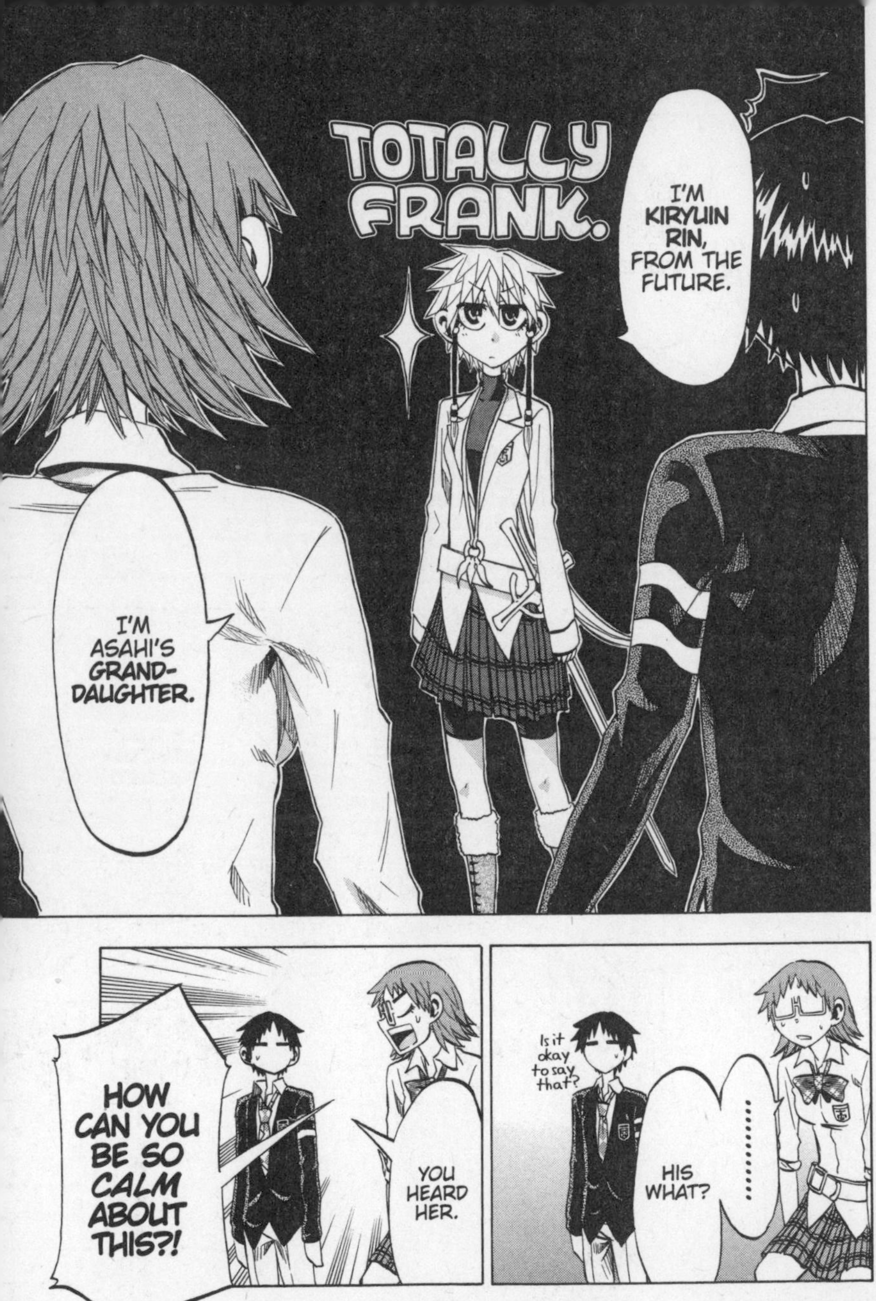
I'M KIRYUIN RIN, FROM THE FUTURE.
TOTALLY FRANK.
I'M ASAHI'S GRAND-DAUGHTER.
......
HIS WHAT?
Is it okay to say that?
YOU HEARD HER.
HOW CAN YOU BE SO CALM ABOUT THIS?!

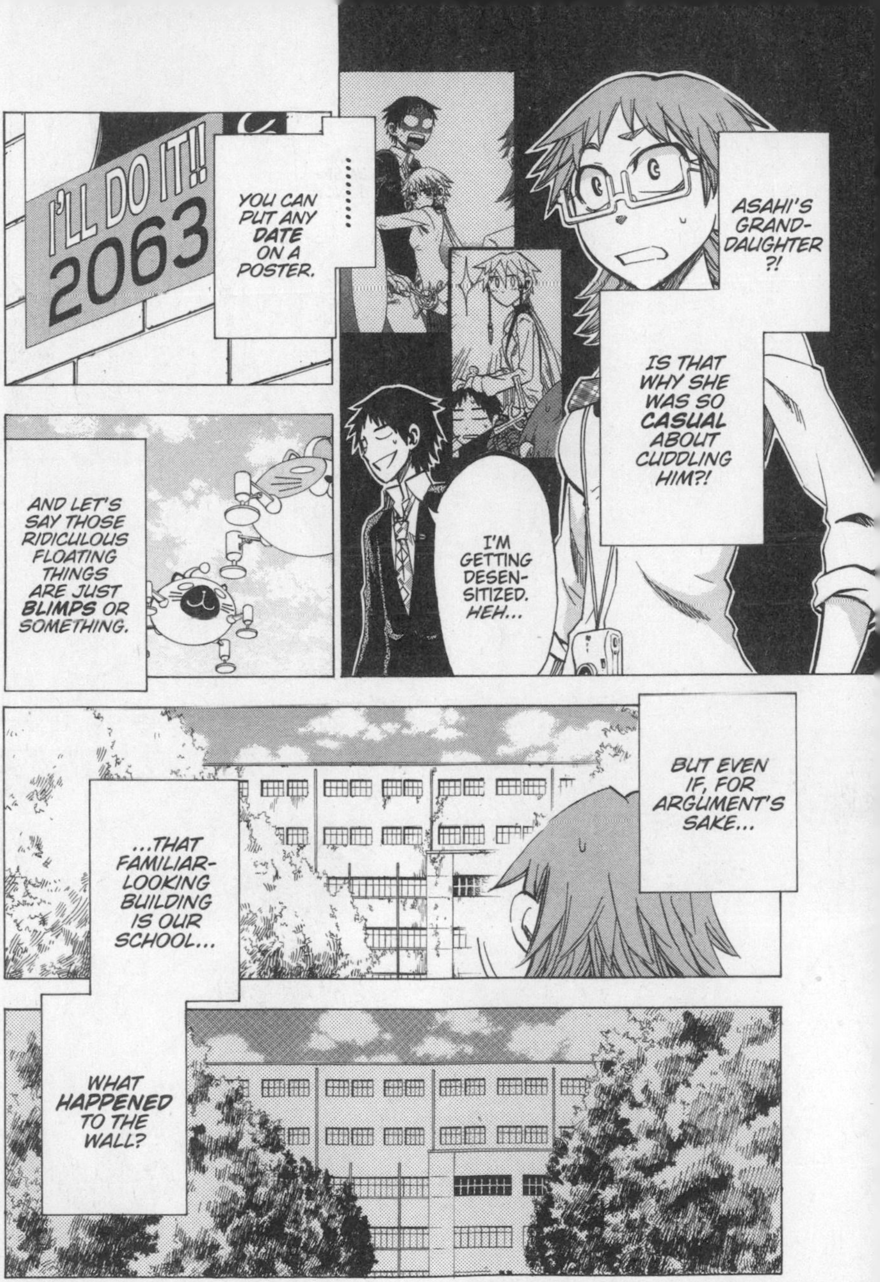

ASAHI'S GRAND-DAUGHTER?!
IS THAT WHY SHE WAS SO CASUAL ABOUT CUDDLING HIM?!
I'M GETTING DESEN-SITIZED. HEH...
I'LL DO IT!! 2063
YOU CAN PUT ANY DATE ON A POSTER.
AND LET'S SAY THOSE RIDICULOUS FLOATING THINGS ARE JUST BLIMPS OR SOMETHING.
BUT EVEN IF, FOR ARGUMENT'S SAKE...
...THAT FAMILIAR-LOOKING BUILDING IS OUR SCHOOL...
WHAT HAPPENED TO THE WALL?

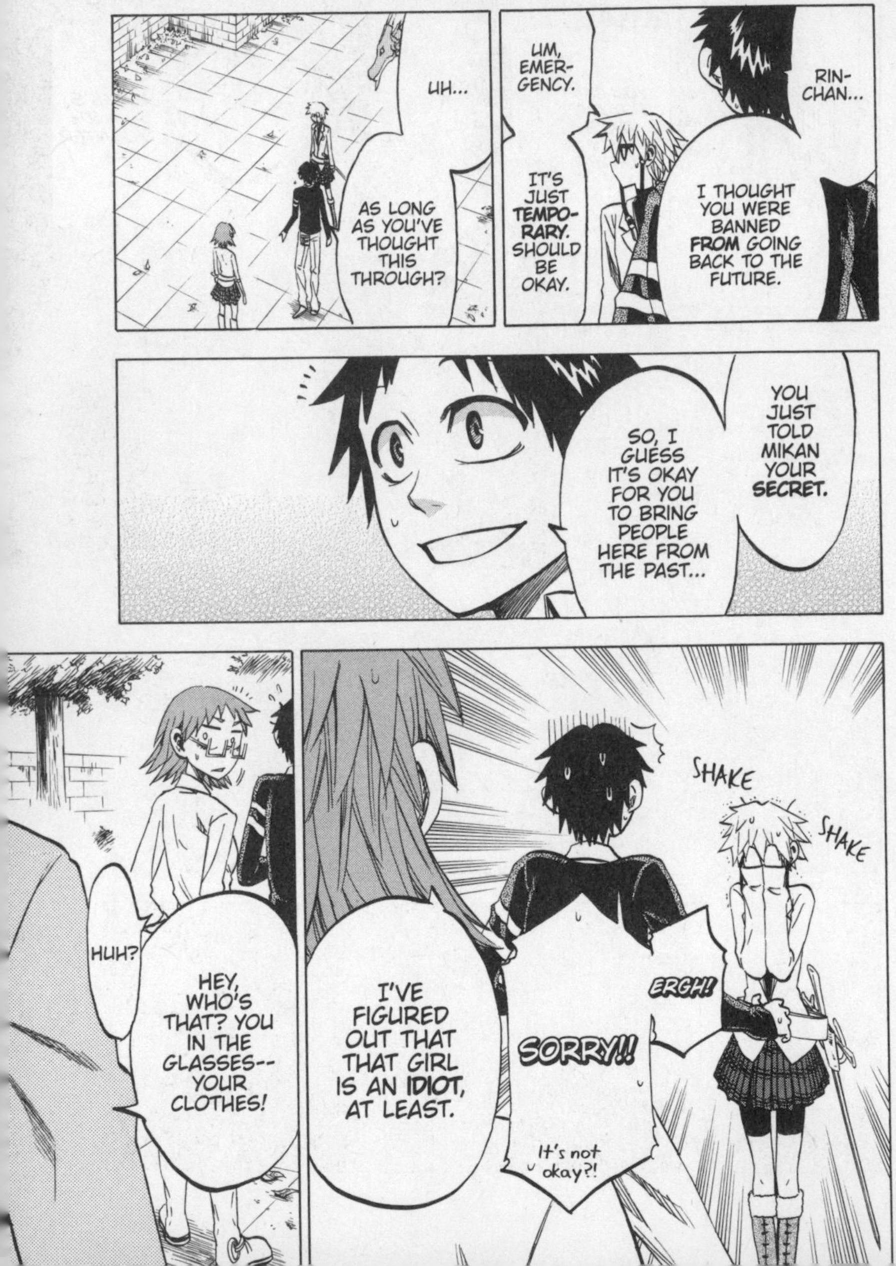
RIN-CHAN...
I THOUGHT YOU WERE BANNED FROM GOING BACK TO THE FUTURE.
UM, EMERGENCY.
IT'S JUST TEMPORARY. SHOULD BE OKAY.
UH...
AS LONG AS YOU'VE THOUGHT THIS THROUGH?
YOU JUST TOLD MIKAN YOUR SECRET.
SO, I GUESS IT'S OKAY FOR YOU TO BRING PEOPLE HERE FROM THE PAST...
SHAKE
SHAKE
ERGH!
SORRY!!
It's not okay?!
I'VE FIGURED OUT THAT THAT GIRL IS AN IDIOT, AT LEAST.
HUH?
HEY, WHO'S THAT? YOU IN THE GLASSES--YOUR CLOTHES!

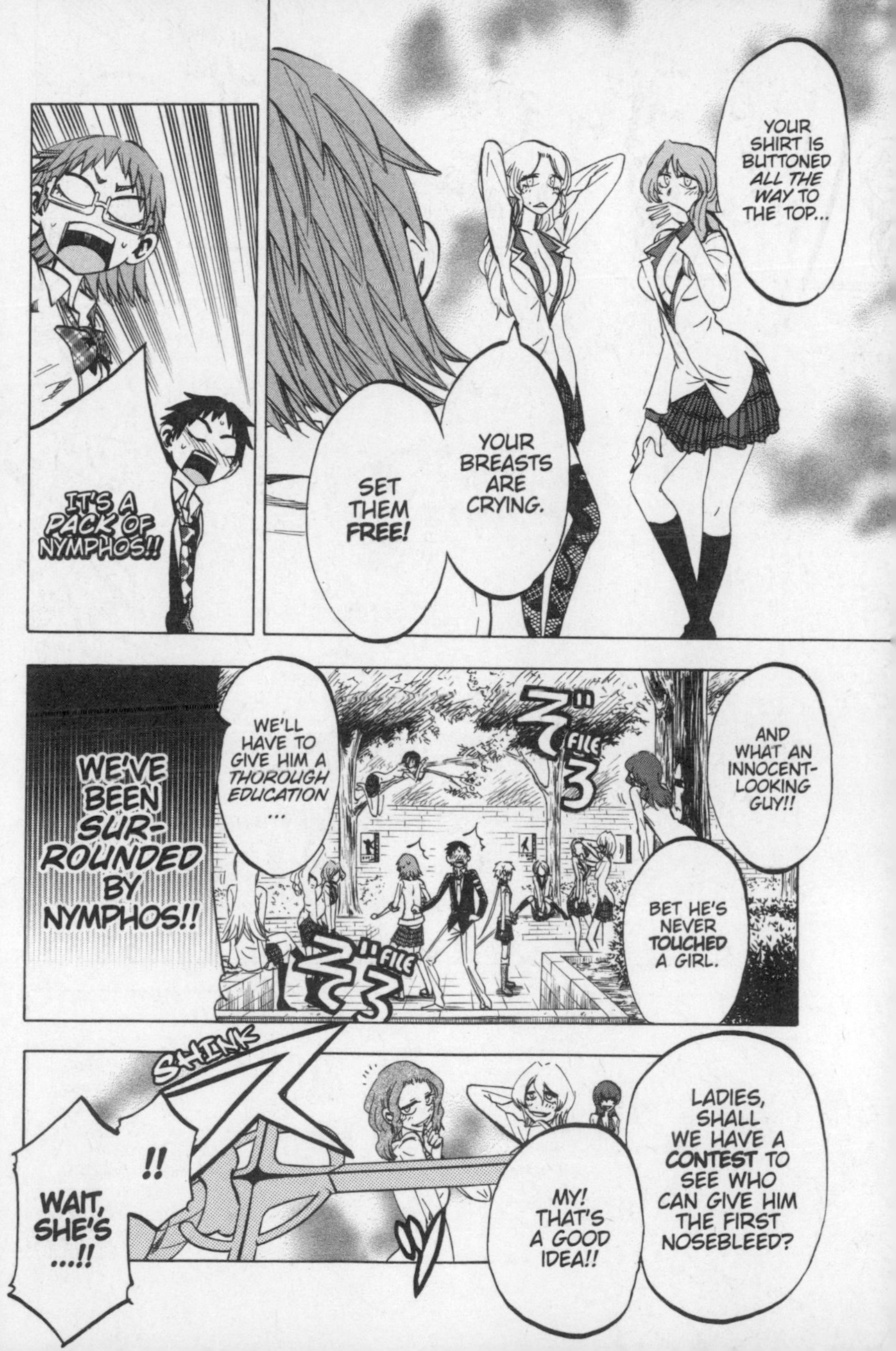
YOUR SHIRT IS BUTTONED *ALL THE WAY* TO THE TOP...
YOUR BREASTS ARE CRYING.
SET THEM **FREE!**
IT'S A *PACK OF* NYMPHOS!!
AND WHAT AN INNOCENT-LOOKING GUY!!
FILE
BET HE'S NEVER **TOUCHED** A GIRL.
WE'LL HAVE TO GIVE HIM A *THOROUGH* EDUCATION ...
FILE
WE'VE BEEN *SUR-ROUNDED* BY NYMPHOS!!
LADIES, SHALL WE HAVE A **CONTEST** TO SEE WHO CAN GIVE HIM THE FIRST NOSEBLEED?
MY! THAT'S A GOOD IDEA!!
SHINK
!!
WAIT, SHE'S ...!!

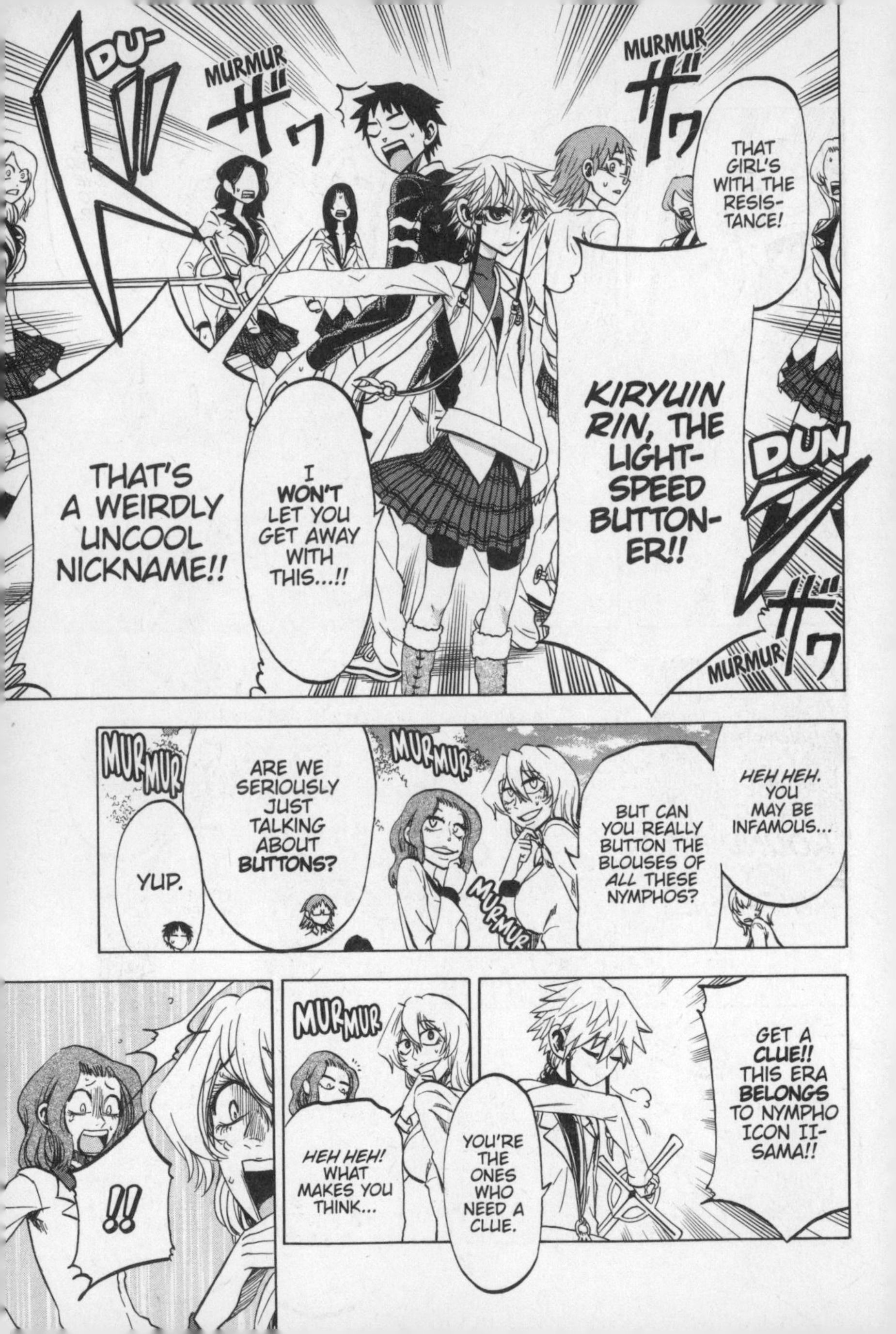
MURMUR ザワ
THAT GIRL'S WITH THE RESISTANCE!
KIRYUIN RIN, THE LIGHT-SPEED BUTTONER!!
DUN
MURMUR ザワ
I WON'T LET YOU GET AWAY WITH THIS...!!
THAT'S A WEIRDLY UNCOOL NICKNAME!!
MURMUR ザワ
DU-
HEH HEH. YOU MAY BE INFAMOUS...
BUT CAN YOU REALLY BUTTON THE BLOUSES OF ALL THESE NYMPHOS?
MURMUR
MURMUR
ARE WE SERIOUSLY JUST TALKING ABOUT BUTTONS?
MURMUR
YUP.
GET A CLUE!! THIS ERA BELONGS TO NYMPHO ICON II-SAMA!!
YOU'RE THE ONES WHO NEED A CLUE.
HEH HEH! WHAT MAKES YOU THINK...
MURMUR
!!

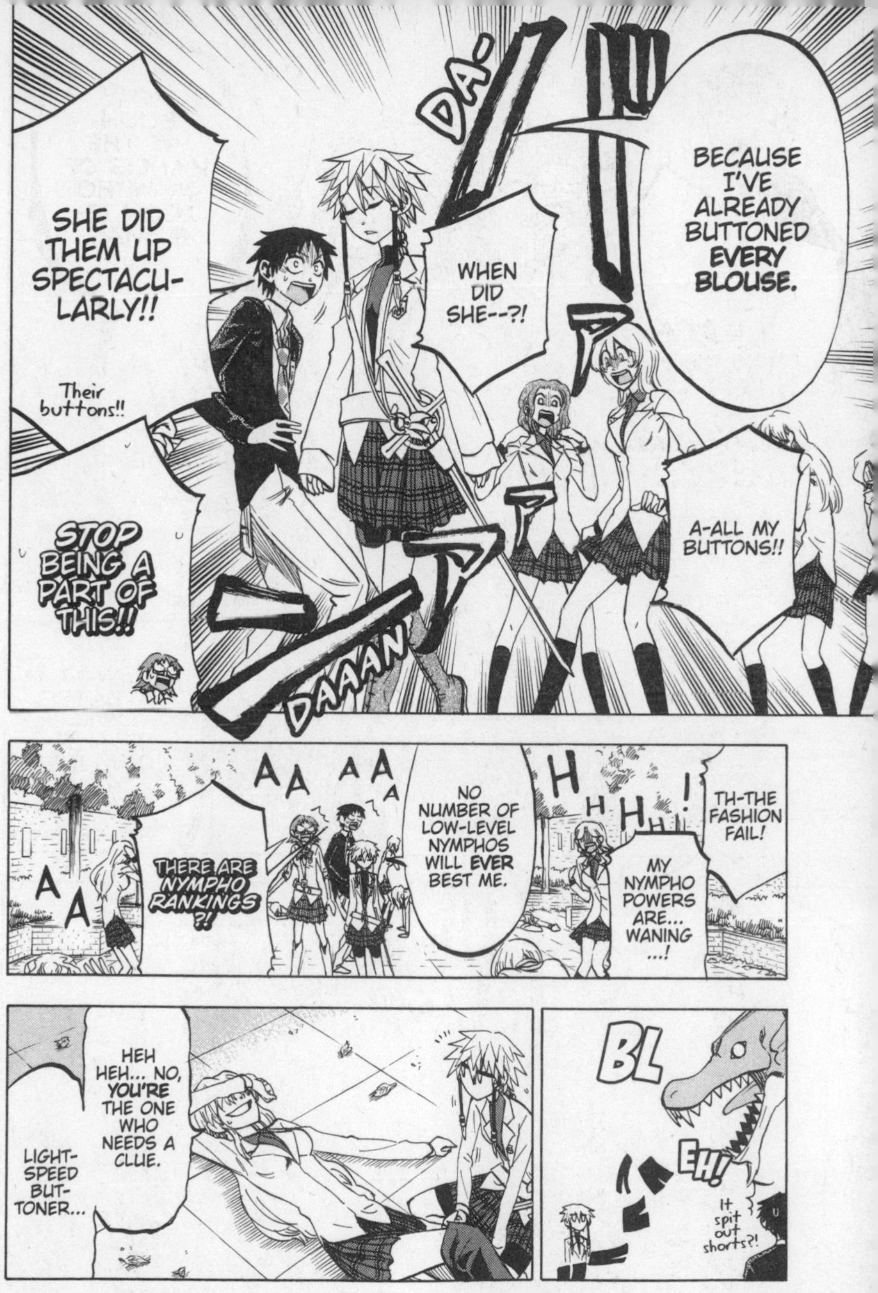
BECAUSE I'VE ALREADY BUTTONED EVERY BLOUSE.
DA-
WHEN DID SHE--?!
SHE DID THEM UP SPECTACU-LARLY!!
Their buttons!!
A-ALL MY BUTTONS!!
STOP BEING A PART OF THIS!!
DAAAAN
TH-THE FASHION FAIL!
HHHHH!
MY NYMPHO POWERS ARE... WANING ...!
NO NUMBER OF LOW-LEVEL NYMPHOS WILL EVER BEST ME.
AAAAA
THERE ARE NYMPHO RANKINGS ?!
AA
BL
EH!
It spit out shorts?!
HEH HEH... NO, YOU'RE THE ONE WHO NEEDS A CLUE.
LIGHT-SPEED BUT-TONER...

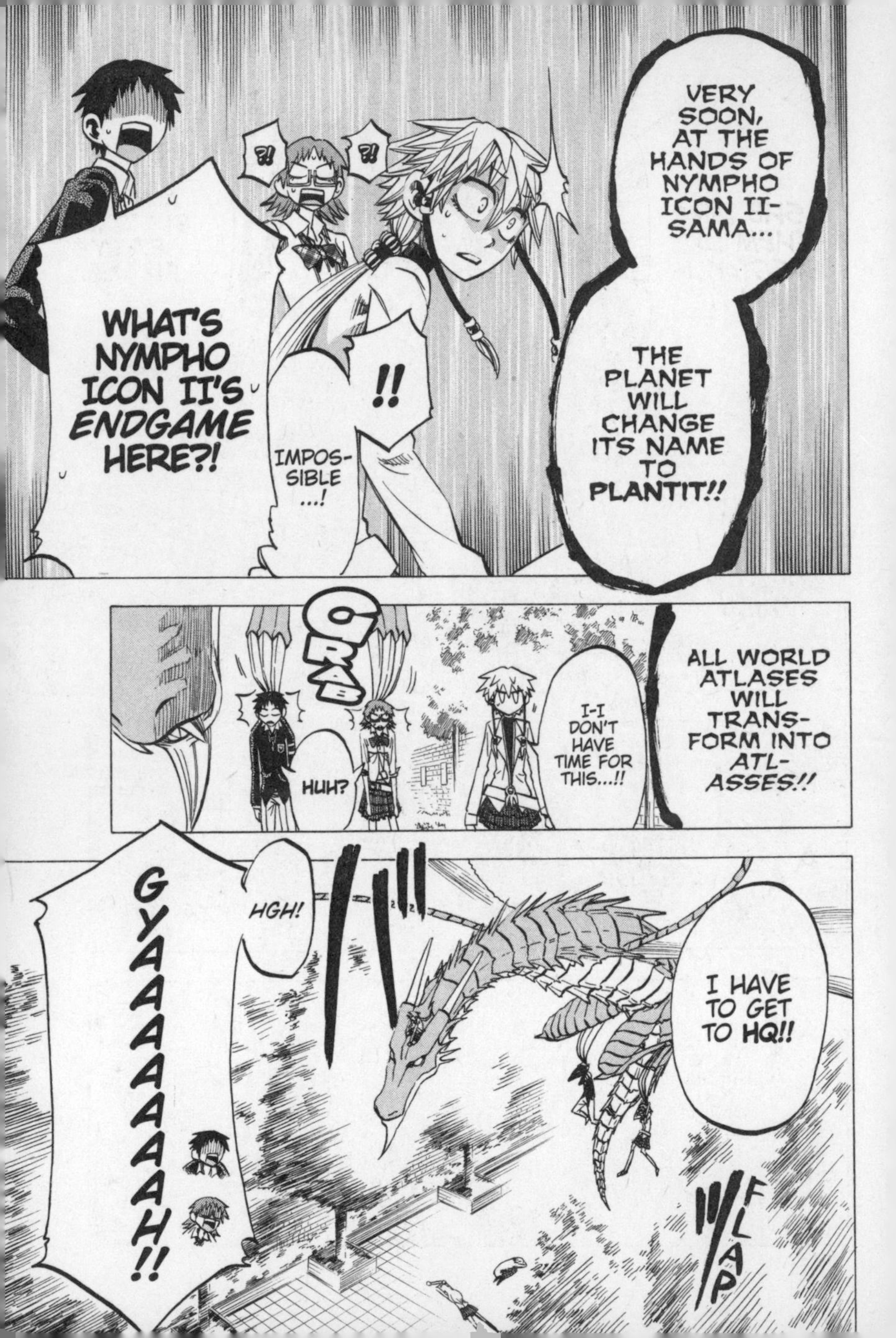
VERY SOON, AT THE HANDS OF NYMPHO ICON II-SAMA...
THE PLANET WILL CHANGE ITS NAME TO PLANTIT!!
!!
IMPOSSIBLE...!
?!
?!
WHAT'S NYMPHO ICON II'S ENDGAME HERE?!
ALL WORLD ATLASES WILL TRANSFORM INTO ATL-ASSES!!
I-I DON'T HAVE TIME FOR THIS...!!
GRAB
HUH?
I HAVE TO GET TO HQ!!
FLAP
HGH!
GYAAAAAAAH!!

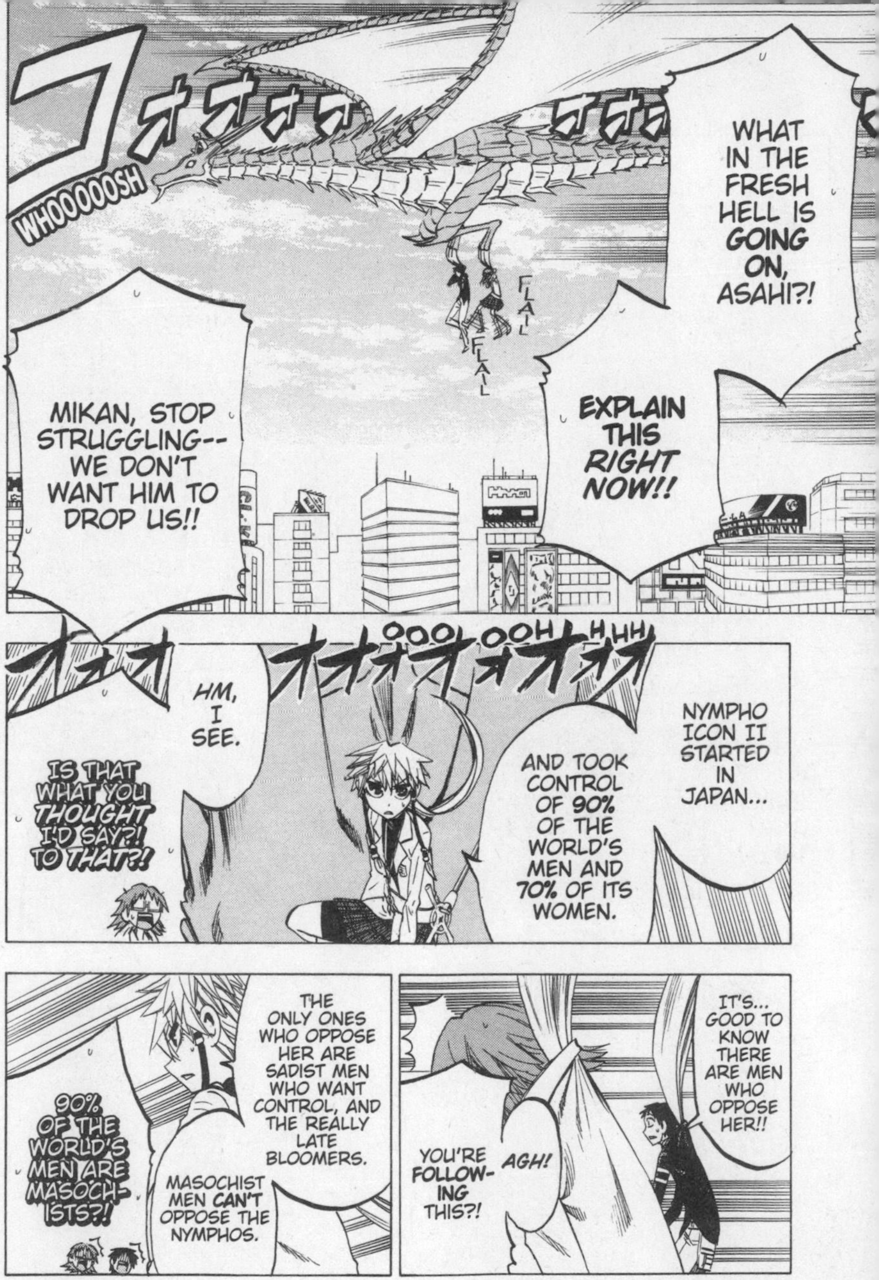
WHAT IN THE FRESH HELL IS GOING ON, ASAHI?!
EXPLAIN THIS RIGHT NOW!!
WHOOOOOSH
FLAIL FLAIL
MIKAN, STOP STRUGGLING-- WE DON'T WANT HIM TO DROP US!!
OOOOOOHHHHH
NYMPHO ICON II STARTED IN JAPAN...
AND TOOK CONTROL OF 90% OF THE WORLD'S MEN AND 70% OF ITS WOMEN.
HM, I SEE.
IS THAT WHAT YOU THOUGHT I'D SAY?! TO THAT?!
IT'S... GOOD TO KNOW THERE ARE MEN WHO OPPOSE HER!!
AGH!
YOU'RE FOLLOWING THIS?!
THE ONLY ONES WHO OPPOSE HER ARE SADIST MEN WHO WANT CONTROL, AND THE REALLY LATE BLOOMERS.
90% OF THE WORLD'S MEN ARE MASOCHISTS?!
MASOCHIST MEN CAN'T OPPOSE THE NYMPHOS.

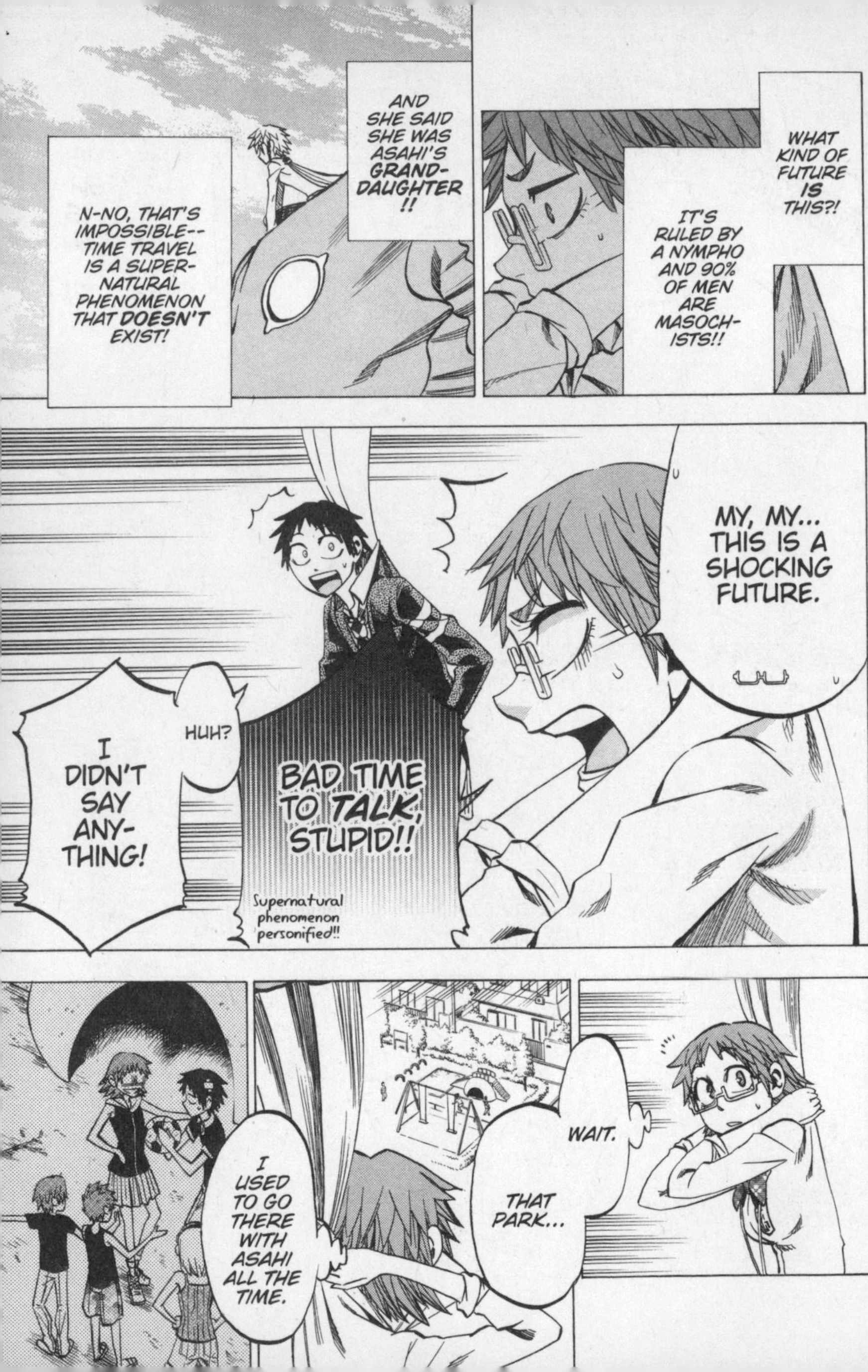
WHAT KIND OF FUTURE IS THIS?!
IT'S RULED BY A NYMPHO AND 90% OF MEN ARE MASOCHISTS!!
AND SHE SAID SHE WAS ASAHI'S GRAND-DAUGHTER!!
N-NO, THAT'S IMPOSSIBLE--TIME TRAVEL IS A SUPER-NATURAL PHENOMENON THAT DOESN'T EXIST!
MY, MY... THIS IS A SHOCKING FUTURE.
BAD TIME TO TALK, STUPID!!
Supernatural phenomenon personified!!
HUH?
I DIDN'T SAY ANY-THING!
WAIT.
THAT PARK...
I USED TO GO THERE WITH ASAHI ALL THE TIME.

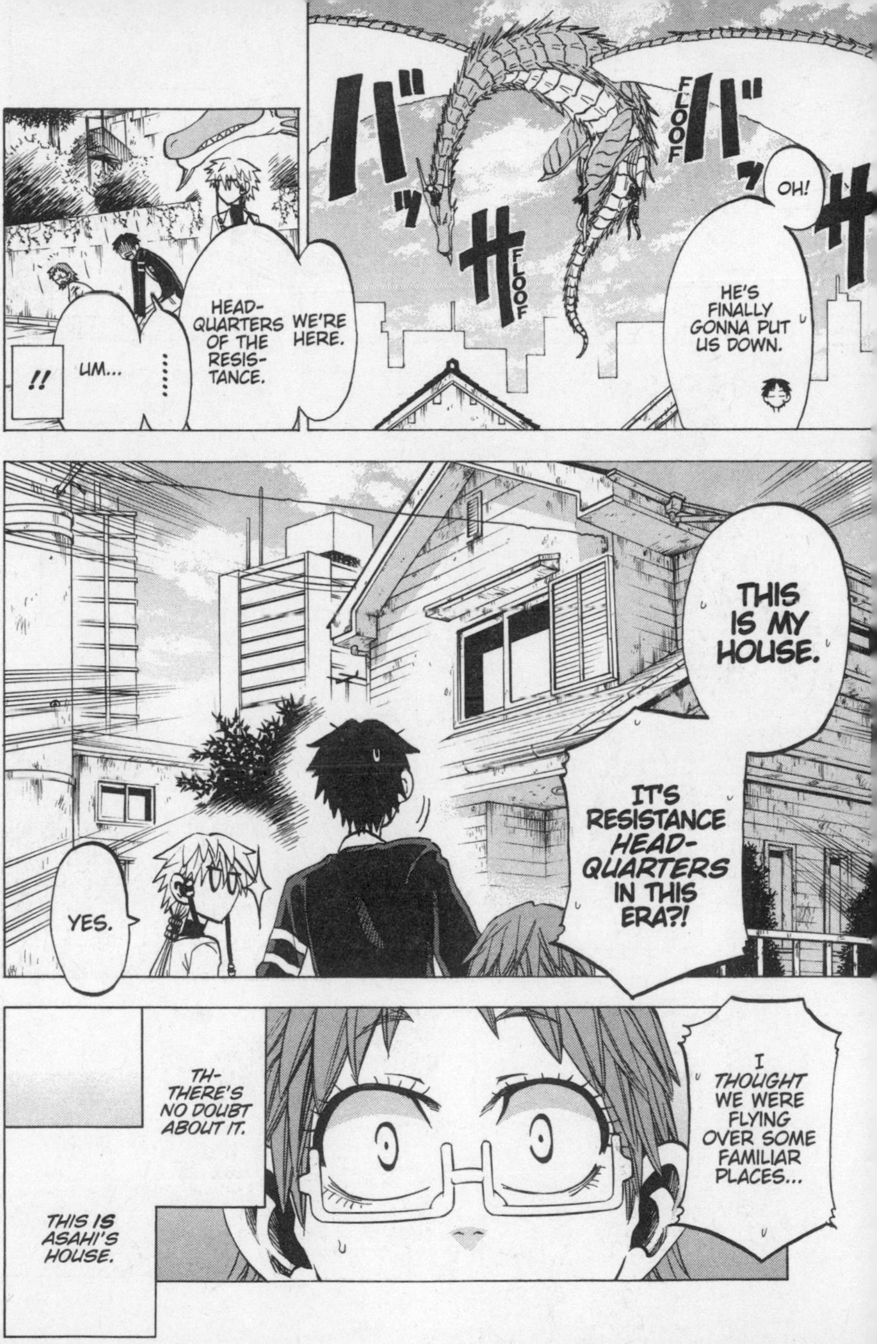

FLOOF
OH!
HE'S FINALLY GONNA PUT US DOWN.
FLOOF
WE'RE HERE.
HEAD-QUARTERS OF THE RESIS-TANCE.
......
UM...
!!
THIS IS MY HOUSE.
IT'S RESISTANCE HEAD-QUARTERS IN THIS ERA?!
YES.
I THOUGHT WE WERE FLYING OVER SOME FAMILIAR PLACES...
TH-THERE'S NO DOUBT ABOUT IT.
THIS IS ASAHI'S HOUSE.

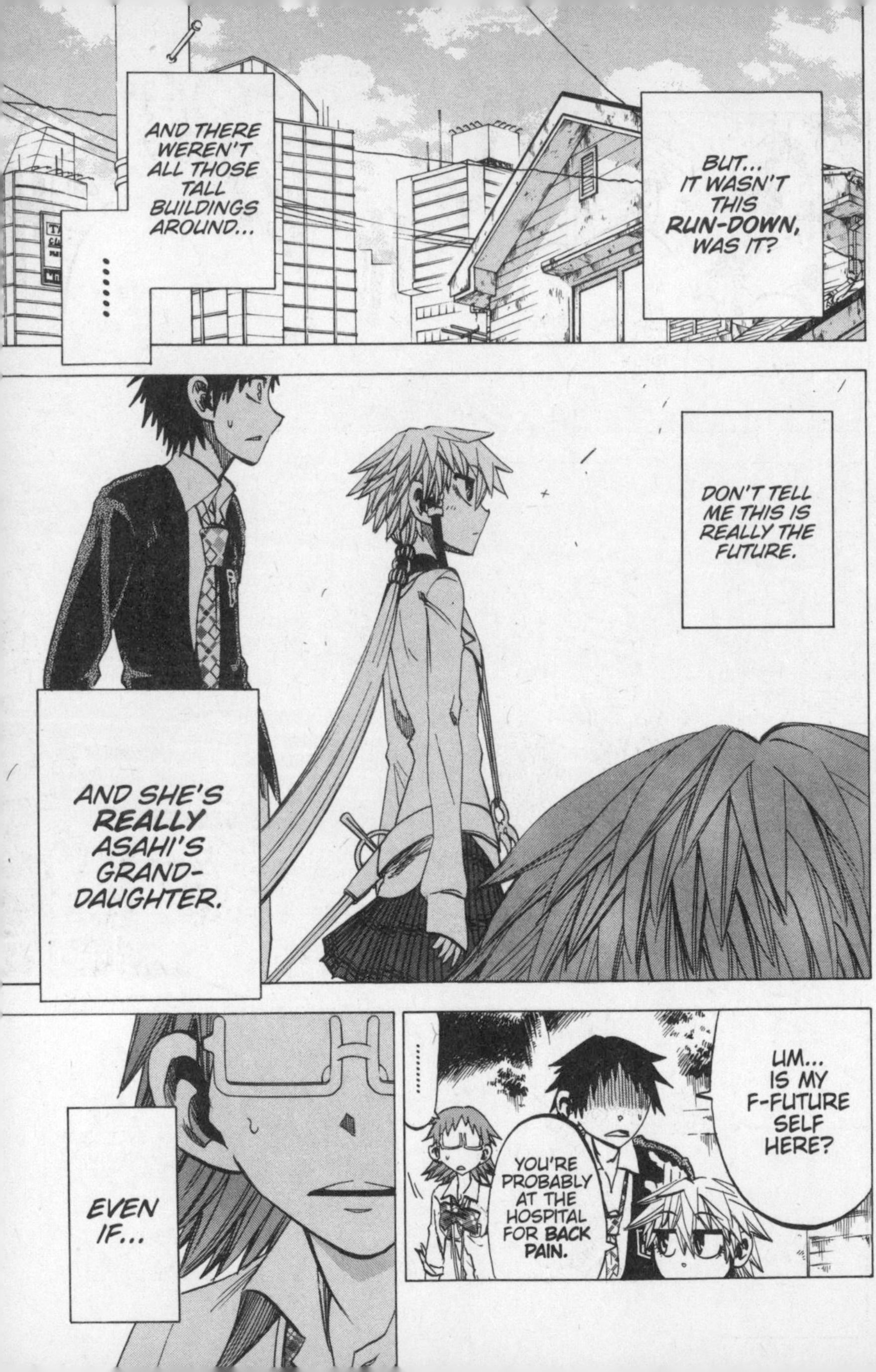
BUT... IT WASN'T THIS RUN-DOWN, WAS IT?
AND THERE WEREN'T ALL THOSE TALL BUILDINGS AROUND...
......
DON'T TELL ME THIS IS REALLY THE FUTURE.
AND SHE'S REALLY ASAHI'S GRAND-DAUGHTER.
UM... IS MY F-FUTURE SELF HERE?
YOU'RE PROBABLY AT THE HOSPITAL FOR BACK PAIN.
......
EVEN IF...

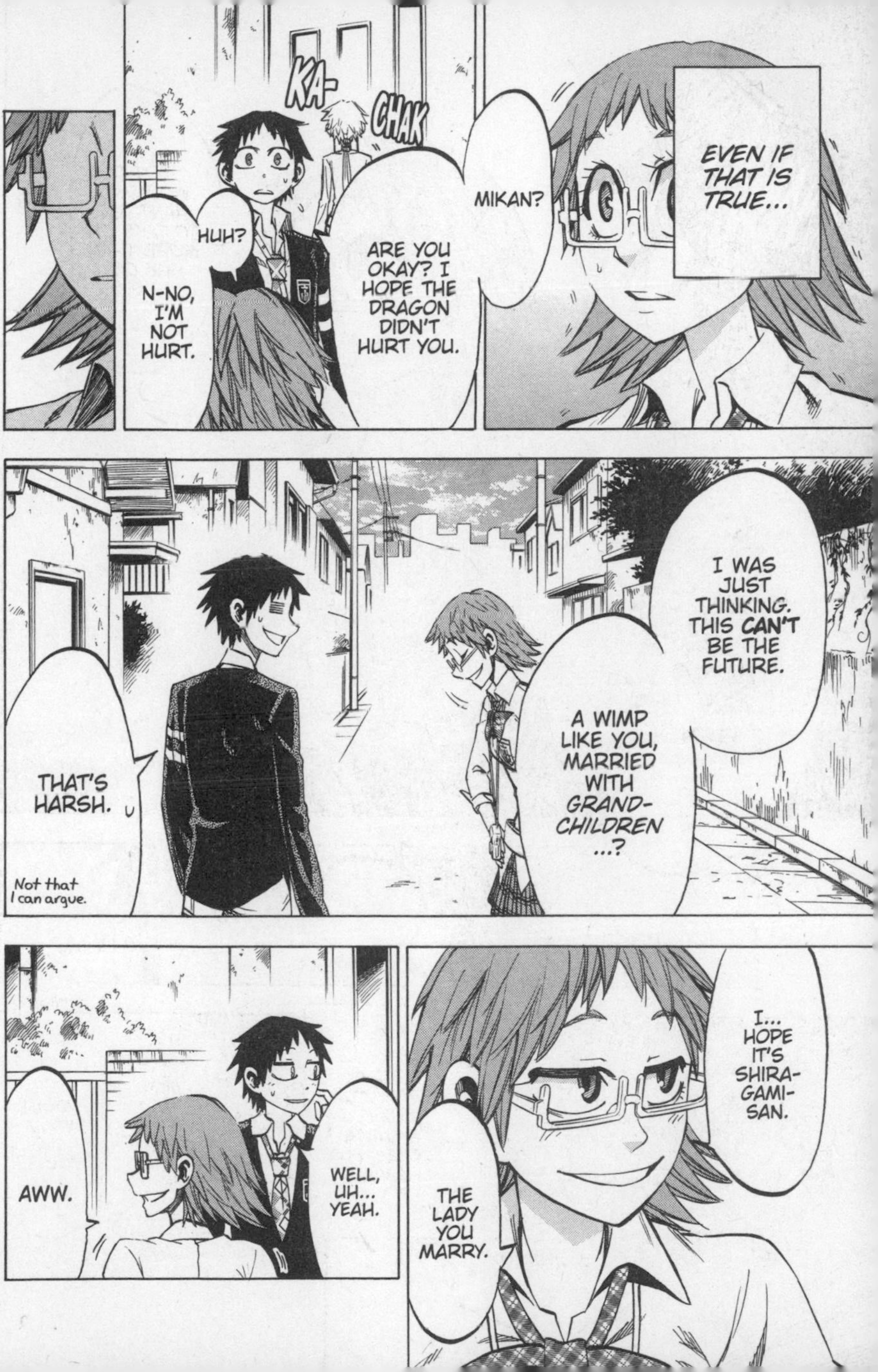
EVEN IF THAT IS TRUE...
MIKAN?
KA-CHAK
ARE YOU OKAY? I HOPE THE DRAGON DIDN'T HURT YOU.
HUH?
N-NO, I'M NOT HURT.
I WAS JUST THINKING. THIS CAN'T BE THE FUTURE.
A WIMP LIKE YOU, MARRIED WITH GRAND-CHILDREN ...?
THAT'S HARSH.
Not that I can argue.
I... HOPE IT'S SHIRA-GAMI-SAN.
THE LADY YOU MARRY.
WELL, UH... YEAH.
AWW.

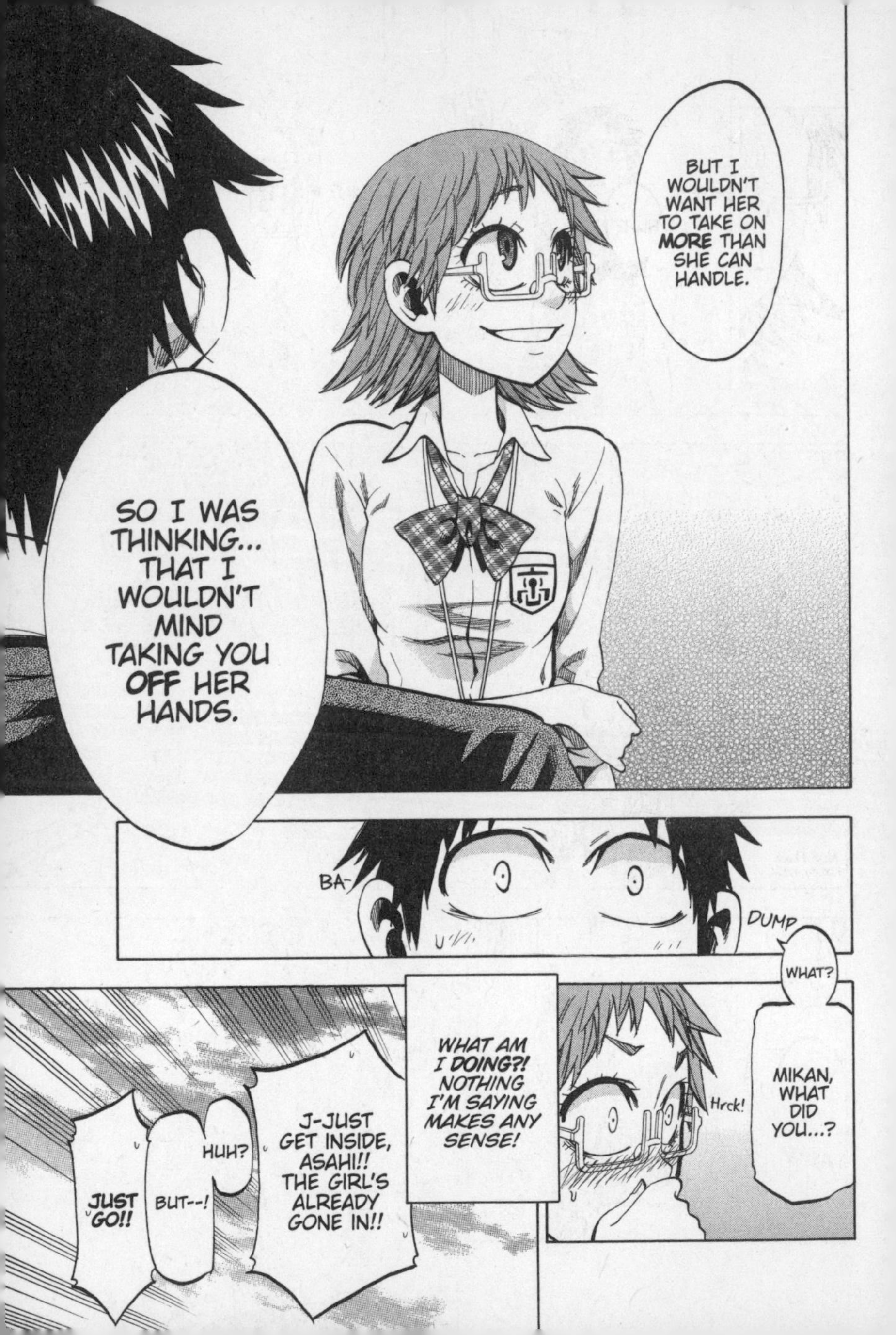

BUT I WOULDN'T WANT HER TO TAKE ON **MORE** THAN SHE CAN HANDLE.
SO I WAS THINKING... THAT I WOULDN'T MIND TAKING YOU **OFF** HER HANDS.
BA-
DUMP
WHAT?
MIKAN, WHAT DID YOU...?
Hrck!
*WHAT AM I **DOING**?! NOTHING I'M SAYING MAKES ANY SENSE!*
J-JUST GET INSIDE, ASAHI!! THE GIRL'S ALREADY GONE IN!!
HUH?
BUT--!
JUST GO!!

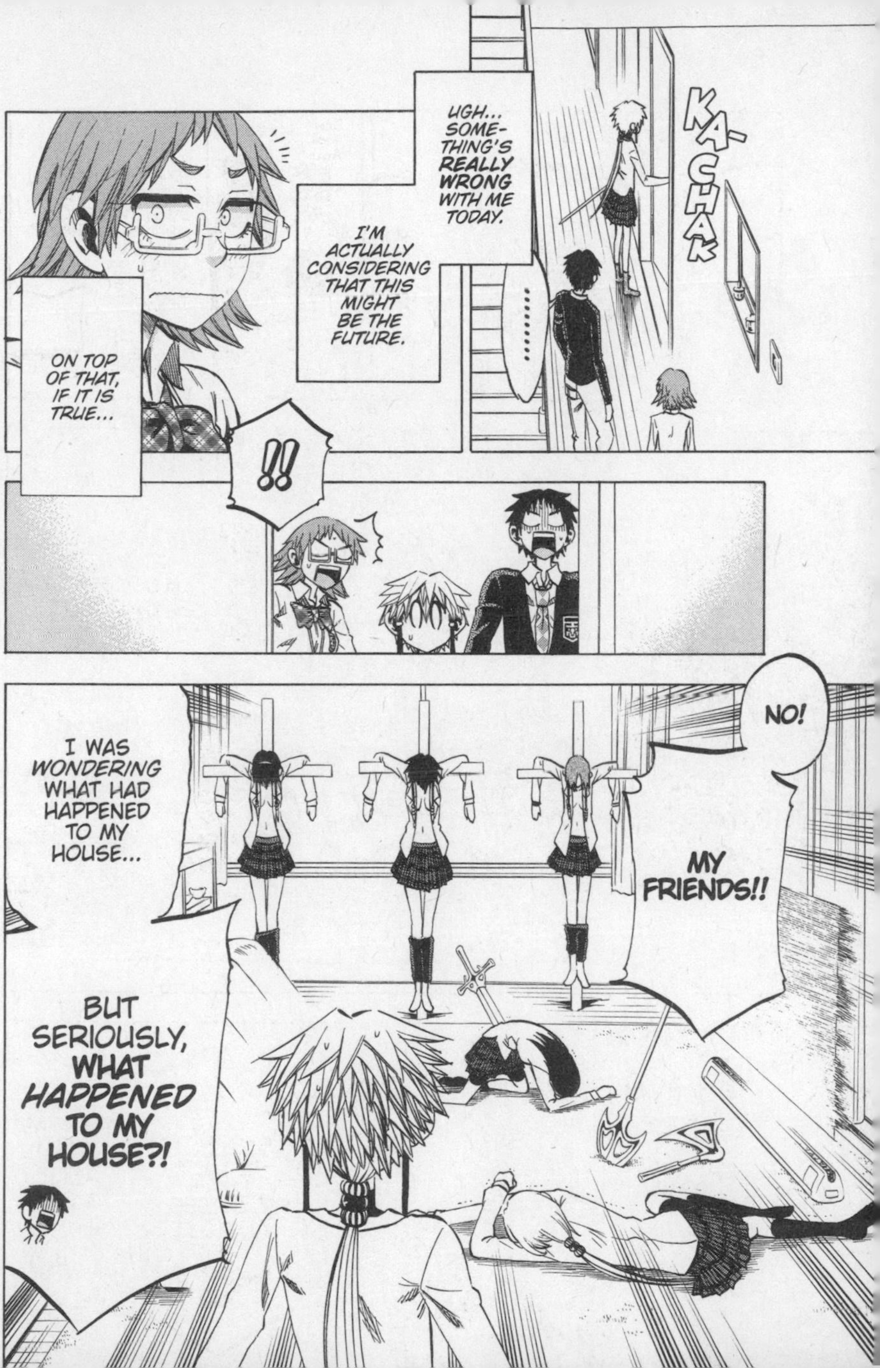
KA-CHAK
UGH... SOME-THING'S REALLY WRONG WITH ME TODAY.
I'M ACTUALLY CONSIDERING THAT THIS MIGHT BE THE FUTURE.
......
ON TOP OF THAT, IF IT IS TRUE...
!!
NO!
MY FRIENDS!!
I WAS WONDERING WHAT HAD HAPPENED TO MY HOUSE...
BUT SERIOUSLY, WHAT HAPPENED TO MY HOUSE?!

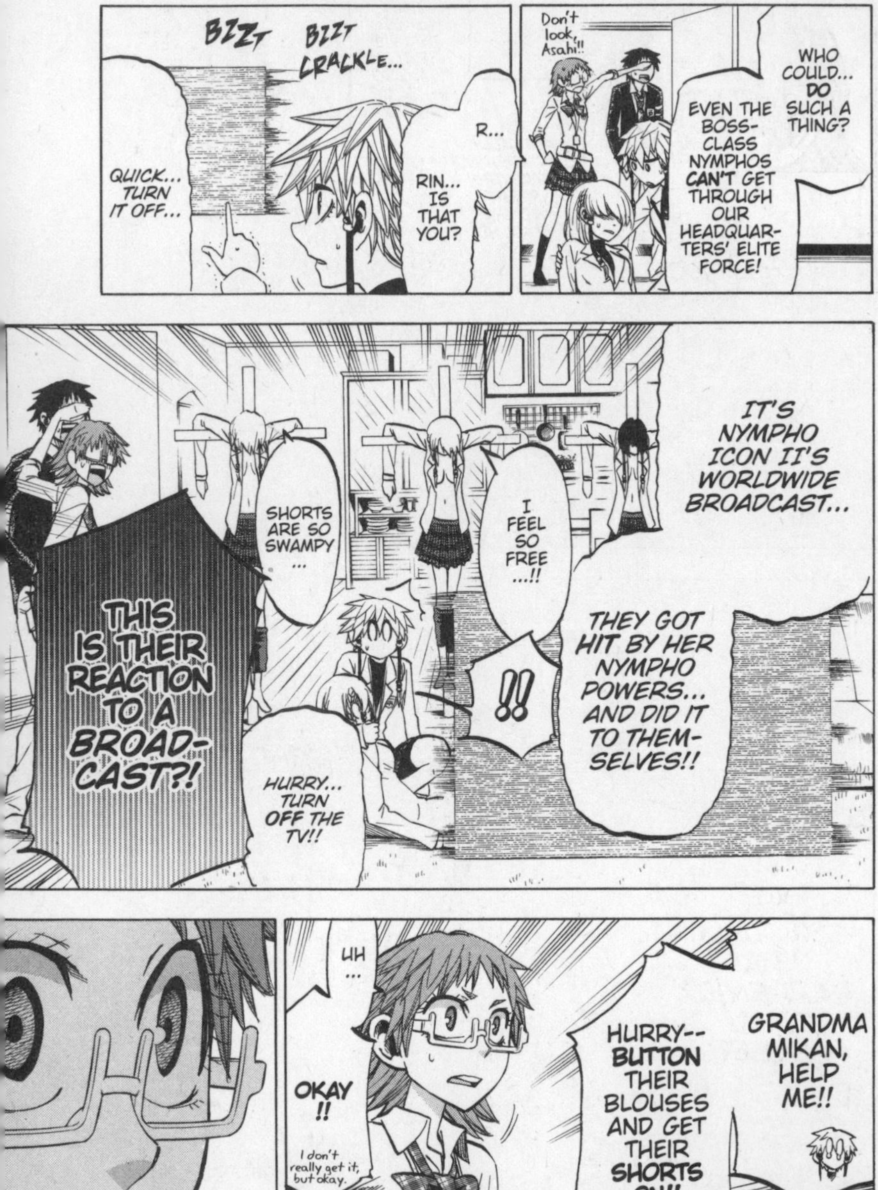
Don't look, Asahi!!
WHO COULD... DO SUCH A THING?
EVEN THE BOSS-CLASS NYMPHOS CAN'T GET THROUGH OUR HEADQUARTERS' ELITE FORCE!
BZZT
BZZT
CRACKLE...
R...
RIN... IS THAT YOU?
QUICK... TURN IT OFF...
IT'S NYMPHO ICON II'S WORLDWIDE BROADCAST...
THEY GOT HIT BY HER NYMPHO POWERS... AND DID IT TO THEMSELVES!!
I FEEL SO FREE...!!
!!
SHORTS ARE SO SWAMPY...
HURRY... TURN OFF THE TV!!
THIS IS THEIR REACTION TO A BROADCAST?!
GRANDMA MIKAN, HELP ME!!
HURRY-- BUTTON THEIR BLOUSES AND GET THEIR SHORTS ON!!
UH...
OKAY!!
I don't really get it, but okay.

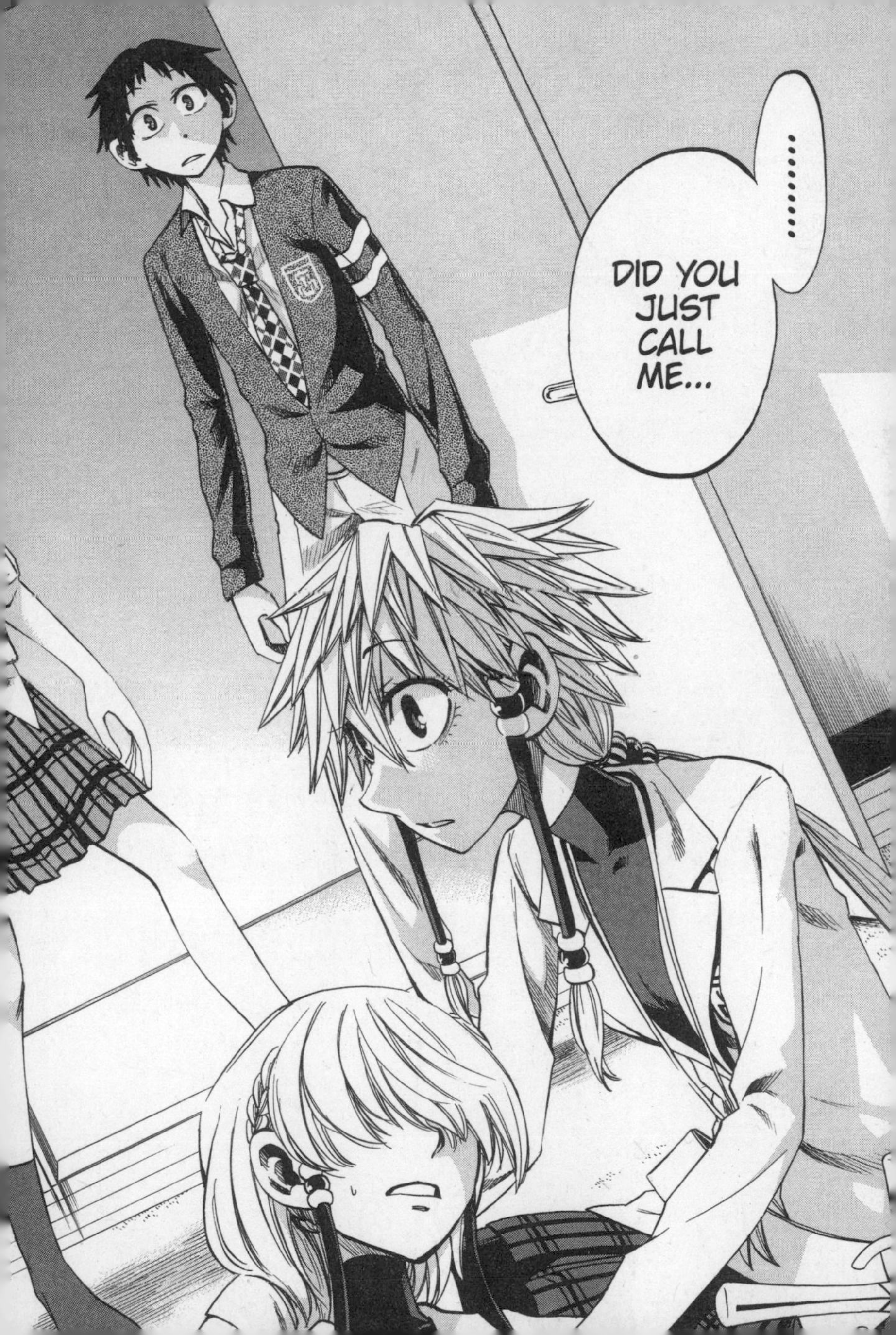
......
DID YOU JUST CALL ME...

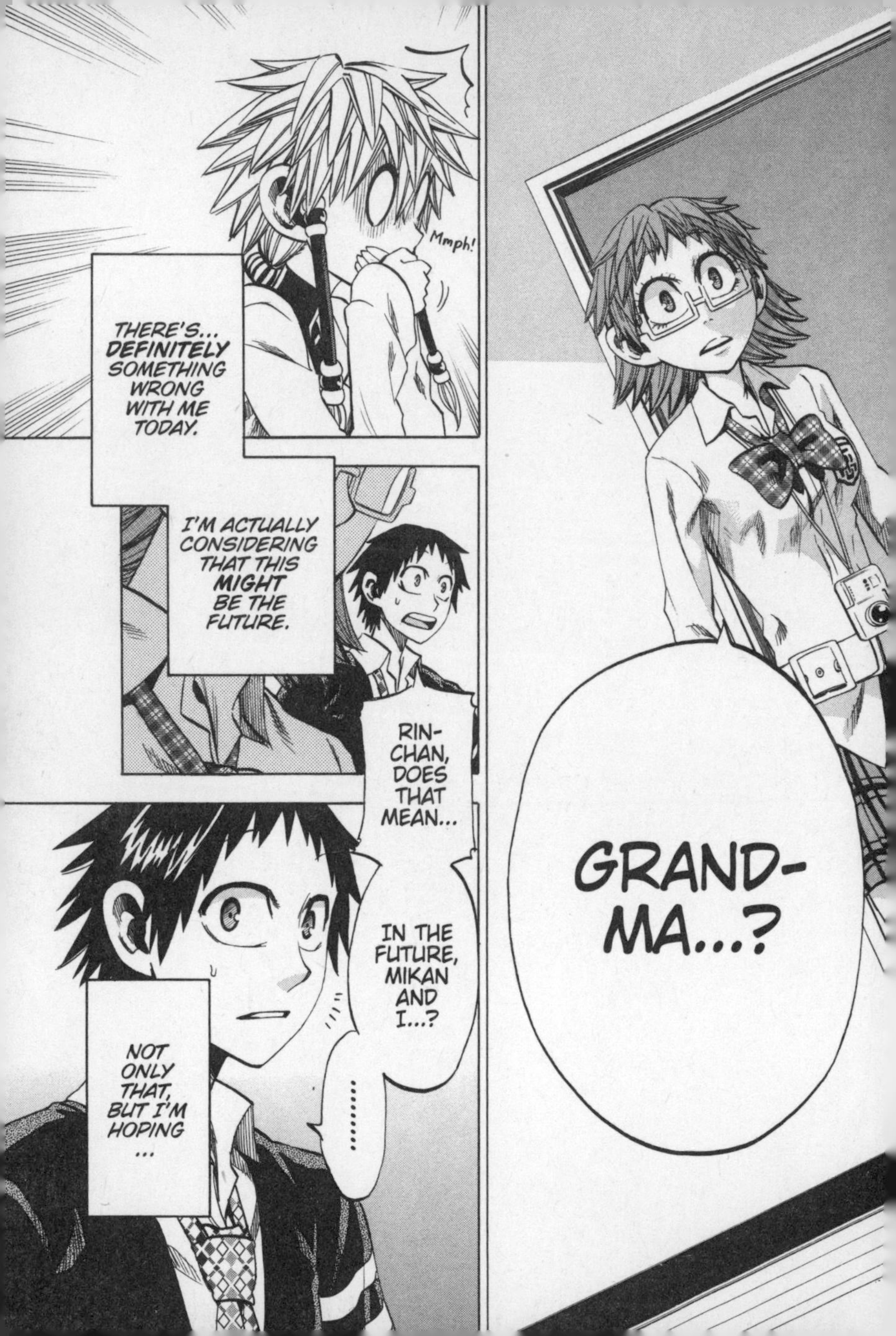
GRAND-MA...?
Mmph!
THERE'S... **DEFINITELY** SOMETHING WRONG WITH ME TODAY.
I'M ACTUALLY CONSIDERING THAT THIS **MIGHT** BE THE FUTURE.
RIN-CHAN, DOES THAT MEAN...
IN THE FUTURE, MIKAN AND I...?
......
NOT ONLY THAT, BUT I'M HOPING ...

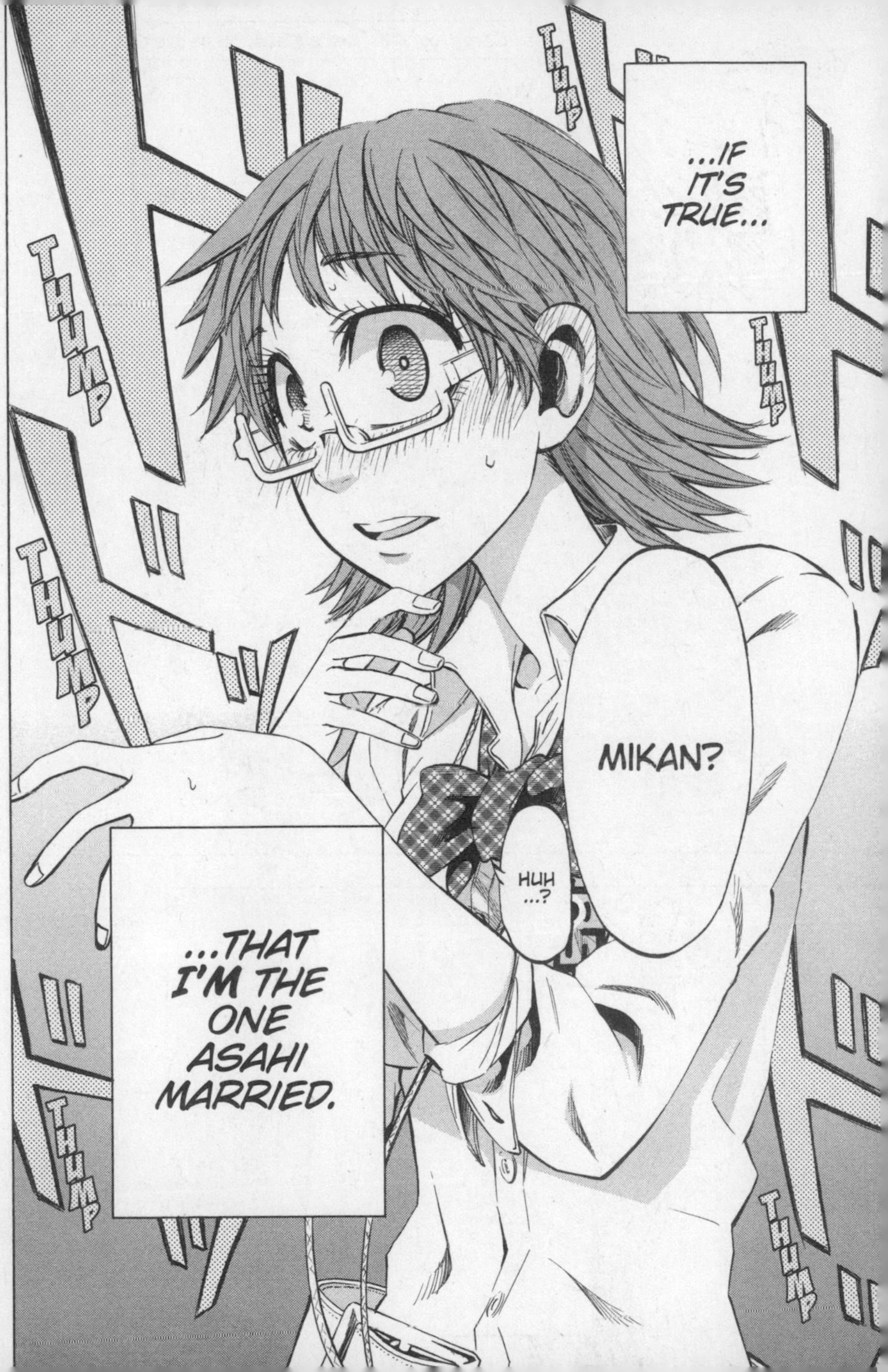
THUMP
...IF IT'S TRUE...
THUMP
THUMP
THUMP
MIKAN?
HUH ...?
...THAT **I'M** THE ONE ASAHI MARRIED.
THUMP
THUMP

Chapter 42: "Let's Look Him in the Eye!"

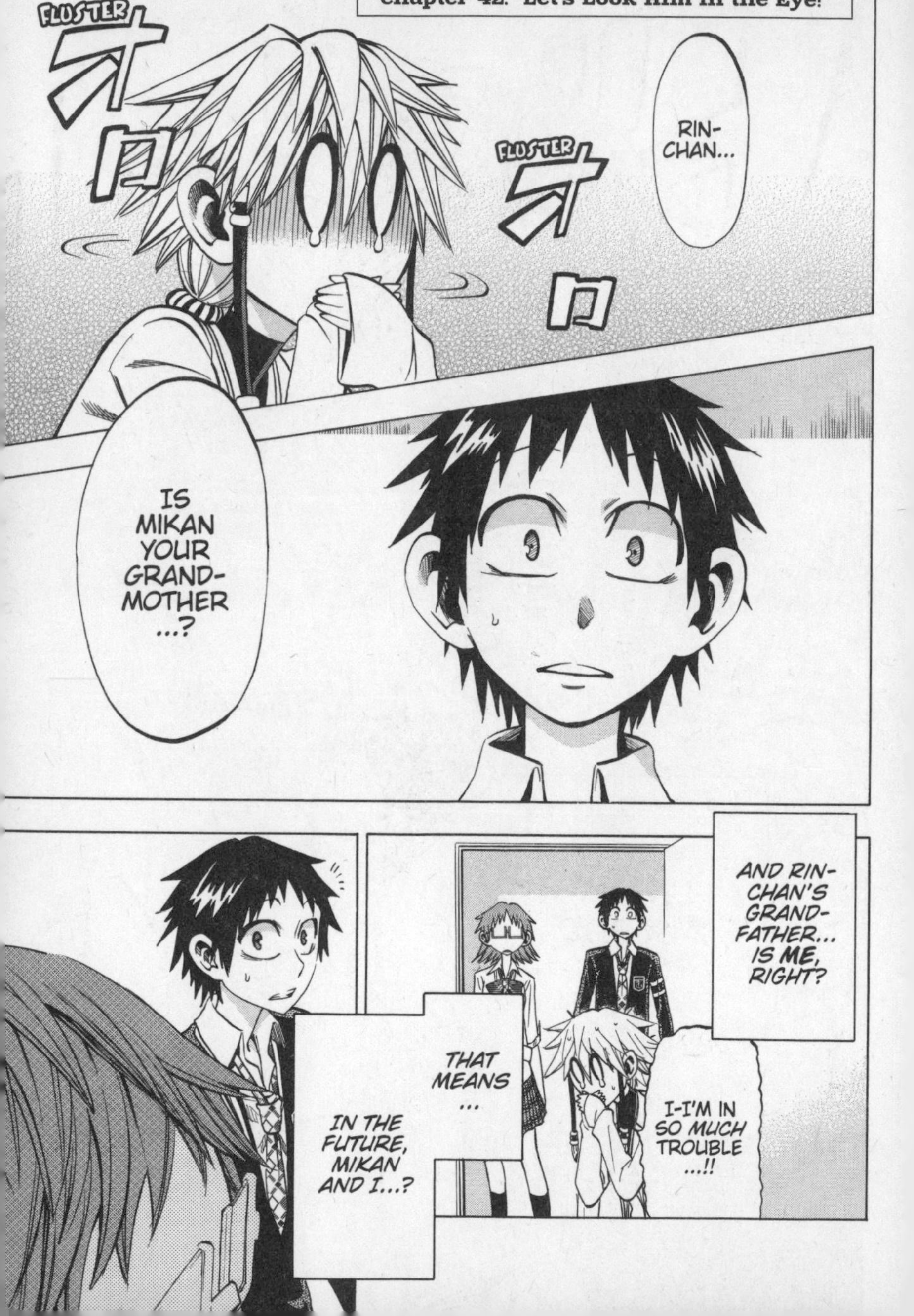
RIN-CHAN...
FLUSTER
FLUSTER
IS MIKAN YOUR GRANDMOTHER...?
AND RIN-CHAN'S GRANDFATHER... IS ME, RIGHT?
I-I'M IN SO MUCH TROUBLE...!!
THAT MEANS...
IN THE FUTURE, MIKAN AND I...?

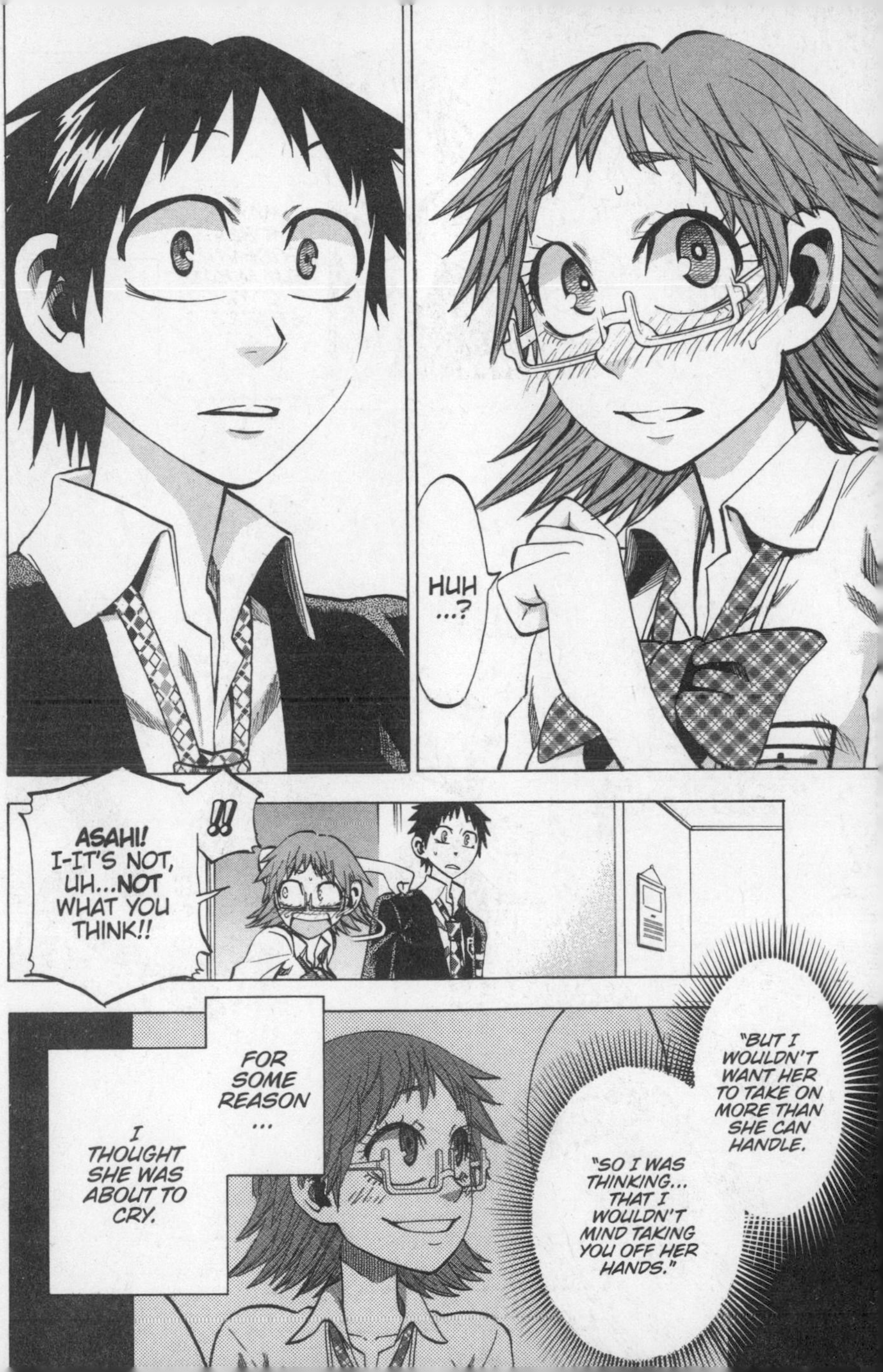
HUH ...?
!!
ASAHI! I-IT'S NOT, UH...NOT WHAT YOU THINK!!
"BUT I WOULDN'T WANT HER TO TAKE ON MORE THAN SHE CAN HANDLE.
"SO I WAS THINKING... THAT I WOULDN'T MIND TAKING YOU OFF HER HANDS."
FOR SOME REASON ...
I THOUGHT SHE WAS ABOUT TO CRY.

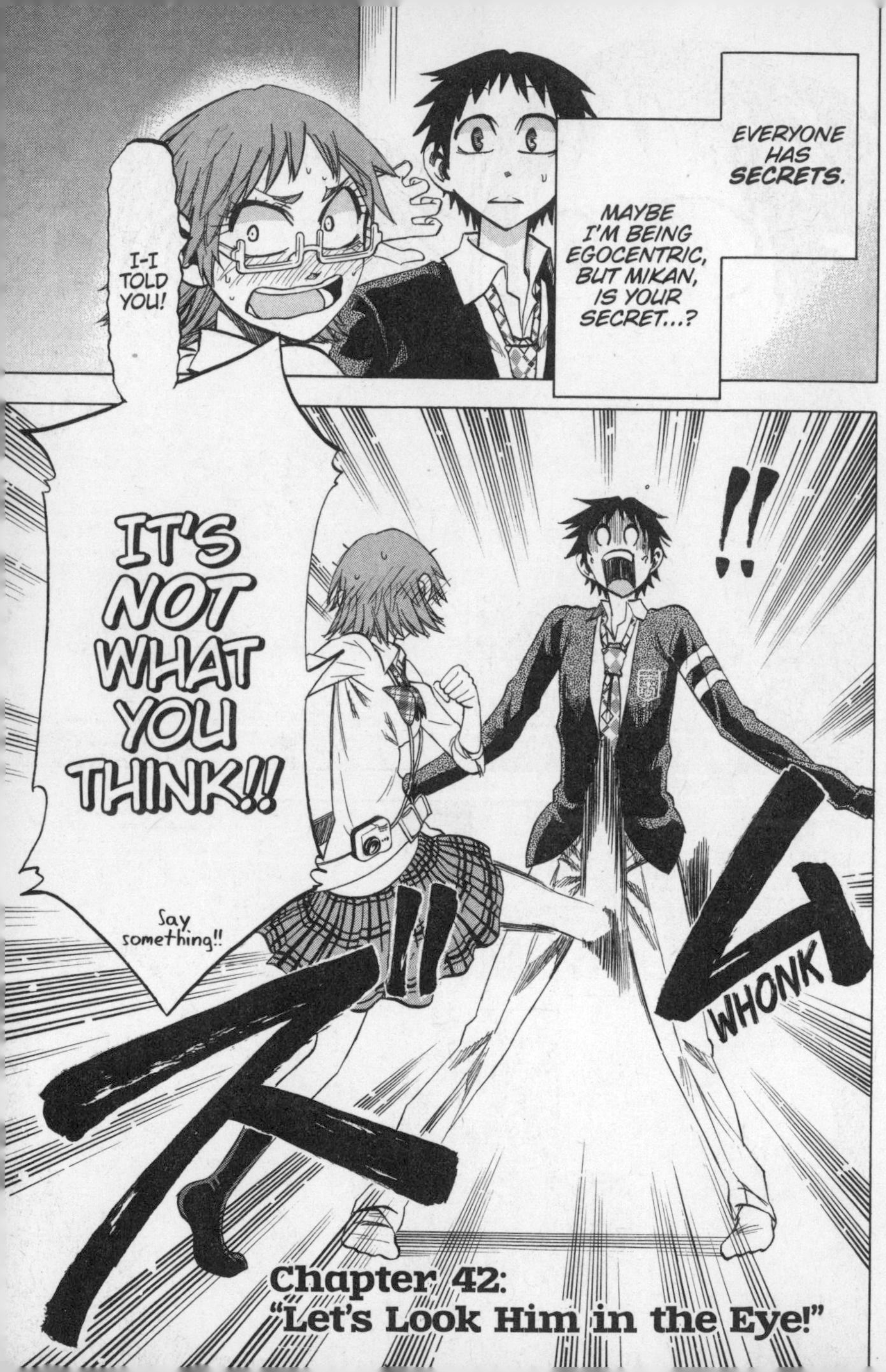
EVERYONE HAS SECRETS.
MAYBE I'M BEING EGOCENTRIC, BUT MIKAN, IS YOUR SECRET...?
I-I TOLD YOU!
IT'S NOT WHAT YOU THINK!!
!!
WHONK
Say something!!
Chapter 42: "Let's Look Him in the Eye!"

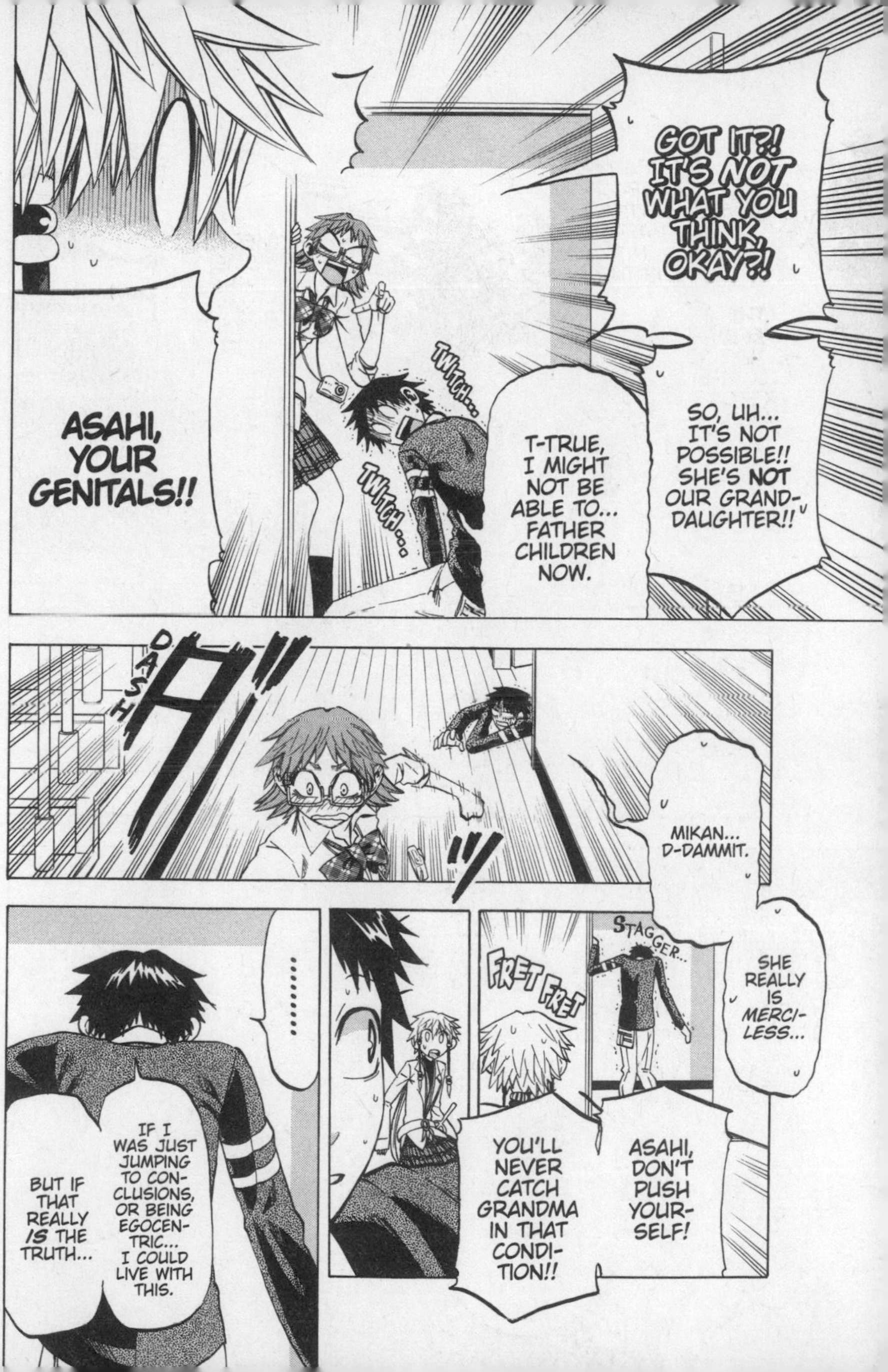
GOT IT?! IT'S NOT WHAT YOU THINK, OKAY?!
SO, UH... IT'S NOT POSSIBLE!! SHE'S NOT OUR GRAND-DAUGHTER!!
T-TRUE, I MIGHT NOT BE ABLE TO... FATHER CHILDREN NOW.
TWITCH...
TWITCH...
ASAHI, YOUR GENITALS!!
MIKAN... D-DAMMIT.
DASH
SHE REALLY IS MERCILESS...
STAGGER...
FRET FRET
ASAHI, DON'T PUSH YOURSELF!
YOU'LL NEVER CATCH GRANDMA IN THAT CONDITION!!
......
IF I WAS JUST JUMPING TO CONCLUSIONS, OR BEING EGOCENTRIC... I COULD LIVE WITH THIS.
BUT IF THAT REALLY *IS* THE TRUTH...

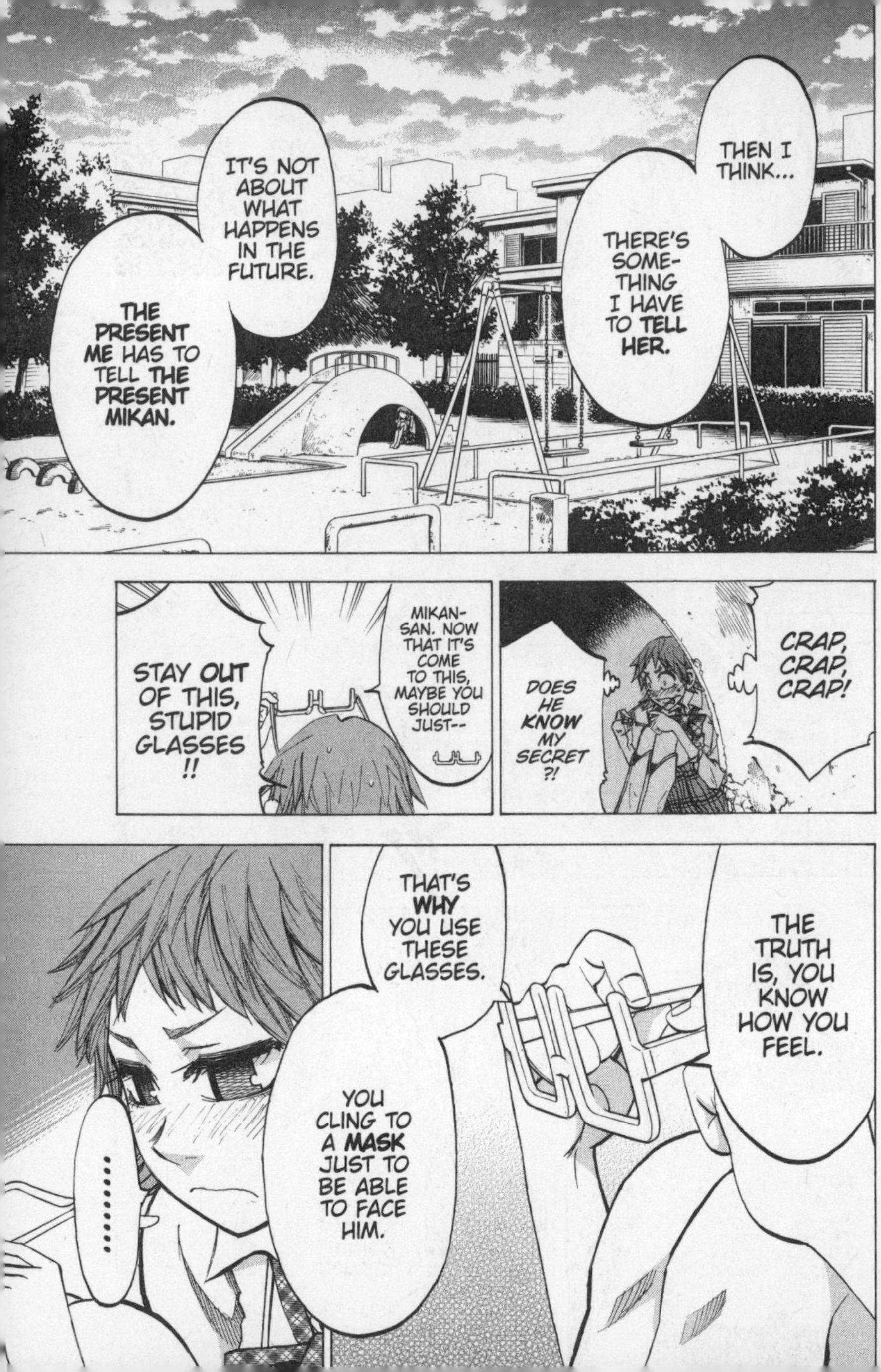
THEN I THINK...
THERE'S SOMETHING I HAVE TO TELL HER.
IT'S NOT ABOUT WHAT HAPPENS IN THE FUTURE.
THE PRESENT ME HAS TO TELL THE PRESENT MIKAN.
CRAP, CRAP, CRAP!
DOES HE KNOW MY SECRET?!
MIKAN-SAN. NOW THAT IT'S COME TO THIS, MAYBE YOU SHOULD JUST--
STAY OUT OF THIS, STUPID GLASSES!!
THE TRUTH IS, YOU KNOW HOW YOU FEEL.
THAT'S WHY YOU USE THESE GLASSES.
YOU CLING TO A MASK JUST TO BE ABLE TO FACE HIM.
....

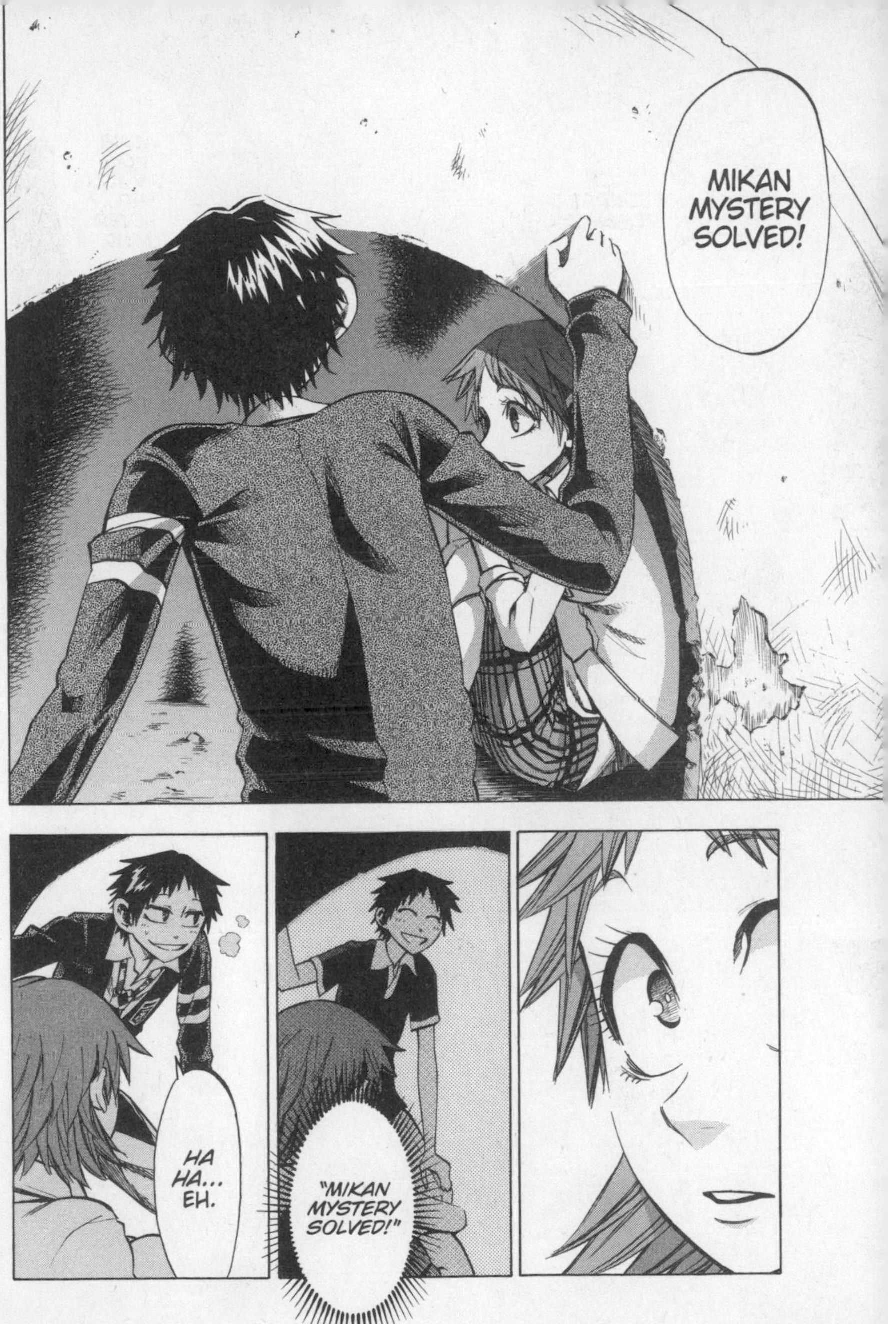

MIKAN MYSTERY SOLVED!
"MIKAN MYSTERY SOLVED!"
HA HA... EH.

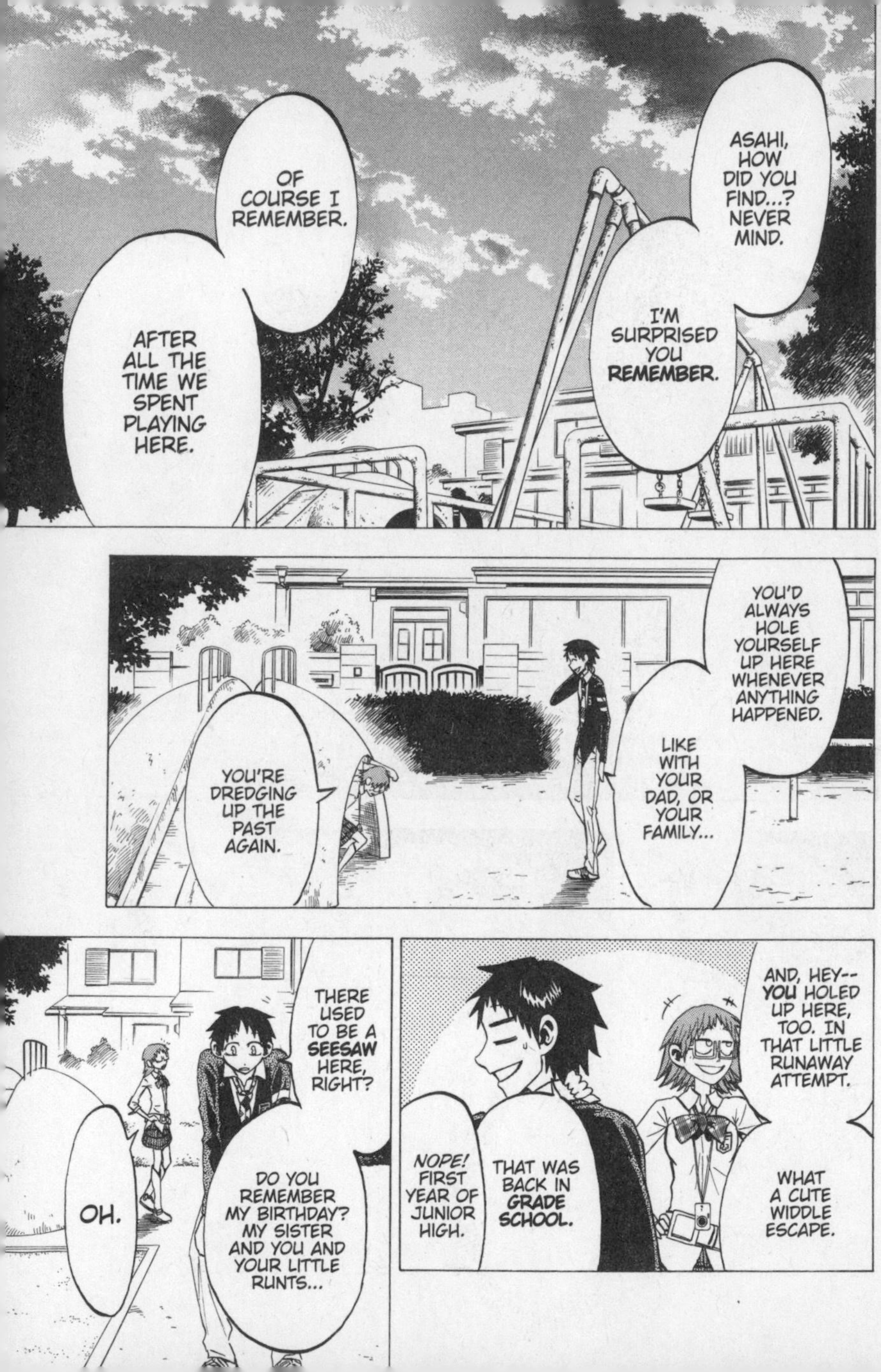
ASAHI, HOW DID YOU FIND...? NEVER MIND.
I'M SURPRISED YOU REMEMBER.
OF COURSE I REMEMBER.
AFTER ALL THE TIME WE SPENT PLAYING HERE.
YOU'D ALWAYS HOLE YOURSELF UP HERE WHENEVER ANYTHING HAPPENED.
LIKE WITH YOUR DAD, OR YOUR FAMILY...
YOU'RE DREDGING UP THE PAST AGAIN.
AND, HEY-- YOU HOLED UP HERE, TOO. IN THAT LITTLE RUNAWAY ATTEMPT.
WHAT A CUTE WIDDLE ESCAPE.
THAT WAS BACK IN GRADE SCHOOL.
NOPE! FIRST YEAR OF JUNIOR HIGH.
THERE USED TO BE A SEESAW HERE, RIGHT?
DO YOU REMEMBER MY BIRTHDAY? MY SISTER AND YOU AND YOUR LITTLE RUNTS...
OH.

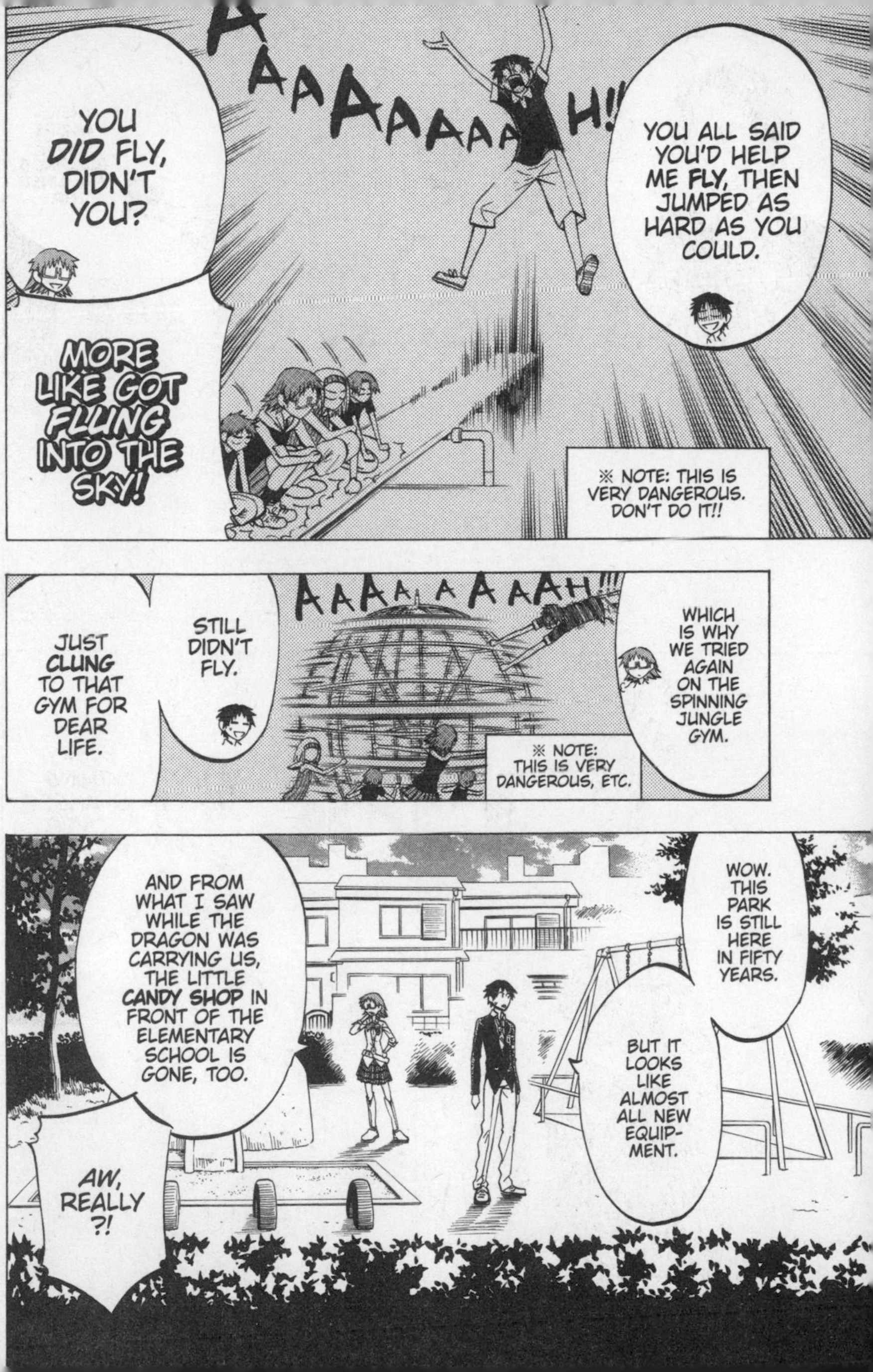
AAAAAAAAAAH!!
YOU ALL SAID YOU'D HELP ME FLY, THEN JUMPED AS HARD AS YOU COULD.
YOU DID FLY, DIDN'T YOU?
※ NOTE: THIS IS VERY DANGEROUS. DON'T DO IT!!
MORE LIKE GOT FLUNG INTO THE SKY!
AAAA AAAAH!!!
WHICH IS WHY WE TRIED AGAIN ON THE SPINNING JUNGLE GYM.
※ NOTE: THIS IS VERY DANGEROUS, ETC.
STILL DIDN'T FLY.
JUST CLUNG TO THAT GYM FOR DEAR LIFE.
WOW. THIS PARK IS STILL HERE IN FIFTY YEARS.
BUT IT LOOKS LIKE ALMOST ALL NEW EQUIPMENT.
AND FROM WHAT I SAW WHILE THE DRAGON WAS CARRYING US, THE LITTLE CANDY SHOP IN FRONT OF THE ELEMENTARY SCHOOL IS GONE, TOO.
AW, REALLY?!

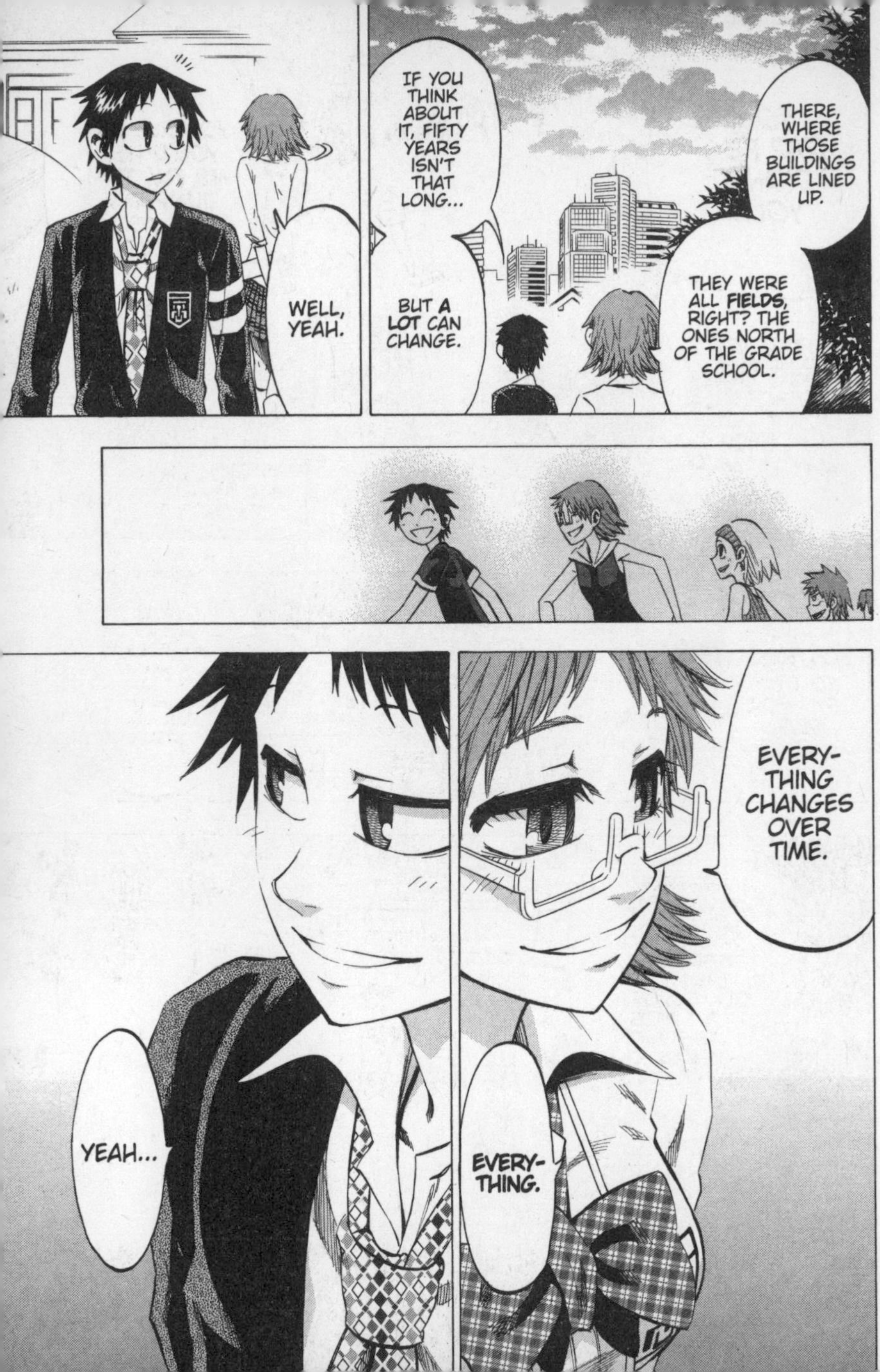
THERE, WHERE THOSE BUILDINGS ARE LINED UP.
THEY WERE ALL **FIELDS**, RIGHT? THE ONES NORTH OF THE GRADE SCHOOL.
IF YOU THINK ABOUT IT, FIFTY YEARS ISN'T THAT LONG...
BUT **A LOT** CAN CHANGE.
WELL, YEAH.
EVERY-THING CHANGES OVER TIME.
EVERY-THING.
YEAH...

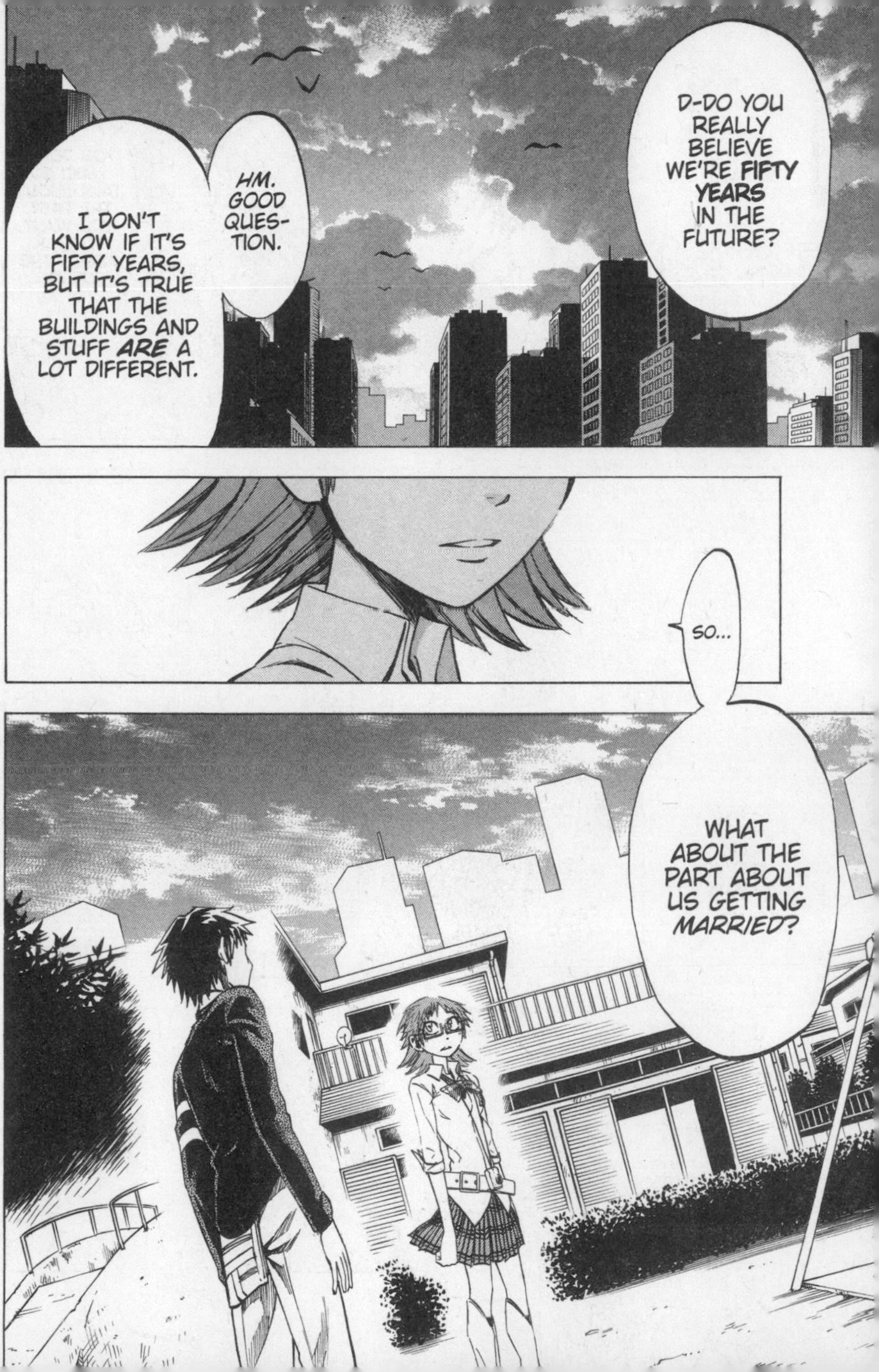
D-DO YOU REALLY BELIEVE WE'RE **FIFTY YEARS** IN THE FUTURE?
HM. GOOD QUES-TION.
I DON'T KNOW IF IT'S FIFTY YEARS, BUT IT'S TRUE THAT THE BUILDINGS AND STUFF ***ARE*** A LOT DIFFERENT.
SO...
WHAT ABOUT THE PART ABOUT US GETTING *MARRIED?*

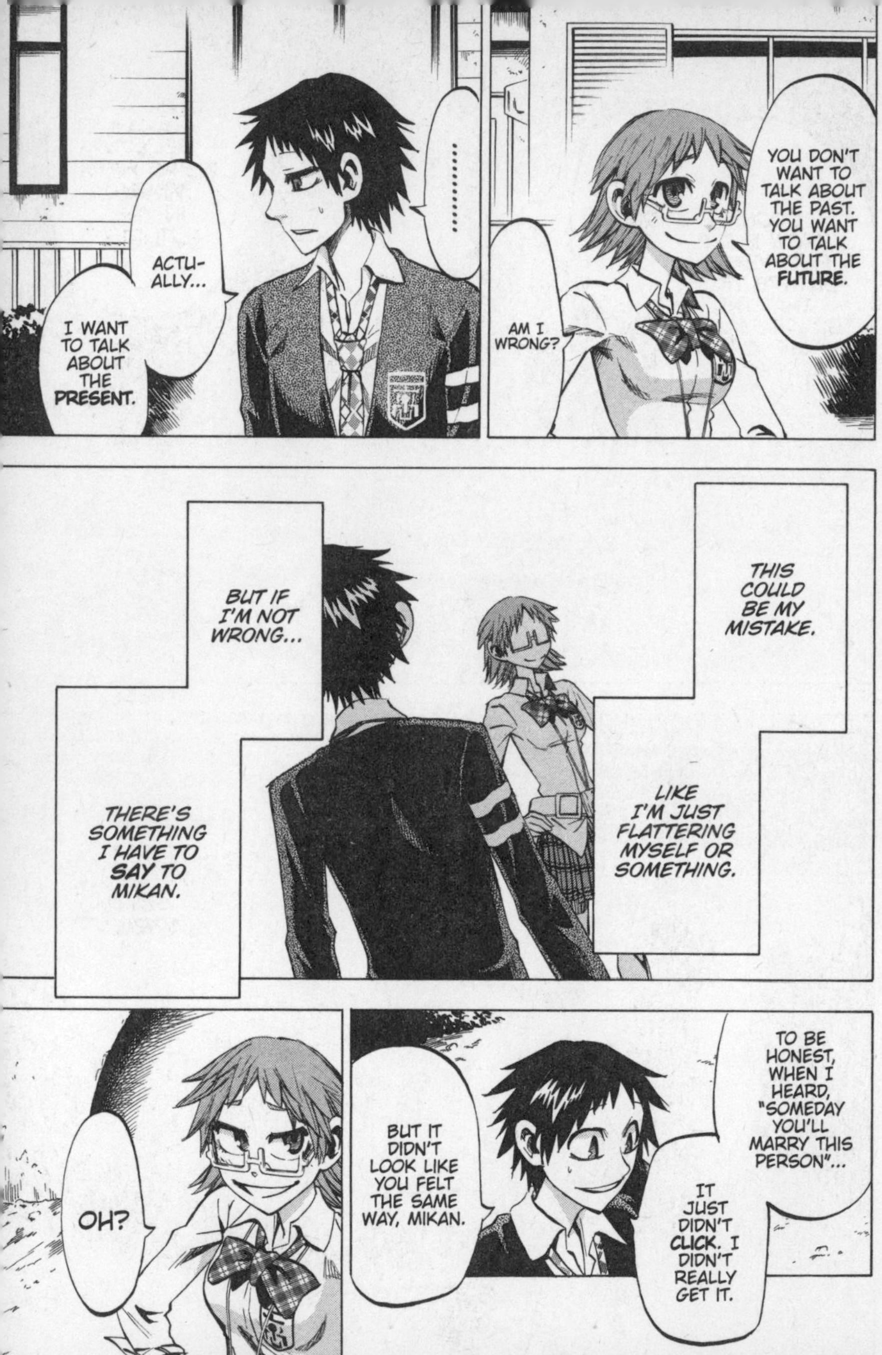

YOU DON'T WANT TO TALK ABOUT THE PAST. YOU WANT TO TALK ABOUT THE FUTURE.
AM I WRONG?
......
ACTU-ALLY...
I WANT TO TALK ABOUT THE PRESENT.
THIS COULD BE MY MISTAKE.
LIKE I'M JUST FLATTERING MYSELF OR SOMETHING.
BUT IF I'M NOT WRONG...
THERE'S SOMETHING I HAVE TO SAY TO MIKAN.
TO BE HONEST, WHEN I HEARD, "SOMEDAY YOU'LL MARRY THIS PERSON"...
IT JUST DIDN'T CLICK. I DIDN'T REALLY GET IT.
BUT IT DIDN'T LOOK LIKE YOU FELT THE SAME WAY, MIKAN.
OH?

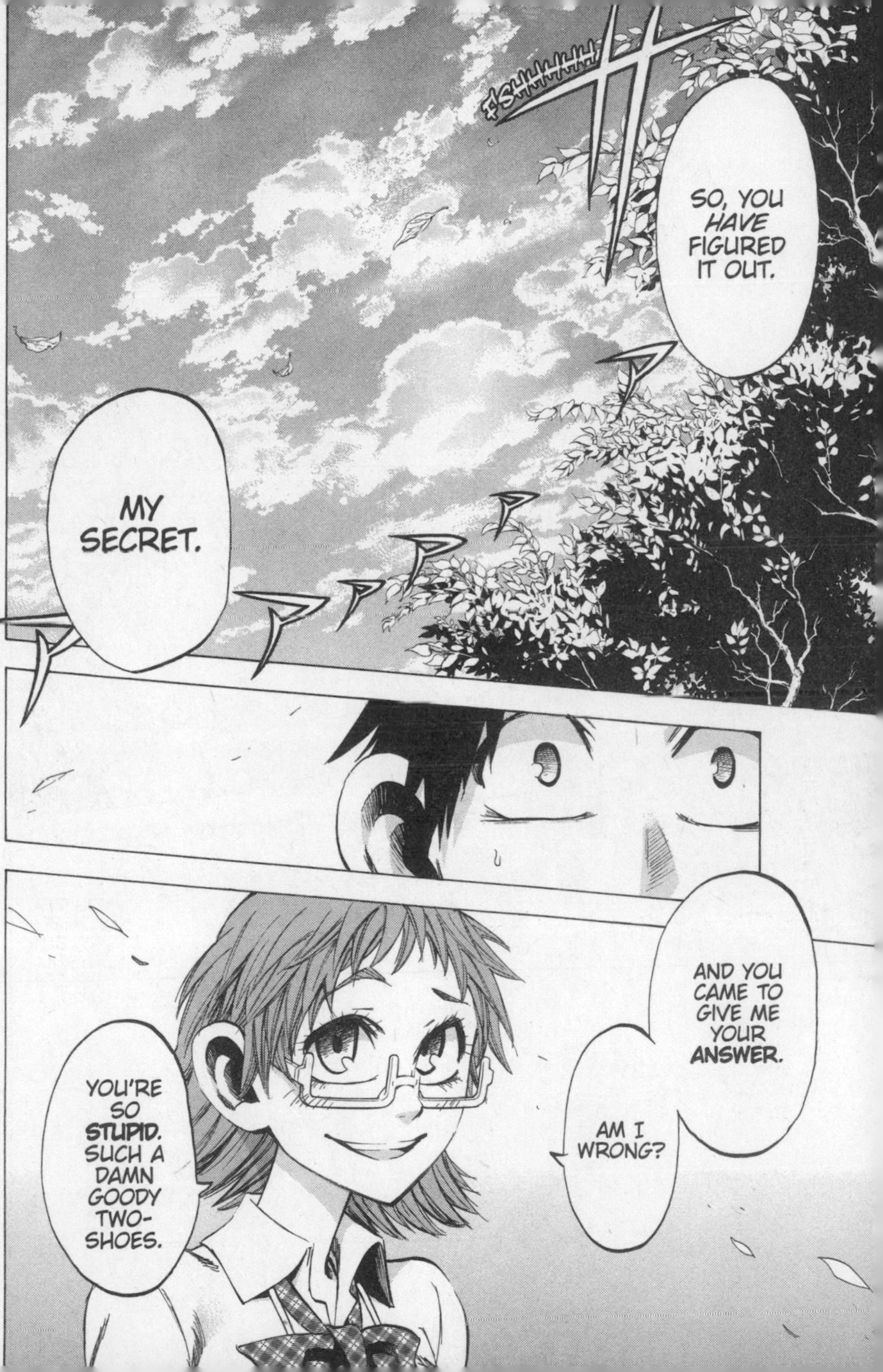
SO, YOU HAVE FIGURED IT OUT.
MY SECRET.
AND YOU CAME TO GIVE ME YOUR ANSWER.
AM I WRONG?
YOU'RE SO STUPID. SUCH A DAMN GOODY TWO-SHOES.

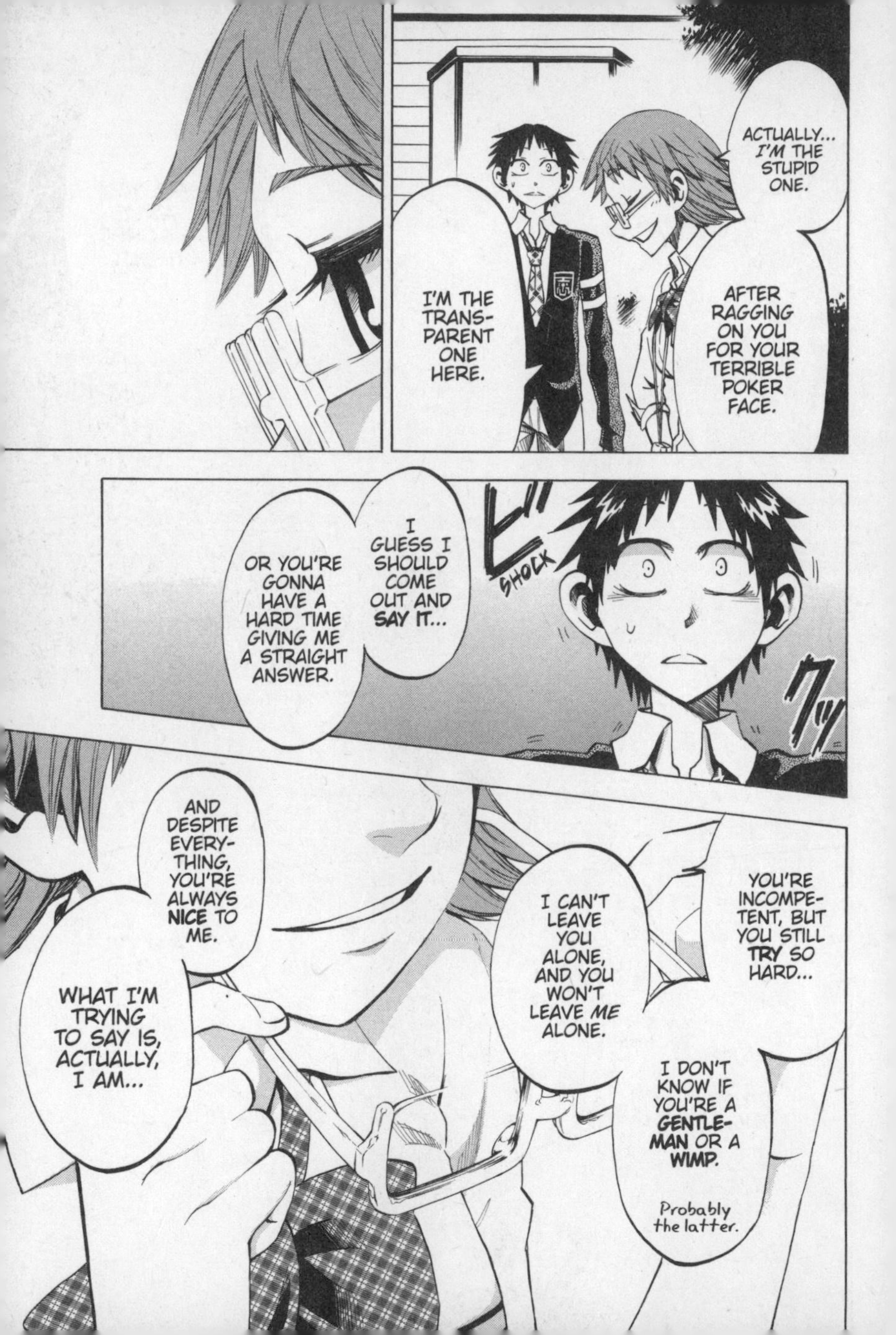
ACTUALLY... *I'M* THE STUPID ONE.
AFTER RAGGING ON YOU FOR YOUR TERRIBLE POKER FACE.
I'M THE TRANSPARENT ONE HERE.
SHOCK
I GUESS I SHOULD COME OUT AND **SAY IT**...
OR YOU'RE GONNA HAVE A HARD TIME GIVING ME A STRAIGHT ANSWER.
YOU'RE INCOMPETENT, BUT YOU STILL **TRY** SO HARD...
I DON'T KNOW IF YOU'RE A **GENTLEMAN** OR A **WIMP**.
Probably the latter.
I CAN'T LEAVE YOU ALONE, AND YOU WON'T LEAVE *ME* ALONE.
AND DESPITE EVERYTHING, YOU'RE ALWAYS **NICE** TO ME.
WHAT I'M TRYING TO SAY IS, ACTUALLY, I AM...

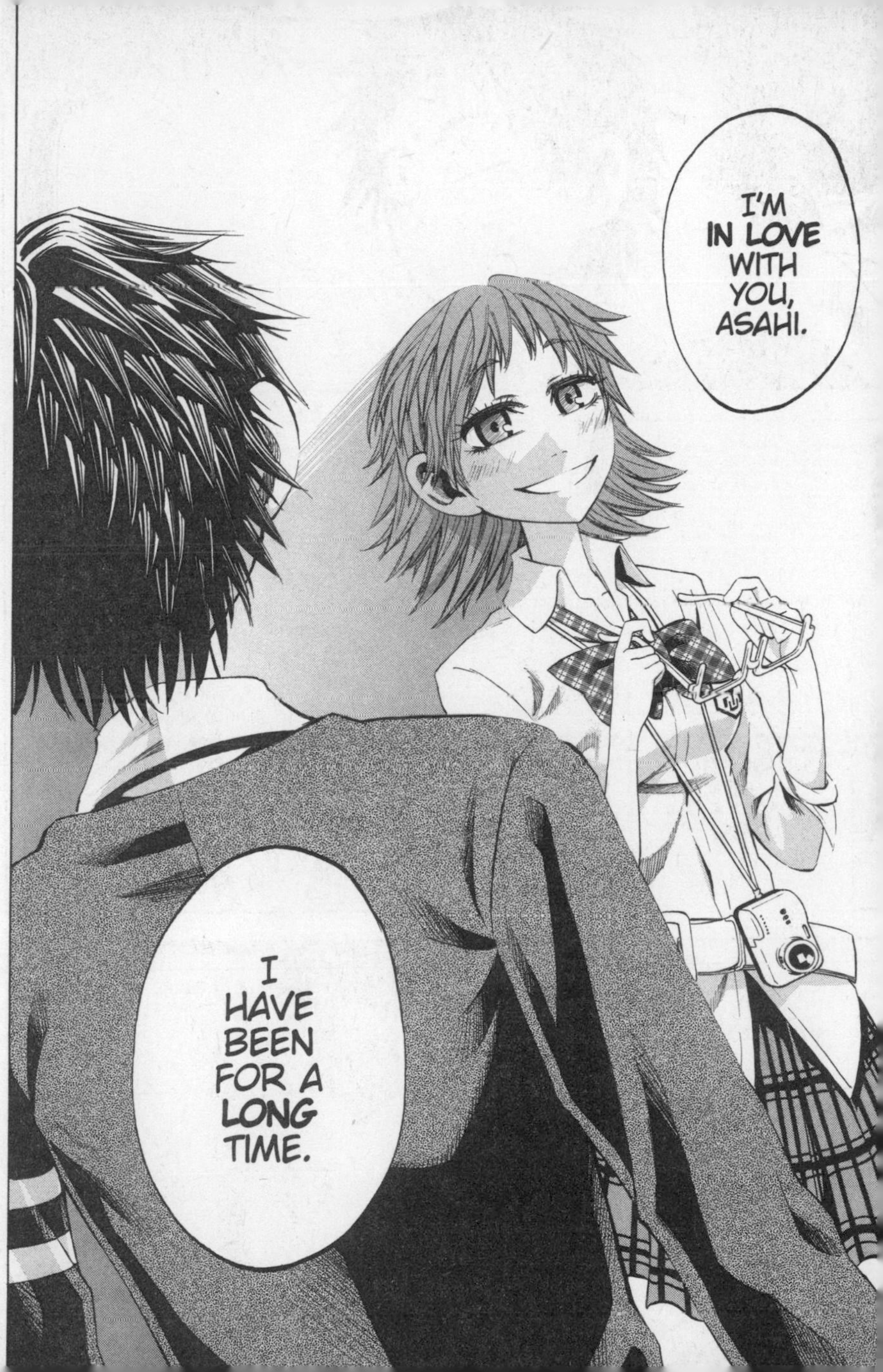
I'M IN LOVE WITH YOU, ASAHI.
I HAVE BEEN FOR A LONG TIME.

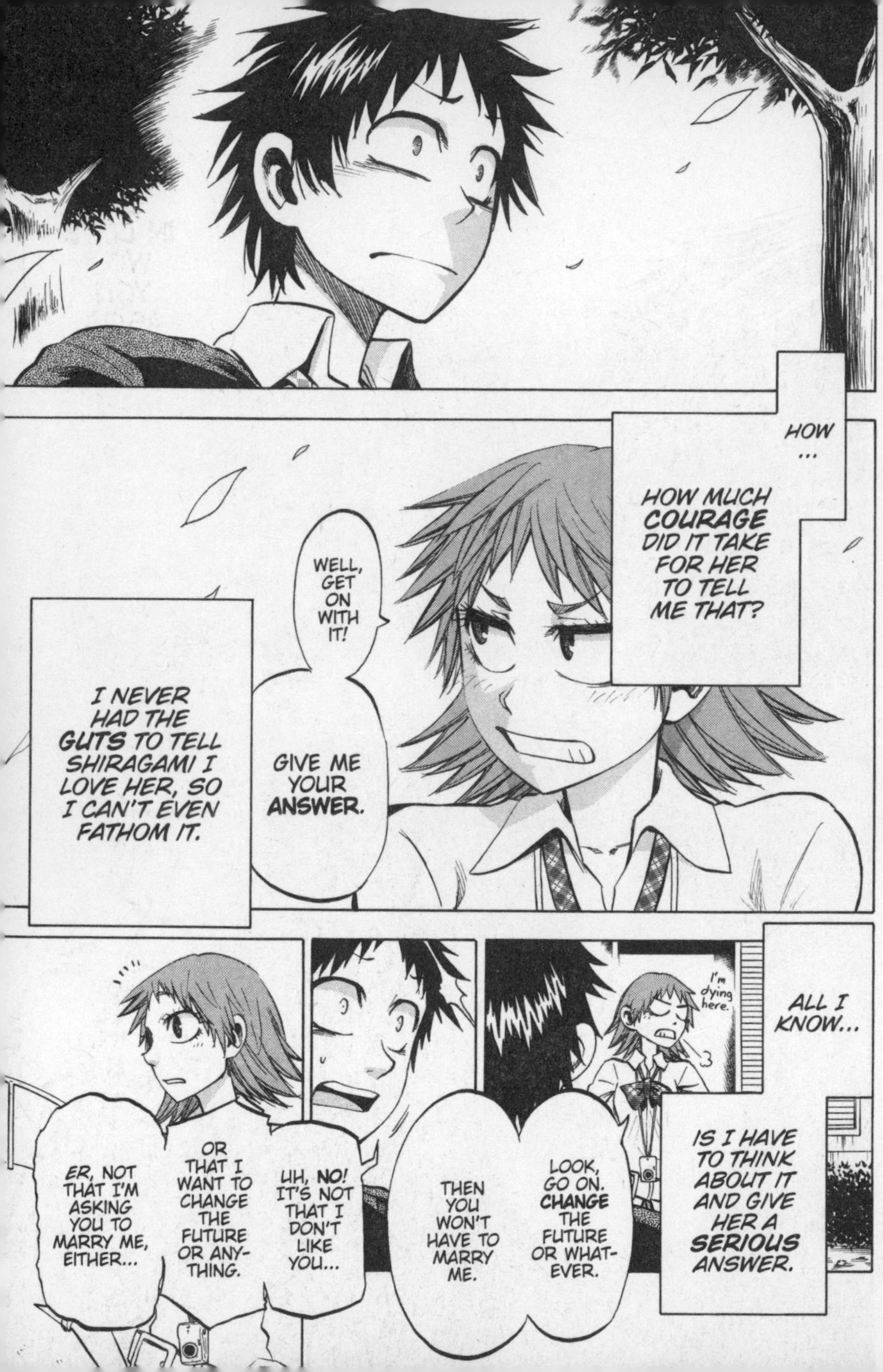

HOW ...
HOW MUCH COURAGE DID IT TAKE FOR HER TO TELL ME THAT?
WELL, GET ON WITH IT!
GIVE ME YOUR ANSWER.
I NEVER HAD THE GUTS TO TELL SHIRAGAMI I LOVE HER, SO I CAN'T EVEN FATHOM IT.
ALL I KNOW...
IS I HAVE TO THINK ABOUT IT AND GIVE HER A SERIOUS ANSWER.
I'm dying here.
LOOK, GO ON. CHANGE THE FUTURE OR WHATEVER.
THEN YOU WON'T HAVE TO MARRY ME.
UH, NO! IT'S NOT THAT I DON'T LIKE YOU...
OR THAT I WANT TO CHANGE THE FUTURE OR ANYTHING.
ER, NOT THAT I'M ASKING YOU TO MARRY ME, EITHER...

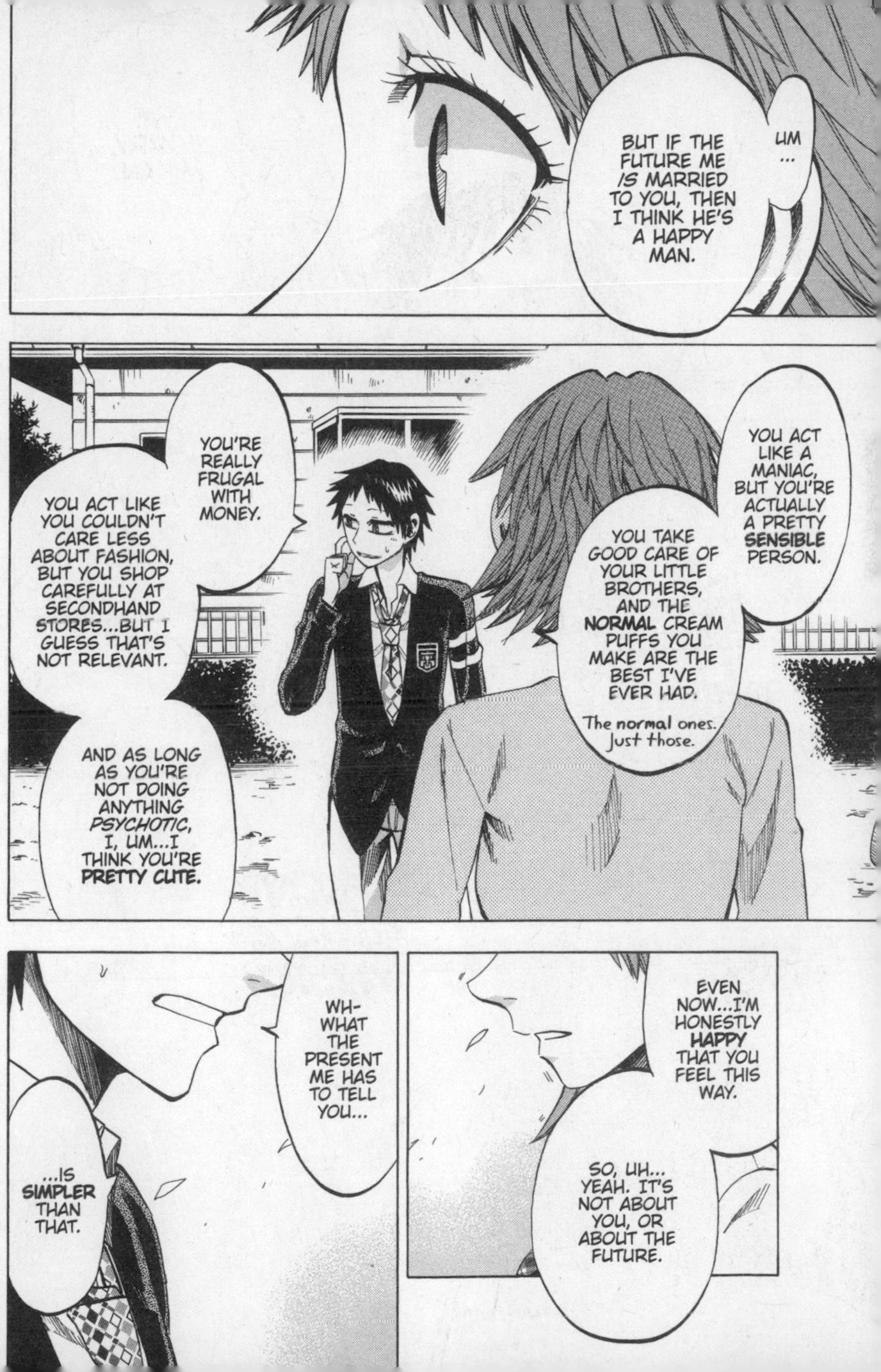
UM ...
BUT IF THE FUTURE ME *IS* MARRIED TO YOU, THEN I THINK HE'S A HAPPY MAN.
YOU ACT LIKE A MANIAC, BUT YOU'RE ACTUALLY A PRETTY **SENSIBLE** PERSON.
YOU TAKE GOOD CARE OF YOUR LITTLE BROTHERS, AND THE **NORMAL** CREAM PUFFS YOU MAKE ARE THE BEST I'VE EVER HAD.
The **normal** ones. Just those.
YOU'RE REALLY FRUGAL WITH MONEY.
YOU ACT LIKE YOU COULDN'T CARE LESS ABOUT FASHION, BUT YOU SHOP CAREFULLY AT SECONDHAND STORES...BUT I GUESS THAT'S NOT RELEVANT.
AND AS LONG AS YOU'RE NOT DOING ANYTHING *PSYCHOTIC*, I, UM...I THINK YOU'RE **PRETTY CUTE.**
EVEN NOW...I'M HONESTLY **HAPPY** THAT YOU FEEL THIS WAY.
SO, UH... YEAH. IT'S NOT ABOUT YOU, OR ABOUT THE FUTURE.
WH- WHAT THE PRESENT ME HAS TO TELL YOU...
...IS **SIMPLER** THAN THAT.

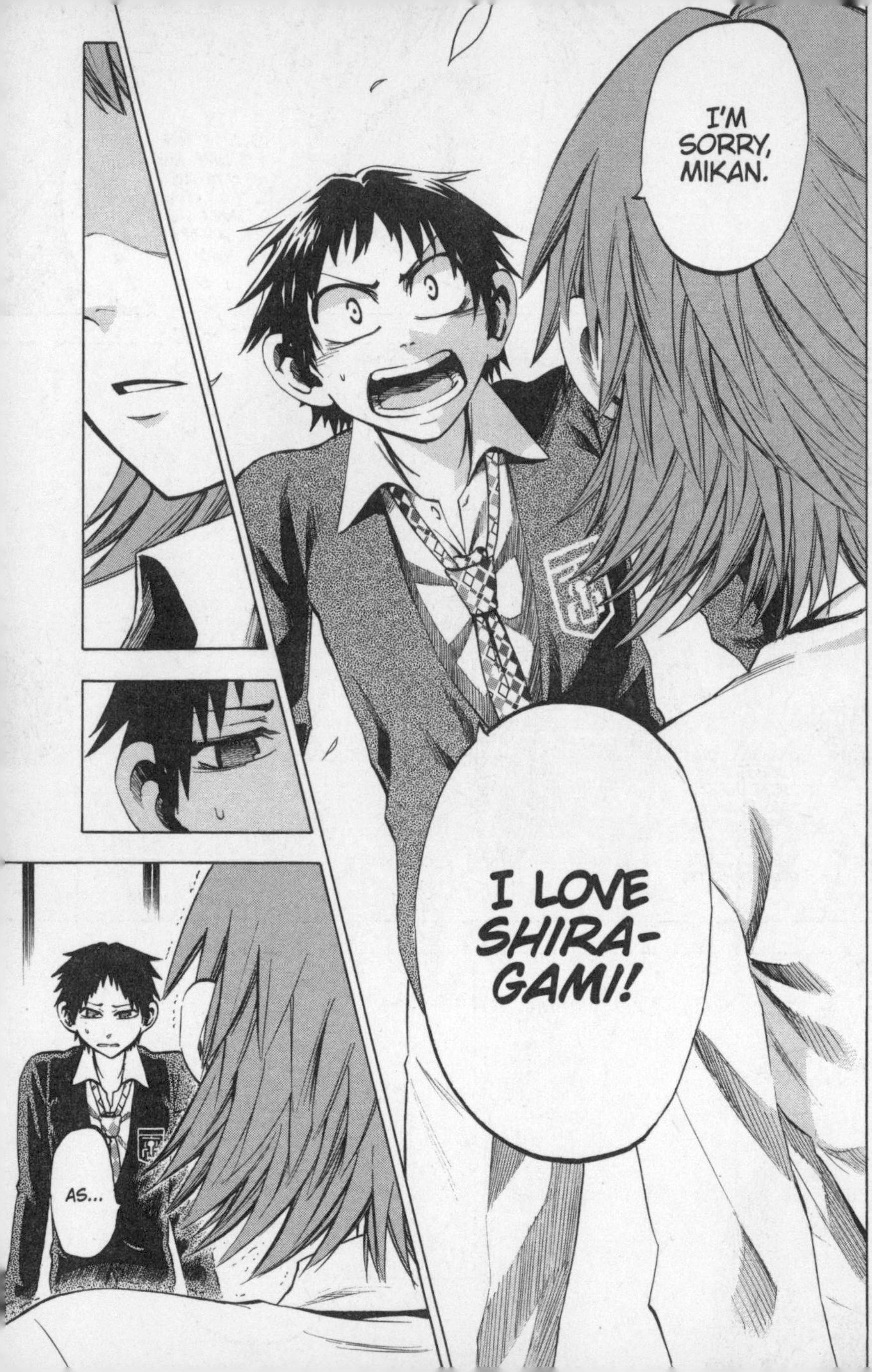
I'M SORRY, MIKAN.
I LOVE SHIRA-GAMI!
AS...

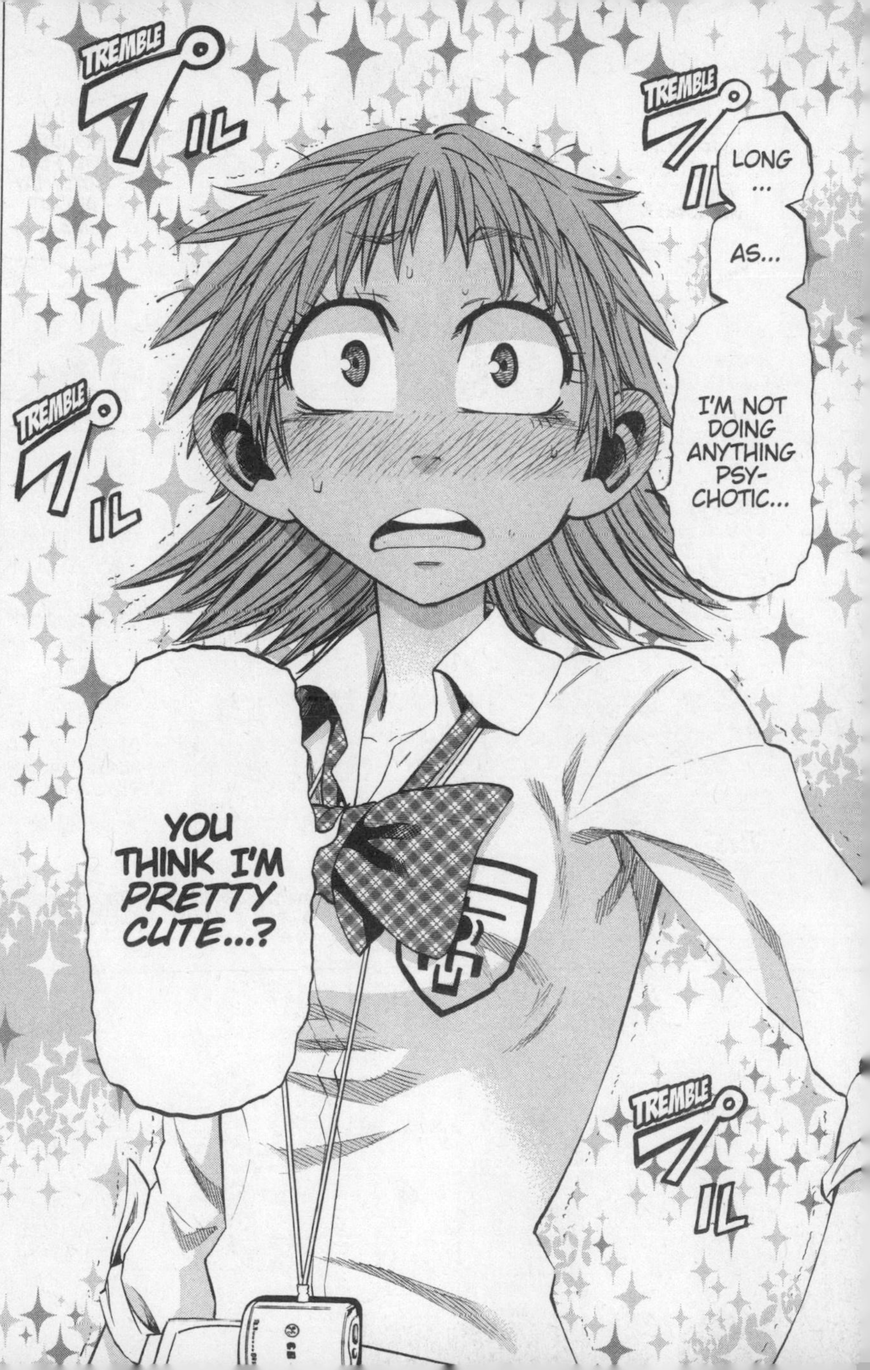
TREMBLE
LONG ... AS...
I'M NOT DOING ANYTHING PSY-CHOTIC...
TREMBLE
TREMBLE
YOU THINK I'M PRETTY CUTE...?
TREMBLE

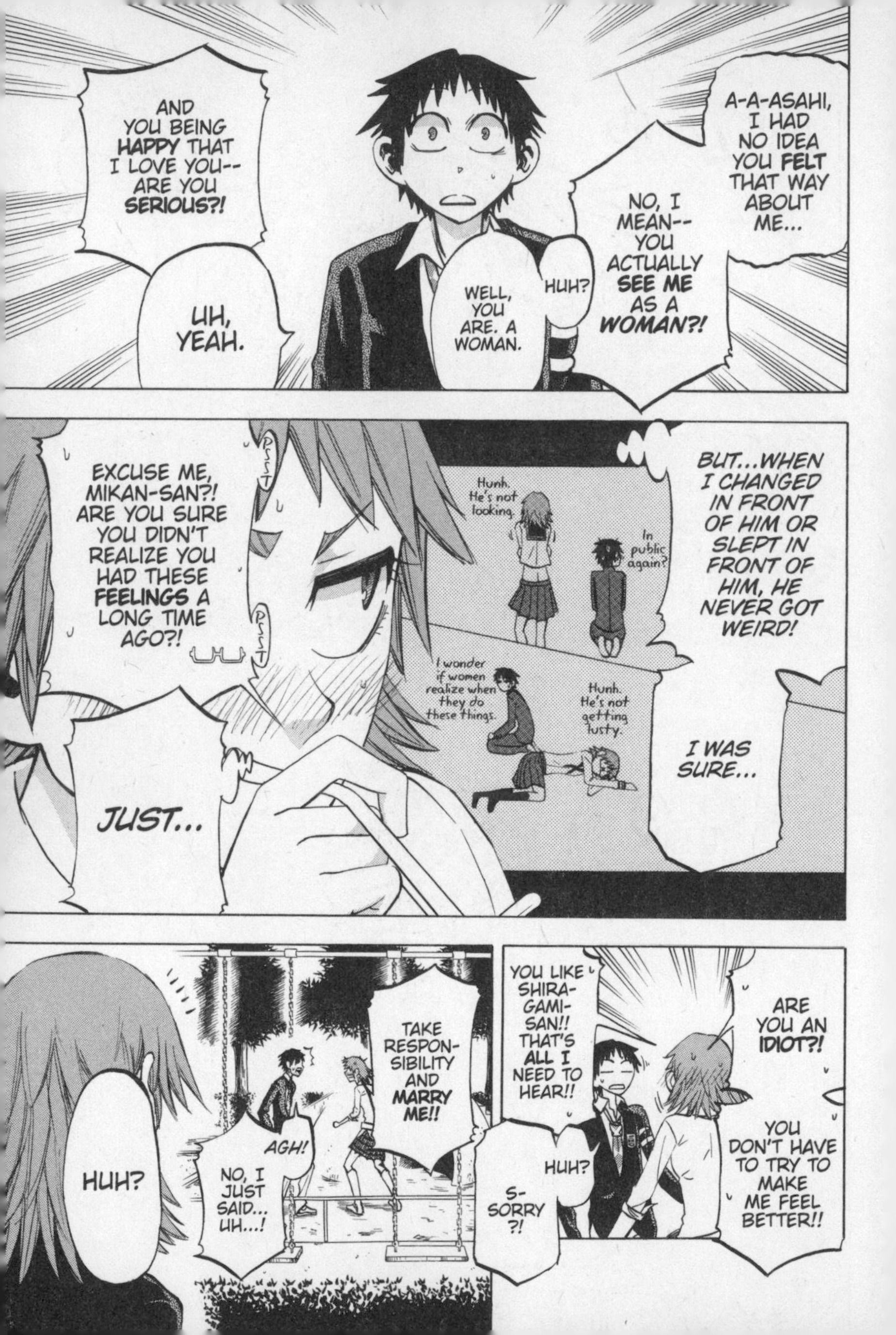
A-A-ASAHI, I HAD NO IDEA YOU FELT THAT WAY ABOUT ME...
NO, I MEAN-- YOU ACTUALLY SEE ME AS A WOMAN?!
HUH?
WELL, YOU ARE. A WOMAN.
AND YOU BEING HAPPY THAT I LOVE YOU-- ARE YOU SERIOUS?!
UH, YEAH.
BUT...WHEN I CHANGED IN FRONT OF HIM OR SLEPT IN FRONT OF HIM, HE NEVER GOT WEIRD!
Hunh. He's not looking.
In public again?
I wonder if women realize when they do these things.
Hunh. He's not getting lusty.
I WAS SURE...
PSST
EXCUSE ME, MIKAN-SAN?! ARE YOU SURE YOU DIDN'T REALIZE YOU HAD THESE FEELINGS A LONG TIME AGO?!
PSST
JUST...
ARE YOU AN IDIOT?!
YOU LIKE SHIRA-GAMI-SAN!! THAT'S ALL I NEED TO HEAR!!
YOU DON'T HAVE TO TRY TO MAKE ME FEEL BETTER!!
HUH?
S-SORRY?!
TAKE RESPON-SIBILITY AND MARRY ME!!
AGH!
NO, I JUST SAID... UH...!
HUH?

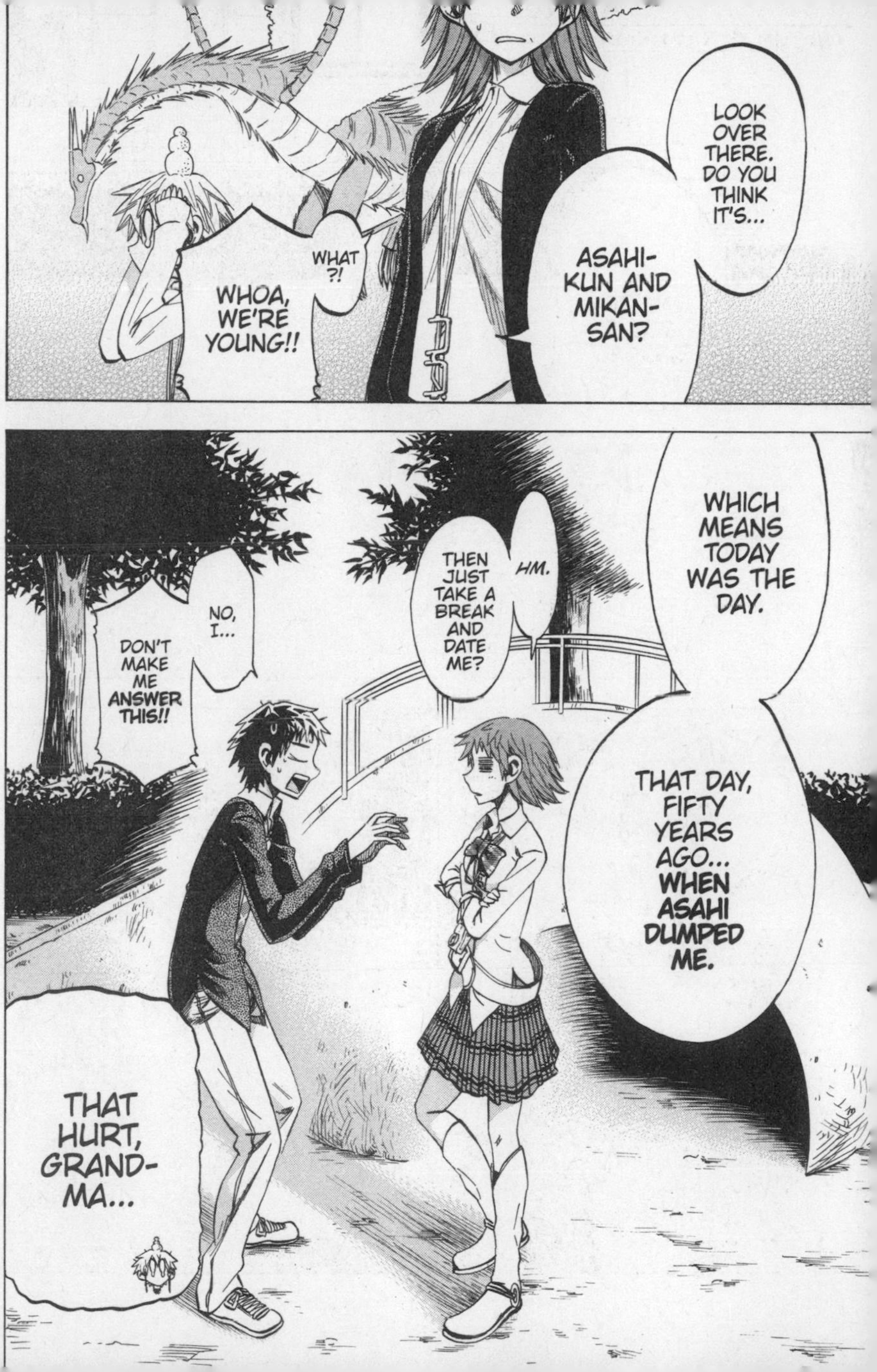
LOOK OVER THERE. DO YOU THINK IT'S...
ASAHI-KUN AND MIKAN-SAN?
WHAT ?!
WHOA, WE'RE YOUNG!!
WHICH MEANS TODAY WAS THE DAY.
THAT DAY, FIFTY YEARS AGO... WHEN ASAHI DUMPED ME.
HM.
THEN JUST TAKE A BREAK AND DATE ME?
NO, I...
DON'T MAKE ME ANSWER THIS!!
THAT HURT, GRANDMA...

Chapter 43: "Let's Make Up Our Mind!"

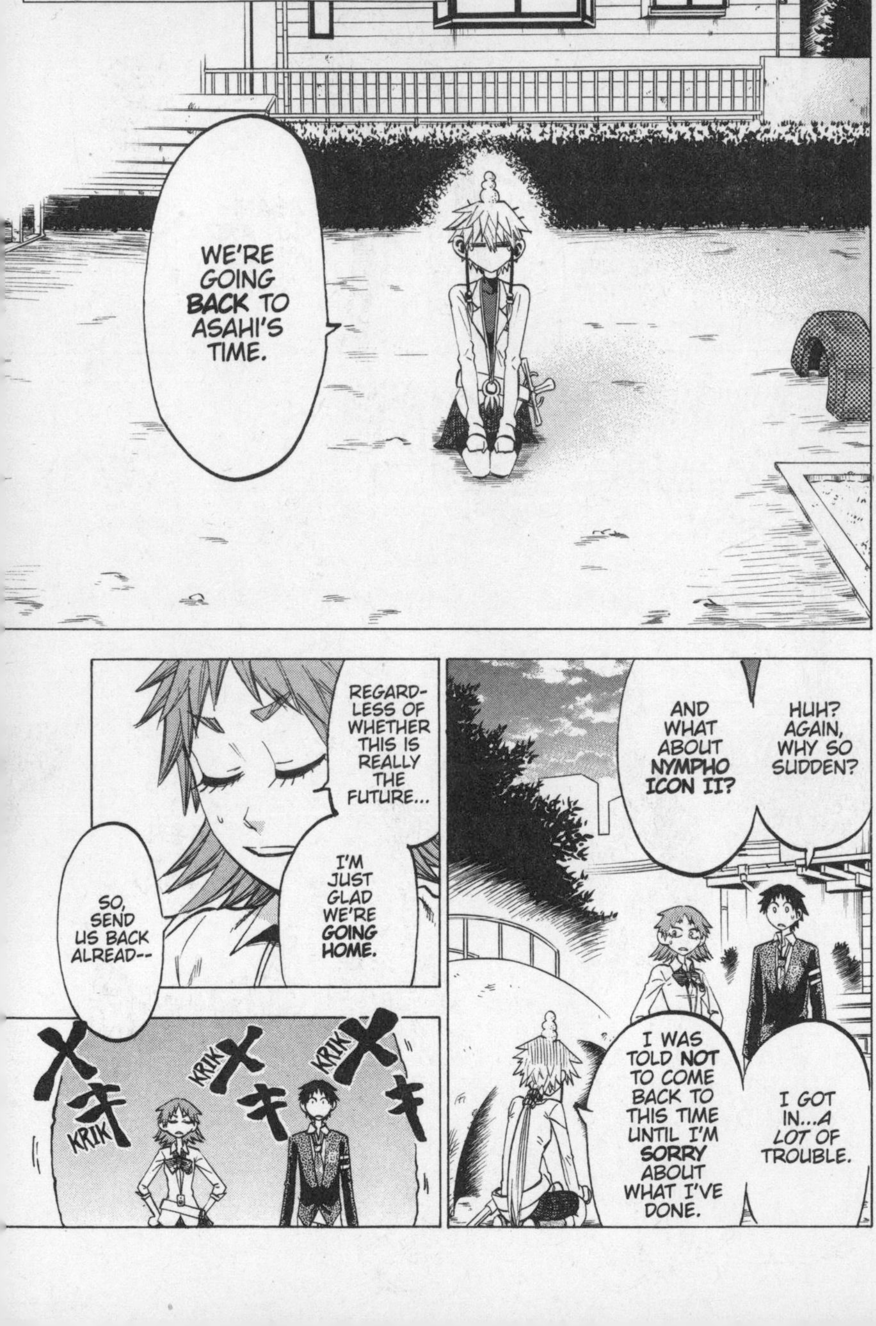
WE'RE GOING BACK TO ASAHI'S TIME.
HUH? AGAIN, WHY SO SUDDEN?
AND WHAT ABOUT NYMPHO ICON II?
I GOT IN...A LOT OF TROUBLE.
I WAS TOLD NOT TO COME BACK TO THIS TIME UNTIL I'M SORRY ABOUT WHAT I'VE DONE.
REGARDLESS OF WHETHER THIS IS REALLY THE FUTURE...
I'M JUST GLAD WE'RE GOING HOME.
SO, SEND US BACK ALREAD--
KRIK
KRIK
KRIK

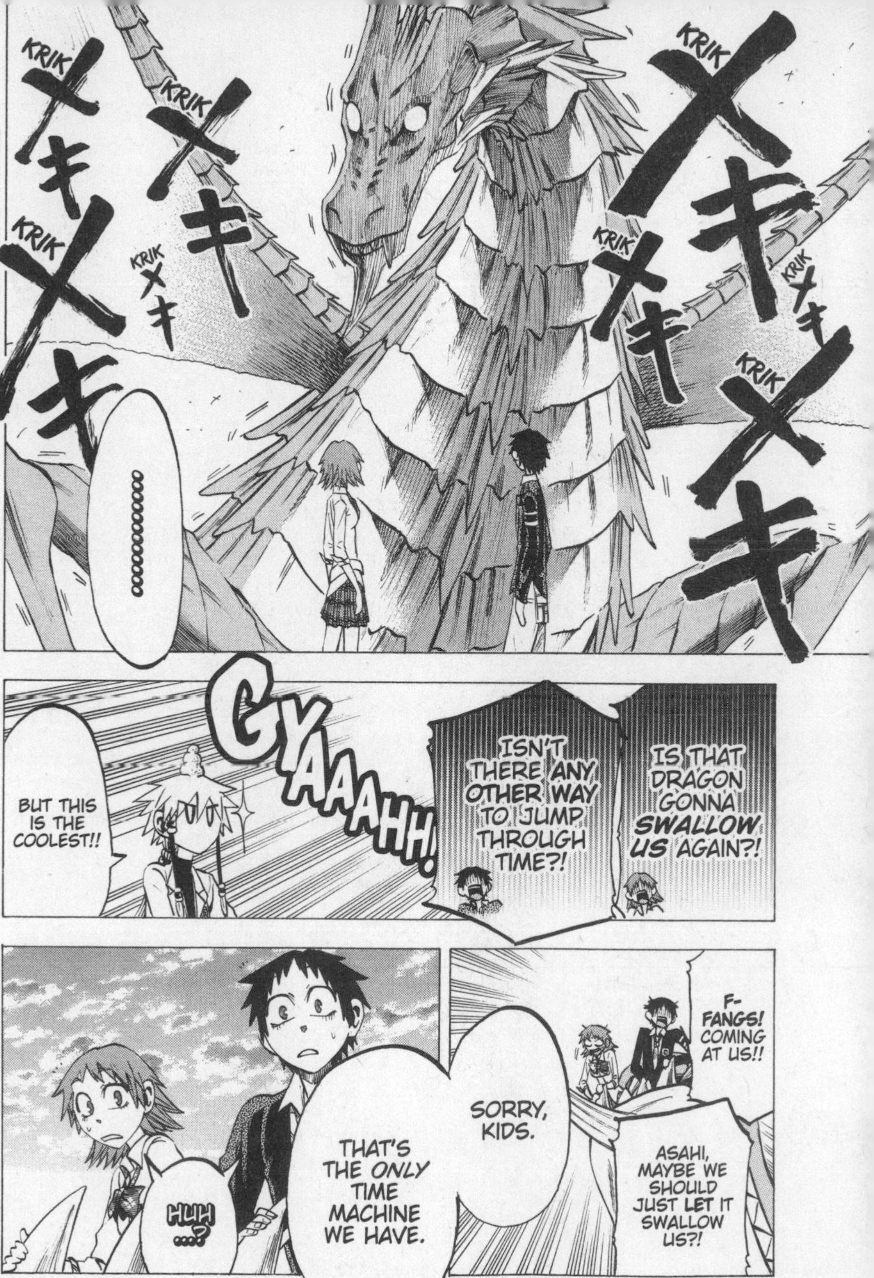
KRIK
KRIK
KRIK
KRIK
KRIK
KRIK
KRIK
KRIK
IS THAT DRAGON GONNA *SWALLOW US* AGAIN?!
ISN'T THERE ANY OTHER WAY TO JUMP THROUGH TIME?!
GYAAAAHH!
BUT THIS IS THE COOLEST!!
F-FANGS! COMING AT US!!
ASAHI, MAYBE WE SHOULD JUST LET IT SWALLOW US?!
SORRY, KIDS.
THAT'S THE *ONLY* TIME MACHINE WE HAVE.
HUH ...?

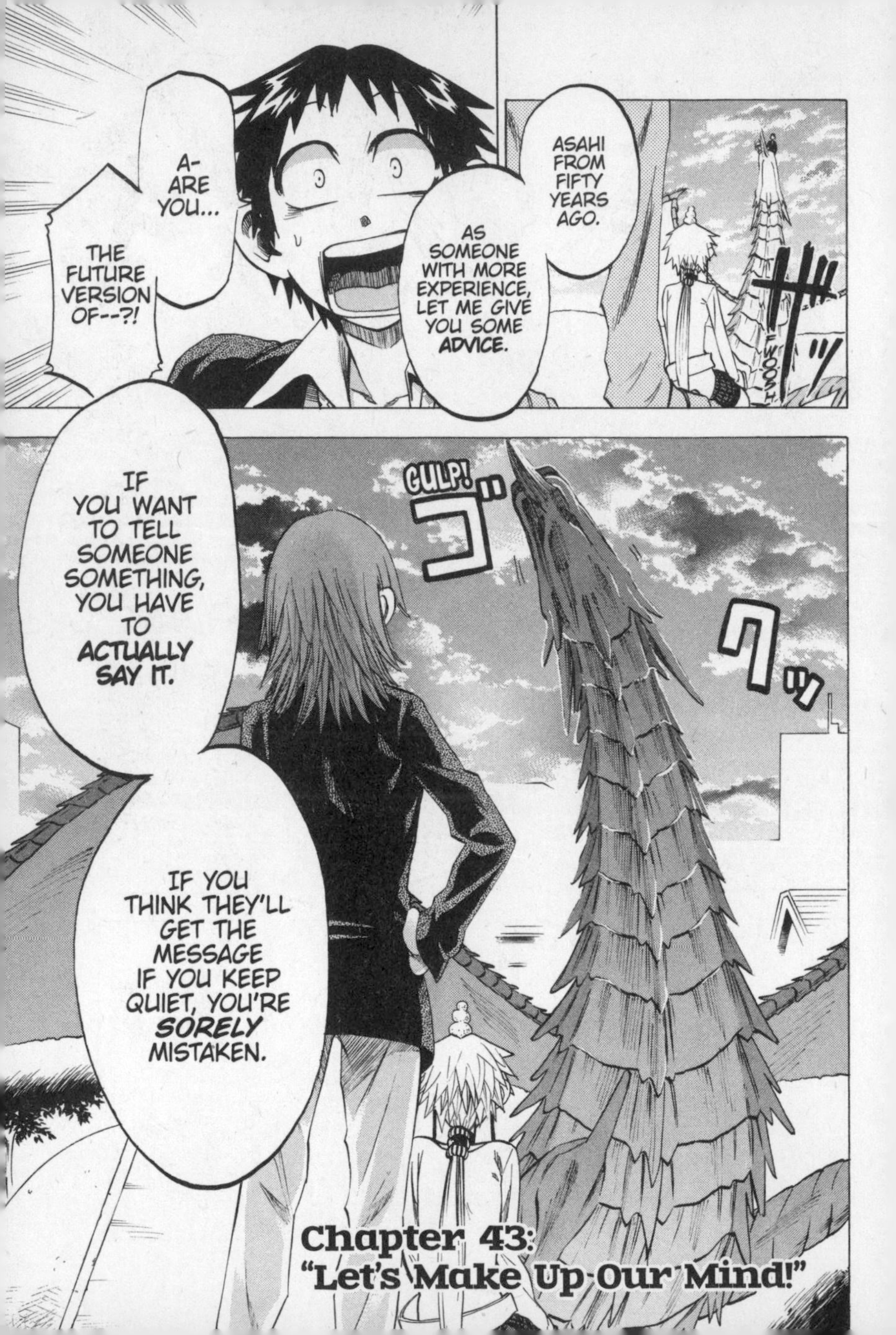
FWOOSH
ASAHI FROM FIFTY YEARS AGO.
A- ARE YOU...
THE FUTURE VERSION OF--?!
AS SOMEONE WITH MORE EXPERIENCE, LET ME GIVE YOU SOME ADVICE.
GULP!
IF YOU WANT TO TELL SOMEONE SOMETHING, YOU HAVE TO ACTUALLY SAY IT.
IF YOU THINK THEY'LL GET THE MESSAGE IF YOU KEEP QUIET, YOU'RE SORELY MISTAKEN.
Chapter 43: "Let's Make Up Our Mind!"

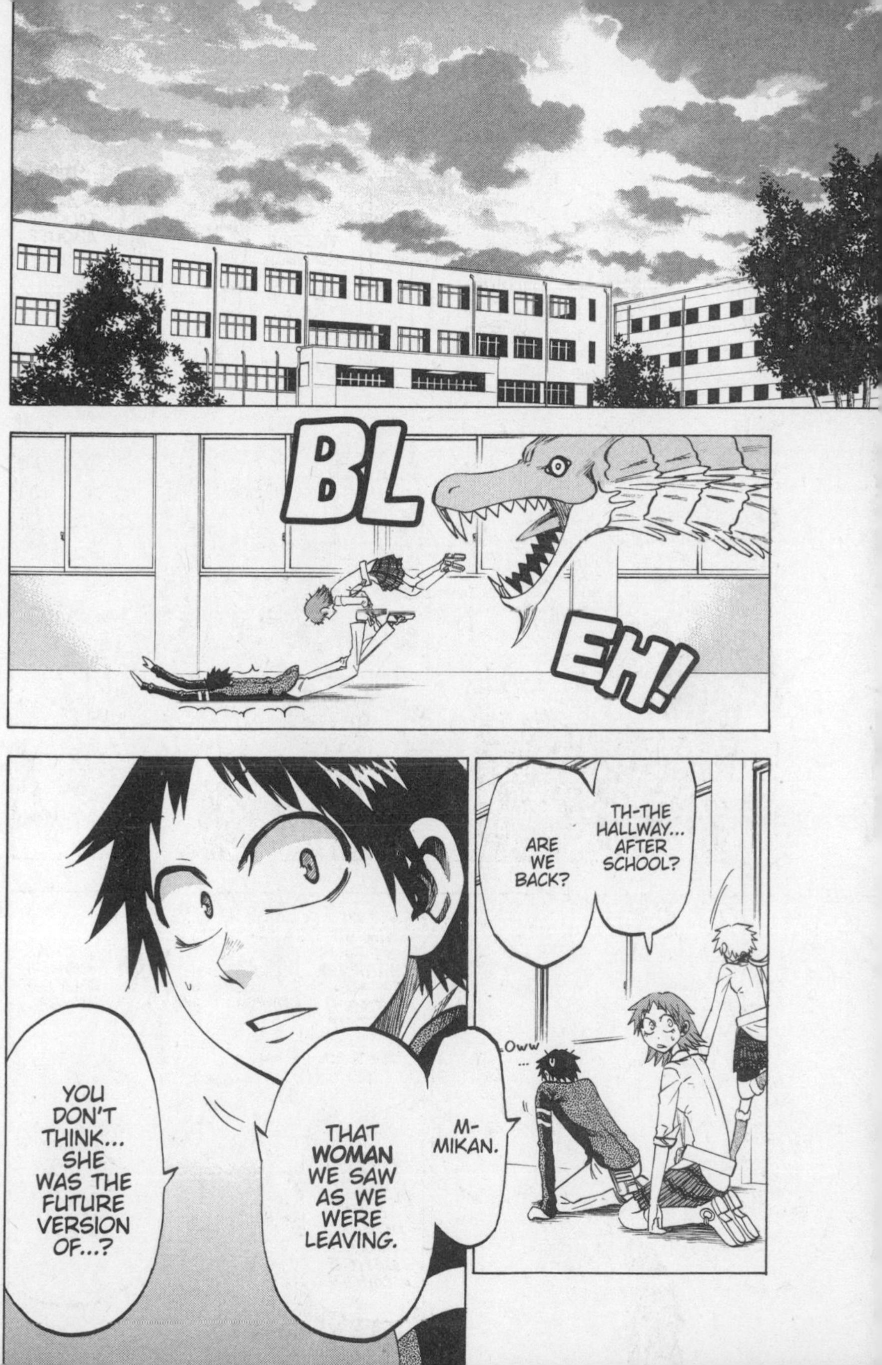
BLEH!
TH-THE HALLWAY... AFTER SCHOOL?
ARE WE BACK?
OWW...
M-MIKAN.
THAT WOMAN WE SAW AS WE WERE LEAVING.
YOU DON'T THINK... SHE WAS THE FUTURE VERSION OF...?

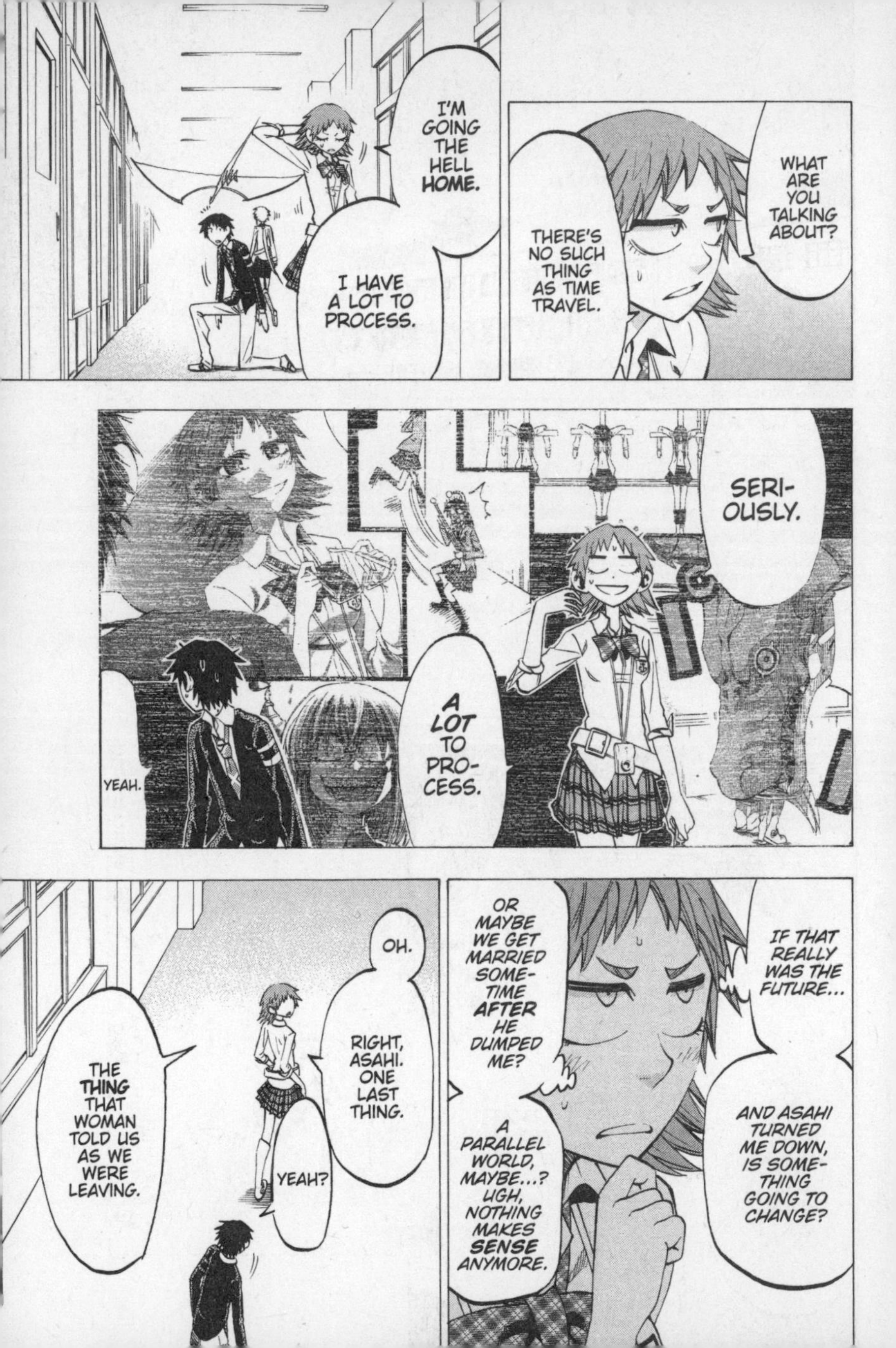
WHAT ARE YOU TALKING ABOUT?
THERE'S NO SUCH THING AS TIME TRAVEL.
I'M GOING THE HELL **HOME.**
I HAVE A LOT TO PROCESS.
SERI-OUSLY.
A LOT TO PRO-CESS.
YEAH.
IF THAT REALLY WAS THE FUTURE...
OR MAYBE WE GET MARRIED SOME-TIME **AFTER** HE DUMPED ME?
AND ASAHI TURNED ME DOWN, IS SOME-THING GOING TO CHANGE?
A PARALLEL WORLD, MAYBE...? UGH, NOTHING MAKES **SENSE** ANYMORE.
OH.
RIGHT, ASAHI. ONE LAST THING.
YEAH?
THE **THING** THAT WOMAN TOLD US AS WE WERE LEAVING.

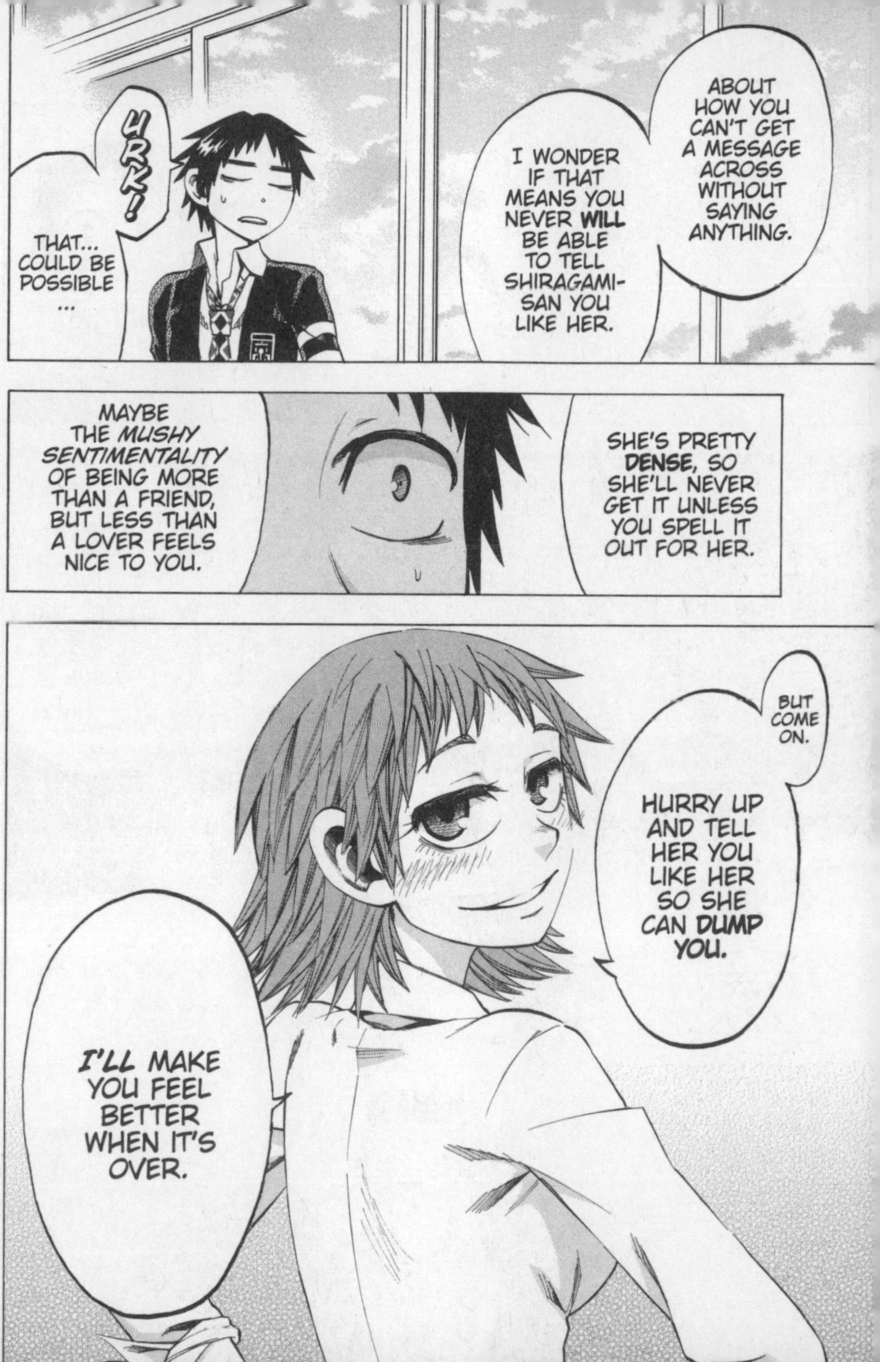
ABOUT HOW YOU CAN'T GET A MESSAGE ACROSS WITHOUT SAYING ANYTHING.
I WONDER IF THAT MEANS YOU NEVER **WILL** BE ABLE TO TELL SHIRAGAMI-SAN YOU LIKE HER.
URK!
THAT... COULD BE POSSIBLE ...
SHE'S PRETTY **DENSE,** SO SHE'LL NEVER GET IT UNLESS YOU SPELL IT OUT FOR HER.
MAYBE THE *MUSHY SENTIMENTALITY* OF BEING MORE THAN A FRIEND, BUT LESS THAN A LOVER FEELS NICE TO YOU.
BUT COME ON.
HURRY UP AND TELL HER YOU LIKE HER SO SHE CAN **DUMP YOU.**
I'LL MAKE YOU FEEL BETTER WHEN IT'S OVER.

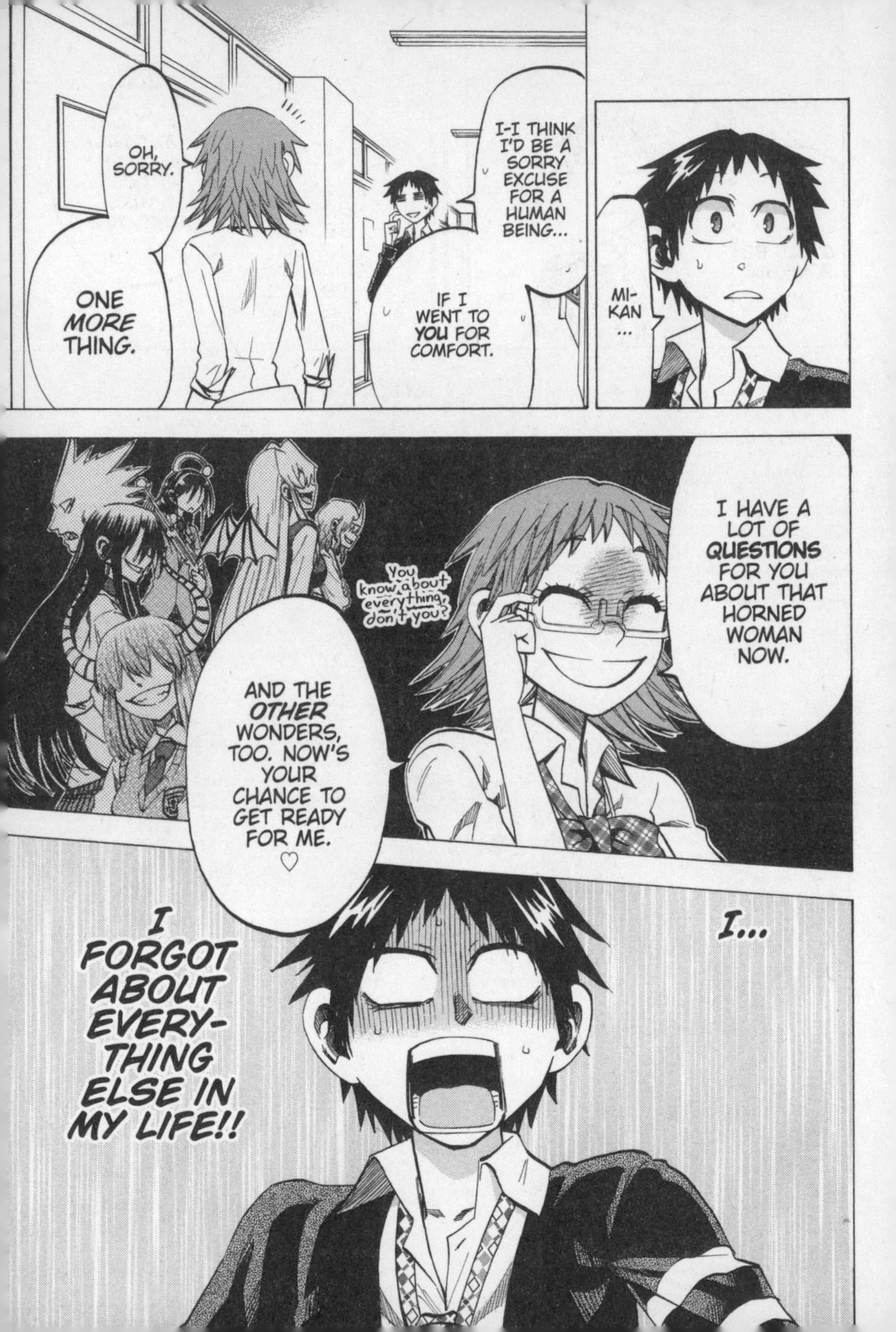
MI-KAN ...
I-I THINK I'D BE A SORRY EXCUSE FOR A HUMAN BEING...
IF I WENT TO YOU FOR COMFORT.
OH, SORRY.
ONE MORE THING.
I HAVE A LOT OF QUESTIONS FOR YOU ABOUT THAT HORNED WOMAN NOW.
You know about everything, don't you?
AND THE OTHER WONDERS, TOO. NOW'S YOUR CHANCE TO GET READY FOR ME. ♡
I...
I FORGOT ABOUT EVERYTHING ELSE IN MY LIFE!!

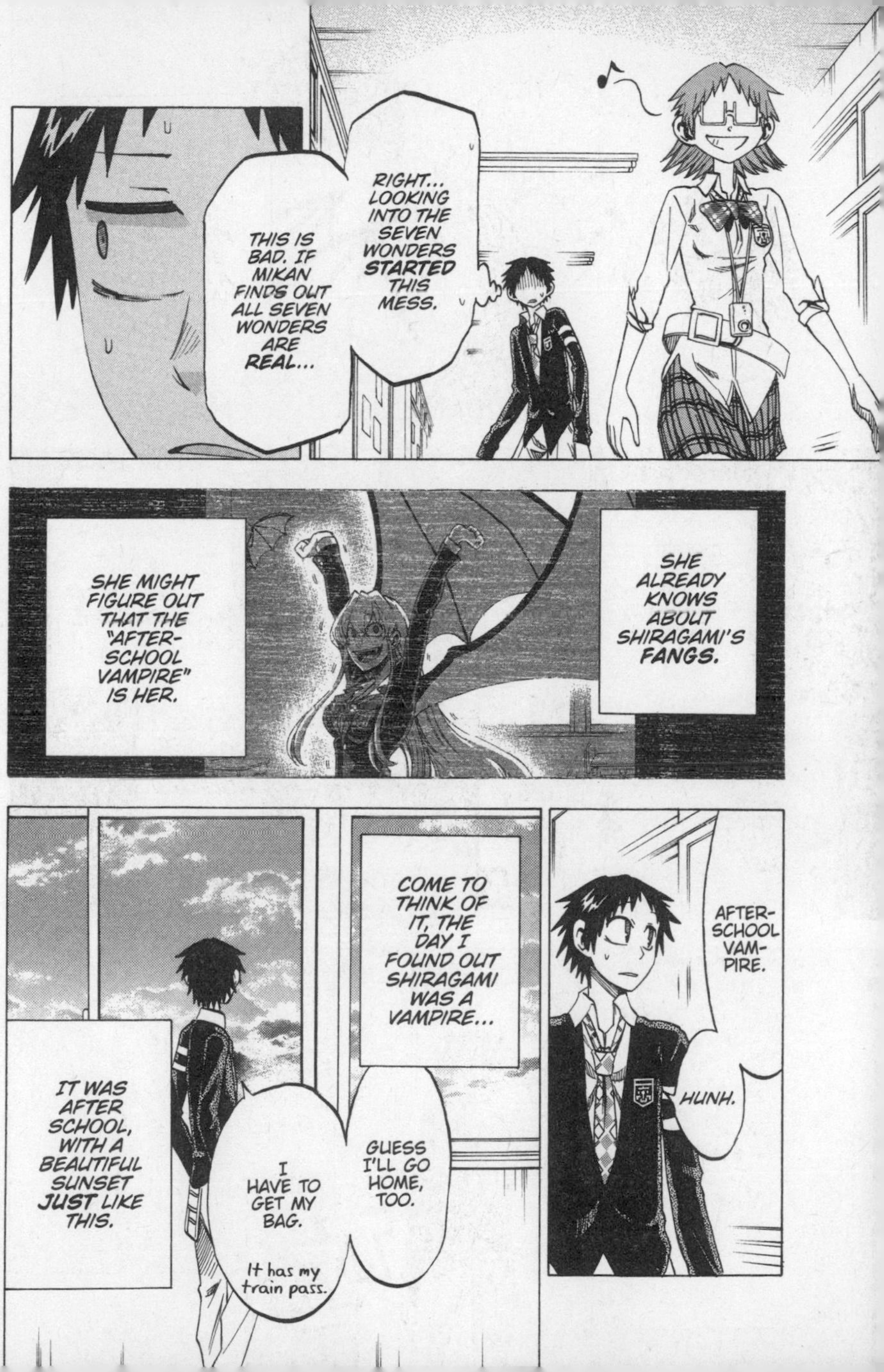
RIGHT... LOOKING INTO THE SEVEN WONDERS STARTED THIS MESS.
THIS IS BAD. IF MIKAN FINDS OUT ALL SEVEN WONDERS ARE REAL...
SHE ALREADY KNOWS ABOUT SHIRAGAMI'S FANGS.
SHE MIGHT FIGURE OUT THAT THE "AFTER-SCHOOL VAMPIRE" IS HER.
AFTER-SCHOOL VAMPIRE.
HUNH.
COME TO THINK OF IT, THE DAY I FOUND OUT SHIRAGAMI WAS A VAMPIRE...
GUESS I'LL GO HOME, TOO.
I HAVE TO GET MY BAG.
It has my train pass.
IT WAS AFTER SCHOOL, WITH A BEAUTIFUL SUNSET JUST LIKE THIS.

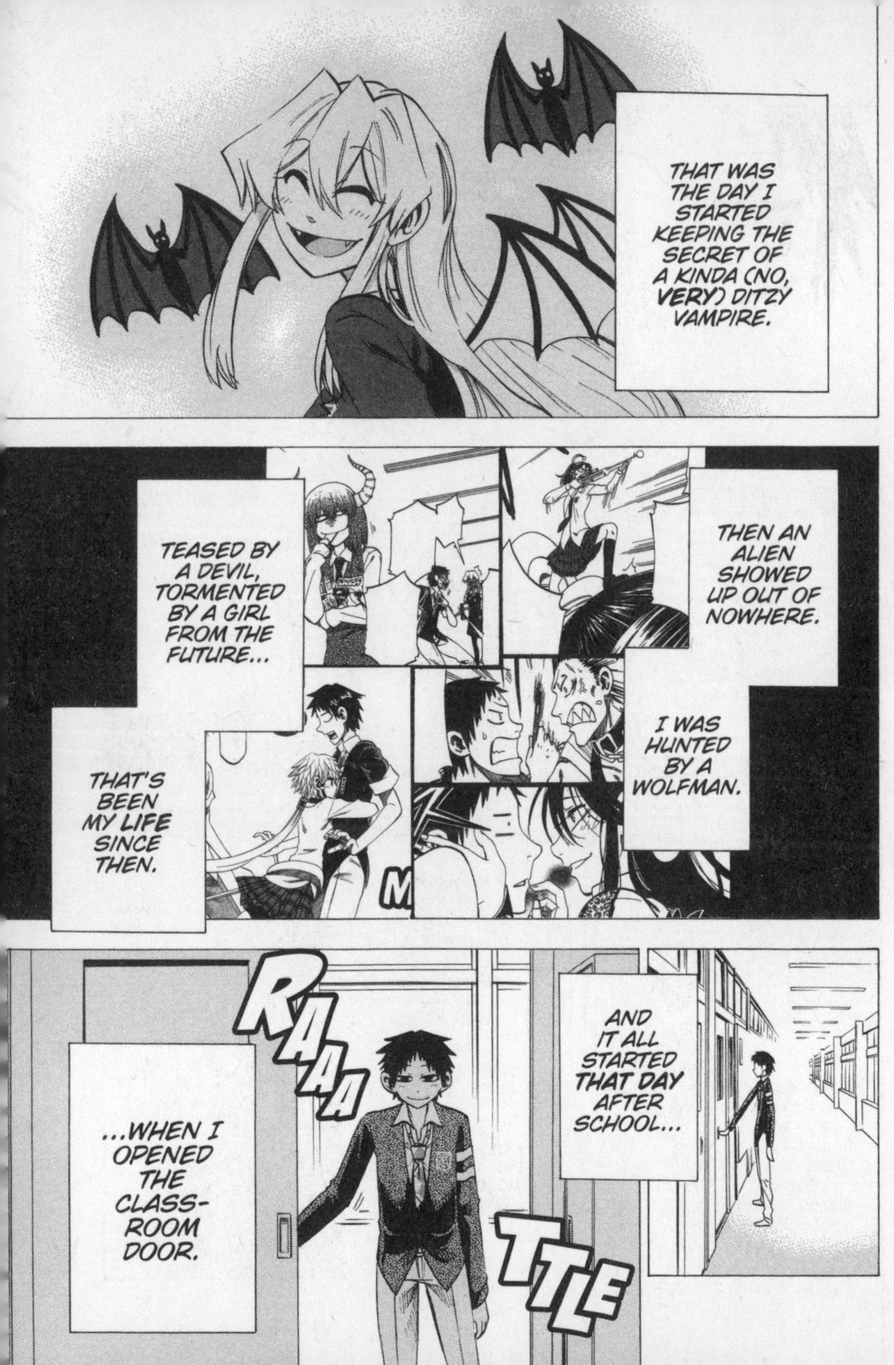
THAT WAS THE DAY I STARTED KEEPING THE SECRET OF A KINDA (NO, VERY) DITZY VAMPIRE.
THEN AN ALIEN SHOWED UP OUT OF NOWHERE.
I WAS HUNTED BY A WOLFMAN.
TEASED BY A DEVIL, TORMENTED BY A GIRL FROM THE FUTURE...
THAT'S BEEN MY LIFE SINCE THEN.
AND IT ALL STARTED THAT DAY AFTER SCHOOL...
RAAAA
TTLE
...WHEN I OPENED THE CLASS-ROOM DOOR.

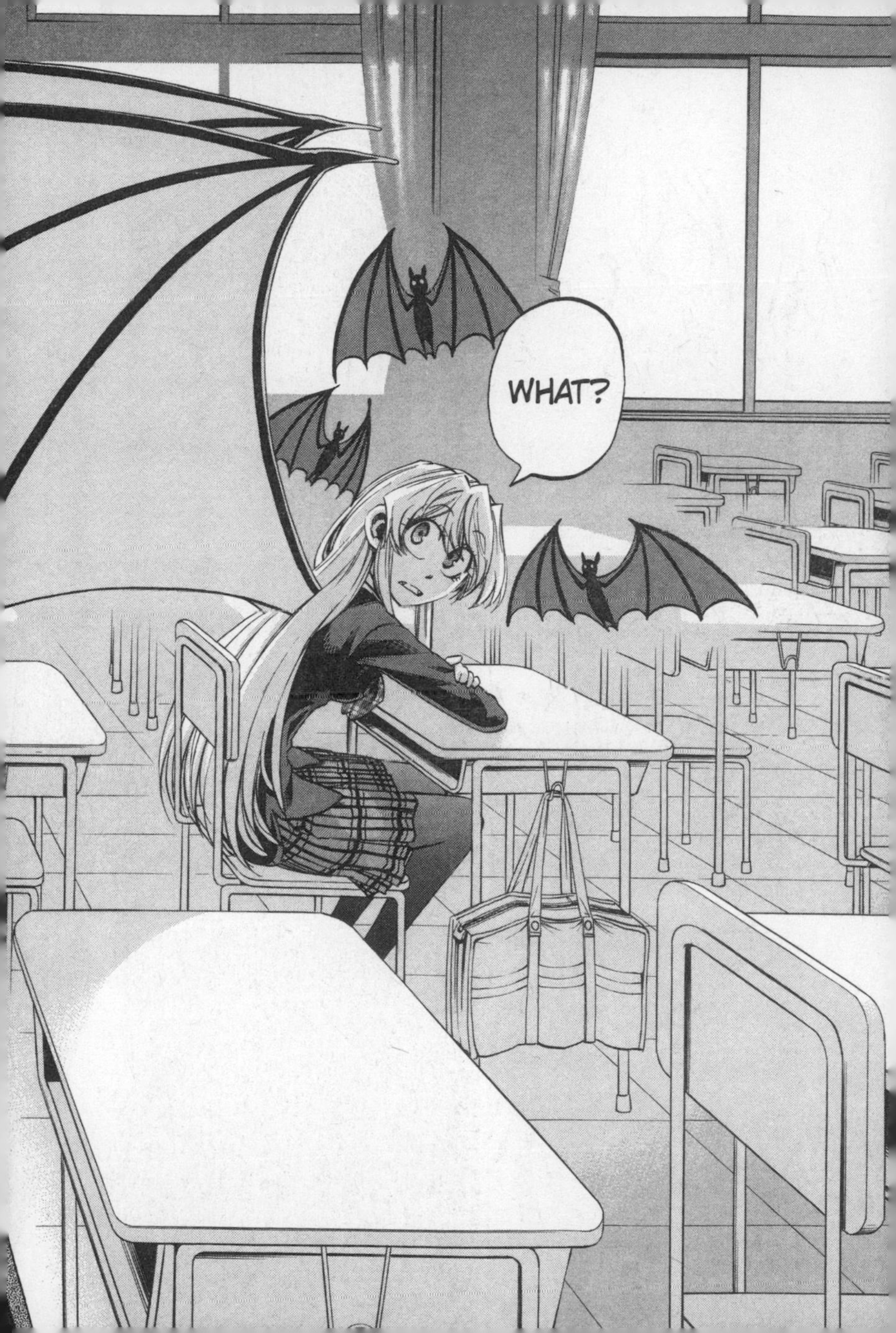
WHAT?

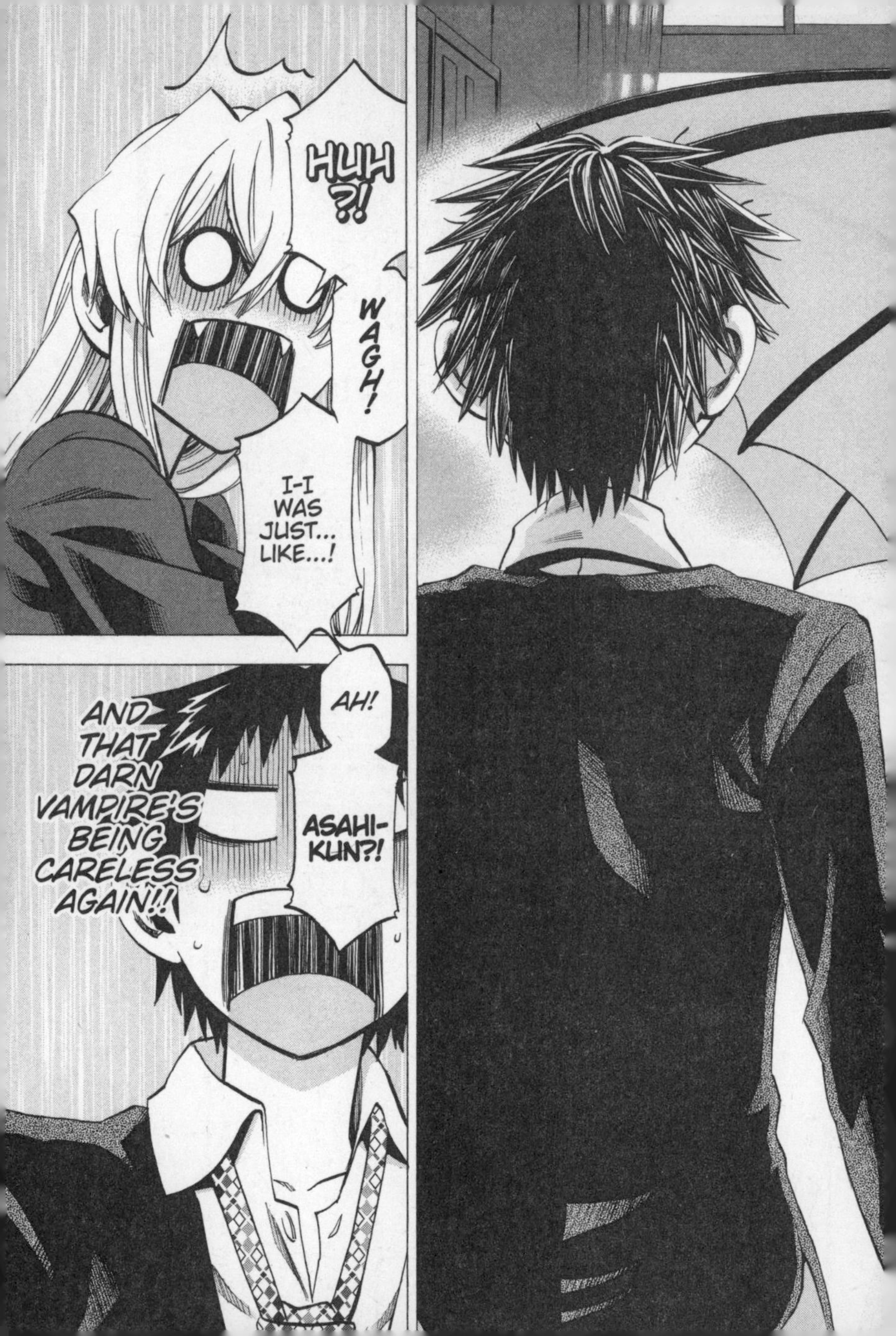
HUH?!
WAGH!
I-I WAS JUST... LIKE...!
AH!
ASAHI-KUN?!
AND THAT DARN VAMPIRE'S BEING CARELESS AGAIN!!

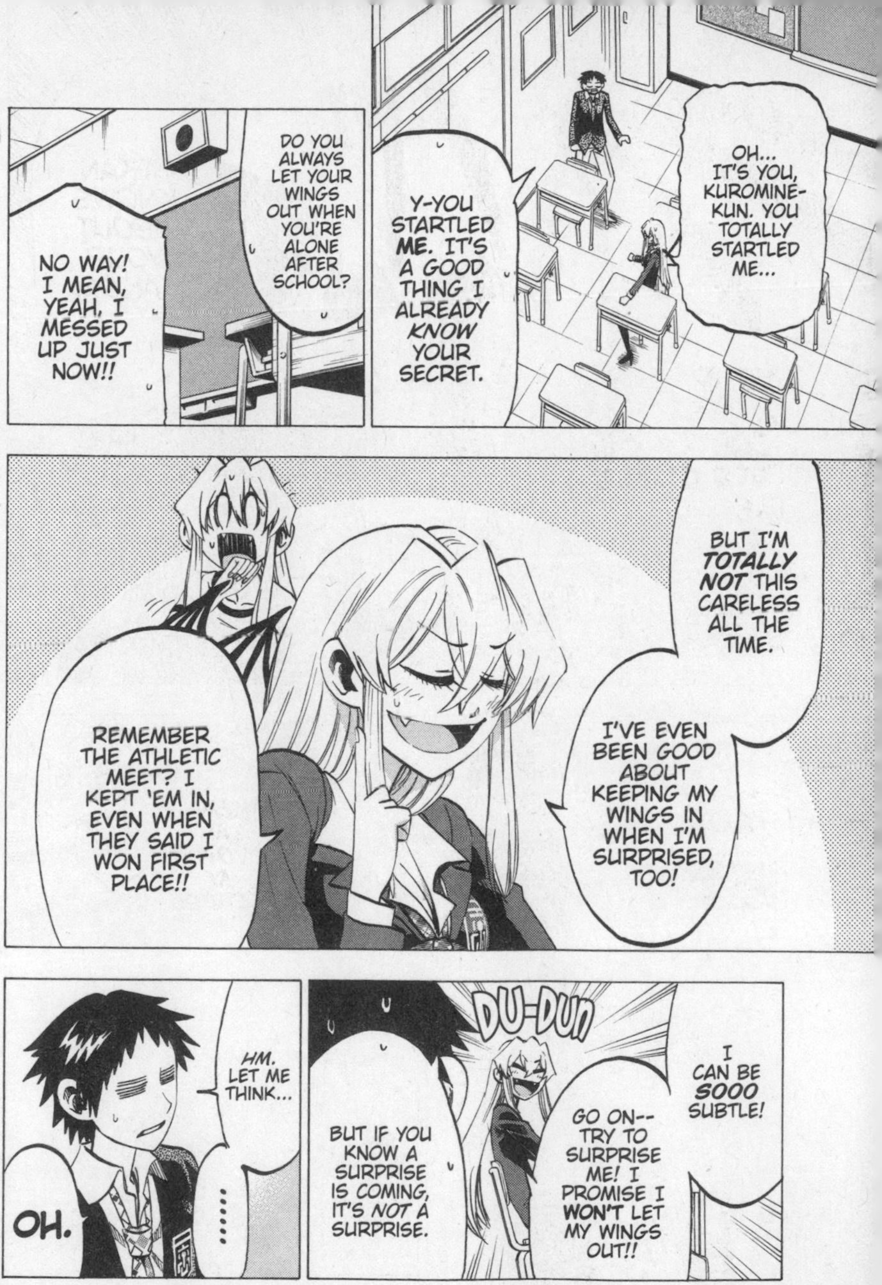
OH... IT'S YOU, KUROMINE-KUN. YOU TOTALLY STARTLED ME...
Y-YOU STARTLED ME. IT'S A GOOD THING I ALREADY KNOW YOUR SECRET.
DO YOU ALWAYS LET YOUR WINGS OUT WHEN YOU'RE ALONE AFTER SCHOOL?
NO WAY! I MEAN, YEAH, I MESSED UP JUST NOW!!
BUT I'M TOTALLY NOT THIS CARELESS ALL THE TIME.
I'VE EVEN BEEN GOOD ABOUT KEEPING MY WINGS IN WHEN I'M SURPRISED, TOO!
REMEMBER THE ATHLETIC MEET? I KEPT 'EM IN, EVEN WHEN THEY SAID I WON FIRST PLACE!!
DU-DUN
I CAN BE SOOO SUBTLE!
GO ON-- TRY TO SURPRISE ME! I PROMISE I WON'T LET MY WINGS OUT!!
BUT IF YOU KNOW A SURPRISE IS COMING, IT'S NOT A SURPRISE.
HM. LET ME THINK...
......
OH.

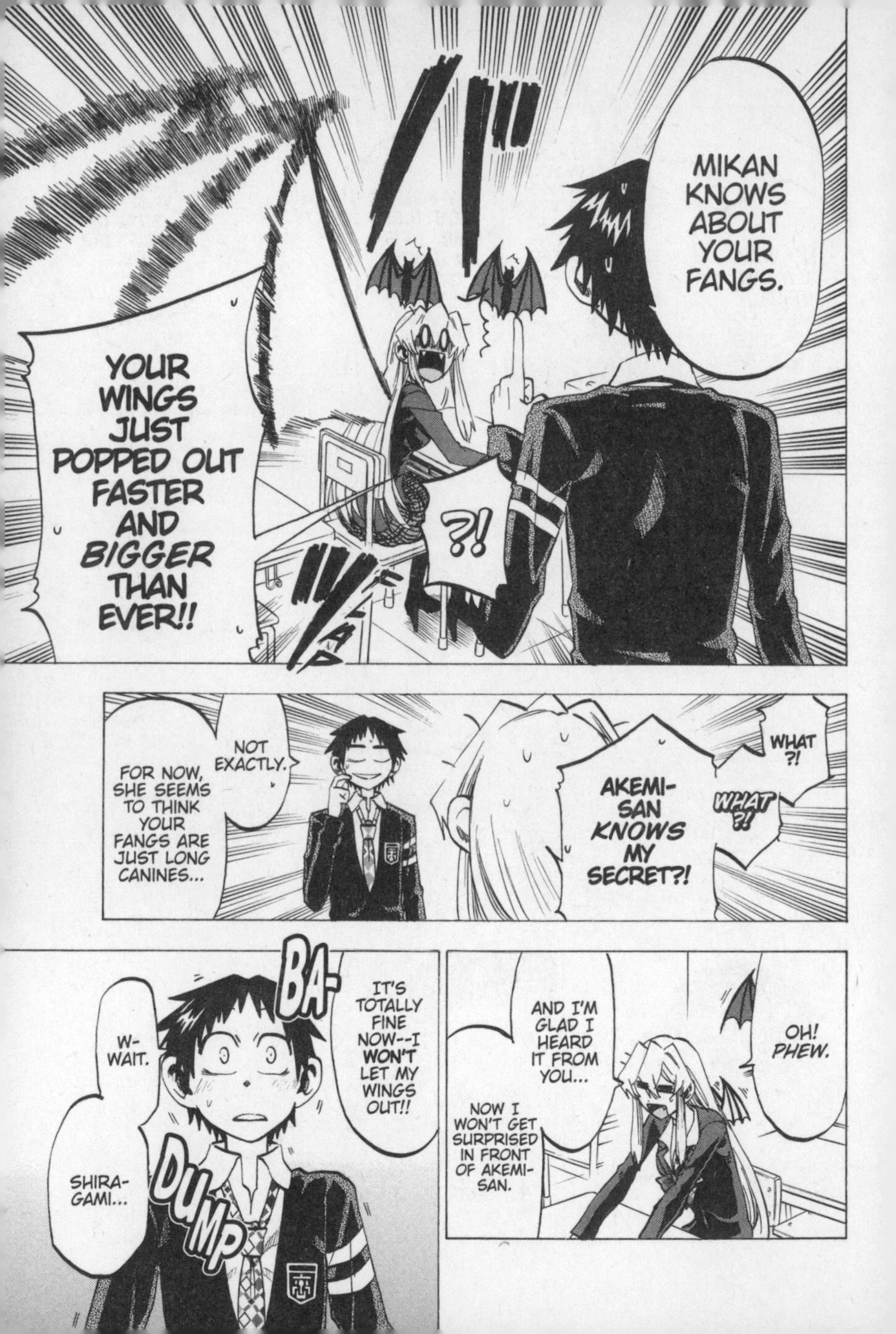
MIKAN KNOWS ABOUT YOUR FANGS.
?!
YOUR WINGS JUST POPPED OUT FASTER AND BIGGER THAN EVER!!
FLAP
WHAT ?!
WHAT ?!
AKEMI-SAN KNOWS MY SECRET?!
NOT EXACTLY.
FOR NOW, SHE SEEMS TO THINK YOUR FANGS ARE JUST LONG CANINES...
OH! PHEW.
AND I'M GLAD I HEARD IT FROM YOU...
NOW I WON'T GET SURPRISED IN FRONT OF AKEMI-SAN.
IT'S TOTALLY FINE NOW--I WON'T LET MY WINGS OUT!!
BA-
W-WAIT.
DUMP
SHIRA-GAMI...

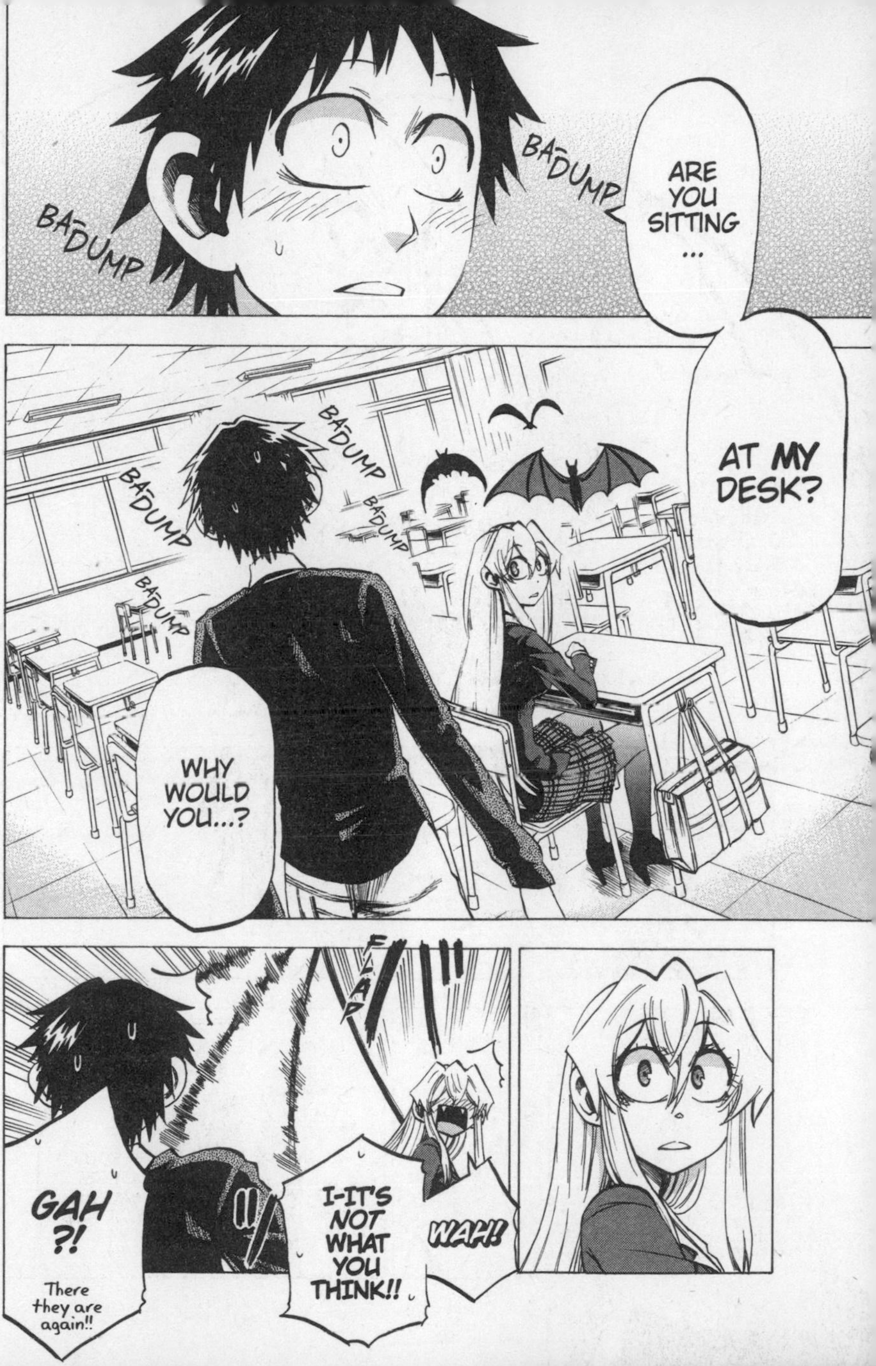
BA-DUMP
BA-DUMP
ARE YOU SITTING ...
AT MY DESK?
BA-DUMP
BA-DUMP
BA-DUMP
BA-DUMP
WHY WOULD YOU...?
FLAP
WAH!
I-IT'S NOT WHAT YOU THINK!!
GAH ?!
There they are again!!

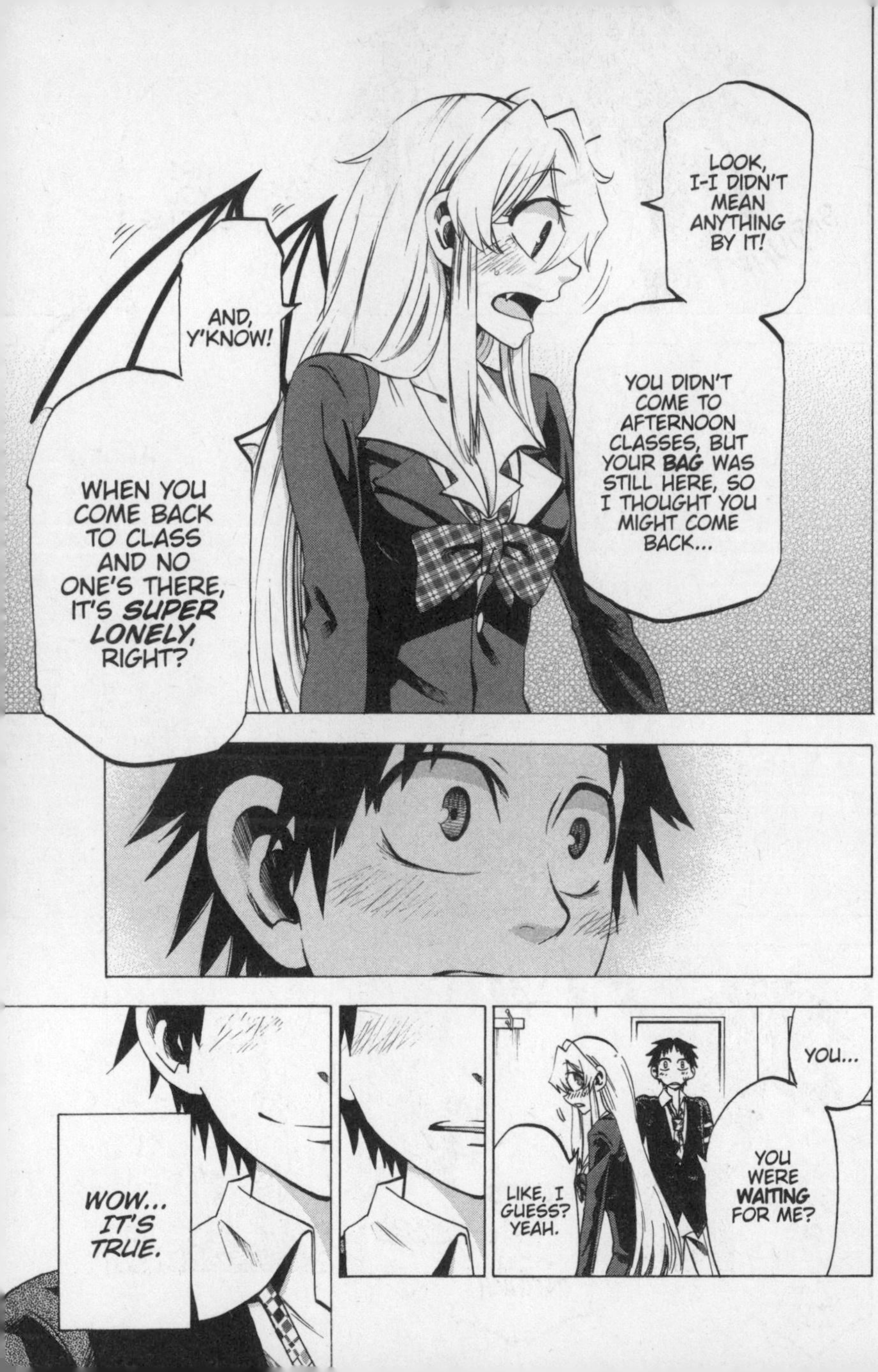
LOOK, I-I DIDN'T MEAN ANYTHING BY IT!
YOU DIDN'T COME TO AFTERNOON CLASSES, BUT YOUR **BAG** WAS STILL HERE, SO I THOUGHT YOU MIGHT COME BACK...
AND, Y'KNOW!
WHEN YOU COME BACK TO CLASS AND NO ONE'S THERE, IT'S ***SUPER LONELY,*** RIGHT?
YOU...
YOU WERE **WAITING** FOR ME?
LIKE, I GUESS? YEAH.
WOW... IT'S TRUE.

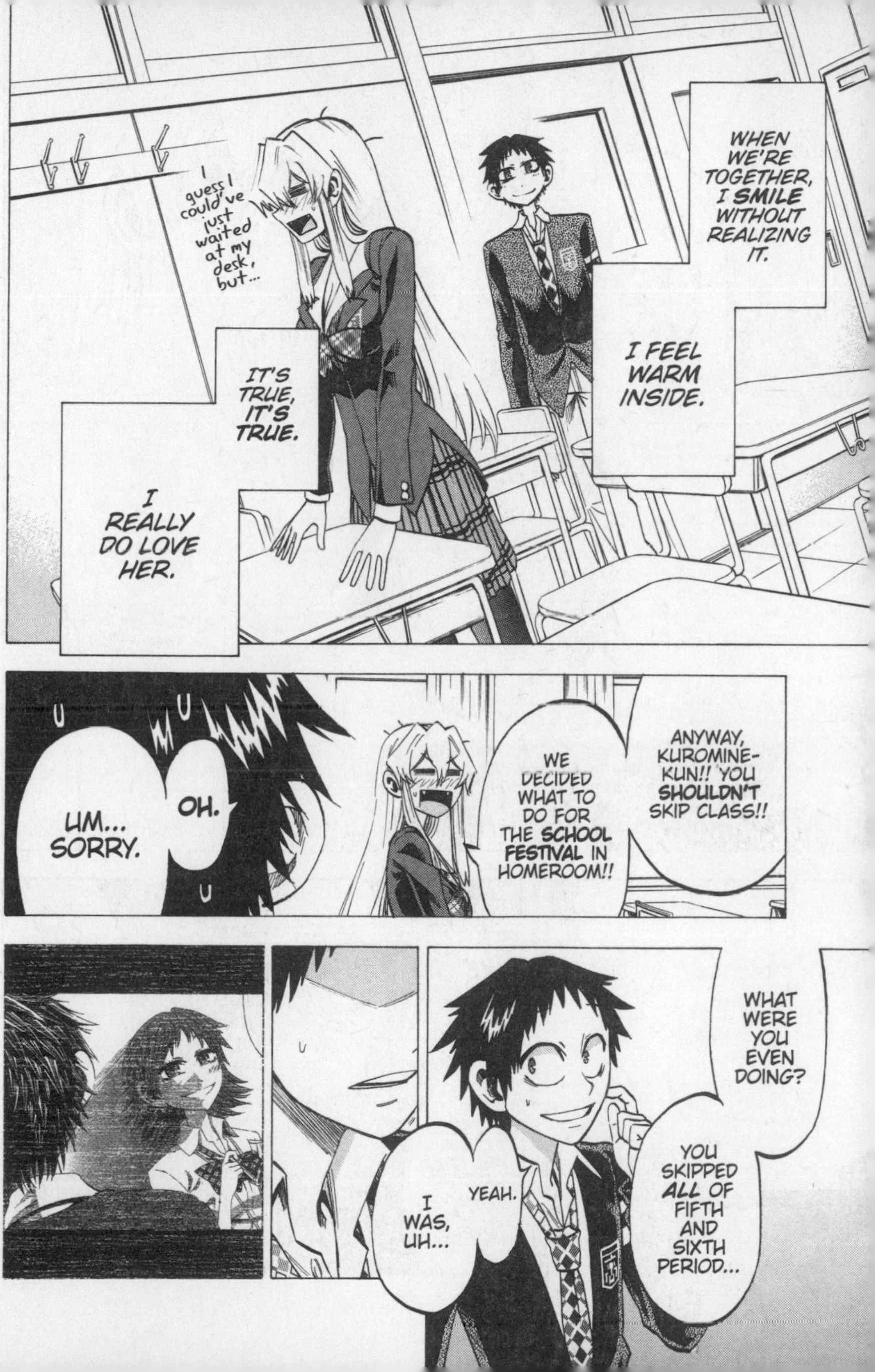
WHEN WE'RE TOGETHER, I SMILE WITHOUT REALIZING IT.
I FEEL WARM INSIDE.
I guess I could've just waited at my desk, but...
IT'S TRUE, IT'S TRUE.
I REALLY DO LOVE HER.
ANYWAY, KUROMINE-KUN!! YOU SHOULDN'T SKIP CLASS!!
WE DECIDED WHAT TO DO FOR THE SCHOOL FESTIVAL IN HOMEROOM!!
OH.
UM... SORRY.
WHAT WERE YOU EVEN DOING?
YOU SKIPPED ALL OF FIFTH AND SIXTH PERIOD...
YEAH.
I WAS, UH...

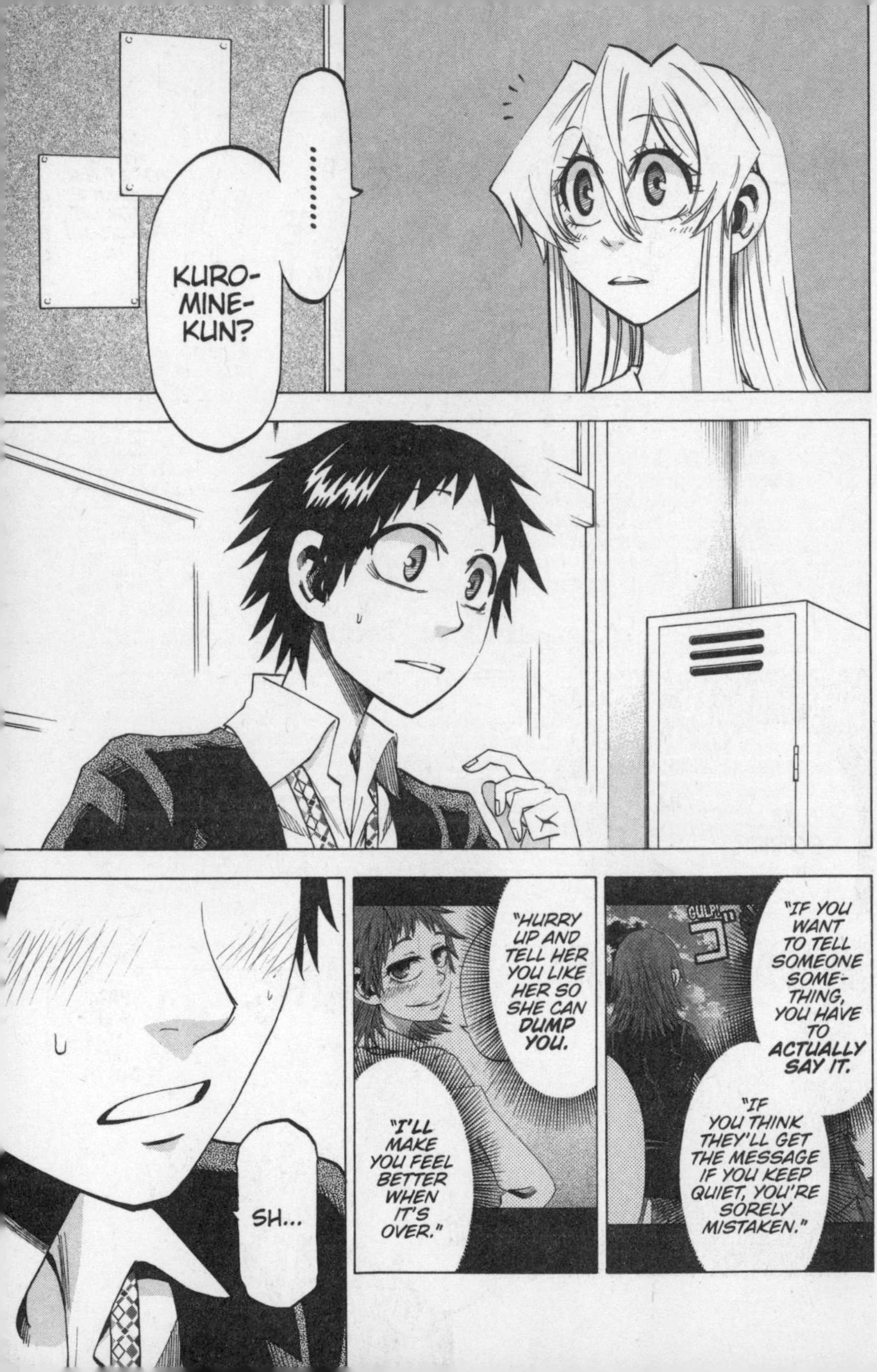

......
KURO-MINE-KUN?
GULP!
"IF YOU WANT TO TELL SOMEONE SOME-THING, YOU HAVE TO ACTUALLY SAY IT.
"IF YOU THINK THEY'LL GET THE MESSAGE IF YOU KEEP QUIET, YOU'RE SORELY MISTAKEN."
"HURRY UP AND TELL HER YOU LIKE HER SO SHE CAN DUMP YOU.
"I'LL MAKE YOU FEEL BETTER WHEN IT'S OVER."
SH...

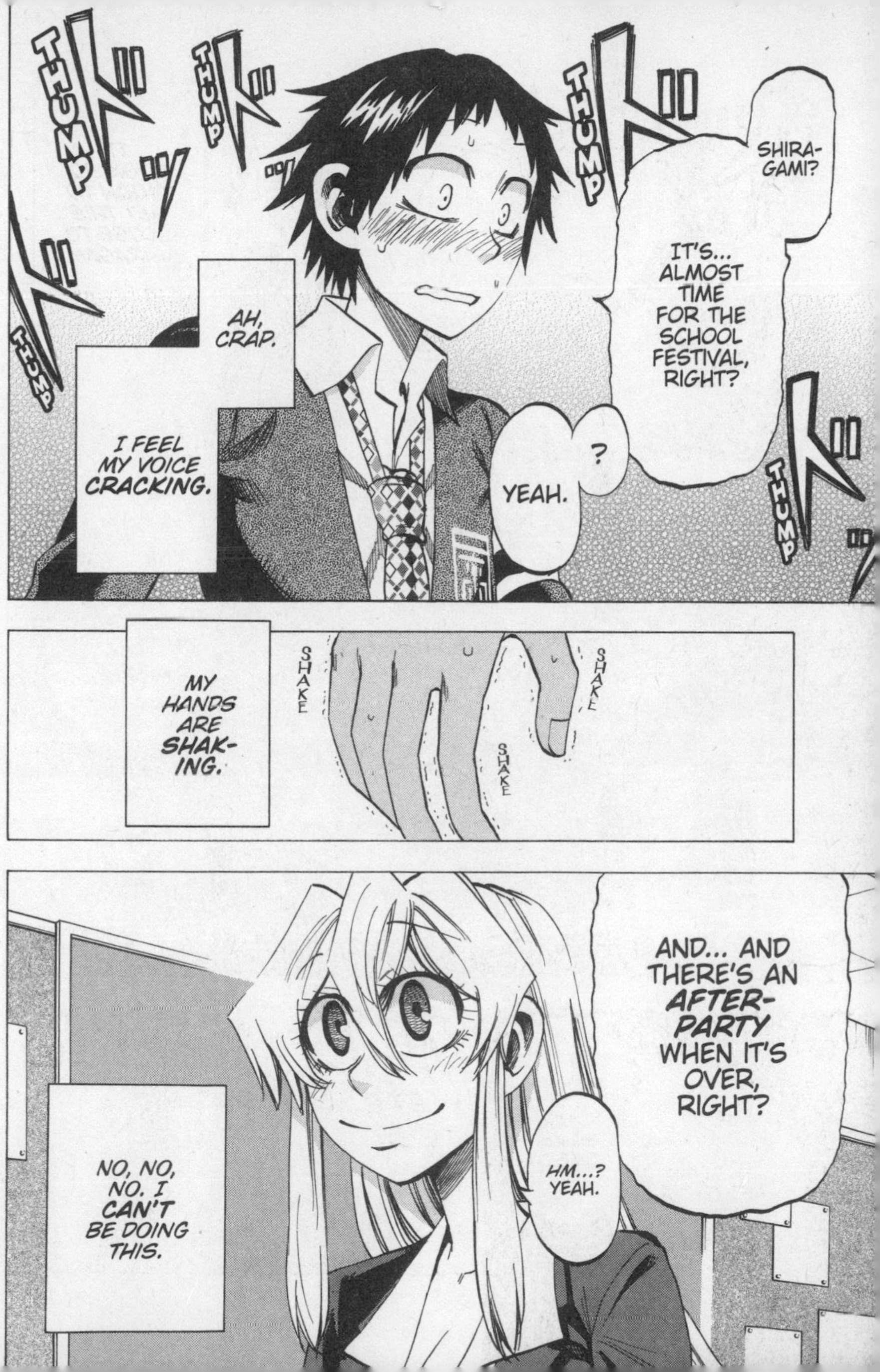
THUMP
THUMP
SHIRA-GAMI?
IT'S... ALMOST TIME FOR THE SCHOOL FESTIVAL, RIGHT?
THUMP
THUMP
THUMP
? YEAH.
AH, CRAP.
I FEEL MY VOICE CRACKING.
SHAKE
SHAKE
SHAKE
MY HANDS ARE SHAK-ING.
AND... AND THERE'S AN AFTER-PARTY WHEN IT'S OVER, RIGHT?
HM...? YEAH.
NO, NO, NO. I CAN'T BE DOING THIS.

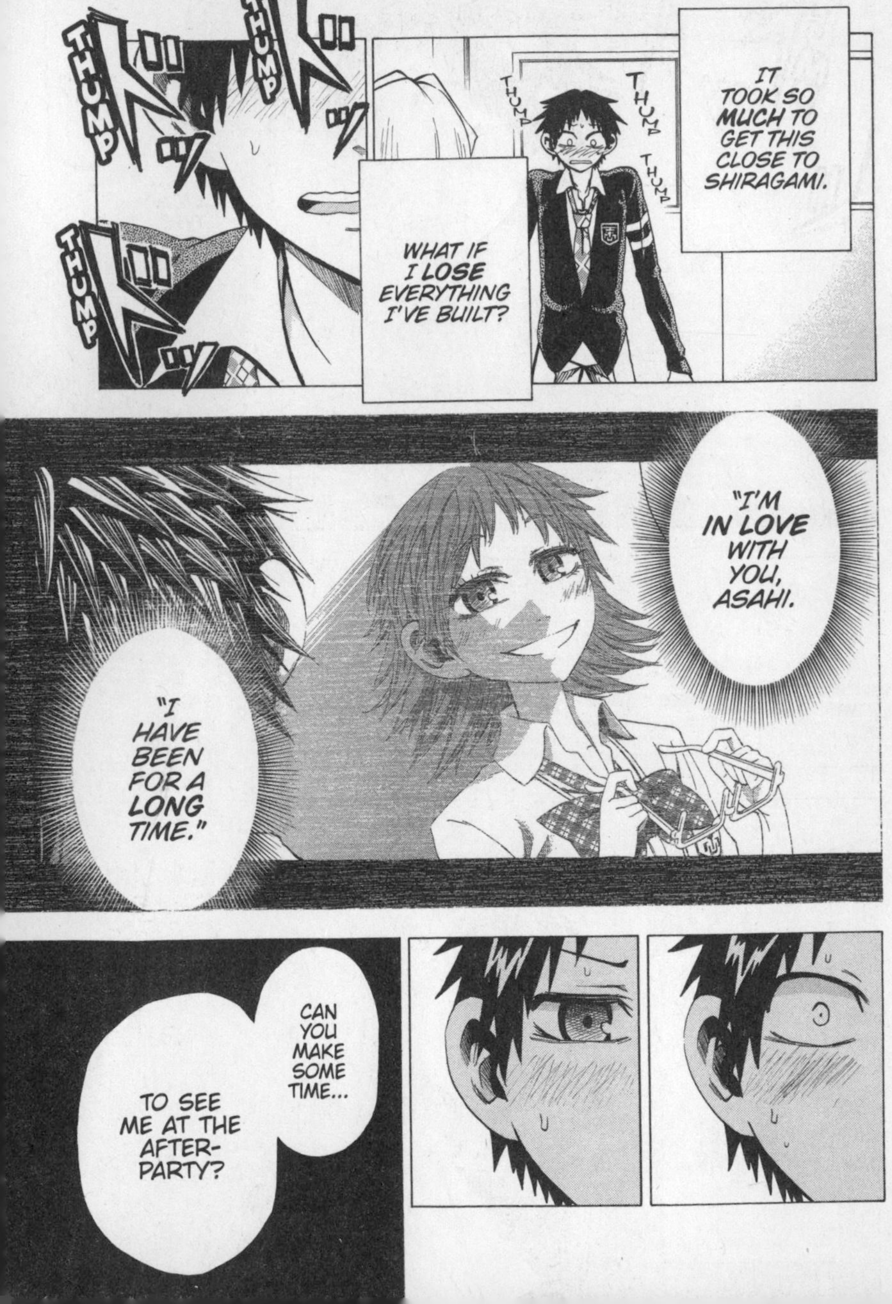
IT TOOK SO MUCH TO GET THIS CLOSE TO SHIRAGAMI.
THUMP
THUMP
THUMP
THUMP
WHAT IF I LOSE EVERYTHING I'VE BUILT?
THUMP
THUMP
THUMP
"I'M IN LOVE WITH YOU, ASAHI.
"I HAVE BEEN FOR A LONG TIME."
CAN YOU MAKE SOME TIME...
TO SEE ME AT THE AFTER-PARTY?

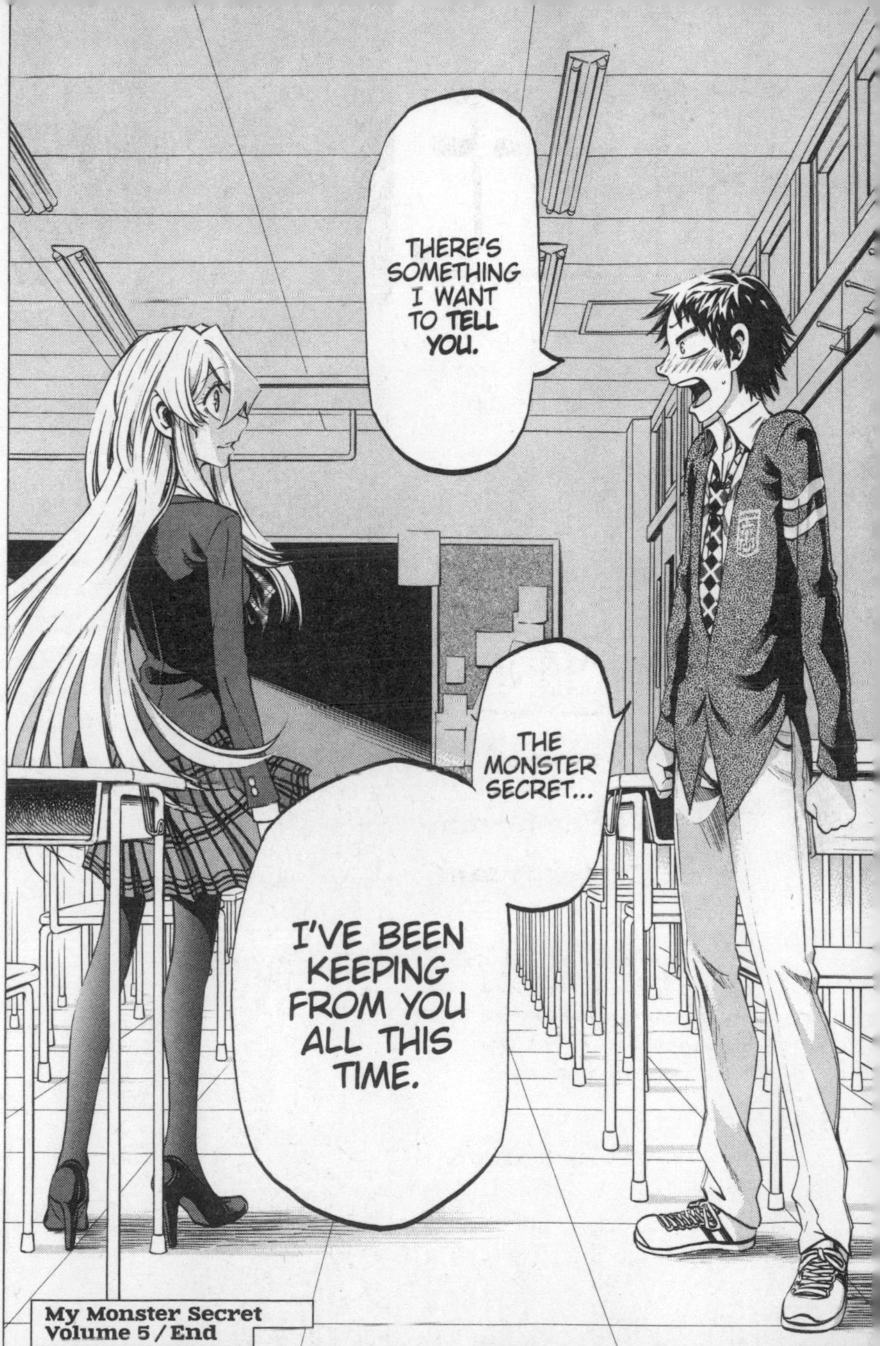
THERE'S SOMETHING I WANT TO TELL YOU.
THE MONSTER SECRET...
I'VE BEEN KEEPING FROM YOU ALL THIS TIME.
My Monster Secret Volume 5 / End

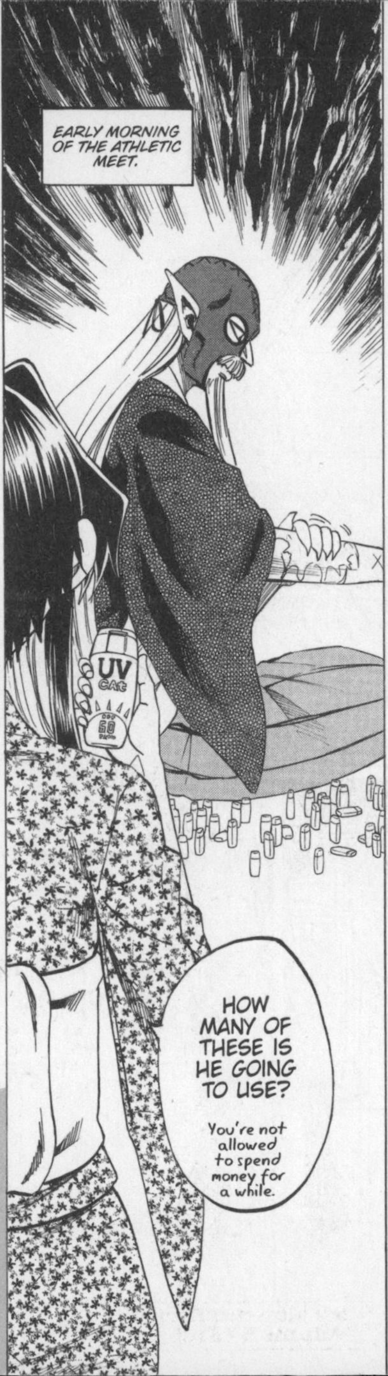
EARLY MORNING OF THE ATHLETIC MEET.
UV
HOW MANY OF THESE IS HE GOING TO USE?
You're not allowed to spend money for a while.

STAFF.

- Akutsu-san
- Shuumeigiku-san
- Seijun Suzuki-san
- Hiroki Minemura-san

(in syllabary order)

SPECIAL THANKS.

- Ayako Matsuda-san

Editor: Mukawa-san, Otsuka-san

I give my thanks to those of you holding this book right now and everyone who let me and this work be a part of their lives.

Eiji Masuda

After the Athletic Meet ①

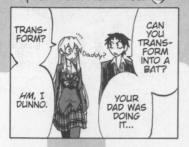

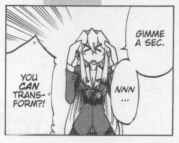

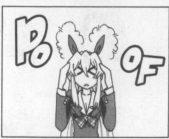

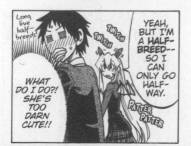

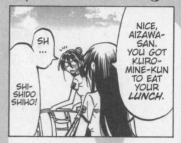

NICE, AIZAWA-SAN. YOU GOT KURO-MINE-KUN TO EAT YOUR LUNCH.
SH ...
SHI-SHIDO SHIHO!
GOOD IDEA.
SHARING WITH EVERY-ONE AT THE MEET.
THE TIERED BOX MADE SENSE.
AND YOU MADE THE SAME AMOUNT AS BEFORE ...
SO THIS TIME, IT WASN'T TOO MUCH!
YES, ABOUT THAT...
MAY I... ASK YOU TO TAKE ONE?
I did it again.
ONE DAY, I'D LIKE TO WATCH YOU MAKE THESE MONSTROS-ITIES.
ZLRRR
YET CLASS REP NEVER THINKS TO FEED HER BROTHER.

After the Athletic Meet ②

CAN YOU TRANS-FORM INTO A BAT?
Daddy?
TRANS-FORM?
YOUR DAD WAS DOING IT...
HM, I DUNNO.
GIMME A SEC.
NNN ...
YOU CAN TRANS-FORM?!
PO OF
YEAH, BUT I'M A HALF-BREED-- SO I CAN ONLY GO HALF-WAY.
TWITCH TWITCH
Long live half-breeds!
WHAT DO I DO?! SHE'S TOO DARN CUTE!!
PATTER PATTER

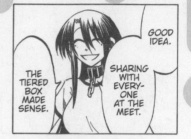

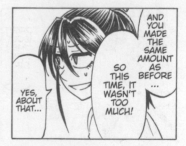

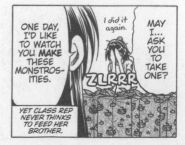

I am 5

After the Athletic Meet ①

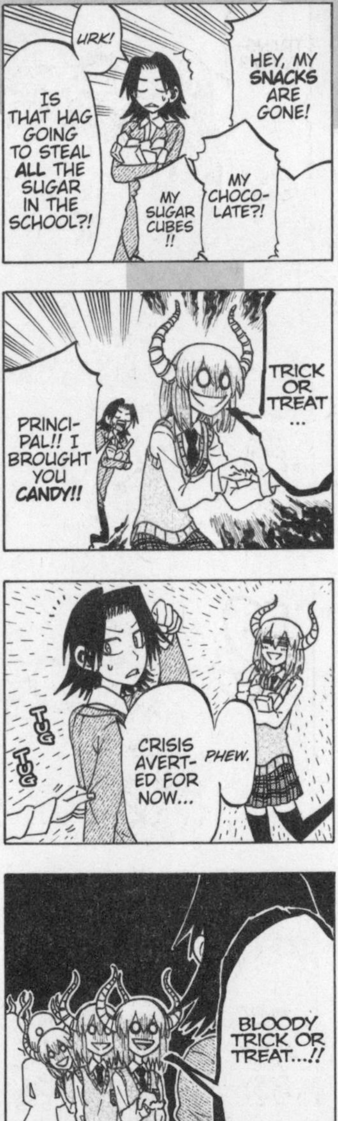
HEY, MY SNACKS ARE GONE!
URK!
MY CHOCOLATE?!
MY SUGAR CUBES !!
IS THAT HAG GOING TO STEAL ALL THE SUGAR IN THE SCHOOL?!
TRICK OR TREAT ...
PRINCIPAL!! I BROUGHT YOU CANDY!!
PHEW.
CRISIS AVERTED FOR NOW...
TUG
TUG
BLOODY TRICK OR TREAT...!!

After the Athletic Meet ②

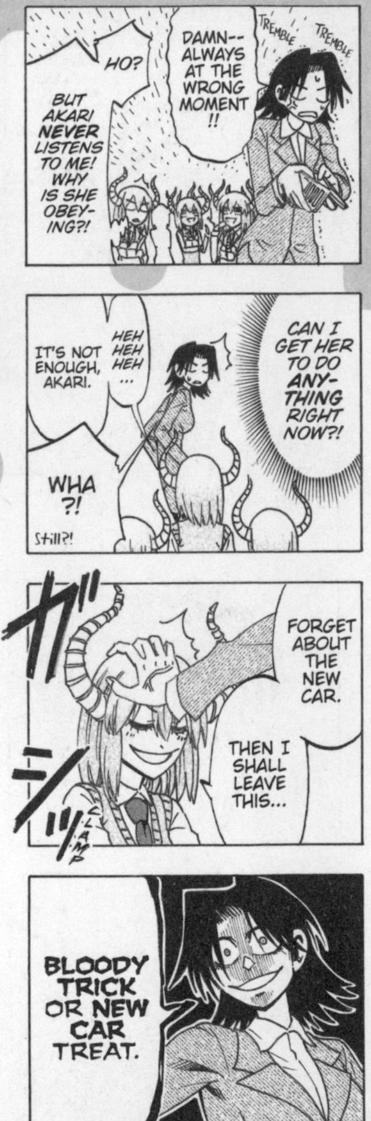
TREMBLE
TREMBLE
DAMN-- ALWAYS AT THE WRONG MOMENT !!
HO?
BUT AKARI NEVER LISTENS TO ME! WHY IS SHE OBEYING?!
CAN I GET HER TO DO ANYTHING RIGHT NOW?!
HEH HEH HEH ...
IT'S NOT ENOUGH, AKARI.
WHA ?!
Still?!
FORGET ABOUT THE NEW CAR.
THEN I SHALL LEAVE THIS...
CLAMP
BLOODY TRICK OR NEW CAR TREAT.

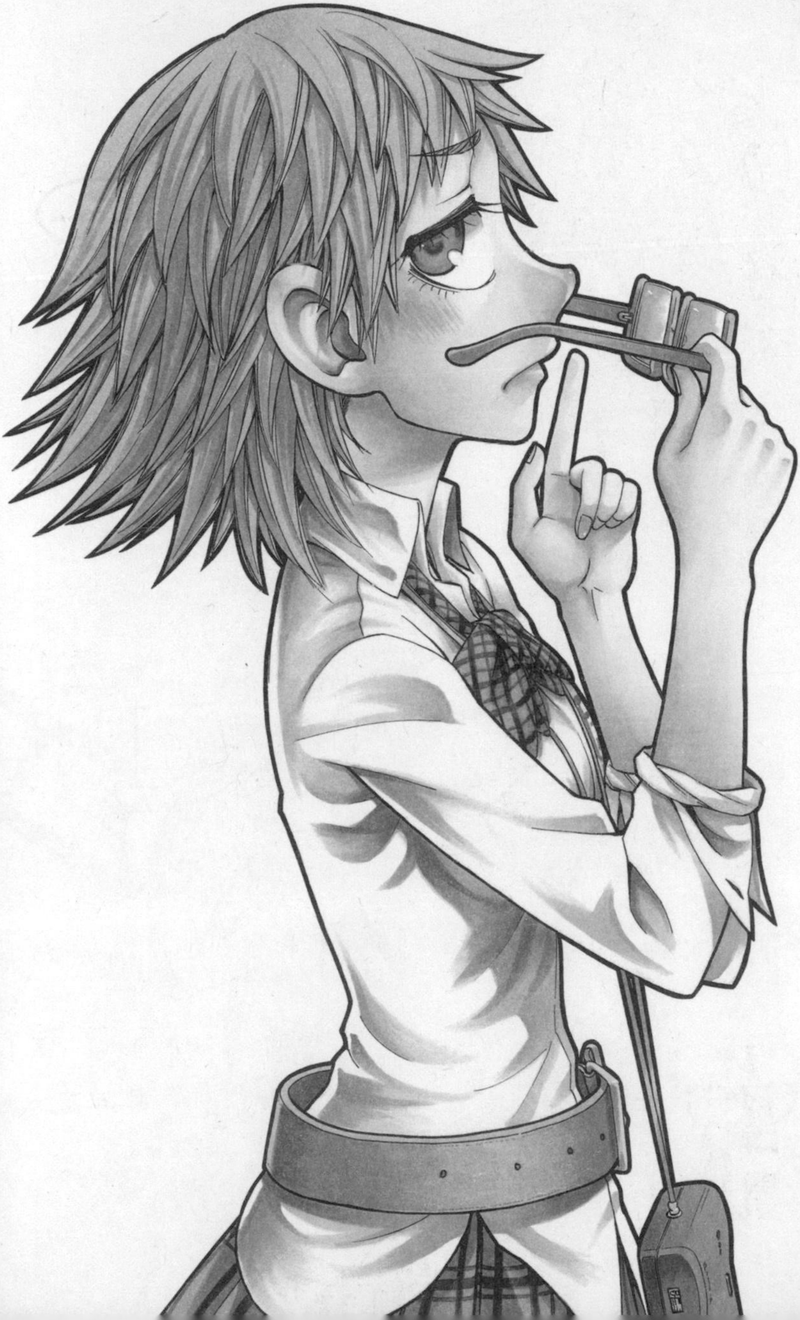

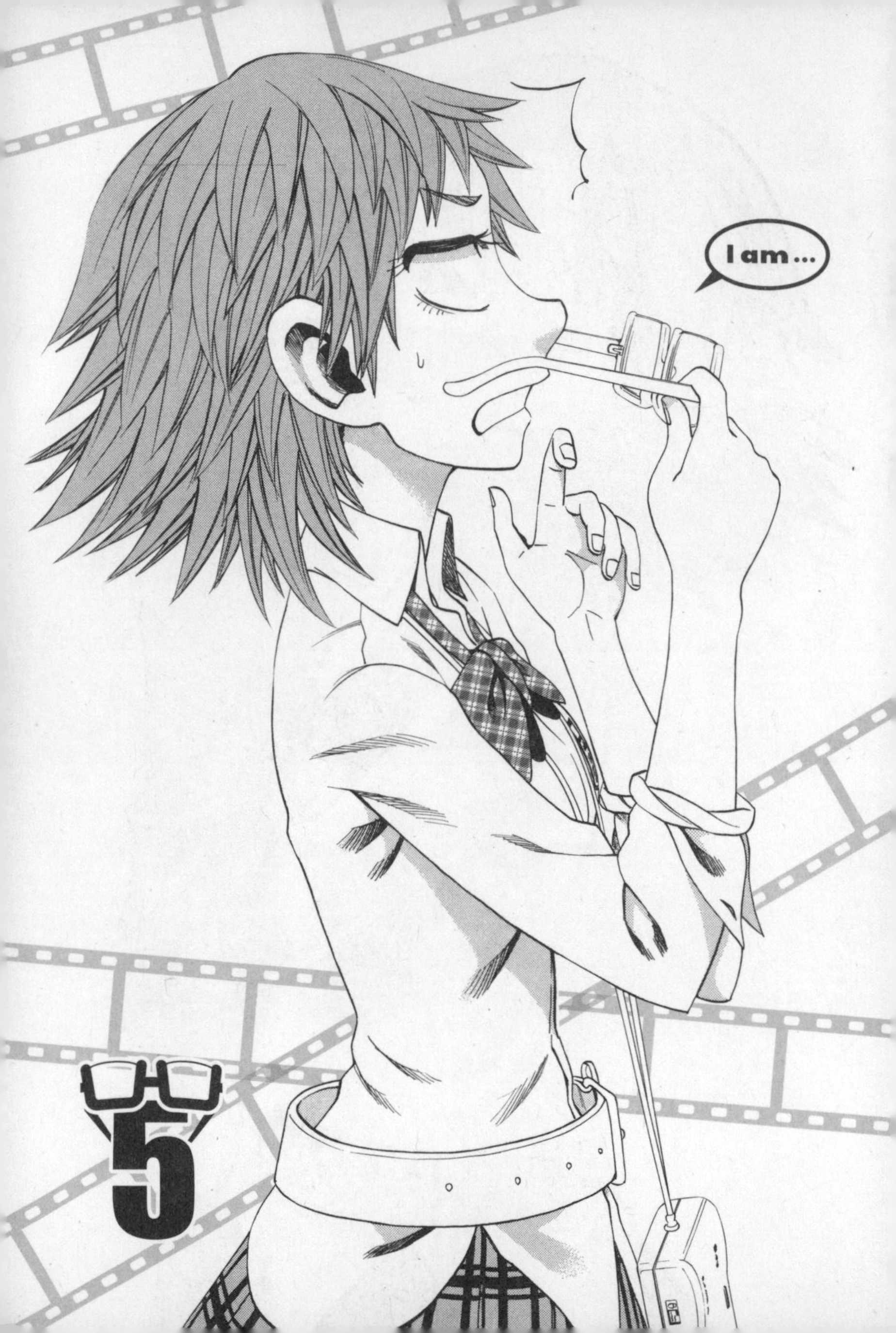
I am...
5

I am... a God of wealth

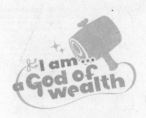

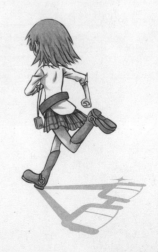